# Generative AI Approaches to Sustainable Development in Higher Education

Eleni Meletiadou
*London Metropolitan University, UK*

IGI Global
Scientific Publishing
Publishing Tomorrow's Research Today

Vice President of Editorial Melissa Wagner
Director of Acquisitions Mikaela Felty
Director of Book Development Jocelynn Hessler
Production Manager Mike Brehm
Cover Design Phillip Shickler

Published in the United States of America by
IGI Global Scientific Publishing
701 East Chocolate Avenue
Hershey, PA, 17033, USA
Tel: 717-533-8845
Fax: 717-533-7115
Website: https://www.igi-global.com E-mail: cust@igi-global.com



Library of Congress Cataloging-in-Publication Data

Names: Meletiadou, Eleni, 1971- editor.
Title: Generative AI approaches to sustainable development in higher education / Edited by Eleni Meletiadou.
Description: Hershey, PA : IGI Global, [2025] | Includes bibliographical references and index. | Summary: "The integration of AI with Education for Sustainable Development (ESD) in Higher Education has sparked a paradigm shift in teaching, learning and assessment offering both incredible opportunities and complex challenges"-- Provided by publisher.
Identifiers: LCCN 2024050848 (print) | LCCN 2024050849 (ebook) | ISBN 9798369356234 (hardcover) | ISBN 9798369356241 (paperback) | ISBN 9798369356258 (ebook)
Subjects: LCSH: Artificial intelligence--Educational applications. | Sustainable development--Study and teaching (Higher)
Classification: LCC LB1028.43 .G465 2025 (print) | LCC LB1028.43 (ebook) | DDC 006.3--dc23/eng/20241106
LC record available at https://lccn.loc.gov/2024050848
LC ebook record available at https://lccn.loc.gov/2024050849
British Cataloguing in Publication Data
A Cataloguing in Publication record for this book is available from the British Library.

# Table of Contents

# Detailed Table of Contents



Generative artificial intelligence has transformed the way educators deliver their lectures and seminars in higher education institutions around the world having an impact on societal norms as well. Despite the impact the adoption of GenAI has had on lecturers and students in higher education, very few research studies have explored lecturers' perceptions of Gen AI and identified sustainable and ethical practices of Gen AI for learning, teaching, and assessment. The current study explored 42 European lecturers' perceptions of the use of innovative Gen AI tools. The current qualitative study used semi-structured interviews to collect data. Convenience sampling was used in this study as the researcher tapped on her network to invite as many lecturers as possible to participate in this study. The data were transcribed and analyzed using the deductive approach for the thematic analysis. The findings revealed that lecturers had an overall positive attitude to adopt and use AI for content creation, debates, assessment and feedback, and conducting research in their respective institutions.



Research indicates that generative artificial intelligence (Gen AI) and its integration into higher education (HE) classes can support the developments in sustainability, and lead to improvements in educational practices, promoting education for social justice, fostering inclusion and accessibility for all students, irrespective of their background, and promoting environmental, i.e., climate awareness and sustainability. These are only some of the ways Gen AI can support and enhance the creation of more effective, inclusive, and sustainable contexts in HE. The current study aimed to explore students' perspectives on Gen AI tools to inform changes that should be implemented in HE to support the more effective use of Gen AI tools by students. One hundred sixty-three students from universities in Greece, Albania, and the UK participated in this study. It is suggested that HE policies and regulations should be modified and reformulated to support sustainable development, while empirical research and its incorporation in HE is a necessity (there is limited focus on practice-oriented/empirical research).



This chapter explores the integration of Generative AI (Gen AI) in higher education (HE) to enhance inclusion, addressing the critical need for a design-oriented and actionable approach to counter inequalities. Applying design thinking, the LivePBL DEEP Method is introduced and structured into four phases: Direction, Education, Event, and Project. This method employs Gen AI to foster inclusive learning environments by aligning AI with policies that view inequalities as diverse, positive opportunities to bridge gaps between pedagogical inequality and equality. Emphasising co-design, the method supports actionable policies at the micro level. It presents use cases from hybrid learning settings, demonstrating practical applications in real-world HE contexts. The chapter concludes with recommendations for scaling and integrating Gen AI to promote inclusion further.



In the context of the growing use of AI in education, this chapter explores the challenges and opportunities of integrating AI with education for sustainable development (ESD) in higher education (HE). It argues that equity, teaching, and assessment practices must be at the heart of this integration to promote social justice and to ensure that the benefits of AI are shared equally. The chapter outlines a vision for AI in ESD that is grounded in equity, pedagogy, and assessment. It explores the potential of AI in supporting the integration of ESD in Higher Education, and the need for innovative and inclusive practices that can help to address it. In the introduction, briefly explain the importance of ESD and the role of AI in supporting it. An overview of the challenges and opportunities associated with using AI in ESD is examined. The role of equity in ESD, and how AI can be used to promote it are

by utilizing the technological pedagogical content knowledge (TPCK) model, which is centrally discussed and implemented in nursing education.



This book chapter aims to establish the generative AI ChatGPT (GPT 3.5) as a valid source for active learning in higher education settings, based on fundamental educational and learning theories that describe efficient active learning methodologies and techniques. The research methodology aims to perform qualitative comparisons of ChatGPT and its various functionalities with the principles of the discussed learning theories. The prompts given to ChatGPT play an important role in how well the AI acts as a learning resource, the quality of the prompt is directly related to the quality of the response given by the AI. Various Prompt Experiments have been included in our case studies that showcase prompts given to the AI and the response received. These experiments will help in consolidating the comparisons between the working of the AI and the principles of the learning theories. Lastly, the chapter discusses the various deficiencies of ChatGPT (GPT 3.5) that need to be taken cautiously when using it as a tool for higher education.



Assessment practices play a crucial role in AI-integrated Education for Sustainable Development (ESD), serving to evaluate student learning outcomes, guide instructional practices, and inform decision-making processes. By leveraging AI technologies, educators can enhance the efficiency, scalability, and effectiveness of assessment practices in sustainable development education. However, it is essential to address the challenges and considerations associated with AI-integrated assessment, including concerns about reliability, validity, bias, ethics, and pedagogy. As we navigate the complexities of the digital age, it is essential to ensure that assessment practices in AI-integrated ESD are aligned with the principles of equity, inclusivity, and social justice, empowering students to become informed, engaged, and responsible global citizens committed to building a more sustainable future.

This chapter explores the transformative impact of digital platforms on work, centring on crowd work as a task-based, online labour model. Through a comprehensive literature review, it examines crowd work's characteristics, benefits such as flexibility and skill development, and challenges like job precarity and algorithmic management powered by artificial intelligence (AI). While AI enhances efficiency in task allocation, it raises ethical concerns about transparency and worker rights. The chapter also addresses how higher education can adapt to the digital economy through curriculum changes, policy advocacy, and collaborative learning spaces to prepare students for digital work. It concludes with future research recommendations, highlighting the need for sustainable labour practices and cross-cultural studies to better understand the evolving gig economy.



This chapter examines the potential of integrating artificial intelligence (AI) in higher education to enhance professional development, assessment, and teaching and learning practices while promoting education for sustainable development (ESD). It explores the latest research, policies, and initiatives that are shaping the future of higher education in the era of AI. The chapter highlights the need for continuous professional development of educators to keep pace with technological advancements and provides insights into the potential uses of AI in assessment and feedback processes to improve student learning outcomes. Additionally, it discusses the integration of AI into teaching and learning practices, including personalised learning, adaptive instruction, and interactive simulations.

# Preface

The integration of Generative Artificial Intelligence (Gen AI) in higher education has emerged as one of the most significant and transformative developments of the 21st century. As we navigate an increasingly digital world, the use of AI in teaching, learning, and assessment presents exciting opportunities for enhancing educational practices, fostering sustainability, and promoting social justice. This edited volume, *Generative AI Approaches to Sustainable Development in Higher Education*, explores how Gen AI is shaping the future of education and how its application can contribute to achieving the Sustainable Development Goals (SDGs) within the context of higher education.

The chapters in this book provide diverse perspectives on how Gen AI can be leveraged to create more inclusive, accessible, and equitable learning environments. The contributions range from the use of AI to promote sustainability and climate awareness to the development of personalized learning pathways for neurodiverse students, offering a comprehensive view of AI's potential in education. This book is organized into several key themes, with each chapter providing empirical insights and theoretical frameworks to highlight the multifaceted role of AI in advancing educational practices for sustainable development.

## CHAPTER OVERVIEW

In Chapter 1, *The Effective Use of Generative AI in Higher Education*, Eleni Meletiadou explores lecturers' perceptions of Gen AI, emphasizing the need for sustainable and ethical AI-powered practices in learning, teaching, and assessment. Through a qualitative study of 42 European lecturers, the chapter discusses the positive impact of AI on content creation, debates, and feedback processes, while underscoring the importance of ethical considerations.

Chapter 2, *Generative Artificial Intelligence for Sustainable Learning Development: Exploring Students' Perspectives*, also by Meletiadou, shifts the focus to students' perspectives on Gen AI tools. Drawing on data from 163 students across Greece, Albania, and the UK, this chapter advocates for policy reforms to support sustainable development through AI in higher education, especially in fostering inclusion and promoting social justice.

In Chapter 3, *Bridging Inequalities in Higher Education with the Use of Gen AI - The LivePBL DEEP Method*, Ying Liu, Yuanyuan Li, and Ting Zhao present the LivePBL DEEP method, a design-oriented approach to bridge inequalities in higher education using Gen AI. The method emphasizes co-design and inclusive learning, offering practical examples from hybrid learning environments.

Doris Chasokela and Aleck Sithole's contribution in Chapter 4, *Equity, Teaching, and Assessment Practices for the Integration of AI, Education for Sustainable Development*, explores how AI can support Education for Sustainable Development (ESD) by addressing equity in teaching and assessment practices, ensuring social justice in AI implementation.

In Chapter 5, *Examining Education for Sustainable Development in Higher Education to Promote Education for Social Justice in ChatGPT*, Özgül Keles investigates how ChatGPT aligns with the SDGs and UNESCO's ESD goals, providing insights into the tool's potential as an educational resource for promoting social justice in higher education.

Chapter 6, *Generative AI - Recent Advances and their Impact on Education*, by Sowmiya Baskar, surveys the advances in Gen AI and its applications in education, particularly its role in creating inclusive learning environments for students with special needs, such as those with neurodiversity.

Subhadip Kowar, Nilav Mukhopadhayay, and Daizy Deb in Chapter 7, *Generative AI Is Changing Personalized Learning to Help Us Build a Sustainable Future*, examine the ability of Gen AI to create personalized learning experiences that foster creativity, empowering students to engage with novel forms of educational content.

Ajibola Waliu and colleagues, in Chapter 8, *Immersive Educational Pedagogy Development: Cloud-Based Adaptive System for Higher Education*, explore the integration of immersive technologies such as Virtual Reality (VR) and Augmented Reality (AR) with AI, highlighting their role in improving learning outcomes and enhancing pedagogical practices.

Ayush Shukla and Unmesh Mandal's Chapter 9, *Inclusive Integration of Generative AI-ChatGPT with Education for Sustainable Development in Higher Education*, investigates ChatGPT's potential for active learning, focusing on how its application can complement educational theories and enhance student engagement.

In Chapter 10, *Intercultural Communication and Assessment Practices in the Integration of AI with Education*, Santhini C, Ruba M, and colleagues delve into the challenges and opportunities of AI-integrated assessment in sustainable development education, emphasizing the importance of fairness and inclusivity in assessment practices.

Teuta Hazizi and Imelda Sejdini's Chapter 11, *Navigating the Digital Economy: Crowd Work, AI Integration, Sustainability, and Higher Education's Response*, explores the growing digital economy and the role of higher education in preparing students for the evolving landscape of crowd work and AI integration, advocating for curriculum reforms and the development of sustainable labor practices.

Finally, in Chapter 12, *Professional Development and Assessment, Teaching and Learning Practices, Policies in Higher Education: Promoting the Integration of AI with Education for Sustainable Development*, Doris Chasokela and Joseph Hlongwane highlight the importance of continuous professional development for educators in leveraging AI, with a focus on its impact on teaching practices, student learning, and assessment.

Each chapter in this book provides a unique perspective on the intersection of AI, education, and sustainability, contributing to a comprehensive understanding of how Gen AI can be harnessed to create a more inclusive, equitable, and sustainable higher education system. Together, these contributions underscore the potential of AI to reshape the educational landscape and advance global sustainability goals.

# Chapter 1
# The Effective Use of Generative AI in Higher Education Exploring Lecturers' Artificial Intelligence Literacy:
## Unveiling Sustainable and Ethical AI-Powered Practices for Learning, Teaching, and Assessment

**Eleni Meletiadou**
https://orcid.org/0000-0003-4833-1450
*London Metropolitan University, UK*

## ABSTRACT

*Generative artificial intelligence has transformed the way educators deliver their lectures and seminars in higher education institutions around the world having an impact on societal norms as well. Despite the impact the adoption of GenAI has had on lecturers and students in higher education, very few research studies have explored lecturers' perceptions of Gen AI and identified sustainable and ethical practices of Gen AI for learning, teaching, and assessment. The current study explored 42 European lecturers' perceptions of the use of innovative Gen AI tools. The current qualitative study used semi-structured interviews to collect data. Convenience sampling was used in this study as the researcher tapped on her network to invite*

DOI: 10.4018/979-8-3693-5623-4.ch001

*as many lecturers as possible to participate in this study. The data were transcribed and analyzed using the deductive approach for the thematic analysis. The findings revealed that lecturers had an overall positive attitude to adopt and use AI for content creation, debates, assessment and feedback, and conducting research in their respective institutions.*

## INTRODUCTION

Generative Artificial Intelligence (Gen AI) can be defined as the ability of a common computer/laptop or a robot-controlled computer to complete tasks that are normally regarded as human. AI (Artificial Intelligence) is designed to learn from experience and practice, reason, or generalize. Its main characteristic is its ability to continuously evolve as it aspires to resolve particularly complex issues. This may lead to a "revolution" that can result in automating many activities normally performed by humans, including the automation of a significant number of human tasks. Lately, AI has moved beyond performing narrow, specialized tasks (e.g. information search), and towards general AI, as it can perform activities similar to those done by humans (Russell & Norvig, 2016). As the range of services using Gen AI is growing, societies are confronted with ethical dilemmas regarding the responsible and ethical use of AI.

Gen AI is based on models i.e., GPT (Generative Pre-trained Transformer), which can produce new, original content, similar to that created by humans. Its most recent version, GPT-4 can also get involved in sophisticated educational debates supporting students in their efforts to understand complex concepts. As it can train on huge data sets, AI is increasingly employed in HE by educators who always strive to create innovative materials to use in their lectures and seminars, quizzes, adaptive quizzes, and tests, or even automatic assessments of assignments. Higher Education is now moving towards a more personalized approach to teaching which fosters student autonomy, more efficient knowledge, and skill acquisition as the skills related to AI use are crucial for the next generation (Pelletier et al., 2022; UNESCO, 2023). Gen AI also allows lecturers to pilot various teaching approaches before using them in their classes by creating synthetic educational data that educators can evaluate before making any further decisions (Brown et al., 2020). Gen AI facilitates various aspects of lecturers' work i.e., administration, TLA, reporting, research etc. (Burns, 2021). Gen AI can now undertake some of the tasks lecturers usually perform on their own and decrease their workload by i.e., monitoring students' progression and progress, predicting it, facilitating students' learning process, and offering tutoring and academic mentor support (Williamson, 2017).

Gen AI can be applied in numerous ways in education to allow personalization of the education process and allow educators to: (a) keep track of students' progress, (b) identify their challenges and mistakes, and provide individualized feedback adapting the level of difficulty to the learners' needs, (c) offer writing support, marking assignments, detecting plagiarism, (d) offer assessment support to lecturers and generally enabling the use of automation of specific educational processes to enable learners to adapt to a universe dominated by algorithmic activities, and (e) offer training for educators to develop their skills while also monitoring the impact of AI on students' creativity and critical thinking (UNESCO, 2023). Educators' work is becoming more efficient as Gen AI is taking over activities that can be automated (i.e., marking) enabling lecturers to spend more time helping students who need special support (inspiration, encouragement, mentoring/coaching) which promotes integration and equalization of educational opportunities, Education for Social Justice and inclusion (Bryant et al., 2020). Gen AI can also support disabled and neurodiverse students who often face exclusion. However, researchers and scholars have raised a great number of ethical dilemmas involved in designing and using Gen AI tools (Floridi et al., 2018). One major issue is that of transparency as students often do not understand how their lecturers use AI to assess their performance. One other major 'thorn' is the privacy of student data as lecturers need to be careful about how this data is stored as it relates to students' progress, preferences, and overall behavior and who has access to it. Finally, this data should only be used for educational purposes (Jobin et al., 2019).

UNESCO offers ethical guidelines that stress the sustainable and fair use of AI in HE, focusing on the significance of responsibility and fairness in the development and implementation of Gen AI (UNESCO, 2021). Gen AI can even replace educators in terms of automatic learning, adapting the level of difficulty, providing answers and information, or offering feedback. From the moment, we put Gen AI into general use, we need to start to realize that we are coming towards the end of classic examination and testing approaches that reflect the essence of academic learning: reasoning, argumentation, and deduction. We also need to consider exams under strict supervision to avoid plagiarism and nonexistent bibliographical sources as is sometimes the norm with texts generated by AI and reconsider how we assess and evaluate our students' learning.

Despite concerns that AI might replace educators, it is believed that AI should be used as a tool to assist lecturers' work as they can now focus on developing students' soft skills i.e., critical thinking, intercultural awareness, and empathy rather than grading and providing personalized feedback. The key challenge yet remains how we can support lecturers' effective, responsible, and sustainable use of AI as individualization of the teaching process using AI is one of the most promising changes in HE (Holstein et al., 2019; Holmes et al., 2019; Luckin et al., 2016). To sum up,

Gen AI can transform the teaching process in HE by increasing its effectiveness, flexibility, and adaptability, considering diverse student needs, which is becoming increasingly important in the context of distance and hybrid education (Hopcan et al., 2023). Potential exclusion of students from the tools related to Gen AI may reduce students' competitiveness in the market and their overall professional development.

The present study explored lecturers' perceptions of the use of AI in HE, their AI literacy, and the range of sustainable and ethical LTA practices using AI tools they have successfully implemented in HE. In this chapter, the relevant literature on lecturers' use of AI in higher education classrooms and their AI literacy will be explored to provide the background of the study. Then, the methodology of the study will be presented in detail to help readers better understand lecturers' perceptions of AI tools in HE. The findings of the study will be examined and then discussed to highlight the benefits and challenges of using AI tools in HE. Implications and recommendations will be analyzed and then limitations and suggestions for further research will be considered to conclude this chapter.

## BACKGROUND

This section will provide the literature review of this study exploring several relevant topics.

### Evolution of AI in Education

Since 1956, Gen AI has transformed HE offering individualized options to enhance student learning while also engaging students in improper usage of AI tools with disastrous effects on their academic performance and creativity (Sanabria-Navarro et al., 2023). Some scholars stress that AI will eventually replace educators while others believe that lecturers are irreplaceable as they can transmit important values to learners and inspire them. Gen AI tools are increasingly in demand lately as they personalize learning and foster better retention and long-term academic performance (Moturu et al., 2023). In the last three decades, the integration of AI in HE has been directly associated with advancements in educational approaches, highlighting the significance of AI-based e-learning applications in transforming the educational context. Changes include supportive student-facing systems, individualized adaptive learning, automatic grading/marking, and tutor feedback. The integration of AI with revolutionary technologies like the Internet of Things and immersive augmented/virtual reality technology is necessary for the future of AI in HE (Tan et al., 2013).

## Lecturers' Attitudes and Perceptions Towards AI

The use of AI tools in HE was either welcomed with enthusiasm as it reduced lecturers' workload or with caution as it generated several problems, i.e., plagiarism. According to Ofosu-Ampong et al. (2024), university teaching staff were enthusiastic about the use of AI tools in their classrooms. However, that study also revealed that lecturers' acceptance was partially due to institutional decisions to integrate AI tools in HE, the ease of use of AI, and the relative support they received. Additionally, the sociocultural context and the continuous professional development opportunities offered always play their role in solidifying lecturers' positive attitudes toward AI. Lecturers are open to tools that can offer significant benefits and ease their everyday lives (Eden et al., 2024).

Previous studies reveal lecturers' attitudes in various contexts as they express their excitement about AI's revolutionary capabilities (Aithal & Aithal, 2023), and its influence on lecturers' and learners' engagement and academic achievement (Huang et al., 2023). Educators express their willingness to explore AI tools and use them in their classes (Pilai et al., 2024; Kim & Kim, 2022; Wang et al., 2021) but some of them also express their concerns about how feasible its integration into certain more traditional HE curricula is (Liu et al., 2023).

## Towards AI Key Themes in Integrating Artificial Intelligence (AI) in Education

### Adaptive and Personalized Learning

AI-powered adaptive and personalized learning also referred to as intelligent tutoring systems (ITS), is a virtual learning environment that tailors LTA approaches to individual students' needs, tastes, and capabilities. It also employs machine learning techniques, self-training algorithms, and neural networks to identify suitable learning content for students depending on their needs (Kabudi et al., 2020). This individualized strategy helps determine each learner's proficiency level and offers appropriate tasks and tests. For instance, Arizona State University used CogBooks, an adaptive learning technology that substituted ordinary books and written material and led to increased passing rates and dropout rates (Contrino et al., 2024). TSAL and WELSA also combine various AI techniques like adaptive learning, automated feedback, grading, and chatbot responses. These AI-powered strategies facilitate Education for Social Justice as they widen access beyond physical institutions. (Bulathwela et al., 2024).

## Automated Grading and Feedback

Lecturers increasingly use AI in grading students' work using i.e., the autograder program, which can evaluate written assignments and multiple-choice tests without human interference (August & Tsaima, 2021). Some other educators use a fusion of AI and virtual reality to assess aspiring dentists' proficiency based on their movements. Gradescope is also employed to digitize and evaluate learners' assignments, decreasing lecturers' workload. On the other hand, lecturers claim that overreliance on AI grading reduces students' creativity and puts certain students at a disadvantage as it promotes uniformity. However, AI programs are consistently used to save educators time and effort in large-scale tests (Al Braiki et al., 2020). Certain platforms like edX are using AI scoring engines that may replicate lecturers' marking and provision of feedback on a large volume of writing assignments. This approach is widely used in online learning environments, but it can restrict students' creative skills and original and innovative thinking in traditional classrooms (Baker, 2021).

## Emotional AI

Students' social and emotional learning is currently measured using Emotional AI (McStay, 2019) and affective computing which focuses on developing systems and devices that can identify and explain students' emotions checking student engagement levels using nonverbal signals assessed by AI technologies (Vistorte et al., 2024). Research indicates that AI tools may use eye, facial expressions, and head movements to evaluate student involvement and further improve engagement and academic performance but there are still serious concerns and reservations for learners with specific disabilities (Barua et al., 2022).

## AI for Equity, Diversity, and Inclusion (EDI)

Research indicates that AI tools that use machine learning algorithms can foster equity and inclusion offering equal opportunities for success to all learners irrespective of their background, tastes, and capabilities (Anis, 2023). As HE Institutions develop their strategic focus on equity and inclusion in AI HE policies, particularly for marginalized students, i.e., BAME, neurodiverse, multilingual, certain initiatives like IBM's Simpler Voice: Overcoming Illiteracy Project help widen access to HE and face challenges such as fairness, accountability, and transparency in AI tools as issues like underdeveloped digital skills and speaking English as a second language may decrease accessibility for certain groups of learners (UNESCO, 2019). Unfortunately, many scholars claim that the use of AI in HE may increase inequalities for marginalized groups and biases. AI tools can support the provision of individualized learning and help students from marginalized groups overcome barriers. Nevertheless, if the algorithms are biased, the solutions offered by AI will also be biased, i.e., Microsoft's Tay, a Twitter chatbot (Dhawan and Batra, 2021). To sum up, responsible and ethical use of AI in HE is the solution to the challenges already mentioned and policymakers must put forward equity, inclusion, and accessibility to increase AI's possibilities of fostering equal and inclusive education (UNESCO, 2021).

## Global Perspectives on AI in HE

Scholars indicate that lecturers' attitudes towards AI depend highly on their context, i.e., country of origin, as this can influence their practices. Lecturers in Estonia, for example, confessed that they need to develop their AI literacy but have been using AI to develop teaching materials and organize their lectures (Chounta, 2022). Another study in the same context revealed that lecturers' previous experience with the use of digital technologies has a significant impact on their personal stances towards AI and the successful use of AI tools in HE (Leoste, 2021). In another continent, Asia, lecturers living in Pakistan are also favorably disposed to the integration of technology in HE as they believe that it increases student engagement and involvement in their own learning (Akram et al., 2022). On the other hand, South Korean educators recognize the need to use AI tools in HE but are deeply concerned as this may influence the development of students' critical thinking skills and learning autonomy (Kim et al., 2022). In Sweden, lecturers claim that there may be issues with fairness, responsibility, and insufficient knowledge and resources for using AI tools in their everyday lectures (McGrath et al., 2023). In North America, university teachers are worried about their own role and the transparency of AI decision-making (Kim, 2022). The overall conclusion one reaches when considering the use of AI globally is that the integration of AI into HE needs to take into consideration the context and consider the challenges and opportunities of each country to enable efficient and inclusive use of AI in HE worldwide. Consequently, collective initiatives informed by the local context and international best practices will have an undeniable impact on shaping the future of the integration of AI tools in HE globally.

Concluding the literature review on the use of AI tools in HE, it is worthwhile mentioning that the main aim of the current study was to answer the following research question:

- How AI literate are HE lecturers nowadays?
- How can lecturers develop sustainable and ethical AI-powered LTA in HE?

## MAIN FOCUS OF THE CHAPTER

### Methodology

#### Participants

The current study used a mixed-method approach and a semi-experimental design. 42 lecturers from various universities across Europe participated in this study. This was a convenience sample as the researcher tapped on her professional network and lecturers' demographic data can be seen in Table 1. The main aim of the study was to explore lecturers' AI literacy and their sustainable and ethical AI-powered LTA practices to inform the readers of this chapter about useful tools they may use in their classes and ensure senior leadership teams are aware of the potential need to develop their academic staff AI literacy.

*Table 1. Demographic details and characteristics of participating lecturers*

| | **Students** | **Frequency** |
|---|---|---|
| **Gender** | Male | 10 |
| | Female | 28 |
| | LGBTQ+ | 4 |
| **Nationality** | UK | 15 |
| | International | 27 |

#### Method and Procedure

The present study utilized an exploratory qualitative approach to explore lecturers' AI literacy and best AI-related practices in HE at 4 HEI in the UK, Greece, Albania, and Cyprus (Ward et al., 2018). It aspired to examine a modern real-life phenomenon within a certain context (Sampson & Johannessen, 2020). The study used a qualitative interviewing data collection method, which is more suitable for exploratory studies that attempt to gain rich insights into a complicated phenomenon like lecturers' AI literacy. In the current study, a semi-structured interview technique was deployed as it matches this exploratory study that implements interpretive philosophy (Saunders, 2016). Its structure allows the researcher to "probe answers and allows a balance between focus and flexibility" (Saunders et al., 2016).

The researcher created different types of open-ended questions that comprised descriptive, structural, contrast, and evaluative content to explore the participants' perspectives and get valid information (Elo et al., 2014). To avoid reflexivity error and response bias, the researcher chose to initiate the interview with a brief discussion to explain the scope of the study in detail and develop intimacy as a strategy to lessen such biases. Case studies have been criticized because they offer little basis for scientific generalization (Yin, 2013). The current study has limitations because it was a qualitative study that used only a specific number of interviewees from a few HEI in Europe. It is closely related to the phenomenological and hermeneutical research approach which points to an internal and thorough awareness of the essence of research, not at generating generalizable outcomes.

The interviews were recorded and transcribed verbatim, based on predetermined semi-structured questions (Yin, 2013). These questions were further elaborated to probe deep into the interviewee's experiences. They aimed to examine their opinions and practices. The semi-structured interview questions were scrutinized taking into consideration an extensive literature review of studies exploring lecturers' AI literacy and included a list of basic questions and some prompts (e.g., exploratory) to promote further discussion. Introductory, barrier, and closing questions were used to allow for a certain kind of progression in the interview procedure and included background demographic questions, experience/behavior questions, opinion/value questions, and feeling questions (Collis & Hussey, 2013). Each interview lasted approximately fifty minutes.

Qualitative research data was collected from non-standardized interviews and analyzed using a prominent approach, thematic analysis (Thornhill et al., 2022). Thematic analysis is adjustable and can provide insight into major resemblances and contrasts on the current topic depending on how these are observed by the interviewees. The research team (the researcher and an assistant) employed a constructivist grounded theory method to analyse the interviews (Ramalho, 2015). The thematic analysis was enhanced by incorporating GenAI into the process (Morgan, 2023).

*Figure 1. Lecturers' AI literacy subfields*

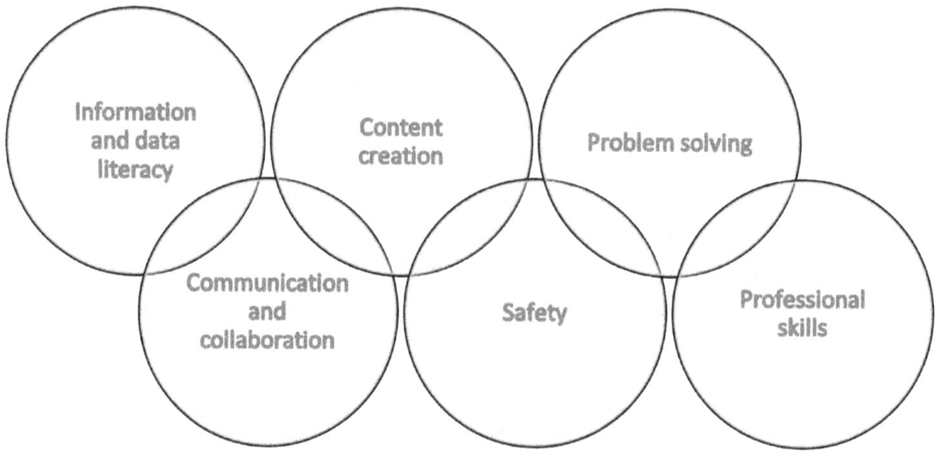


## Findings

The researcher analysed all findings taking into consideration the research questions of the current study and detected the following major themes which were repeated by more than 30 lecturers.

### Lecturers as enthusiastic adopters of AI tools

Many lecturers confessed that their knowledge of AI tools was limited but were eager to learn and experiment with new AI techniques which could potentially decrease their workload, increase students' engagement, and promote Social Justice for low-achieving students. However, they expressed their concerns about the impact of AI on students' critical thinking, creative and problem-solving skills.

> *"AI is a new friend we have to get to know better. We have been using it for seeking new information and proofreading our work, but we need to learn other ways in which we can use AI tools to support all our students irrespective of their background, and make our lectures more engaging. I look forward to using AI as an assessment tool as well as it will help us dedicate our marking time to students in need. HEI should invest money and time in developing our AI literacy. This would be a wise investment for our own and our students' future."*

Lecturers also discussed imaginative ways in which they were using AI to inspire their students and develop autonomous learners, responsible for their own and their peers' learning.

> *"I love exploring new ways to use AI tools. At first, I was using Chat GPT and grammar checkers for proofreading as they help expedite processes like article and research paper writing as well as grammar verification. I then used Chat GPT in statistical analysis expanding students' capabilities beyond the usual methods. I also encouraged students to use AI for exam preparation when they needed assistance in solving problems or needed to better understand our course materials. Finally, I used chatbots and digital assistants as they are widely accessible and provide excellent student learning opportunities and rapid guidance and support."*

## Lecturers as cautious adopters of AI tools

Some lecturers also highlighted the fact that Chat GPT can be used as a supplementary tool rather than as a primary teaching approach. They believed in maintaining a balanced approach and facilitating a gradual adoption of AI in HE learning and teaching. The main goal was to ensure that students did not depend on them too much as this would have an impact on the development of crucial personal and professional skills. AI tools can be used to provide additional practice for students who need it especially before exams fostering analytical skills and allowing low-achieving students or students with disabilities to receive additional support if needed.

> *"Cautious optimism may allow gradual successful and meaningful integration of AI techniques in AI classes without compromising traditional pedagogical values. I have used Chat GPT in my classes as an additional resource for students and can assure you that it increased student engagement and autonomy. The use of AI tools for targeted tasks or supplementary material supports students as they receive additional practice and is a valuable assistance for low-achieving students. Lecturers should always pilot AI tools before using them systematically in their classes and receive extensive 365 feedback to ensure they achieve the goals for which they are used without creating additional problems. Even tried-out AI tools need to be introduced with caution to different groups of learners as their needs and tastes vary."*

Some lecturers were even more skeptical about the use of AI tools as they are not always accurate and reliable. This may result in offering students the wrong information and this ultimately has a direct impact on student learning. Students need to be warned to be cautious and further verify all information they receive.

*"AI tools can offer misleading information. I have seen it in my classes. Students should learn to critically assess all information they receive from AI tools. They should not rely on AI to do their coursework and resolve all their problems. That kind of dependency should be avoided. Therefore, the use of AI tools should be carefully monitored and students' AI literacy should also be developed before using AI tools in the classroom. Students should be aware that plagiarism is a serious academic offense and AI tools should not be used to offer readymade solutions to potentially 'lazy' students."*

To sum up, the findings from the current study indicated that lecturers expressed their wish to develop their own AI literacy and that of their students but also expressed their ethical and pedagogical concerns about using AI tools systematically in their classes as they want to avoid students and their own overdependence on AI and the potential underdevelopment of their creative and critical thinking skills due to excessive use of AI in their everyday lives.

## Discussion and Implications

The current study explored lecturers' perceptions of how AI literate educators in HE are at the moment and how they could develop sustainable and ethical AI-powered LTA in HE. The outcomes indicated that the majority of the lecturers currently use AI even to perform simple tasks, i.e., searching for new information and materials, correcting work, and creating new materials confirming previous research (Jafari & Keykha, 2024; Rudolph et al., 2023; Ou et al., 2024). Lecturers have indicated that they are trying to familiarize themselves with the new AI tools and they see great potential but need additional guidance and support. Many lecturers express their concerns about the ethical concerns of using AI to generate answers as the credibility of the generated material is often questionable. They also point out the benefits of the use of AI tools by multilingual students in translation and proofreading. This fosters equity for marginalized students who do not speak English as their first language. Lecturers in our study also seem worried about keeping up with the evolution of technology and preparing students for using AI in their work in the future. They believe that training in the ethical use of AI should be mandatory as students and lecturers often use AI in their research.

Participants in this study highlighted that Gen AI tools are invaluable as they can provide immediate and detailed feedback to students - which is impossible for lecturers to do - enhancing student academic performance and engagement. These outcomes align with previous research stressing how useful and effective Gen AI tools can be in HE (He et al., 2025; Khlaif et al., 2024; Lau & Guo, 2023; Moorhouse et al., 2023). However, they also identified several pitfalls as both lecturers and students lack the necessary skills to make full and responsible use of AI tools.

They also need continuous professional development to become instantly aware of new developments (Fakhar et al., 2024). Lecturers also seem unaware of effective ways in which they can integrate AI tools in their teaching. They also report their concerns for integrity and the fear for AI-generated content to undermine traditional assessment approaches. They stressed the necessity of developing improved AI detection techniques and awareness programs to eliminate the chances of plagiarism and academic dishonesty (Tripathi & Thakar, 2024).

To sum up, the findings of this research highlight the complexity lecturers are faced with when using AI tools in HE. The findings highlight both the potential benefits and challenges linked with integrating AI tools, offering valuable insights for lecturers, policymakers, senior leaders and managers, and HEIs. The contribution of this study lies in the way participants reported different procedures used to improve the integration of AI tools with LTA in HE. The study wishes to offer recommendations for the development of successful, ethical, and sustainable AI-powered practices and for continuously developing lecturers' AI literacy to be able to effectively guide their students and develop their AI-related professional skills.

## CONCLUSION

This research offers a thorough understanding of the factors influencing the use of generative artificial intelligence (Gen AI) by lecturers in HE and offers valuable insights into their perceptions of their AI literacy. The study also presents several sustainable and ethically powered LTA practices that educators currently use in HE. Even though there are evident benefits, such as instant and personalized feedback for students, challenges related to ease of use and academic integrity need to be addressed. By leveraging these insights, HEIs, senior leadership teams, and policymakers can develop strategies to help lecturers efficiently integrate Gen AI, thereby improving both their own LTA practices and student learning experiences and outcomes.

### Limitations and Directions for Future Research

The current study has several limitations and offers directions for future research. First, the study included a limited number of participants from European HEIs only. Therefore, the results may not apply to other educational contexts. The cultural, technological, and educational differences across different European countries may have an impact on these lecturers' adoption and successful integration of Gen AI tools in their classes. Moreover, the current research relied on self-reported data from the interviewees, which are susceptible to several biases such as social desirability and recollection bias. The lecturers may also have inflated or understated their use and perceptions of Gen AI tools, potentially impacting the outcomes' accuracy.

This study used a cross-sectional approach, collecting data at a single point in time. This technique limits the ability to infer causality or track changes in perceptions and behaviors over time. More longitudinal studies would be more efficient in capturing the evolution of educators' perceptions and the long-term impacts of Gen AI integration in HE.

Furthermore, this research did take into consideration the variability in the types and functionalities of Gen AI tools employed by the interviewees. Different tools may have varying levels of effectiveness and user-friendliness, influencing educators' perceptions and experiences. These studies should use longitudinal designs to track changes in educators' perceptions, attitudes, and use of Gen AI tools over time. This would provide additional insights into the long-term effects of Gen AI in HE settings. In addition, conducting comparative studies across different countries, educational levels, and cultural contexts could help to identify universal and context-specific factors influencing Gen AI adoption. This would enhance the generalizability of the findings and inform tailored implementation strategies.

Future studies should also include a broader range of individuals, including those who are skeptical about or neutral towards Gen AI techniques. Understanding the barriers and facilitators for different groups can provide a more complete picture of the problems and potential of integrating Gen AI into HE. As Gen AI technologies continue to evolve, future research should examine the latest advancements and their implications for educational assessment. Studies should investigate the integration of emerging technologies, such as augmented-reality learning systems, with Gen AI tools to improve educational experiences. Additional research is needed to explore the ethical implications of utilizing Gen AI in HE, including concerns about data privacy and academic integrity and the potential of AI bias. Creating comprehensive ethical rules and policies will be critical to the responsible use of Gen AI capabilities.

Finally, exploring the efficiency of different training and support programs for lecturers using Gen AI tools can offer insights into best sustainable practices for continuous professional development. Future research should investigate the most effective approaches to develop educators' digital competencies and self-confidence in utilizing AI-powered techniques. By addressing these limitations and investigating the recommended future research topics, researchers can contribute to a more comprehensive understanding of Gen AI integration in HE contexts and its potential to enhance HE LTA fostering social justice.

## REFERENCES


Aithal, P. S., & Aithal, S. (2023). Optimizing the use of artificial intelligence-powered GPTs as teaching and research assistants by professors in higher education institutions: A study on smart utilization. *International Journal of Management, Technology, and Social Sciences*, *8*(4), 368–401. DOI: 10.47992/IJMTS.2581.6012.0326

Akram, H., Abdelrady, A. H., Al-Adwan, A. S., & Ramzan, M. (2022). Teachers' perceptions of technology integration in teaching-learning practices: A systematic review. *Frontiers in Psychology*, *13*, 920317. DOI: 10.3389/fpsyg.2022.920317 PMID: 35734463

Al Braiki, B., Harous, S., Zaki, N., & Alnajjar, F. (2020). Artificial intelligence in education and assessment methods. *Bulletin of Electrical Engineering and Informatics*, *9*(5), 1998–2007. DOI: 10.11591/eei.v9i5.1984

Anis, M. (2023). Leveraging artificial intelligence for inclusive English language teaching: Strategies and implications for learner diversity. *Journal of Multidisciplinary Educational Research*, *12*(6), 54–70.

August, S. E., & Tsaima, A. (2021). Artificial intelligence and machine learning: an instructor's exoskeleton in the future of education. *Innovative Learning Environments in STEM Higher Education: Opportunities, Challenges, and Looking Forward*, 79-105.

Baker, R. S. (2021). Artificial intelligence in education: Bringing it all together. *Digital education outlook: Pushing the frontiers with AI, blockchain, and robots*, 43-54.

Barua, P. D., Vicnesh, J., Gururajan, R., Oh, S. L., Palmer, E., Azizan, M. M., Kadri, N. A., & Acharya, U. R. (2022). Artificial intelligence enabled personalised assistive tools to enhance education of children with neurodevelopmental disorders—A review. *International Journal of Environmental Research and Public Health*, *19*(3), 1192. DOI: 10.3390/ijerph19031192 PMID: 35162220

Brown, T. B., Mann, B., Ryder, N., Subbiah, M., Kaplan, J., Dhariwal, P., . . . Amodei, D. (2020). Language Models are Few-Shot Learners. *arXiv preprint arXiv:2005.14165.*

Bryant, J., Heitz, C., Sanghvi, S., & Wagle, D. (2020). *How artificial intelligence will impact K-12 teachers*. McKinsey & Company.

Bulathwela, S., Pérez-Ortiz, M., Holloway, C., Cukurova, M., & Shawe-Taylor, J. (2024). Artificial intelligence alone will not democratise education: On educational inequality, techno-solutionism and inclusive tools. *Sustainability (Basel), 16*(2), 781. DOI: 10.3390/su16020781

Burns, M. (2021). Technology in education. Background paper prepared for the 2023 Global Education Monitoring Report on Technology in Education. https://www.researchgate.net/publication/358358065_Technology_in_Education_Background_Paper_for_2023_Global_Education_Monitoring_Report

Chounta, I. A., Bardone, E., Raudsep, A., & Pedaste, M. (2022). Exploring teachers' perceptions of artificial intelligence as a tool to support their practice in Estonian K-12 education. *International Journal of Artificial Intelligence in Education, 32*(3), 725–755. DOI: 10.1007/s40593-021-00243-5

Contrino, M. F., Reyes-Millán, M., Vázquez-Villegas, P., & Membrillo-Hernández, J. (2024). Using an adaptive learning tool to improve student performance and satisfaction in online and face-to-face education for a more personalized approach. *Smart Learning Environments, 11*(1), 6. DOI: 10.1186/s40561-024-00292-y

Eden, C. A., Chisom, O. N., & Adeniyi, I. S. (2024). Integrating AI in education: Opportunities, challenges, and ethical considerations. *Magna Scientia Advanced Research and Reviews, 10*(2), 6-13.

Elo, S., Kääriäinen, M., Kanste, O., Pölkki, T., Utriainen, K., & Kyngäs, H. (2014). Qualitative content analysis: A focus on trustworthiness. *SAGE Open, 4*(1). DOI: 10.1177/2158244014522633

Fakhar, H., Lamrabet, M., Echantoufi, N., & Ajana, L. (2024). Towards a New Artificial Intelligence-based Framework for Teachers' Online Continuous Professional Development Programs: Systematic Review. *International Journal of Advanced Computer Science and Applications, 15*(4). Advance online publication. DOI: 10.14569/IJACSA.2024.0150450

Floridi, L., Cowls, J., Beltrametti, M., Chatila, R., Chazerand, P., Dignum, V., Luetge, C., Madelin, R., Pagallo, U., Rossi, F., Schafer, B., Valcke, P., & Vayena, E. (2018). AI4People—an ethical framework for a good AI society: Opportunities, risks, principles, and recommendations. *Minds and Machines, 28*(4), 689–707. DOI: 10.1007/s11023-018-9482-5 PMID: 30930541

He, A. J., Zhang, Z., Anand, P., & McMinn, S. (2025). Embracing generative artificial intelligence tools in higher education: A survey study at the hong kong university of science and technology. *Journal of Asian Public Policy, 18*(1).

Holmes, W., Bialik, M., & Fadel, C. (2019). *Artificial intelligence in education: Promises and implications for teaching and learning*. Centre for Curriculum Redesign.

Holstein, K., McLaren, B. M., & Aleven, V. (2019). Designing for complementarity: Teacher and student needs for orchestration support in AI-enhanced classrooms. *Artificial Intelligence in Education: 20th International Conference, AIED 2019, Chicago, IL, USA, June 25-29, 2019Proceedings*, *20*(Part I), 157–171.

Hopcan, S., Polat, E., Ozturk, M. E., & Ozturk, L. (2023). Artificial intelligence in special education: A systematic review. *Interactive Learning Environments*, *31*(10), 7335–7353. DOI: 10.1080/10494820.2022.2067186

Huang, A. Y., Lu, O. H., & Yang, S. J. (2023). Effects of artificial Intelligence–Enabled personalized recommendations on learners' learning engagement, motivation, and outcomes in a flipped classroom. *Computers & Education*, *194*, 104684. DOI: 10.1016/j.compedu.2022.104684

Jafari, F., & Keykha, A. (2024). Identifying the opportunities and challenges of artificial intelligence in higher education: A qualitative study. *Journal of Applied Research in Higher Education*, *16*(4), 1228–1245. DOI: 10.1108/JARHE-09-2023-0426

Jobin, A., Ienca, M., & Vayena, E. (2019). The global landscape of AI ethics guidelines. *Nature Machine Intelligence*, *1*(9), 389–399. DOI: 10.1038/s42256-019-0088-2

Kabudi, T., Pappas, I., & Olsen, D. H. (2021). AI-enabled adaptive learning systems: A systematic mapping of the literature. *Computers and Education: Artificial Intelligence*, *2*, 100017. DOI: 10.1016/j.caeai.2021.100017

Khlaif, Z. N., Ayyoub, A., Hamamra, B., Bensalem, E., Mitwally, M. A., Ayyoub, A., Hattab, M. K., & Shadid, F. (2024). University teachers' views on the adoption and integration of generative AI tools for student assessment in higher education. *Education Sciences*, *14*(10), 1090. DOI: 10.3390/educsci14101090

Kim, J., Lee, H., & Cho, Y. H. (2022). Learning design to support student-AI collaboration: Perspectives of leading teachers for AI in education. *Education and Information Technologies*, *27*(5), 6069–6104. DOI: 10.1007/s10639-021-10831-6

Kim, N. J., & Kim, M. K. (2022, March). Teacher's perceptions of using an artificial intelligence-based educational tool for scientific writing. *Frontiers in Education*, *7*, 755914. DOI: 10.3389/feduc.2022.755914

Lau, S., & Guo, P. (2023, August). From" Ban it till we understand it" to" Resistance is futile": How university programming instructors plan to adapt as more students use AI code generation and explanation tools such as ChatGPT and GitHub Copilot. In *Proceedings of the 2023 ACM Conference on International Computing Education Research-Volume 1* (pp. 106-121). DOI: 10.1145/3568813.3600138

Leoste, J., Jõgi, L., Õun, T., Pastor, L., San Martín López, J., & Grauberg, I. (2021). Perceptions about the future of integrating emerging technologies into higher education—The case of robotics with artificial intelligence. *Computers, 10*(9), 110. DOI: 10.3390/computers10090110

Liu, M., Ren, Y., Nyagoga, L. M., Stonier, F., Wu, Z., & Yu, L. (2023). Future of education in the era of generative artificial intelligence: Consensus among Chinese scholars on applications of ChatGPT in schools. *Future in Educational Research, 1*(1), 72–101. DOI: 10.1002/fer3.10

Luckin, R. W., Holmes, M., & Griffiths, L. B. (2016). *Forcier Intelligence Unleashed: An Argument for AI in Education*. Pearson London.

Moorhouse, B. L., Yeo, M. A., & Wan, Y. (2023). Generative AI tools and assessment: Guidelines of the world's top-ranking universities. *Computers and Education Open, 5*, 100151. DOI: 10.1016/j.caeo.2023.100151

Morgan, D. L. (2023). Exploring the use of artificial intelligence for qualitative data analysis: The case of ChatGPT. *International Journal of Qualitative Methods, 22*, 1–10. DOI: 10.1177/16094069231211248

Moturu, V. R., & Nethi, S. D. (2022). Artificial intelligence in education. In *Emerging IT/ICT and AI Technologies Affecting Society* (pp. 233–244). Springer Nature Singapore.

Ofosu-Ampong, K. (2024). Beyond the hype: Exploring faculty perceptions and acceptability of AI in teaching practices. *Discover Education, 3*(1), 38. DOI: 10.1007/s44217-024-00128-4

Ou, A. W., Stöhr, C., & Malmström, H. (2024). Academic communication with AI-powered language tools in higher education: From a post-humanist perspective. *System, 121*, 103225. DOI: 10.1016/j.system.2024.103225

Pelletier, K., Brown, M., Brooks, D. C., McCormack, M., Reeves, J., Arbino, N., Bozkurt, A., Crawford, S., Czerniewicz, L., Gibson, R., Linder, K., Mason, J., & Mondelli, V. (2021). *2021 EDUCAUSE horizon report teaching and learning edition*. EDUCAUSE.

Pillai, R., Sivathanu, B., Metri, B., & Kaushik, N. (2024). Students' adoption of AI-based teacher-bots (T-bots) for learning in higher education. *Information Technology & People*, *37*(1), 328–355. DOI: 10.1108/ITP-02-2021-0152

Ramalho, R., Adams, P., Huggard, P., & Hoare, K. (2015). Literature review and constructivist grounded theory methodology. In Ramalho, R., Adams, P., Huggard, P., & Hoare, K. (Eds.), *Forum Qualitative Sozialforschung/Forum: Qualitative Social Research, 16* (Vol. 3).

Rudolph, J., Tan, S., & Tan, S. (2023). ChatGPT: Bullshit spewer or the end of traditional assessments in higher education? *Journal of Applied Learning and Teaching, 6*(1), 342-363.

Russell, S. J., & Norvig, P. (2016). *Artificial intelligence: a modern approach.* Pearson.

Sampson, H., & Johannessen, I. A. (2020). Turning on the tap: The benefits of using 'real-life' vignettes in qualitative research interviews. *Qualitative Research*, *20*(1), 56–72. DOI: 10.1177/1468794118816618

Sanabria-Navarro, J. R., Silveira-Pérez, Y., Pérez-Bravo, D. D., & de-Jesús-Cortina-Núñez, M. (2023). Incidences of Artificial Intelligence in Contemporary Education. *Comunicar: Media Education Research Journal*, *31*(77), 93–103. DOI: 10.3916/C77-2023-08

Saunders, L. (2016). Teaching the reference interview through practice-based assignments. *RSR. Reference Services Review*, *44*(3), 390–410. DOI: 10.1108/RSR-04-2016-0025

Tan, S. (2013). Harnessing Artificial Intelligence for Innovation in Education. In *Learning Intelligence: Innovative and Digital Transformative Learning Strategies* (pp. 335–363). Springer.

Thornhill, E., Sanderson, C., & Gupta, A. (2022). A grounded theory analysis of care-coordinators' perceptions of family growth associated with an experience of first episode psychosis. *Psychosis*, *14*(4), 355–367. DOI: 10.1080/17522439.2021.1971743

Tripathi, A., & Thakar, S. V. (2024). Ethical Use of AI for Academic Integrity: Preventing Plagiarism and Cheating. *Ethical Frameworks in Special Education: A Guide for Researchers, 91.*

UNESCO (Ed.). (2019). Artificial Intelligence in education: Challenges and opportunities for sustainable development. UNESCO Working Papers on Education Policy. https://bit.ly/3z6BQvN

UNESCO. (2020). *AI in Education: Change at the Speed of Learning*. UNESCO IITE Policy Brief.

UNESCO. (2021). International Forum on AI and the futures of education developing competencies for the AI era.

UNESCO. (2023). *Global Education Monitoring Report. Technology in Education. A Tool on Whose Terms?* UNESCO.

Vistorte, A. O. R., Deroncele-Acosta, A., Ayala, J. L. M., Barrasa, A., López-Granero, C., & Martí-González, M. (2024). Integrating artificial intelligence to assess emotions in learning environments: A systematic literature review. *Frontiers in Psychology, 15*, 1387089. DOI: 10.3389/fpsyg.2024.1387089 PMID: 38966729

Wang, Y., Liu, C., & Tu, Y. F. (2021). Factors affecting the adoption of AI-based applications in higher education. *Journal of Educational Technology & Society, 24*(3), 116–129.

Ward, J. K., Comer, U., & Stone, S. (2018). On qualifying qualitative research: Emerging perspectives and the "Deer"(descriptive, exploratory, evolutionary, repeat) paradigm. *Interchange, 49*(1), 133–146. DOI: 10.1007/s10780-018-9313-x

Williamson, B. (2017). Big data in Education. *Sage (Atlanta, Ga.).*

Yin, L. W. (2013). *Inclusive leadership and employee voice: Mediating roles of psychological safety and leader-member exchange*. PhD Thesis. Hong Kong Baptist University.

## ADDITIONAL READING

Meletiadou, E. (2011). *Peer assessment of writing in secondary education: Its impact on learners' performance and attitudes. M.A. in Applied Linguistics*. University of Cyprus.

Meletiadou, E. (2012). The impact of training adolescent EFL learners on their perceptions of peer assessment of writing. *RPLTL, 3*(1), 240–251.

Meletiadou, E. (2013). EFL learners' attitudes towards peer assessment, teacher assessment and the process writing' (Vol. M.A.). In D. Tsagari (Ed.) *Language Testing and Evaluation Series, 28* (pp. 312-330). Frankfurt am Main: Peter Lang GmbH.

Meletiadou, E. (2021a). Exploring the impact of peer assessment on EFL students' writing performance. *IAFOR Journal of Education*, *9*(3), 77–95. DOI: 10.22492/ije.9.3.05

Meletiadou, E. (2021a). Opening Pandora's box: How does peer assessment affect EFL students' writing quality? *Languages (Basel, Switzerland)*, *6*(3), 115. DOI: 10.3390/languages6030115

Meletiadou, E. (2021b). Exploring the impact of peer assessment on EFL students' writing performance. *IAFOR Journal of Education*, *9*(3), 77–95. DOI: 10.22492/ije.9.3.05

Meletiadou, E. (2021c). Using Padlets as e-portfolios to develop undergraduate students' writing skills and motivation. *IAFOR Journal of Undergraduate Education*, *9*(4), 67–83. DOI: 10.22492/ije.9.5.04

Meletiadou, E. (2022). The utilisation of peer-Assisted learning/mentoring and translanguaging in Higher Education. *IAFOR Journal of Education. Language Issue*, *10*(1), 135–154.

Meletiadou, E. (2022a). The Use of Peer Assessment as an Inclusive Learning Strategy in Higher Education Institutions: Enhancing Student Writing Skills and Motivation.

Meletiadou, E. (2022b). *Learners' perceptions of peer assessment: Implications for their willingness to write in an EFL classroom.* International Journal of Teacher Education and Professional Development. IGI. DOI: 10.4018/IJTEPD.295539

Meletiadou, E. (2022c). The lived experiences of female educational leaders in Higher Education in the UK: Academic resilience and gender.

Meletiadou, E. (2022d). Profiling the writing competency of BAME undergraduate students: Fostering Inclusion and academic success to improve retention in Tertiary Education.

Meletiadou, E. (accepted). Using Educational Digital Storytelling to enhance multilingual students' writing skills in Higher Education. *IAFOR Journal of Education. Technology Issue.*

Meletiadou, E., & Tsagari, D. (2012). Investigating the attitudes of adolescent EFL learners towards peer assessment of writing. In Tsagari, D. (Ed.), *Research on English as a foreign language in Cyprus* (Vol. II, pp. 225–245). University of Nicosia Press.

Meletiadou, E., & Tsagari, D. (2014). An exploration of the reliability and validity of peer assessment of writing in secondary education. In Tsagari, D. (Ed.), *Major trends in theoretical and applied linguistics 3* (pp. 235–250). De Gruyter Open Poland. DOI: 10.2478/9788376560915.p14

Meletiadou, E., & Tsagari, D. (2016). The washback effect of peer assessment on adolescent EFL learners in Cyprus. In Tsagari, D. (Ed.), *Classroom-based assessment in L2 contexts*. Cambridge Scholars Publishing.

Meletiadou, E., & Tsagari, D. (2022a). Exploring teachers' perceptions of the use of peer assessment in EFL test-dominated writing classes. *Recent Development in Language Testing and Assessment Special Issue.Languages (Basel, Switzerland)*, *7*(1), 16. DOI: 10.3390/languages7010016

## KEY TERMS AND DEFINITIONS

**AI Literacy:** The ability to understand the basic techniques and concepts behind AI in different products and services.

**Artificial Intelligence:** The theory and development of computer systems able to perform tasks normally requiring human intelligence, such as visual perception, speech recognition, decision-making, and translation between languages.

**Student Engagement:** A term used to describe an individual's interest and enthusiasm. for school, which impacts their academic performance and behavior.

Chapter 2

# Generative Artificial Intelligence for Sustainable Learning Development:

## Exploring Students' Perspectives in Higher Education

**Eleni Meletiadou**
https://orcid.org/0000-0003-4833-1450
*London Metropolitan University, UK*

## ABSTRACT

*Research indicates that generative artificial intelligence (Gen AI) and its integration into higher education (HE) classes can support the developments in sustainability, and lead to improvements in educational practices, promoting education for social justice, fostering inclusion and accessibility for all students, irrespective of their background, and promoting environmental, i.e., climate awareness and sustainability. These are only some of the ways Gen AI can support and enhance the creation of more effective, inclusive, and sustainable contexts in HE. The current study aimed to explore students' perspectives on Gen AI tools to inform changes that should be implemented in HE to support the more effective use of Gen AI tools by students. One hundred sixty-three students from universities in Greece, Albania, and the UK participated in this study. It is suggested that HE policies and regulations should be modified and reformulated to support sustainable development, while empirical research and its incorporation in HE is a necessity (there is limited focus on practice-oriented/empirical research).*

DOI: 10.4018/979-8-3693-5623-4.ch002

## INTRODUCTION

Generative Artificial Intelligence (Gen AI) techniques, i.e., ChatGPT have been recently used as omnipotent digital technology strategies in Higher Education Institutions (HEIs) contexts. Gen AI can be utilized to boost the use of digital pedagogy in HE in so many ways unclosing individualized learning, automated assessment and feedback creation, virtual assistants and chatbots, content creation, resource suggestion, time management, language translation and support, proofreading, editing, research assistance, simulations and virtual labs (Chiu, 2024; Crawford et al., 2023; Nikolopoulou, 2025). Scholars also claim that Gen AI can promote cooperation and communication, widen accessibility, develop students' emotional intelligence, and foster inclusivity, and digital literacy (Bender, 2024; Chiu, 2024; Kazanidis & Pellas, 2024). However, there are also challenges and risks involved when lecturers try to implement Gen AI in HE. For instance, overreliance on automated feedback could mean that students miss out on educators' input which fosters the development of students' creative and critical thinking skills and allows human, social and emotional connection which is crucial for some students, i.e., those facing mental health issues, directly putting them at a disadvantage. Moreover, Gen AI supports content creation and resource guidance, it may reinforce biases depending on the data used as input and often ignores the context of any specific problem, often oversimplifying complex processes and concepts leading to a lack of academic depth (Wei et al., 2025; Bhandari, 2023). Gen AI tools are also unable to detect culture-specific issues which often leads to misinterpretation and mistakes in language translation when used by multilingual students (Bender, 2024); human-language learning interactions are crucial for developing students' emotional intelligence and intercultural awareness as well as their linguistic skills (Voss et al., 2023). Lecturers and students in HE also state that reliance on simulations, VR, and augmented reality may lead to lack of experiential learning which is crucial for developing professionals as AI tools cannot replicate extraordinary events that may take place in real-life (Bozkurt et al., 2023). Gen AI-mediated activities also lack the spontaneity of face-to-face interaction, human touch and humor as these are experienced in real-life situations preventing team building and bonding which may lead to students' decreased engagement (Li et al., 2024).

Being freely available via Chat GPT, Gen AI tools can be combined with other forms of digital technology to support students in their academic learning journey as long as students are aware of how these can be used to support their learning. Therefore, developing students' AI and digital literacy skills seems a pre-requisite in order to address the risks and challenges associated with Gen AI misuse. Gen AI can transform students' academic outcomes and enhance their engagement as it offers the possibility of a more flexible, adaptive, personalized, captivating learning and assessment experience for HE learners (Nguyen et al., 2024), and in fostering sustainable learning development (Shwedeh et al., 2024; Sywelem, 2024). The use of Gen AI tools in HE can help HEIs advance their sustainability by improving student academic outcomes, the relevant operational systems, increasing student engagement, improving student continuation etc. Gen AI's ability to create new content, find new resources, and offer individualized learning or scenario building and simulations (i.e., VR-powered labs) are directly linked to sustainable learning development in HE as it widens student access to HE fostering inclusion. Gen AI- powered systems can create flexible lesson plans, tests, quizzes, case scenarios or simulations related to intercultural sustainability enhancing student autonomy and involvement in their own learning process and their awareness of prominent sustainability issues. The use of digital technology can also enhance students' learning experience as students investigate various sustainability strategies used by companies around the world to increase i.e., intercultural awareness allowing students to better comprehend the impact and the implications of sustainable practices in real-life.

The current chapter offers valuable insights regarding students' perceptions of Gen AI and how Gen AI tools can be used in HE to increase sustainable learning development for all learners irrespective of their background, needs, or tastes. It aspires to contribute to the ongoing debate on the effective and ethical use of Gen AI tools in HE where the use of sustainable educational practices is now required to support the development of students' professional skills. Sustainability needs to be integrated into lecturers' everyday educational practices to support students in becoming aware and helping tackle major sustainability issues i.e., climate change and critical thinking about global challenges, as well as responsible use of resources as the implementation of Gen AI into HE is associated with sustainability and has become a priority for HEIs (Miao et al, 2021). This is perfectly aligned with the 2030 Agenda for Sustainable Development and its sustainable development goal 4 (SDG-4) which supports the incorporation of AI tools into HE (Uğraş et al., 2024).

## BACKGROUND

This section will provide the literature review of this study exploring several topics.

### AI in Higher Education

Gen AI has been considered a priority in HE nowadays taking into consideration its potential to increase students' academic performance and engagement increasing student achievement and productivity. According to various scholars, Gen AI tools aim to aid lecturers -not to replace them- and supplement their work decreasing their workload (Chaika, 2023; Nguyen et al., 2022). As new technologies are continuously evolving, lecturers and students need to keep up with the new updates, and students and lecturers need to become pioneers in the integration of new techniques i.e., AI to ensure safe and ethical use to support learning and teaching (Alam, 2023; Schiff, 2022). Several AI tools have been used in HE and they all have their advantages and disadvantages. Some of them, i.e., Chat GPT, have become students' best friends as they facilitate individualized learning (Sajja et al., 2024). Students love them as they support autonomous learning and allow them to develop their knowledge on any given topic at their own pace. Students can then improve their academic performance, and pass their courses but also genuinely write more cohesively and insightfully (Marzuki et al., 2023). AI tools can also be used for research purposes, i.e., brainstorming, literature reviews and data analysis (Casal & Kessler, 2023). Gen AI tools can be incorporated in HE teaching and learning to promote critical and creative thinking as they try to solve real-world challenges. However, Gen AI tools when used without caution can prevent the development of lower-level cognitive skills (How et al., 2023). University students have also been using AI unfairly and have committed academic crimes, i.e., plagiarism as students are often unaware of how to use AI tools ethically (Chan, 2024).

## Students' Perceptions and Concerns About AI

An exploration of HE students' perceptions and concerns about AI can offer significant insights into how they use Gen AI tools and their potential influence on their academic performance and professional ventures. Students who have positive dispositions towards Gen AI techniques experiment with them, use them frequently, and try to integrate them into their own learning as they can improve their academic performance. They firmly believe that the development of their AI literacy is vital if they want to increase their chances of finding employment post-graduation which is a significant indicator of Gen AI's pedagogical value (Chan & Hu, 2023; T¸ ala ˘ et al., 2024). Several studies have explored HE students' perceptions of Gen AI revealing that postgraduate students feel relatively comfortable with Gen AI and are well aware of the ethical issues related to Gen AI use (Ivanov et al., 2024; Lin & Chen, 2024; Nikolic et al., 2024). They also express their wish to further explore Gen AI tools and are only moderately concerned about the risks posed by Gen AI (Amooozadeh et al., 2024; Kilzilcec et al., 2024). Many studies indicate that the majority of university students use it for homework and academic assignments while many students also use it during tests and to create articles (Zhang et al., 2024). They perceive Gen AI tools as more beneficial than risky (Jain et al., 2024). The above findings are true for the Global North but the situation is slightly different in the Global South and its developing countries as there was a significant lack of awareness due to limited use of Gen AI tools in education (Demaidi, 2023). Research studies reveal that the main reasons why Gen AI tools are not used in developing countries are: limited language options, cases of academic dishonesty, bias and lack of accountability, and a general lack of interest among both students and lecturers (Mollura et al., 2020). Moreover, some students express their concerns about privacy, power dynamics, and control related to the use of Gen AI although they admit their utility, user-friendly interface and the quick feedback on their performance they often receive (Allen & Weill, 2024). While students admit that they offer personalized support and additional possibilities for communication, they also highlight concerns about responsibility, agency, and surveillance issues. To sum up, more research is needed to offer additional insights into students' perceptions and concerns about the use of AI tools in HE.

The main aim of the current study was to answer the following research questions:

- What are students' perceptions of the use of Gen AI tools in HE?
- What are students' perceptions of their own AI literacy in HE?

## MAIN FOCUS OF THE CHAPTER

### Methodology

#### Participants

The study focused on exploring HE students' perspectives on Gen AI. Data was gathered using a qualitative approach through an electronic survey with open-ended questions. Participant recruitment used a combination of snowball and convenience sampling methods. To reach a wider audience, the survey link was shared through various online platforms such as Facebook, Twitter, and WhatsApp groups. Identified respondents were encouraged to further distribute the survey link among their peers. All participants received consent forms and detailed information about the study prior to their participation. They were given the opportunity to review and understand the information before providing their consent. Participants were also assured that they could withdraw from the study at any point without facing any consequences. Throughout the study, confidentiality and anonymity of the participants were prioritized. Their identities were kept undisclosed, and their responses were treated with the utmost privacy and confidentiality.

The participants of this study were 163 undergraduate students who studied in the UK, Albania, and Greece. The demographic information of the participating students is included in Table 1. All data were analysed using thematic analysis.

Two coders manually generated codes. After reading the entire dataset, each coder was assigned the same subset of 50 responses to identify potential themes. In cases where the coders disagreed, they discussed the discrepancies and reached an agreement. Finally, a codebook was created based on consensus and utilized to code the remaining responses.

*Table 1. Demographic details and characteristics of participating students*

| | Students | Frequency |
|---|---|---|
| **Gender** | Male | 82 |
| | Female | 78 |
| | LGBTQ+ | 3 |
| **Nationality** | Domestic | 63 |
| | International | 100 |

## FINDINGS

The researcher analysed all findings taking into consideration the research questions of the current study and detected the following major themes which were repeated by more than 120 students.

### Individualized and Instant Learning Support

Low-achieving students confessed that they used Gen AI tools as virtual tutors as they could get immediate answers to any questions they might have. Multilingual students also said that they used Gen AI tools like Grammarly to check their written assignments and offer suggestions. They are not always helpful but students use their own critical thinking skills to make decisions. They helped them by increasing their understanding and allowing them to see things from another perspective. Lecturers cannot possibly offer students feedback every time they need it. Gen AI tools offer students more options to enhance their learning process and overcome barriers they may be facing i.e., due to language. Lecturers cannot provide students with feedback several times per day as is the case with Gen AI tools. Therefore, it can safely be used to reduce lecturers' workload allowing them to focus their attention on weak students who need it the most. Gen AI tools develop students' autonomy and their problem-solving skills revolutionizing traditional teaching methods. These are valuable professional skills students will need when they graduate.

*"Gen AI is my best friend. I always turn to it when in doubt. Lecturers are not always there to support us all. It is impossible. Gen AI also provides feedback on my work and useful suggestions. They really make my life easier."*

## Academic Writing and Brainstorming Support

Students reported using Gen AI tools, i.e., Chat GPT as a writing companion. It helped them brainstorm new ideas and increased their creativity. They also find new sources of inspiration as they can interact with these tools. Students need encouragement and support at the beginning and they frequently get it from Gen AI as lecturers are not omnipresent. Gen AI tools also offer technical support by helping them gather citations and create bibliographic lists thus improving their efficiency. Students often use Gen AI tools to improve their writing skills as GEN AI tools often provide rich feedback and can help improve their assignments by offering very helpful suggestions.

*"I speak English as a second language and I am not confident when I write assignments. I cannot always ask my lecturer for feedback. I cannot make always appointments with academic mentors as well. Using Gen AI tools is so fast and efficient. It has almost become a routine to ask for help in terms of proofreading. I can safely say that I have improved my skills ever since I have started using Gen AI. It is also brilliant for helping me come up with new ideas. When people ask me a question, I often do not understand a word or two. When I get help from Gen AI, I can then come up with incredible ideas. I just need some help initially."*

## Research and Analysis Support

Some of the participants claimed that Gen AI techniques help postgraduate students with their research projects as they are amazing tools when students look up studies to create their literature reviews or need to summarise their readings. They can even help students fomr hypotheses based on the data their research projects have generated. As Gen AI tools have access to an incredible amount of data and information, they can indicate new research methods that young researchers are sometimes unaware of and even help them with data collection and analysis. As Gen AI tools can process large amounts of data incredibly fast, students can get their preliminary analysis results in their hands very fast and reflect on the contribution of their research projects.

*"Gen AI techniques are unbelievably helpful to final year undergraduate and postgraduate students as they can help them create their literature reviews, find additional sources, analyse their data and even make decisions about the*

*usefulness of their study by looking at their preliminary results very fast. This helps PhD students complete their studies in no time..."*

## Visual and Audio Multi-Media Support

Students also use Gen AI tools to create artwork as if they were graphic designers and do monotonous work they would rather avoid. Students need support as they often need to meet multiple deadlines. STEM students can get considerable help by just using a prompt. These tools are also very helpful in creating slides, audios and videos frequently needed to be submitted as assignments by students in HEI. Gen AI is an amazing content creator offering valuable insights and ideas.

*"Sometimes, you run out of ideas or you do not want to do the 'dirty work'. You simply do not have enough time for everything. Gen AI tools can offer a hand offering insightful ideas and incredible new possibilities. Things have changed for the better for HE students...It was about time..."*

## Challenges Regarding Accuracy and Transparency

Students often rely on Gen AI tools but the information they provide is not always accurate. These tools frequently make mistakes, i.e., in terms of semantics and culture. Students state that the information provided is often misleading and they cannot often tell the difference. Studenst are also afraid of Gen AI tools as they do not understand who is behind them and how they reach the decisions they do. They are still a mystery.

*"Who knows who stands behind Gen AI. It is like a myth. There are issues of transparency and lack of trust. Moreover, AI tools are not perfect. We need to assess the information they provide as it is not always true."*

All in all, students were able to detect numerous advantages for players but also offer suggestions to improve the overall implementation of the DEERs in HE.

## Challenges Regarding Privacy and Ethical Issues

Students also expressed their concerns about privacy and ethical issues as AI can gather information from their messages and use it in unpredictable ways. AI tools can get students' private information and this poses a number of security risks as we do not know who has access to all this information. A further issue which is also a major concern for lecturers is plagiarism a form of academic misconduct. The fast evolution of Gen AI tools makes it difficult for academic institutions to find ways to detect plagiarized information in students' assignments.

*"Distinguishing what students can write from what they can get from Gen AI is straight forward for the time being but as technological advancements move so fast, it will surely become impossible to detect or prove what information has been misused by 'lazy students'. This is not fair for other students who devote so much time and energy on their assignments. There are also privacy issues as we do not know where all that information we are providing is stored and who has access to it. We are scared..."*

## Challenges Regarding Lack of Clear Policies and Procedures

Students also complain about the lack of policies and regulation in HE regarding the use of AI. They are concerned about governance as obscure regulations often result in misuse and taking unnecessary risks which no one in HEIs can afford as it has a direct impact on all students. Students expressed their wish for clear guidelines and for the development of their AI literacy to be able to use Gen AI more efficiently.

*"I am afraid. How do we know we are using technology in the right way? Who talked to us about strategies, regulations and policies? Noone. Things are so unclear and risky. We need to receive more information about the safe and ethical use of GenAI, as we do want to use these tools in our everyday life. It is a must..."*

## Concerns About Human Values

Participants also referred to risks related to social issues and their own values. Gen AI may increase social inequalities and hinder inclusion for certain groups of students. It might widen the gap among gifted and low-achieving students, white and blacks, rich and poor. Another concern is how it will affect the lecturer-student relationship as students get more dependent on Gen AI tools and lose their respect for educators.

*"AI may become dangerous...A threat to our own values as they do not align well. Some people do not use it with their assignment. This is not fair for them. What do we do then? Who do we trust? AI or our lecturers? Who knows best?"*

## Concerns About Career Prospects

Finally, students believe that Gen AI is neither a friend nor a foe. Gen AI can replace many humans in countless jobs, including educators. What will happen then? Jobs are disappearing as Gen AI has a deep impact on societies and the workplace. This will test future graduates' nerves as people not aware of Gen AI technologies will fall behind.

*"Insecurity is everywhere. I wanted to become a lecturer but Gen AI will soon replace us all. What job to choose, I do not know. Shall it exist in a decade from now? Who knows?"*

To sum up, the findings from the current study indicated that students had mixed feelings about Gen AI and expressed their need for continuous development of their Gen AI literacy to be able to follow the fast evolvement of technology and the opportunities it provides for teaching and learning.

## DISCUSSION AND IMPLICATIONS

The current study reveals the highly complex and mixed responses of HE students to the use of Gen AI as students confessed both their passion and eagerness to learn more and systematically use AI tools to enhance their academic journey but also their reservations for using these techniques widely. The outcomes of the current study offer a comprehensive description and understanding of our HE students' views. Students seem to be familiar with some AI tools but hesitant about how they are allowed to use them in terms of their studies. Students request support from their lecturers to develop their AI literacy skills to meet the demands posed by their future employers as these are widely used in various industries. Frequency of use varies among students depending on their age, cultural background and country of origin when these are international students. Ou study also stresses the benefits and challenges of utilizing AI in HE in terms of teaching and learning. Students were also aware of the different ways they could use AI techniques but also of their limitations and revealed their fears about the reliability, privacy, ethical issues, and vague policies related to GenAI, and its relative influence on students' personal development, career prospects, and societal values.

The present research project showed that how frequently students use AI tools and how aware of their capabilities are depends on how frequently they experiment with it and how open they are to innovative tools in teaching and learning. Therefore, familiarization of students with new techniques may support the development of positive dispositions towards Gen AI and the development of students' AI literacy. However, students seem to have too high expectations thinking that Gen AI tools may resolve magically all their problems. Students need to become more aware of the risks Gen AI tools may pose as i.e., the use of AI tools for the provision of individualized support has certain limitations as these tools cannot always support students' needs around the clock. Although students need support to improve their writing skills in terms of content rather than grammar and proofreading as Atlas's study has indicated (2023), this is not always feasible. Students also expect AI tools to support them beyond offering support in terms of literature reviews and help them create hypotheses and keep themselves updated with the modern trends in their field (Berg, 2023). Gen AI is breaking barriers in HE teaching, learning and assessment by fostering inclusion, catering for all students' needs and tastes, improving students' academic performance and enhancing their learning motivation and engagement.

Students need to avoid overdependency on Gen AI tools and take into consideration concerns that have been widely raised regarding accuracy, transparency, privacy, and ethics in relation to the use of Gen AI in HE learning and teaching. For instance, students often face the challenge of plagiarism as they do not know what information provided by Gen AI tools is original and cannot determine any mistakes in the data provided by Gen AI thus requiring support from their lecturers and more experienced members of staff (Lubowitz, 2023; Peres et al., 2023). Our study confirms previous research indicating that all students have reservations against Gen AI tools no matter how positively disposed they are towards innovative learning strategies in HE (also in Dahmash et al., 2020). Students also recognise that Gen AI may limit the developments of the critical, analytical and creative skills although they do have a direct impact on the career opportunities they may have (Ghotbi et al., 2022; Gong et al., 2019; Park et al., 2020) and can be misaligned with important human values (Gillissen et al., 2022; Jha et al., 2022). Senior leadership teams in HEIs, senior leaders in the industry and policymakers need to take into consideration students' attitudes towards Gen AI as it is crucial to secure their acceptance as users to enhance teaching and learning outcomes facilitating the integration of Gen AI tools into HE. Finally, the use of Gen AI is expected to have a deep impact on students' sustainable learning and issues of equity and inclusion in HE, e.g., ensure equitable access to HE and promotion of accessibility and inclusion, as Gen AI tools are able to identify barriers to access, indicate interventions to improve inclusivity, and help students via personalized learning systems.

## CONCLUSION

Gen AI technology has brought about incredible advances over the last decades and continues to change and transform our HEIs and societies at an incredible pace (Beckingham et al., 2024) as it generates innovative educational opportunities aiming to transform the educational practices. Digital transformation has a deep and significant impact on sustainable HEIs (Mohamed Hashim et al., 2022). To increase its efficacy in learning, teaching and assessment, Gen AI utilization needs to be sustainable, safe, and ethical (Beckingham et al., 2024). The current study - despite its obvious limitations (small scale study) - explored students' attitudes toward Gen AI tools which aim to foster sustainable learning development in HE. These can improve educational practices, graduate outcomes and student engagement and improve educational procedures by improving the utilization of digital resources supporting research and innovation. Since the integration of Gen AI in HE may create incredible opportunities for students, future research is needed to examine the transformative prospects and impact of Gen AI for sustainability in HE.

## REFERENCES


Alam, A. (2023). Developing a Curriculum for Ethical and Responsible AI: A University Course on Safety, Fairness, Privacy, and Ethics to Prepare Next Generation of AI Professionals. In *Intelligent Communication Technologies and Virtual Mobile Networks* (pp. 879–894). Springer Nature Singapore. DOI: 10.1007/978-981-99-1767-9_64

Allen, D., & Weyl, E. G. (2024). The real dangers of generative ai. *Journal of Democracy*, *35*(1), 147–162. DOI: 10.1353/jod.2024.a915355

Amoozadeh, M., Daniels, D., Nam, D., Kumar, A., Chen, S., Hilton, M., & Alipour, M. A. (2024, March). Trust in Generative AI among students: An exploratory study. In *Proceedings of the 55th ACM Technical Symposium on Computer Science Education* V. 1 (pp. 67-73). DOI: 10.1145/3626252.3630842

Atlas, S. (2023). ChatGPT for higher education and professional development: A guide to conversational AI.

Beckingham, S., Lawrence, J., Powell, S., & Hartley, P. (Eds.). (2024). *Using generative AI effectively in higher education: Sustainable and ethical practices for learning, teaching and assessment*. Routledge. DOI: 10.4324/9781003482918

Bender, S. M. (2024). Awareness of artificial intelligence as an essential digital literacy: ChatGPT and Gen-AI in the classroom. *Changing English*, *31*(2), 161–174. DOI: 10.1080/1358684X.2024.2309995

Berg, C. (2023). The case for generative AI in scholarly practice.

Bhandari, A. (2023). Bias in AI: A comprehensive examination of factors and improvement strategies. *International Journal on Computer Science and Engineering*, *10*(6), 9–14. DOI: 10.14445/23488387/IJCSE-V10I6P102

Bozkurt, A., Junhong, X., Lambert, S., Pazurek, A., Crompton, H., Koseoglu, S., & Romero-Hall, E. (2023). Speculative futures on ChatGPT and generative artificial intelligence (AI): A collective reflection from the educational landscape. *Asian Journal of Distance Education*, *18*(1), 53–130.

Casal, J. E., & Kessler, M. (2023). Can linguists distinguish between ChatGPT/AI and human writing?: A study of research ethics and academic publishing. *Research Methods in Applied Linguistics*, *2*(3), 100068. DOI: 10.1016/j.rmal.2023.100068

Chaika, O. (2023). The role of artificial intelligence in higher education. *Молодь і ринок*, (6/214), 69-74.

Chan, C. K. Y. (2024). Students' perceptions of 'AI-giarism': Investigating changes in understandings of academic misconduct. *Education and Information Technologies*, 1–22. DOI: 10.1007/s10639-024-13151-7

Chan, C. K. Y., & Hu, W. (2023). Students' voices on generative AI: Perceptions, benefits, and challenges in higher education. *International Journal of Educational Technology in Higher Education*, *20*(1), 43. DOI: 10.1186/s41239-023-00411-8

Chiu, T. K. (2024). Future research recommendations for transforming higher education with generative AI. Computers and Education: Artificial Intelligence, 6, Article 100197.

Crawford, J., Cowling, M., & Allen, K. (2023). Leadership is needed for ethical ChatGPT: Character, assessment, and learning using artificial intelligence (AI). *Journal of University Teaching & Learning Practice*, *20*(3), 02. DOI: 10.53761/1.20.3.02

Demaidi, M. N. (2023). Artificial intelligence national strategy in a developing country. *AI & Society*, 1–13. DOI: 10.1007/s00146-023-01779-x

Ghotbi, N., Ho, M. T., & Mantello, P. (2022). Attitude of college students towards ethical issues of artificial intelligence in an international university in Japan. *AI & Society*, *37*(1), 283–290. DOI: 10.1007/s00146-021-01168-2

Gillissen, A., Kochanek, T., Zupanic, M., & Ehlers, J. (2022). Medical students' perceptions towards digitalization and artificial intelligence: A mixed-methods study. *Health Care*, *10*(4), 723. PMID: 35455898

Gong, B., Nugent, J. P., Guest, W., Parker, W., Chang, P. J., Khosa, F., & Nicolaou, S. (2019). Influence of artificial intelligence on Canadian medical students' preference for radiology specialty: A national survey study. *Academic Radiology*, *26*(4), 566–577. DOI: 10.1016/j.acra.2018.10.007 PMID: 30424998

How, M. L., Cheah, S. M., Chan, Y. J., Khor, A. C., & Say, E. M. P. (2023). Artificial Intelligence for Advancing Sustainable Development Goals (SDGs): An Inclusive Democratized Low-Code Approach. In *The Ethics of Artificial Intelligence for the Sustainable Development Goals* (pp. 145–165). Springer International Publishing. DOI: 10.1007/978-3-031-21147-8_9

Ivanov, S., Soliman, M., Tuomi, A., Alkathiri, N. A., & Al-Alawi, A. N. (2024). Drivers of generative AI adoption in higher education through the lens of the Theory of Planned Behaviour. *Technology in Society*, *77*, 102521. DOI: 10.1016/j.techsoc.2024.102521

Jain, K. K., & Raghuram, J. N. V. (2024). Gen-AI integration in higher education: Predicting intentions using SEM-ANN approach. *Education and Information Technologies, 29*(13), 1–41. DOI: 10.1007/s10639-024-12506-4

Jha, N., Shankar, P. R., Al-Betar, M. A., Mukhia, R., Hada, K., & Palaian, S. (2022). Undergraduate medical students' and interns' knowledge and perception of artificial intelligence in medicine. *Advances in Medical Education and Practice, 13*, 927–937. DOI: 10.2147/AMEP.S368519 PMID: 36039185

Kazanidis, I., & Pellas, N. (2024). Harnessing generative artificial intelligence for digital literacy innovation: A comparative study between early childhood education and computer science undergraduates. *AI, 5*(3), 1427–1445. DOI: 10.3390/ai5030068

Kizilcec, R. F., Huber, E., Papanastasiou, E. C., Cram, A., Makridis, C. A., Smolansky, A., Zeivots, S., & Raduescu, C. (2024). Perceived impact of generative AI on assessments: Comparing educator and student perspectives in Australia, Cyprus, and the United States. *Computers and Education: Artificial Intelligence, 7*, 100269. DOI: 10.1016/j.caeai.2024.100269

Li, J., Cao, H., Lin, L., Hou, Y., Zhu, R., & El Ali, A. (2024, May). User experience design professionals' perceptions of generative artificial intelligence. In *Proceedings of the CHI Conference on Human Factors in Computing Systems* (pp. 1-18). DOI: 10.1145/3613904.3642114

Lin, H., & Chen, Q. (2024). Artificial intelligence (AI)-integrated educational applications and college students' creativity and academic emotions: Students and teachers' perceptions and attitudes. *BMC Psychology, 12*(1), 487. DOI: 10.1186/s40359-024-01979-0 PMID: 39285268

Lubowitz, J. H. (2023). ChatGPT, an artificial intelligence chatbot, is impacting medical literature. *Arthroscopy, 39*(5), 1121–1122. DOI: 10.1016/j.arthro.2023.01.015 PMID: 36797148

Marzuki, W., Widiati, U., Rusdin, D., Darwin, , & Indrawati, I. (2023). The impact of AI writing tools on the content and organization of students' writing: EFL teachers' perspective. *Cogent Education, 10*(2), 2236469. DOI: 10.1080/2331186X.2023.2236469

Miao, F., Holmes, W., Huang, R., & Zhang, H. (2021). *AI and education–Guidance for policy-makers*. United Nations Educational, Scientific and Cultural Organization.

Mohamed Hashim, M., Tlemsani, I., & Duncan Matthews, R. (2022). A sustainable university: Digital transformation and beyond. *Education and Information Technologies, 27*(7), 8961–8996. DOI: 10.1007/s10639-022-10968-y PMID: 35340534

Mollura, D. J., Culp, M. P., Pollack, E., Battino, G., Scheel, J. R., Mango, V. L., Elahi, A., Schweitzer, A., & Dako, F. (2020). Artificial intelligence in low-and middle-income countries: Innovating global health radiology. *Radiology*, *297*(3), 513–520. DOI: 10.1148/radiol.2020201434 PMID: 33021895

Nguyen, A., Kremantzis, M., Essien, A., Petrounias, I., & Hosseini, S. (2024). Enhancing student engagement through artificial intelligence (AI): Understanding the basics, opportunities, and challenges. *Journal of University Teaching & Learning Practice*, *21*(06). Advance online publication. DOI: 10.53761/caraaq92

Nguyen, T. H., Tran, D. N., Vo, D. L., Mai, V. H., & Dao, X. Q. (2022). AI-powered university: Design and deployment of robot assistant for smart universities. *Journal of Advances in Information Technology, 13*(1).

Nikolic, S., Wentworth, I., Sheridan, L., Moss, S., Duursma, E., Jones, R. A., Ros, M., & Middleton, R. (2024). A systematic literature review of attitudes, intentions and behaviours of teaching academics pertaining to AI and generative AI (GenAI) in higher education: An analysis of GenAI adoption using the UTAUT framework. *Australasian Journal of Educational Technology*. Advance online publication. DOI: 10.14742/ajet.9643

Nikolopoulou, K. (2025). Generative artificial intelligence and sustainable higher education: Mapping the potential. *Journal of Digital Educational Technology*, *5*(1), ep2506. DOI: 10.30935/jdet/15860

Park, C. J., Yi, P. H., & Siegel, E. L. (2020). Medical student perspectives on the impact of artificial intelligence on the practice of medicine. *Current Problems in Diagnostic Radiology*, *50*(5), 614–619. DOI: 10.1067/j.cpradiol.2020.06.011 PMID: 32680632

Peres, R., Shreier, M., Schweidel, D., & Sorescu, A. (2023). On ChatGPT and beyond: How generative artificial intelligence may affect research, teaching, and practice. *International Journal of Research in Marketing*, *40*(2), 269–275. DOI: 10.1016/j.ijresmar.2023.03.001

Sajja, R., Sermet, Y., Cikmaz, M., Cwiertny, D., & Demir, I. (2024). Artificial intelligence-enabled intelligent assistant for personalized and adaptive learning in higher education. *Information (Basel)*, *15*(10), 596. DOI: 10.3390/info15100596

Schiff, D. (2022). Education for AI, not AI for education: The role of education and ethics in national AI policy strategies. *International Journal of Artificial Intelligence in Education*, *32*(3), 527–563. DOI: 10.1007/s40593-021-00270-2

Shwedeh, F., Salloum, S. A., Aburayya, A., Fatin, B., Elbadawi, M. A., Al Ghurabli, Z., & Al Dabbagh, T. (2024). AI adoption and educational sustainability in higher education in the UAE. In A. Al-Marzouqi, S. A. Salloum, M. Al-Saidat, A. Aburayya, & B. Gupta, B. (Eds.), Artificial intelligence in education: The power and dangers of ChatGPT in the classroom (pp. 201–229). Springer. DOI: 10.1007/978-3-031-52280-2_14

Sywelem, M. M. G. (2024). Artificial intelligence and the sustainability of educational services: An overview. *World Journal of Social Sciences and Humanities*, *10*(1), 8–17. DOI: 10.12691/wjssh-10-1-2

Tala, M. L., Müller, C. N., Nastase, I. A., State, O., & Georghe, G. (2024). Exploring university students' perceptions of generative artificial intelligence in education. Amfiteatru Economic Journal, 26(65), 71–88.

Voss, E., Cushing, S. T., Ockey, G. J., & Yan, X. (2023). The use of assistive technologies including generative AI by test takers in language assessment: A debate of theory and practice. *Language Assessment Quarterly*, *20*(4-5), 520–532. DOI: 10.1080/15434303.2023.2288256

Wei, X., Kumar, N., & Zhang, H. (2025). Addressing bias in generative AI: Challenges and research opportunities in information management. *Information & Management*, *62*(2), 104103. DOI: 10.1016/j.im.2025.104103

Zhang, Z., Dong, Z., Shi, Y., Price, T., Matsuda, N., & Xu, D. (2024, March). Students' perceptions and preferences of generative artificial intelligence feedback for programming. *Proceedings of the AAAI Conference on Artificial Intelligence*, *38*(21), 23250–23258. DOI: 10.1609/aaai.v38i21.30372

## ADDITIONAL READING

Meletiadou, E. (2011). *Peer assessment of writing in secondary education: Its impact on learners' performance and attitudes. M.A. in Applied Linguistics*. University of Cyprus.

Meletiadou, E. (2012). The impact of training adolescent EFL learners on their perceptions of peer assessment of writing. *RPLTL*, *3*(1), 240–251.

Meletiadou, E. (2013). EFL learners' attitudes towards peer assessment, teacher assessment and the process writing' (Vol. M.A.). In D. Tsagari (Ed.) *Language Testing and Evaluation Series, 28* (pp. 312-330). Frankfurt am Main: Peter Lang GmbH.

Meletiadou, E. (2021a). Exploring the impact of peer assessment on EFL students' writing performance. *IAFOR Journal of Education*, *9*(3), 77–95. DOI: 10.22492/ije.9.3.05

Meletiadou, E. (2021a). Opening Pandora's box: How does peer assessment affect EFL students' writing quality? *Languages (Basel, Switzerland)*, *6*(3), 115. DOI: 10.3390/languages6030115

Meletiadou, E. (2021b). Exploring the impact of peer assessment on EFL students' writing performance. *IAFOR Journal of Education*, *9*(3), 77–95. DOI: 10.22492/ije.9.3.05

Meletiadou, E. (2021c). Using Padlets as e-portfolios to develop undergraduate students' writing skills and motivation. *IAFOR Journal of Undergraduate Education*, *9*(4), 67–83. DOI: 10.22492/ije.9.5.04

Meletiadou, E. (2022). The utilisation of peer-Assisted learning/mentoring and translanguaging in Higher Education. *IAFOR Journal of Education. Language Issue*, *10*(1), 135–154.

Meletiadou, E. (2022a). The Use of Peer Assessment as an Inclusive Learning Strategy in Higher Education Institutions: Enhancing Student Writing Skills and Motivation.

Meletiadou, E. (2022b). *Learners' perceptions of peer assessment: Implications for their willingness to write in an EFL classroom.* International Journal of Teacher Education and Professional Development. IGI. DOI: 10.4018/IJTEPD.295539

Meletiadou, E. (2022c). The lived experiences of female educational leaders in Higher Education in the UK: Academic resilience and gender.

Meletiadou, E. (2022d). Profiling the writing competency of BAME undergraduate students: Fostering Inclusion and academic success to improve retention in Tertiary Education.

Meletiadou, E. (accepted). Using Educational Digital Storytelling to enhance multilingual students' writing skills in Higher Education. *IAFOR Journal of Education. Technology Issue.*

Meletiadou, E., & Tsagari, D. (2012). Investigating the attitudes of adolescent EFL learners towards peer assessment of writing. In Tsagari, D. (Ed.), *Research on English as a foreign language in Cyprus* (Vol. II, pp. 225–245). University of Nicosia Press.

Meletiadou, E., & Tsagari, D. (2014). An exploration of the reliability and validity of peer assessment of writing in secondary education. In Tsagari, D. (Ed.), *Major trends in theoretical and applied linguistics 3* (pp. 235–250). De Gruyter Open Poland. DOI: 10.2478/9788376560915.p14

Meletiadou, E., & Tsagari, D. (2016). The washback effect of peer assessment on adolescent EFL learners in Cyprus. In Tsagari, D. (Ed.), *Classroom-based assessment in L2 contexts*. Cambridge Scholars Publishing.

Meletiadou, E., & Tsagari, D. (2022a). Exploring teachers' perceptions of the use of peer assessment in EFL test-dominated writing classes. *Recent Development in Language Testing and Assessment Special Issue.Languages (Basel, Switzerland)*, *7*(1), 16. DOI: 10.3390/languages7010016

## KEY TERMS AND DEFINITIONS

**Gen AI:** It refers to deep-learning models that can generate high-quality text, images, and other content based on the data they were trained on.

**Sustainability:** It refers to the ability to be maintained at a certain rate or level.

# Chapter 3
# Bridging Inequalities in Higher Education With the Use of Gen AI:
## The LivePBL DEEP Method

**Ying Liu**
*London School of Science and Technology, UK*

**Yuanyuan Li**
*Capital Normal University, Beijing, China*

**Ting Zhao**
*Beijing Youth and Politics Vocational College, China*

## ABSTRACT

*This chapter explores the integration of Generative AI (Gen AI) in higher education (HE) to enhance inclusion, addressing the critical need for a design-oriented and actionable approach to counter inequalities. Applying design thinking, the LivePBL DEEP Method is introduced and structured into four phases: Direction, Education, Event, and Project. This method employs Gen AI to foster inclusive learning environments by aligning AI with policies that view inequalities as diverse, positive opportunities to bridge gaps between pedagogical inequality and equality. Emphasising co-design, the method supports actionable policies at the micro level. It presents use cases from hybrid learning settings, demonstrating practical applications in real-world HE contexts. The chapter concludes with recommendations for scaling and integrating Gen AI to promote inclusion further.*

DOI: 10.4018/979-8-3693-5623-4.ch003

## INTRODUCTION

Higher Education (HE) confronts profound equality, diversity, and inclusion challenges. Sustainable Development Goal 4 (SDG 4), which was adopted by 184 UNESCO Member States on November 4, 2015, in Paris, states:

> *By 2030, ensure equal access for all women and men to affordable and quality technical, vocational, and tertiary education, including university (UNESCO, 2015).*

HE must share, if not lead, this responsibility. Significant evidence has raised concerns that despite well-intentioned policies and frameworks, the pace of change has been sluggish (Bergan et al., 2018; Smith & Chen, 2024). There are noticeable disparities between the aspirations outlined in these policies and the actual practices observed (Marginson, 2016; Patel & Martinez, 2024).

While policies may mandate equal access, their practical action often falls short (Jones & Williams, 2024; Tight, 2020) due to inadequate funding, lack of infrastructure, societal biases, a lack of accountability, and efforts that were said to promote diversity but are superficial rather than substantive. Significant gaps exist in the consistent implementation of strategies across different regions and institutions around the globe (Garcia et al., 2022; Lumby & Foskett, 2016). For example, there are challenges in fulfilling the commitments under SDG 4 and translating them into real-world outcomes (Li & Johnson, 2024; McCowan, 2019).

This chapter concerns critical issues arising to accelerate HE efforts to close these gaps. It argues that the

- Current design methods are insufficient to orientate implementations in inclusion and diversity;
- The strategies are often poorly or loosely designed in terms of disciplinary and digital technology applications, and that
- HE must enhance strategic design thinking.

The chapter introduces and discusses the "LivePBL DEEP Method," designed to guide the use of Gen AI tools, such as ChatGPT, to bridge the existing gaps. However, before making it clear what LivePBL DEEP and Gen AI encompass, it is essential first to establish the context of why constructing this method is necessary.

### Inequality and Equality: Gaps on Both Sides

The argument that delays in aligning policy with practice undermine equitable access to HE is well-supported by recent research (Wilcox & Lawson, 2024). These delays often result in continued barriers for marginalised communities, including those from racial, socio-economic, and cultural backgrounds. For instance, studies (Neimann et al., 2022) have highlighted that despite policies aimed at equity, practical implementation issues continue to restrict access to quality education, particularly for disadvantaged groups. However, large-scale studies (Diaz et al., 2023 ; Jain et al., 2023; OECD-iLibrary, 2018) demonstrate that while expansion in HE systems has increased overall access, it has not necessarily addressed broader and deeper inequalities. These inequalities are often rooted in earlier stages of education and socio-technologic and socio-economic backgrounds, leading to disparities in outcomes. Most current policies are on equality or inclusion in HE, which predominantly focus on the institutional side (Diaz et al., 2023 ; Jain et al., 2023) rather than addressing the diversity and inequality sides of the equation, neglecting the broader context of inequality that students from marginalised backgrounds face.

Inequality in HE highlights the differences and barriers various groups face, leading to disadvantages for some. In contrast, equality focuses on removing these barriers to provide equal opportunities and outcomes for all, aiming for a fair and just educational environment. Addressing inequality involves identifying and reducing specific disparities while promoting equality by creating policies and practices (Kottmann et al., 2019; Wang, 2023). To effectively bridge the gap, solutions must also engage, motivate, and provide personalised or adaptive learning support for these students (Salas-Pilco et al., 2022). There should also be more efforts to address the external barriers and challenges that hinder students' access to and success in HE (Spricigo et al., 2023). The policies remain insufficient without this dual approach to overview both sides (i.e., equality and inequality).

It is noticeable that the recent development in HE has increasingly recognised the importance of integrating a social dimension to

1. Address the diverse needs of students,
2. Ensure that education systems contribute not only to academic growth but also to
3. Take action in social equity and personal development and
4. Create more holistic learning experiences.

Furthermore, a growing recognition that formal education, typically characterised by structured curriculum and assessments within educational institutions, must be complemented by non-formal education (Colley et al., 2019; Langa & David, 2021). Non-formal education includes a wide range of learning activities outside traditional academic settings, such as community-based programs, online courses, workshops, and extracurricular activities (Mok & Neubauer, 2020). These forms of education are increasingly valued for their flexibility, relevance, and ability to foster skills like critical thinking, creativity, and social awareness. Fragoso et al.

(2024) acknowledge and call for ensuring that HE is a vehicle for social inclusion, that formal education must be complemented by non-formal education, and that a non-formal approach takes more social considerations to enhance educational outcomes and support social mobility.

## Digital Technology and Gen AI in Bridging the Gaps

Digital technology has played a crucial role in bridging formal and non-formal learning. Online platforms, open educational resources, and digital credentials are increasingly important in providing accessible learning opportunities and recognising achievements across different educational contexts.

One of the significant contributions of digital technology is the creation of hybrid learning environments that blend formal and non-formal education (Garcia et al., 2022). Online platforms and virtual classrooms have expanded access to educational resources beyond the traditional classroom, enabling students to learn at their own pace and in their own space. This flexibility is crucial for students facing geographic, economic, or social barriers to accessing traditional campus-based education. According to Garcia et al. (2022), hybrid models facilitate collaborative learning, where students from diverse backgrounds can engage with one another, share experiences, and gain new perspectives, thus fostering a more inclusive learning community. Similarly, Sorensen and Andersen (2022) highlight that digital platforms play a critical role in promoting social mobility by connecting students from various socio-economic backgrounds.

Technology has advanced rapidly in Gen AI. Gen AI refers to a class of artificial intelligence models designed to generate new content, including text, images, music, and other forms of data (SpringerOpen, 2024). Unlike traditional AI, which focuses on pattern recognition and prediction, Gen AI creates novel outputs based on learned patterns and structures from existing data. This capability stems from advanced machine learning techniques. Gen AI Tools are specific applications or platforms that leverage Gen AI technology to perform tasks such as content creation, data synthesis, and personalised recommendations. Notable examples of Gen AI tools include ChatGPT-3 and ChatGPT-4, which can generate coherent text, and DALL-E (McKinsey&Company, 2024), which can create images from textual descriptions.

Many point out that Gen AI can offer transformative potential in HE by providing personalised, scalable, and engaging learning experiences (Duarte et al., 2023). Its ability to tailor content to individual student needs addresses diverse learning preferences and supports those requiring additional assistance (Garcia et al., 2022; Sahin & Ozkan, 2024). Gen AI can assist access to quality learning, particularly for remote or underserved areas, and enhances engagement through interactive materials (Collis & van der Wende, 2023; Sorensen & Andersen, 2022). It can also support inclusivity by offering content in multiple formats, catering to students with disabilities. Moreover, Gen AI assists educators by automating administrative tasks, allowing them to focus on teaching and mentoring (Nguyen & Bui, 2023).

## Tackling HE Inequality through Design

Design thinking (DT) views the educational landscape by offering a flexible, iterative process emphasising empathy, creativity, and problem-solving. It provides an in-depth exploration of the role of design pedagogy in higher education, offering valuable insights for integrating creative and innovative approaches into academic curricula. DT is often understood to elicit users' needs, define challenges, ideate solutions, prototyping, and testing. However, arguably, DT involves more fundamentals.

DT encourages active learning and critical thinking, allowing students to engage with real-world problems. For instance, the Harvard Graduate School of Education has integrated DT into its curriculum, utilising tools such as brainstorming kits and prototyping materials to enhance creative problem-solving and promote inclusive, student-centred learning environments (Lake et al., 2024; Razzouk & Shute, 2012). The focus on empathy in DT (Chen et al., 2023; Efilti & Gelmez, 2024) helps educators understand and address students' diverse experiences, thereby enriching the learning process and fostering more engaging educational experiences.

DT offers a structured framework that facilitates collaboration and innovative thinking, enabling institutions to tackle complex issues. For example, Arizona State University has leveraged DT to align its educational research initiatives with local and global needs, such as sustainable development and technological advancements (Brown & Katz, 2011; Martin, 2014). This alignment not only enhances actionable policymaking but also ensures that the curriculum remains relevant and prepares students for future challenges.

The use of DT helps break down traditional academic silos, promoting interdisciplinary learning and research that are critical in today's complex world (Lake et al., 2024; Rowe, 1987). DT aligns with Gen AI applicational developments in HE policymaking, where "user-centred" policies

1. Identify the diverse needs of students, faculty, and other stakeholders.
2. Foster more equitable and effective educational practices by continuously iterating on policies based on real-world feedback.
3. Enable iterative processes to allow institutions to swiftly adapt to changing HE landscapes and societal demands and
4. Ensure that policies remain relevant and responsive.

Post-COVID-19, research on design thinking has surged to address HE inequality gaps, such as disparities in social engagement between students from different socioeconomic backgrounds (Martin, 2014; Razzouk & Shute, 2012). Many have explored and demonstrated DT in bridging these gaps by using technologies focusing on empathy and "user-centred" design. Empathy should be articulated and prioritised. DT should encourage a deep understanding of the challenges faced by different groups within the academic community, leading to more inclusive and just-in-need policies (Razzouk & Shute, 2012); thereby, educators and policymakers can better understand and address the challenges these students face.

## Exploring Gen AI through LivePBL DEEP Method to Bridge the Gaps

LivePBL, which stands for Live Project-Based Learning. LivePBL emerged in 2020, when COVID-19 started, as an innovative hybrid educational model to address the challenges in music education, especially in developing countries. The platform integrates PBL with Continuous Professional Development (CPD) to create a holistic learning environment (Zhang et al., 2022; Zhou et al., 2023). Developed by educators from the Music College at Capital Normal University in Beijing, LivePBL focuses on enhancing teaching practices and student engagement (Liu et al., 2022; Wang et al., 2020). However, LivePBL is not the primary focus of this chapter because there is a more essential range of multidisciplinary areas that current research needs to synthesise and cross the boundaries.

*Figure 1. LivePBL DEEP Method*

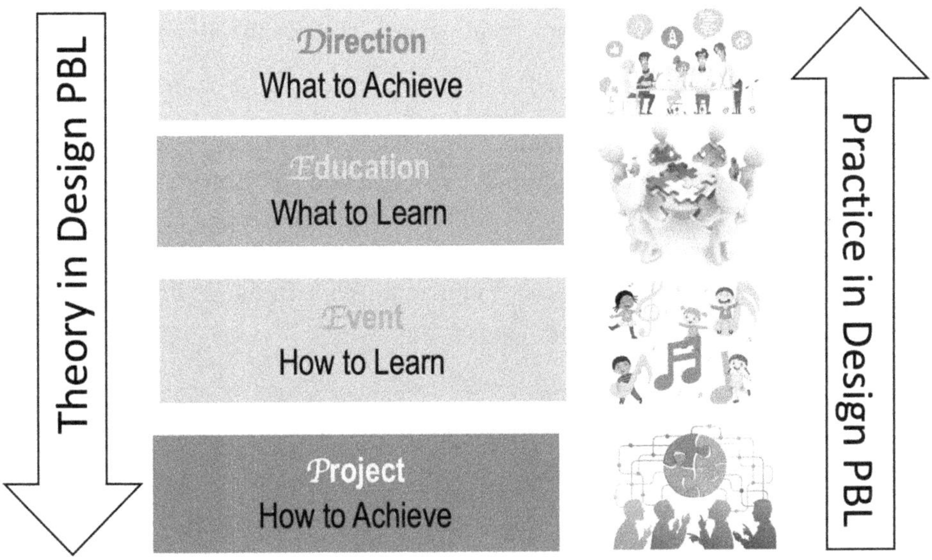


The DEEP Method (Develop, Education, Event, Project) evolved with four phases (Figure 1 illustrates LivePBL DEEP Method):

1. Direction (What to achieve): This phase involves setting goals and defining desired outcomes to address inequalities, focusing on a roadmap that aligns with stakeholders' needs.
2. Education (What to learn): This phase identifies educational contexts of inequality and designs curricula and resources that leverage digital technologies and Gen AI for co-learning opportunities.
3. Event (How to learn): This phase focuses on engaging activities and experiences, using Gen AI to enhance learning through personalised pathways.
4. Project (How to achieve): This phase frames and implements practical projects that apply learned skills to real-world issues, aiming to bridge the gaps between inequality and equality in HE.

In this chapter, the terms “dimension” and “phase” are used interchangeably: “dimension” pertains to aspects of the design model, while 'phase' refers to stages in the design project. The integration of Gen AI in HE provides a sustainable approach to bridging inequality, which requires the design on the four orientations:

1. Disadvantaged Stakeholders: Identifying those underserved by HE policies.

2. Pedagogical Inequalities: Recognizing inequalities in teaching and learning.
3. Engaging Actions: Developing motivating actions for these groups.
4. Policy Transition Projects: Implementing projects that shift HE practices toward equality.

The use cases of the DEEP Method are illustrated to explore ChatGPT, which assists the co-design. The rest of the chapter is structured as follows: Section 2 outlines the foundations of the DEEP Method in addressing HE inequalities; Section 3 discusses the qualitative research methodology; Section 4 presents use cases of the method in practice; and Section 5 concludes with findings, limitations, and future directions.

*Figure 2. The DEEP Method Designed to Bridge the Gap from Inequality to Equality*

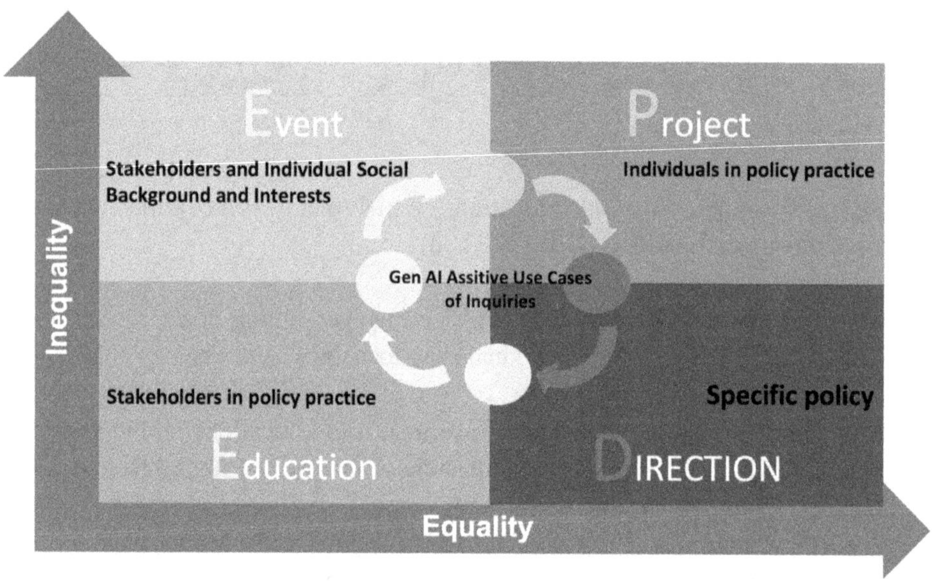


## FOUNDATIONS OF LIVEPBL DEEP METHOD FOR EXPLORING GEN AI BETWEEN INEQUALITY AND EQUALITY

This section explores the aspects that are foundational to constructing the DEEP Method. The main focus is on how the method can be applied to

1. Utilise Gen AI,

2. Address the gaps from equality to inequality in HE,
3. Examine the strategic design orientations necessary for integrating Gen AI into educational practices and
4. Synthesise the need for a comprehensive design approach.

Figure 2 illustrates the DEEP Method designed to bridge the gap from inequality to equality.

## Tackling Pedagogical Inequality and Achieving Pedagogical Equality in HE

In the current research, the term "pedagogical equality" is an institutionally driven approach that aims to provide equal educational opportunities for all students, ensuring fair access to quality education regardless of individual backgrounds. Institutions focus on creating systems and environments where resources, teaching practices, and support are evenly distributed (Amaral et al., 2021; Wilcox & Lawson, 2022). For example, universities implementing inclusive policies and using adaptive learning technologies strive to foster diverse learning needs, ensuring every student receives the required support (Laurillard et al., 2023). As Figure 3 shows, design orientations for equality and inequality are addressed by policy frameworks and global initiatives, but require different design approaches to implement, especially in the social dimension.

*Figure 3. The Differences in Design Orientations between Equality and Inequality*

| = equal **Equality** ≠ not equal | > greater than ≥ greater than or equal **Inequality** < less than ≤ less than or equal |
|---|---|
| **Key Differences in Design Orientation between Equality and Inequality** | |
| **Universal Access**: Ensuring that all students, regardless of background, have equal access to higher education opportunities. | **Scope and Focus**: Inequality-focused designs often zero in on specific groups and their unique challenges, whereas equality-focused designs aim to create a level playing field for everyone. |
| **Inclusive Policies**: Creating policies and practices that promote inclusivity and diversity within the entire student body, faculty, and staff. | **Resource Allocation**: Addressing inequality may require disproportionate investment in disadvantaged groups, while promoting equality might focus on more evenly distributed resources and opportunities. |
| **Holistic Support Systems**: Developing support systems that cater to the diverse needs of all students, such as counseling, academic advising, and inclusive teaching practices. | **Interventions vs. Systems**: Inequality solutions may involve targeted, remedial interventions, whereas equality solutions emphasize systemic changes that benefit everyone. |
| **Equal Opportunity Initiatives**: Implementing initiatives that ensure all students have equal opportunities to succeed, such as equitable admissions processes, diverse curricula, and inclusive campus cultures. | |
| **Long-term Cultural Change**: Fostering a culture of inclusivity and respect for diversity within higher education institutions that benefits all stakeholders. | |

Hence, pedagogical inequality (Ryynänen & Nivala, 2019) is characterised by disparities in teaching quality, resource access, and support. It mainly impacts disadvantaged groups, and limited support can hinder their academic progress and inclusion. Online resources like MOOCs, OERs, and virtual libraries partially address these issues by democratising access to quality materials worldwide. However, the accessibility of these resources varies significantly across different socio-techno and social-economic groups. According to (Garcia et al., 2022), the online resources enable students to tailor their learning experiences to focus on areas where they need the most support. The self-directed learning approach that bridges the gaps is often in traditional settings that lack support for critical thinking and self-motivation (Collis & van der Wende, 2023). Furthermore, Brighouse and Swift (2008) argue that there must be a balance between pedagogical equality and other societal values, such as family and economic growth.

The social dimension in HE aims to create equitable access and participation, particularly for underrepresented groups, as emphasised by initiatives like the Bologna Process (Altbach et al., 2019; EHEA, 2015; Tomusk, 2021). Integrating formal and non-formal education—such as community programs, online courses, and extracurricular activities—provides flexibility and relevance, fostering critical thinking, creativity, and social awareness (Colley et al., 2019; European-Commission, 2020; Langa & David, 2021; UNESCO, 2016). Global initiatives like UNESCO's

Education 2030 Framework for Action advocate for lifelong learning and emphasise recognising skills and competencies acquired outside traditional education settings. Implementing these frameworks requires both formal and non-formal learning experiences, ensuring quality and coherence in educational delivery (Altbach et al., 2019; Colley et al., 2019; EHEA, 2015; Mok & Neubauer, 2020).

The latest research shows that Gen AI bridges pedagogical inequality by offering personalised learning, adapting content to individual styles, and providing customised feedback that boosts engagement, especially for students struggling with traditional methods (Nguyen & Bui, 2023). Additionally, Gen AI can identify at-risk students early, offering targeted interventions to prevent dropouts and promote academic success (Sahin & Ozkan, 2024). Integrating digital technologies with Gen AI should provide scalable solutions that meet the diverse needs of students (Duarte et al., 2023; Sahin & Ozkan, 2024).

## Design Orientations in Exploring Gen AI

As discussed in the previous section, pedagogical inequality highlights the challenges marginalised groups face, while pedagogical equality aims to provide equal opportunities for all. Integrating Gen AI tools requires design orientations. The term "design orientation" is referred to as being the emphasis on functional elements in the creation of products or systems. Pedagogically, design orientation in HE emphasises adopting design thinking in teaching practices (Hatt et al., 2023; McLaughlin et al., 2022). According to (Buchanan, 2020), balancing artistic expression with practical usability needs a design orientation that navigates the design that is not only pleasing to look at but also efficient and user-friendly. From a strategic perspective, design orientation involves aligning design principles with business objectives to drive innovation and competitive advantage.

There has been a rapidly growing research and development to orientate HE through design as a User-Centred Approach (AnNing et al., 2024), emphasising the importance of focusing on the "end-user's" needs, preferences, and experiences. So that the design for HE also involves iterative piloting and feedback loops to refine designs that effectively solve users' problems. Norman (2013) highlights that a user-centred design orientation prioritises empathy and understanding the user context, ensuring that products and services are intuitive, accessible, and satisfying.

Design orientation can signify either the primary focus (Hatt et al., 2023), guiding a design process, such as user-centred, aesthetic, or functional priorities, or it can refer to the spatial arrangement and navigational aspects, guiding how users move through and interact with a space or interface (Verganti, 2009). The orientation involves not only the technological aspects of Gen AI assistance but also the holistic consideration of the diverse needs of students and educational stakeholders.

In conclusion, the design orientations for Gen AI in education are multifaceted and complex, reflecting a balance navigated between technological innovation and educational values as Gen AI continues to evolve (McDonald et al., 2024).

## Personalisation and Adaptability

One of the most prominent orientations in Gen AI applications is the emphasis on personalisation and adaptability in learning. According to Nguyen and Bui (2023), personalised approaches can significantly enhance student engagement and motivation by offering customised feedback and tailored learning pathways. This focus prioritises the learner's experience, striving to make education more inclusive by accommodating diverse learning styles (Duarte et al., 2023). However, balancing this personalisation with the standardisation needed for educational assessment and accreditation presents a significant challenge (Chen et al., 2021).

## Equity and Access

Another essential design orientation is on equity and access. Gen AI can democratise education by providing high-quality resources to students, regardless of their geographic location or socio-economic status. Garcia et al. (2022) note that online platforms leveraging Gen AI can deliver scalable educational solutions, reaching underrepresented and marginalised groups. This focus aims to reduce disparities in educational opportunities and outcomes (Collis & van der Wende, 2023). However, the digital divide remains a significant obstacle, as students from lower socio-economic backgrounds may lack access to necessary technology and internet connectivity (Zhong, 2020). To address these challenges, comprehensive policies and infrastructure investments are required to ensure that the advantages of Gen AI are available to all students (Deng & Xie, 2019).

## Pedagogical Alignment

Aligning Gen AI applications with pedagogical principles is another crucial orientation. The goal is to integrate Gen AI in a way that supports, rather than replaces, traditional teaching methods. AI can augment teaching by offering educators valuable insights into student performance and recommending personalised interventions (Mavroudi et al., 2024). However, an over-reliance on AI could weaken the teacher-student relationship, which is fundamental to effective learning. This orientation stresses the importance of designing AI systems that complement and enhance current educational practices, promoting critical thinking, creativity, and collaboration (Winne & Baker, 2018).

## Technological Integration and Scalability

The design of Gen AI in education focuses on seamless technological integration and scalability. Successful implementation requires Gen AI applications to accommodate diverse, large student bodies (Zailer & Barak-Medina, 2024). The challenge is designing the use of Gen AI that is both scalable and adaptable to different educational contexts and needs (Holmes et al., 2019).

## Lifelong Learning and Non-formal Education

Gen AI's role in lifelong learning and non-formal education constitutes another important design orientation. Gen AI technologies can offer flexible opportunities encompass professional development, skills training, and personal enrichment courses. The emphasis is on developing Gen AI that supports informal learning experiences and validates various skills and competencies (Langa & David, 2021).

## Exploring Gen AI Applications for HE Inclusion at Micro Levels in Real-world

This section explores Gen AI for HE inclusion at micro levels that some would call grassroots, operational, or implementation levels in the real world through actionable policies. It particularly addresses the gaps between:

1. Differentiated instructions based on equality and differentiated learning from the side of the inequality,
2. Enhanced support based on equality and personalised support from the side of the inequality,
3. Differentiated instruction that is from an equality viewpoint, and
4. Implementing and managing the policy practices.

Bridging these gaps often occurs at macro levels and is generally understood as "good education". Students are requested to make progress within the same curriculum system. However, the system should be designed and needs pedagogic differentiation planning to enable students to achieve learning objectives. More or less challenging content for more or less capable learners (Langa & David, 2021) is not reflected in the design in the first place. Differentiated instruction must have "enhanced support". It is designed to provide a multi-professional and collaborative team effort to support students in providing various students' personal, physical, cognitive, social and emotional needs for support (Asriadi et al., 2023).

Adapting the learning needs can have a different design orientation. Instead of considering the differentiating stages of instruction, designing a differentiated learning environment based on inequality among students has been rapidly growing (Nkambou et al., 2023). Living in a future society that needs a future-oriented design has proven challenging and motivating for teachers worldwide. Embracing students' differences and engaging them to learn, collaborate, and become co-learners who are both personally and socially responsible should be pursued in HE (Finkelstein et al., 2019; Sakarneh & Nair, 2014).

The micro-level policy strategy accommodates various teaching and learning strategies that use Gen AI (Chan, 2023; Järvelä, 2006). Key capabilities include active learning, critical thinking, relating to others, using language, symbols, ICT, and self-management. Successful inclusion entails accepting differences with a positive attitude (Chan, 2023; Järvelä, 2006), where they argue that a positive attitude towards inclusive HE is critical for building successful inclusion policies. Moreover, Colucci et al. (2022) note that HE institutions must develop competencies to modify teaching approaches, particularly in inclusive non-formal education. Co-teaching and collaboration between general and special education teachers, along with multi-professional teams, have been areas of significant focus (Friend et al., 2022). Differentiation poses challenges due to the complexity of its implementation because it operates at both macro and micro levels.

While macro-level differentiation involves pre-planning curriculum content, micro-level differentiation occurs during instruction (Gheyssens et al., 2024). Gheyssens et al. (2024) highlight that co-teaching processes must be facilitated at a micro level to build a shared professional identity and knowledge. Kang et al. (2023) discuss inclusive teacher professionalism in teacher education. Exploring Gen AI can help overcome barriers to scaling AI applications in education, though current applications are fragmented (Haefner et al., 2023). The frameworks reviewed emphasise inclusive approaches to AI learning design, integrating culturally responsive teaching and diverse assessments (Samuel et al., 2023).

## RESEARCH METHODOLOGY OF THE DEEP METHOD

This section introduces the background of LivePBL's research setting and then discusses the methodology behind the DEEP Method, which employs interpretive design using qualitative research methodology.

## LivePBL Research Setting

Our study utilised ChatGPT 4.0 in project-based learning (PBL) collaborative design. The LivePBL program, which adopts a hybrid PBL model, serves as a framework for research and development, engaging various stakeholders. Launched during the COVID-19 pandemic, this initiative brings together university faculty, school headteachers, and community leaders from the Dalian Shuxiang social community, involving participants from the UK, Nepal, and China. The collaboration encompasses university and college students under the mentorship of academic faculty, school children and club members led by headteachers, and families participating in community-based learning activities. For more information, refer to LivePBL publications (Liu et al., 2022; Wang et al., 2020; Zhang et al., 2022; Zhou et al., 2023).

Based in China, Capital Normal University, which specialises in training future teachers, struggles with providing practical teaching experience due to constraints in mobility and resources. Furthermore, teacher training programs frequently lack international perspectives, hindering the incorporation of innovative teaching methods. By integrating the DEEP method and ChatGPT into non-formal educational contexts, these challenges are addressed, equipping students with the necessary skills to navigate the complexities of contemporary education, including adaptability, cultural sensitivity, and proficiency in critical 21st-century skills. The program is supported by digital platforms such as Zoom and a learning management system (LMS) operated by The Support School in Liverpool, UK. This setup allows PBL to be explored through sociocultural activities, providing a platform for experimenting with new educational strategies and technologies. Feedback from participants is systematically gathered through structured interviews, surveys, and direct observations, ensuring a thorough evaluation of the program's impact.

## Research Approach

A qualitative research methodology with the following focuses:

1. The research led by interpretive design,
2. Constructing the DEEP Method,
3. Applying the DEEP Method to identify the gaps between HE inequalities and
4. Exploring Gen AI by the DEEP Method in HE practices bridging the gaps

In the similar design principles Akpan et al. (2020), which constructs the design through “what is taught, to whom and in what ways”, the DEEP Method expands and is constructed by

1. What to achieve (on Direction)
2. What to learn (on Education)
3. How to learn (on Event)
4. How to Achieve (on Project)

*Figure 4. LivePBL DEEP Method Design Orientation*

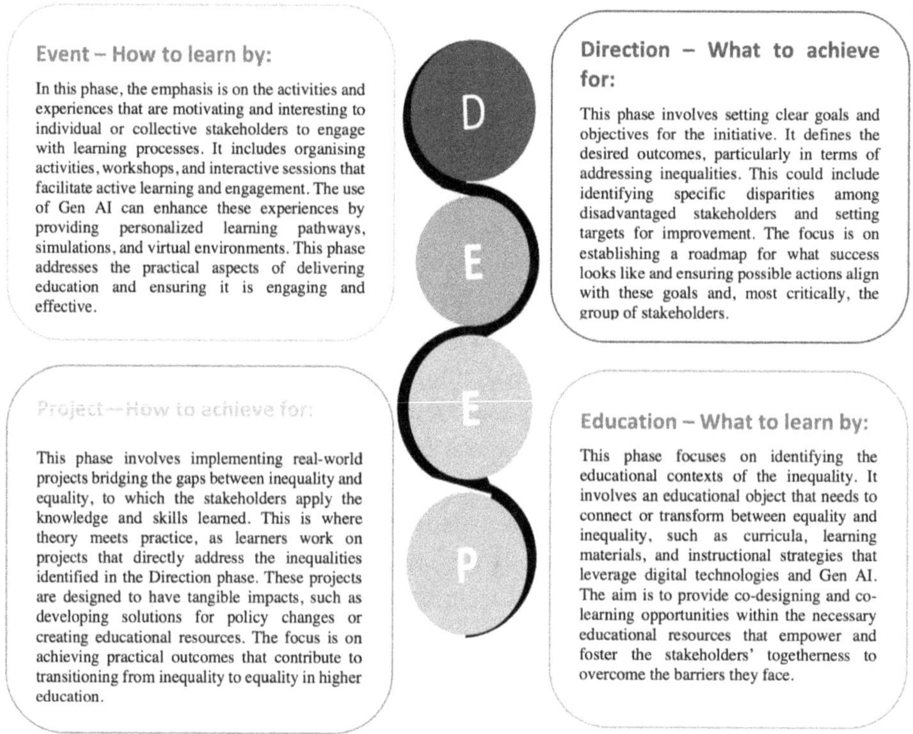


The DEEP Method has been applied in hybrid formal and non-formal learning settings. This contributes to educational epistemologies in social sciences, as Cohen et al. (2011) point out:

*The social work can only be understood from the standpoint of the individuals who are part of the ongoing action being investigated, and their model of a person is an autonomous one (p. 41).*

The policy practice strategy needs to accommodate the design orientations, particularly the orientation in dynamic and evolving changing contexts. As Berliner (2002) argues, positivist approaches are not purposefully orientated to provide HE institutional or learner strategies. Yanow (2000) points out that many possibilities of multiple interpretations characterise social policies. Study cases should create or innovate a design method for events and situations to engage broader policy implementations. The inclusion of diversity can be better achieved by both sides of inequality when designing a process to engage and bridge both sides. The DEEP Method is a method that orientates the design on these four levels of inequalities to use Gen AI tools to provide possibilities and opportunities, thereby bridging the gaps to implement equality. In summary, the DEEP Method orientates (or navigates) Project-Based Learning (PBL) in four phases interacting with Gen AI: Direction, Education, Event, and Project. Figure 4 illustrates the design orientation of the DEEP Method with Gen AI applications.

## USE CASES OF THE DEEP METHOD

This section explores the DEEP Method's practical applications, demonstrating how each phase—Direction, Education, Event, and Project—can be implemented to address specific challenges on both sides of inequality and equality.

### Direction: Identification of Inequality - Recognising Groups that Are Disadvantaged by Current HE Policies

To foster more equitable educational environments, it is essential to identify groups disadvantaged by current policies. The case studies from China reveal the challenges marginalised groups face, emphasising the need for targeted interventions. For example, existing equality policies often fall short, leaving rural students underserved. The urban-rural divide significantly impacts access to HE for these students, who frequently encounter barriers such as limited secondary education, financial constraints, and lower expectations.

A study by Li et al. (2021) found that rural students are underrepresented in top-tier universities, highlighting the gap in educational opportunities between urban and rural regions. This disparity is exacerbated by the household registration system (hukou), which restricts access to academic resources and opportunities based on one's residence. Zhou (2011) highlighted that ethnic minority students often struggle with the Mandarin-centric curriculum and examination system, which does not accommodate their linguistic needs. Socio-economic factors further complicate this situation, as minority regions are usually poor, limiting students' access to quality education and resources. Despite existing equality policies, practical barriers continue to impede progress. Policies must be implemented effectively and with targeted support for marginalised groups to bridge these gaps. Appendix I presents use cases for the Direction dimension of the DEEP Method. The prompt formula explores specific policies, stakeholders in practice, and their individual and local social contexts, using the following structure:

*How does [Specific Policy] affect [Stakeholders in Policy Practice], considering their [Stakeholders' Individual and Local Social Background]?*

These inquiries provide a structured way to explore the impact of specific policies, the role of various stakeholders in implementing these policies, and how individual and local social backgrounds shape stakeholders' experiences and outcomes.

## Education: Pedagogical Inequality - Addressing Disparities in Teaching and Learning Settings

Appendix II illustrates use cases on the dimension Education of the DEEP Method. The Prompt formula is

*How does [Specific Policy] address pedagogical inequalities for [Stakeholders in Policy Practice], considering their [Stakeholders' Individual and Local Social Background]?*

Gen AI assists in examining how specific policies and stakeholder roles address pedagogical inequalities. A significant concern is a disparity in instructional quality; marginalised students often faceless experienced educators, impacting their academic outcomes. In rural China, for example, there is a notable shortage of qualified teachers compared to urban areas (Liu, 2020). This discrepancy is partly due to the unequal distribution of educational resources and the challenges in attracting and retaining skilled educators in less affluent areas. Curriculum relevance is another critical aspect of pedagogical inequality. In many academic settings, curricula are not designed to reflect students' diverse cultural and socio-economic backgrounds. This can lead to a disconnect between students' lived experiences and the educational content they encounter, which can hinder engagement and learning (Zhou, 2011). Access to academic resources also plays a significant role in perpetuating pedagogical inequalities. This digital divide became particularly evident during the COVID-19 pandemic when remote learning highlighted the disparities in access to digital devices and the Internet (Zhong, 2020). Creating supportive learning environments is critical to addressing pedagogical inequalities.

## Actionable Engagement: Specifying Actions that Disadvantaged Groups Can Take to Overcome Inequalities

Actionable engagement is essential for policies aimed at overcoming educational inequalities. By defining specific actions—such as capacity-building, accessing resources, advocacy, and leveraging cultural capital—policies can empower disadvantaged groups to overcome barriers and achieve educational goals. During policy design, focusing on actionable engagement clarifies the roles of policymakers and institutions and enables affected communities to bridge academic gaps actively. Appendix III illustrates use cases on the dimension Event of the DEEP Method. The Prompt Formula is

*What specific actions are facilitated by [Specific Policy] for [Stakeholders in Policy Practice] to enable [Stakeholders' Individual and Local Social Background] in overcoming educational inequalities?*

These inquiries explore practical actions of educational policies, stakeholder roles, and how diverse individuals engage to overcome inequalities in the following areas:

- Capacity Building and Skill Development
- Access to Resources and Support Networks
- Advocacy and Representation
- Leveraging Community and Cultural Capital
- Utilising Technology for Inclusive Learning

## Project: Policy Practice Project - Implementing Practice Projects to Achieve Equality

Appendix IV illustrates the use cases on the dimension of Project in DEEP Method. The Prompt Formula is

*How does [Specific Policy] guide the implementation of practical projects involving [Stakeholders in Policy Practice], considering their [Stakeholders' Individual and Local Social Background], to achieve educational equality?*

The Project phase turns policy strategies into actionable initiatives, aiming for equality in HE. Projects can address immediate inequalities and drive long-term systemic change by setting clear objectives, fostering collaboration, efficiently managing resources, and ensuring sustainability. This phase translates theoretical frameworks into measurable actions, ensuring policies become practical solutions directly impacting target groups. Gen AI assists co-designed project in the following areas:

- Defining the scope and objectives of the project
- Collaborative design and implementation: Co-design and Project-Based Learning
- Resource Allocation and Management
- Learning by Experience and Doing with Gen AI Assistance
- Monitoring and Evaluation
- Scaling and Sustainability

After a project's success, scaling and sustainability are critical. Practical projects should be adaptable to other contexts, like using Gen AI across various subjects or levels. Sustainability involves integrating Gen AI tools into curricula, ongoing educator training, and continuous technical support. Documenting case studies and best practices is crucial for knowledge sharing. For example, a Gen AI project to enhance student engagement can guide other institutions. Detailed documentation of strategies, challenges, and outcomes provides insights for future initiatives while showcasing improved learning outcomes to support broader adoption.

## CONCLUSION

The LivePBL DEEP Method, using Gen AI, offers a design approach to bridge gaps in HE to enhance inclusion. This approach targets both micro and macro levels: at the micro level, it supports marginalised students—such as those from rural, low-income, and minority backgrounds—who face barriers to resources and opportunities; at the macro level, it involves policymakers, educators, and administrators who shape the educational landscape. The method's four phases—Direction, Education, Event, and Project—provide a structured design approach for developing inclusive HE policies. Through setting goals (Direction), identifying curriculums and resources (Education), engaging students in practical activities (Event), and applying skills to real-world issues (Project), it aims to explore both sides from HE inequality to equality. Use cases demonstrate that Gen AI can enhance personalised learning, provide tailored feedback and early intervention for at-risk students, thereby fostering a more inclusive educational environment.

However, the research reported in this chapter has limitations, including managing the co-design feedback, the digital divide that limits access for disadvantaged students and various ethical issues such as over-reliance on Gen AI that may hinder interpersonal skill development. Future research should focus on enhancing the design's scalability and accessibility to benefit diverse student demographics. This requires robust policies and infrastructure to ensure accountability in incorporating non-formal educational elements. Emphasising hybrid learning environments will also be vital in fostering a flexible and inclusive educational system. As Gen AI and digital technologies evolve, thoughtful and accountable design can positively navigate the exploration of HE inequalities on more diversified HE landscapes.

## REFERENCES


Akpan, V. I., Igwe, U. A., Mpamah, I. B. I., & Okoro, C. O. (2020). Social constructivism: Implications on teaching and learning. *British Journal of Educational Technology*, *8*(8), 49–56.

Altbach, P. G., Reisberg, L., & Rumbley, L. E. (2019). *Trends in Global Higher Education: Tracking an Academic Revolution.*

Amaral, A., Tavares, O., Sá, C., & Sin, C. (2021). Equity in Higher Education: Evidence, Policies and Practices. Setting the Scene. In *Equity Policies in Global Higher Education: Reducing Inequality and Increasing Participation and Attainment*. Palgrave Macmillan.

Asriadi, M. A., Hadi, S., Istiyono, E., & Retnawati, H. (2023). Does Differentiated Instruction Affect Learning Outcome? Systematic Review and Meta-Analysis. *Journal of Pedagogical Research*, *7*(5), 18–33.

Bergan, S., Gallagher, T., & Harkavy, I. (2018). *Higher Education for Diversity, Social Inclusion and Community*. Council of Europe.

Brighouse, H., & Swift, A. (2008). Putting educational equality in its place. *Education Finance and Policy*, *3*(4), 444–466. DOI: 10.1162/edfp.2008.3.4.444

Brown, T., & Katz, B. (2011). Change by Design. *Journal of Product Innovation Management*, *28*(3), 381–384. DOI: 10.1111/j.1540-5885.2011.00806.x

Buchanan, B. (2020). Artificial Intelligence and Ethics: A Systematic Review of Bias and Fairness. *AI & Society*, *35*(4), 837–856.

Chan, C. K. Y. (2023). A comprehensive AI policy education framework for university teaching and learning. *International Journal of Educational Technology in Higher Education*, *20*(38), 1–25. DOI: 10.1186/s41239-023-00408-3

Chen, K., Chen, J., & Wang, C. (2023). The roles of empathy and motivation in creativity in design thinking. *Knowledge Management & E-Learning*, *15*(3), 468–486.

Chen, X., Zou, D., & Cheng, G. (2021). Exploring the Integration of Artificial Intelligence into Education: A Review and Outlook. *Journal of Educational Technology & Society*, *24*(4), 83–97.

Cohen, L., Manion, L., & Morrison, K. (2011). *Research Methods in Education.* Routledge.

Colley, H., Hodkinson, P., & Malcolm, J. (2019). *Non-formal Learning: Mapping the Conceptual Terrain*. Springer.

Collis, B., & van der Wende, M. (2023). Designing the Future of Learning with AI: From Personalization to Global Inclusion. *Journal of Educational Technology & Society*, *45*(2), 112–126.

Colucci, E., Davies, H., Korhonen, J., & Gaebel, M. (2022). Recognising and valuing non-formal and informal learning outcomes in higher education. *European Journal of Education*, *57*(3), 387–405.

Deng, L., & Xie, J. (2019). The Digital Divide in Education: Issues and Solutions in the Context of AI. *International Journal of Information Management*, *50*, 47–56.

Diaz, J., Gusto, C., Narine, L. K., Jayaratne, K. S. U., & Silvert, C. (2023). Toward Diversity, Equity, and Inclusion Outreach and Engagement in Extension Education: Expert Consensus on Barriers and Strategies. *Journal of Extension*, *6*(1), 21. DOI: 10.34068/joe.61.01.21

Duarte, J., Morais, M., & Pereira, R. (2023). Hybrid Learning Environments: A Pathway to Inclusive Higher Education. *Journal of Educational Technology & Society*, *26*(2), 75–88.

Efilti, P., & Gelmez, K. (2024). A deep dive into the impacts of empathy on design learning and teaching. *International Journal of Technology and Design Education*, *34*(2), 809–852. DOI: 10.1007/s10798-023-09835-9

EHEA. (2015). *The Bologna Process Revisited: The Future of the European Higher Education Area*.

European-Commission. (2020). *European Education Area*.

Finkelstein, S., Sharma, U., & Furlonger, B. (2019). The inclusive practices of classroom teachers: A scoping review and thematic analysis. *International Journal of Inclusive Education*, *25*, 1–28.

Fragoso, A., Javrh, P., Kelava, P., Kramberger, T., Ličen, N., Radovan, M., Rotar, D. B., Ermenc, K. S., Vidmar, T., Žagar, I. Ž., Žiljak, T., & Žnidaršič Žagar, S. (2024). *From Formal to Non-Formal: Education, Learning and Knowledge*. Cambridge Scholars Publishing.

Friend, M., Cook, L., Hurley-Chamberlain, D., & Shamberger, C. (2022). Co-Teaching: Principles, Practices, and Pragmatics in Inclusive Classrooms. *The Journal of Special Education*, *55*(2), 90–103.

Garcia, P., Smith, A., & Li, Y. (2022). The Democratization of Education: Online Learning Resources and Equity in Higher Education. *Journal of Higher Education Policy and Management, 44*(3), 239–255.

Gheyssens, E., Coubergs, C., & DeMaeyer, S. (2024). Differentiated Instruction as an Approach to Establish Effective Teaching in Inclusive Classrooms. *The Journal of Educational Research, 62*, 23–45.

Haefner, N., Parida, V., Gassmann, O., & Wincent, J. (2023). Implementing and scaling artificial intelligence: A review, framework, and research agenda. *Technological Forecasting and Social Change, 197*, 1–11. DOI: 10.1016/j.techfore.2023.122878

Hatt, L., Davidson, J., & Carrion-Weiss, J. (2023). Design Thinking as Pedagogy in Practice. *International Journal of Management and Applied Research, 10*(2), 95–105.

Holmes, W., Blalik, M., & Fadel, C. (2019). *Artificial Intelligence in Education: Promise and Implications for Teaching and Learning*. Center for Curriculum Redesign.

Jain, D., Herrera, A., & Bernal, S. (2023). Decolonizing Higher Education: Addressing Equity, Diversity, and Inclusion in Academia, Innovate. *Journal of Education, Ageing, and Digital Technologies, 7*, 985–1001.

Järvelä, S. (2006). *Personalised Learning? New Insights into Fostering Learning Capacity*. OECD Publishing.

Jones, R., & Williams, K. (2024). Diversity and Inclusion in Higher Education: A Comparative Analysis of Policy Implementation. *Higher Education Quarterly, 34*(1), 77–84.

Kang, J., Lim, S., & Park, H. (2023). Inclusive Teacher Professionalism: New Approaches in Teacher Education. *International Journal of Educational Research, 101*, 112–125.

Kottmann, A., Vossensteyn, J. J., Kolster, R., Veidemane, A., Blasko, Z., Biagi, F., & Sánchez-Barrioluengo, M. (2019). *Social Inclusion Policies in Higher Education: Evidence from the EU. Overview of major widening participation policies applied in the EU 28.*

Lake, D., Guo, W., Chen, E., & McLaughlin, J. (2024). Design Thinking in Higher Education: Opportunities and Challenges for Decolonized Learning. *Teaching & Learning Inquiry, 12*(1), 40–50. DOI: 10.20343/teachlearninqu.12.4

Langa, P. V., & David, M. E. (2021). *Crossing Boundaries in Higher Education: Rethinking Inclusion and Social Justice*. Routledge.

Laurillard, D., Rowe, F. A., & Rafferty, J. A. (2023). Enhancing Inclusive Learning through Digital Innovation: A Case Study in Optometry Education. *Journal of Inclusive Practice in Further and Higher Education, 15*(3), 245–250.

Li, H., Whalley, J., & Xing, C. (2021). Urban-rural inequality and higher education access in China. *China Economic Review, 67*, 101–115.

Li, X., & Johnson, D. (2024). The Impact of Institutional Policies on Student Diversity and Inclusion Outcomes. *Studies in Higher Education, 49*(2), 50–68.

Liu, Y. (2020). Challenges and Opportunities in Rural Education: The Case of China. *Journal of Rural Studies, 78*, 150–158.

Liu, Y., Li, Y., Yang, S., Ren, T., Li, H., Hogg, A., Shah, P., Li, J., Zhang, Y., & Chhetri, A. (2022). A hybrid and non-formal music education connecting China's local family communities and cultures with Nepal. [IJI]. *International Journal for Infonomics, 15*(1), 6. DOI: 10.20533/iji.1742.4712.2022.0218

Lumby, J., & Foskett, N. (2016). *International Perspectives on Leading and Managing Educational Institutions*. Bloomsbury Academic.

Marginson, S. (2016). *Higher Education and the Common Good*. Melbourne University Publishing.

Martin, R. (2014). *The Design of Business: Why Design Thinking is the Next Competitive Advantage*. Harvard Business Review Press.

Mavroudi, E., Holmes, W., & Ibáñez, M. (2024). *Exploring the Impact of Artificial Intelligence in Teaching and Learning of Science: A Systematic Review of Empirical Research*. Springer.

McCowan, T. (2019). *Higher Education for and Beyond the Sustainable Development Goals*. Palgrave Macmillan. DOI: 10.1007/978-3-030-19597-7

McDonald, N., Johri, A., Ali, A., & Hingle, A. (2024). Generative Artificial Intelligence in Higher Education: Evidence from an Analysis of Institutional Policies and Guidelines. arXiv. McKinsey&Company. (2024). What is ChatGPT, DALL-E, and generative AI?

McLaughlin, J. E., Chen, E., Lake, D., Guo, W., Skywark, E. R., & Liu, T. (2022). Design thinking teaching and learning in higher education: Experiences across four universities. *PLoS One, 17*(3).

Mok, K. H., & Neubauer, D. (2020). *Higher Education in Asia: Equity, Access and the Social Dimension*. Springer.

Neimann, T., Felix, J. J., Shliakhovchuk, E., & Hindman, L. L. (2022). *Policy and Practice Challenges for Equality in Education*. IGI Global.

Nguyen, L. T., & Bui, T. D. (2023). Personalized Learning through Generative AI in Higher Education: Challenges and Opportunities. *Computers & Education*, •••, 182.

Nkambou, R., Panagiotopoulos, I., Kalou, A., Pierrakeas, C., & Kameas, A. (2023). *Adaptive Learning Spaces with Context-Awareness*. Lecture Notes in Computer Science. Springer.

Norman, D. A. (2013). *The Design of Everyday Things*. Basic Books.

OECD-iLibrary. (2018). *PISA 2018 Results* (Vol. II). Where All Students Can Succeed.

Patel, A., & Martinez, L. (2024). Bridging Policy and Practice: Challenges in Implementing Equity in Higher Education. *Journal of Educational Policy and Administration*, *29*(2), 89–105.

Razzouk, R., & Shute, V. (2012). What is Design Thinking and Why is it Important? *Review of Educational Research*, *82*(3), 330–348. DOI: 10.3102/0034654312457429

Rowe, P. G. (1987). *Design Thinking*. MIT Press.

Ryynänen, S., & Nivala, E. (2019). Inequality as a social pedagogical question. *International Journal of Social Pedagogy*, *7*(1), 1–16. DOI: 10.14324/111.444.ijsp.2019.v7.1.008

Sahin, E., & Ozkan, M. (2024). The Role of AI in Supporting At-Risk Students: A Case Study of Generative AI in Higher Education. *Artificial Intelligence in Education*, *30*(1), 105–120.

Sakarneh, M. A., & Nair, N. S. A. (2014). Effective Teaching in Inclusive Classroom: Literature Review. *Journal of Education and Practice*, *5*, 28–34.

Salas-Pilco, S. Z., Xiao, K., & Hu, X. (2022). Artificial Intelligence and Learning Analytics in Teacher Education: A Systematic Review. *Education Sciences*, *12*(8), 12. DOI: 10.3390/educsci12080569

Samuel, Y., Brennan-Tonetta, M., Samuel, J., Kashyap, R., Kumar, V., Krishna-Kaashyap, S., Chidipothu, N., Anand, I., & Jain, P. (2023). Cultivation of human centered artificial intelligence: Culturally adaptive thinking in education (CATE) for AI. *Frontiers in Artificial Intelligence*, *6*, 6. DOI: 10.3389/frai.2023.1198180 PMID: 38106981

Smith, J., & Chen, Y. (2024). The Evolving Role of Higher Education in Promoting Social Justice. *International Journal of Higher Education and Policy*, *22*(3), 45–62.

Sorensen, E. K., & Andersen, L. K. (2022). Collaborative Learning and Social Mobility: The Role of Digital Platforms in Higher Education. *International Journal of Educational Technology*, *39*(4), 200–215.

Spricigo, C. B., Camilotti, B. M., Graham, C. R., & Baptista, R. (2023). An exploration of institutional and personal barriers to online academic engagement at a Brazilian university. *Educación XX1, 26*(2), 17-50.

SpringerOpen. (2024). Unveiling the evolution of generative AI (GAI): A comprehensive and investigative analysis toward LLM models (2021–2024) and beyond. *Journal of Electrical Systems and Information Technology, 11*(2), 101–125.

Tight, M. (2020). *Education for All? The Legacy of International Commitment*. Routledge.

Tomusk, V. (2021). *The Bologna Process: A Critical Sociology of Higher Education in Europe*. Routledge.

UNESCO. (2015). *Education 2030: Incheon Declaration and Framework for Action*. UNESCO.

UNESCO. (2016). *Education for People and Planet: Creating Sustainable Futures for All.*

Verganti, R. (2009). *Design-Driven Innovation: Changing the Rules of Competition by Radically Innovating What Things Mean*. Harvard Business Press.

Wang, L. (2023). *Equity, inclusion and the transformation of higher education*. UNESCO.

Wang, Y., Liu, X., Zhang, Y., Sang, X., & Wang, M. (2020). The first model of family education on the delivery of bilingual British NCC digital literacy qualifications in Dalian, China — Engaging and motivating children'. *Proceedings of the International Conference on Education in Mathematics, Science and Technology (ICEMST)*, Istanbul, Turkey, 21-24 March.

Wilcox, K. C., & Lawson, H. A. (2022). Advancing Educational Equity Research, Policy, and Practice. *Education Sciences*, *12*(12), 894. DOI: 10.3390/educsci12120894

Wilcox, K. C., & Lawson, H. A. (2024). Advancing Educational Equity Research, Policy, and Practice. *Education Sciences*, *12*(12), 894–914. DOI: 10.3390/educsci12120894

Winne, P. H., & Baker, R. S. (2018). The Potentials of Learning Analytics and AI to Improve Educational Practice. *British Journal of Educational Technology*, *49*(4), 610–626.

Yanow, D. (2000). *Conducting Interpretive Policy Analysis*. Sage Publications. DOI: 10.4135/9781412983747

Zailer, G., & Barak-Medina, E. (2024). Strategies for integrating generative AI into higher education: Navigating challenges and leveraging opportunities. *Education Sciences*, *14*(5), 503–509. DOI: 10.3390/educsci14050503

Zhang, L., Ren, T., Xie, Y., Tian, Z., Tang, T., & Li, Y. (2022). Student Choirs and Virtual Social Practices by LivePBL: Linking Vocal Education with Project Based Learning. *Literacy Information and Computer Education Journal*, *13*(1), 7. DOI: 10.20533/licej.2040.2589.2022.0482

Zhong, R. (2020). Digital Divide in Education: Challenges and Solutions during the COVID-19 Pandemic. *Journal of Educational Technology & Society*, *60*(6), 18–24.

Zhou, M. (2011). The ethnic minority-majority gap in China's higher education. *Asian Ethnicity*, *12*(2), 145–156.

Zhou, Y., Ren, T., Chen, N., Li, J., Lu, K., Li, Y., Acharya, A., Shah, P., Hogg, A., & Liu, Y. (2023). Student virtual social practices between China and Nepal. *International Journal of Technology and Inclusive Education*, *12*(1), 6.

# APPENDIX I

*Figure 5. Use cases on the dimension direction of livepbl deep method*

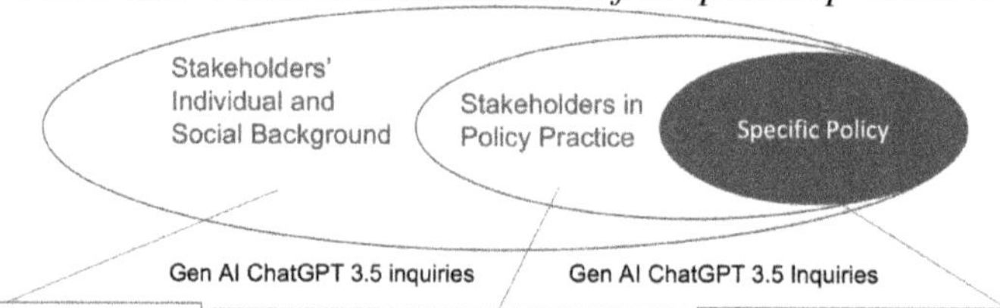


1. How do students from low socio-economic backgrounds perceive the benefits of the financial aid provided under the "Education for All" initiative?
2. In what ways do cultural practices of ethnic minority students influence their engagement with the "Special Programs for Ethnic Minorities" policy?
3. How do first-generation college students from rural areas navigate the challenges posed by the current HE policies in China?
4. How does the social stigma associated with disabilities affect the experiences of students with disabilities under the "Regulation on the Education of Persons with Disabilities"?
5. What impact do local economic conditions have on the participation of students in higher education following the Gaokao reform?

1. How have university administrators responded to the mandates of the "Special Programs for Ethnic Minorities" in enhancing campus diversity?
2. What roles do local government officials play in implementing the National Plan for Medium and Long-term Education Reform and Development (2010-2020) in remote areas?
3. How do faculty members perceive the effectiveness of the "Education for All" initiative in addressing academic inequalities in higher education?
4. How have student advocacy groups contributed to the enforcement of the "Regulation on the Education of Persons with Disabilities" in Chinese universities?
5. What challenges do secondary school teachers face in aligning their curriculum with the goals of the Gaokao reform?

1. How does the National Plan for Medium and Long-term Education Reform and Development (2010-2020) impact the quality of education provided in rural Chinese schools?
2. In what ways has the "Special Programs for Ethnic Minorities" policy influenced university admission rates among ethnic minority students in China?
3. What are the implications of the "Education for All" initiative on the provision of financial aid to students from low-income families in Chinese higher education?
4. How effective has the "Regulation on the Education of Persons with Disabilities" been in improving campus accessibility in Chinese universities?
5. How has the introduction of China's Gaokao reform affected the inclusion of students from underrepresented regions?

# APPENDIX II

*Figure 6. Use cases on the dimension education of livepbl deep method*

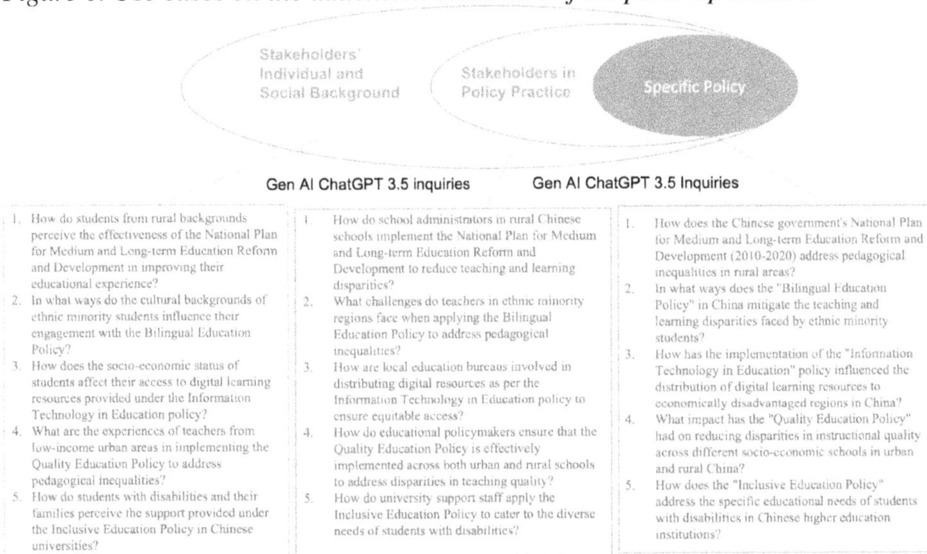

# APPENDIX III

*Figure 7. Use cases on the dimension event of livepbl deep method*

Gen AI ChatGPT 3.5 inquiries

1. What specific actions can students from rural backgrounds take to utilize the opportunities provided by the National Plan for Medium and Long-term Education Reform and Development?
2. How can ethnic minority students engage with the Bilingual Education Policy to enhance their academic performance and integration into mainstream education?
3. What proactive steps can students with disabilities take to access the accommodations and support outlined in the Inclusive Education Policy?
4. How can low-income students navigate the processes involved in accessing financial aid and scholarships under the Financial Aid and Scholarship Policy?
5. What initiatives can students from underprivileged regions undertake to maximize the benefits of the Digital Education Strategy for their academic growth?

1. How can school administrators implement the National Plan for Medium and Long-term Education Reform and Development to encourage actionable engagement among disadvantaged students?
2. What role do teachers play in executing the Bilingual Education Policy to support ethnic minority students in overcoming language-related challenges?
3. How can university disability services leverage the Inclusive Education Policy to provide actionable support to students with disabilities?
4. What responsibilities do financial aid offices have under the Financial Aid and Scholarship Policy to ensure equitable distribution of resources to low-income students?
5. How can IT support staff in educational institutions promote the use of digital tools as part of the Digital Education Strategy to assist students from low-income backgrounds?

Gen AI ChatGPT 3.5 Inquiries

1. What actions does the National Plan for Medium and Long-term Education Reform and Development (2010-2020) outline to empower rural students to overcome educational inequalities?
2. How does the "Bilingual Education Policy" in China facilitate actionable engagement for ethnic minority students to navigate language barriers in education?
3. What specific measures are provided by the "Inclusive Education Policy" to enable students with disabilities to access higher education on an equitable basis?
4. How does the "Financial Aid and Scholarship Policy" assist low-income students in overcoming the financial barriers to higher education in China?
5. What actions are promoted by the "Digital Education Strategy" to ensure that students from underprivileged regions can access online learning resources?

## APPENDIX IV

*Figure 8. Design orientations on dimension project livepbl deep method*

### Direction: Engagement Praxes

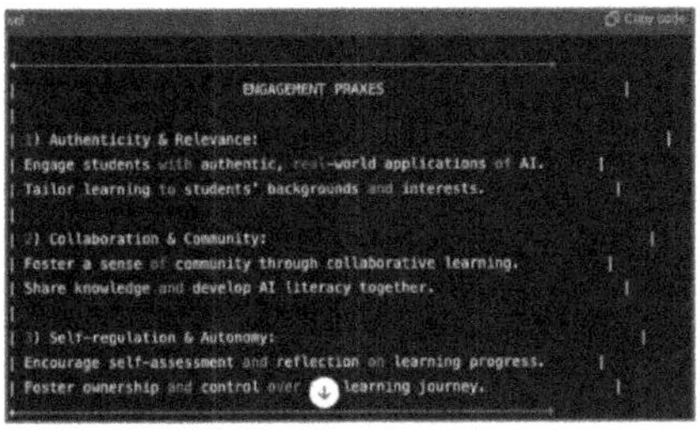


The "engagement" praxes focus on the motivations and reasons behind learning AI, emphasizing how to keep students invested in the learning process. Key elements include:

**Authenticity & Relevance:** Engaging students by making learning activities authentic and relevant to their lives helps sustain interest and motivation. Personalized learning, tailored to students' backgrounds and interests, is crucial. For example, Project-Based Learning (PBL) enables students to work on projects that apply AI technologies to real-world problems, making the learning experience more meaningful and relevant.

**Collaboration & Community:** Building a sense of community and encouraging collaboration among students fosters a supportive learning environment. By creating AI-focused learning communities and providing opportunities for collaborative learning, students can share knowledge and develop AI literacy together. This social aspect of learning helps sustain effort and persistence.

**Self-regulation & Autonomy:** Encouraging self-regulation and autonomy in students is vital for maintaining long-term engagement. In AI education, students can practice these skills through self and peer evaluations, where they assess their learning artifacts and reflect on their progress. This process helps students set and adjust their goals, fostering a sense of ownership and control over their learning journey.

### Education: Learning Praxes

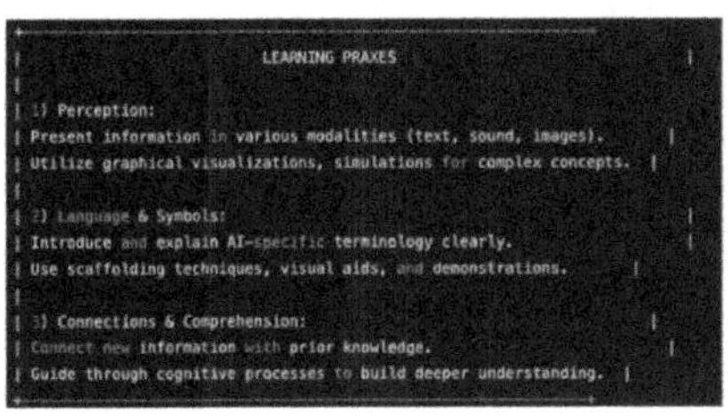


The "representation" praxes focus on the content and materials provided to learners, ensuring they are accessible and comprehensible:

**Perception:** Information should be presented in various modalities (text, sound, images) and formats to accommodate different learning styles. In AI education, using graphical visualizations, simulations, and interactive demonstrations can help students understand complex concepts. For example, tools like Teachable Machine can visualize AI processes, making them more accessible.

**Language & Symbols:** AI learning often involves new and unfamiliar terminology. It is crucial to introduce and explain these terms clearly, using scaffolding techniques before advancing to more complex concepts. Visual aids and interactive demonstrations can also support the understanding of AI-specific language and symbols.

**Connections & Comprehension:** To help students build a deeper understanding of AI, it is important to connect new information with prior knowledge and guide them through the cognitive processes involved in learning. The explain-ability of AI systems, such as visualizing decision-making processes, is essential. This transparency helps demystify AI and makes its operations more comprehensible, aiding students in constructing meaningful knowledge.

## APPENDIX V

*Figure 9. Design orientations for exploring gen ai at a micro level within higher education (he) to foster inclusivity*

### Direction: Engagement Praxes

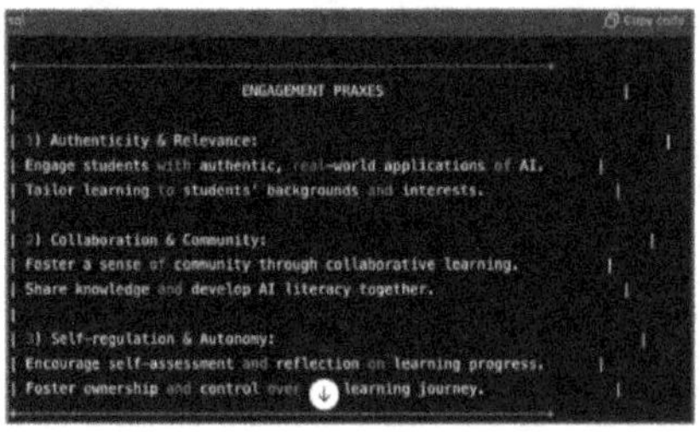


The "engagement" praxes focus on the motivations and reasons behind learning AI, emphasizing how to keep students invested in the learning process. Key elements include:

**Authenticity & Relevance:** Engaging students by making learning activities authentic and relevant to their lives helps sustain interest and motivation. Personalized learning, tailored to students' backgrounds and interests, is crucial. For example, Project-Based Learning (PBL) enables students to work on projects that apply AI technologies to real-world problems, making the learning experience more meaningful and relevant.

**Collaboration & Community:** Building a sense of community and encouraging collaboration among students fosters a supportive learning environment. By creating AI-focused learning communities and providing opportunities for collaborative learning, students can share knowledge and develop AI literacy together. This social aspect of learning helps sustain effort and persistence.

**Self-regulation & Autonomy:** Encouraging self-regulation and autonomy in students is vital for maintaining long-term engagement. In AI education, students can practice these skills through self and peer evaluations, where they assess their learning artifacts and reflect on their progress. This process helps students set and adjust their goals, fostering a sense of ownership and control over their learning journey.

### Education: Learning Praxes

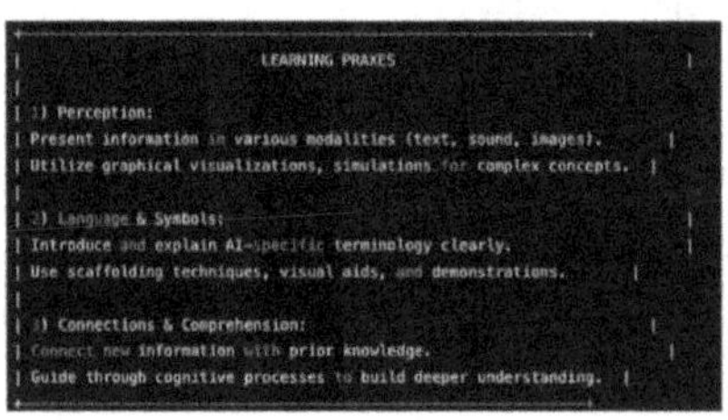


The "representation" praxes focus on the content and materials provided to learners, ensuring they are accessible and comprehensible:

**Perception:** Information should be presented in various modalities (text, sound, images) and formats to accommodate different learning styles. In AI education, using graphical visualizations, simulations, and interactive demonstrations can help students understand complex concepts. For example, tools like Teachable Machine can visualize AI processes, making them more accessible.

**Language & Symbols:** AI learning often involves new and unfamiliar terminology. It is crucial to introduce and explain these terms clearly, using scaffolding techniques before advancing to more complex concepts. Visual aids and interactive demonstrations can also support the understanding of AI-specific language and symbols.

**Connections & Comprehension:** To help students build a deeper understanding of AI, it is important to connect new information with prior knowledge and guide them through the cognitive processes involved in learning. The explain-ability of AI systems, such as visualizing decision-making processes, is essential. This transparency helps demystify AI and makes its operations more comprehensible, aiding students in constructing meaningful knowledge.

Chapter 4

# Equity, Teaching, and Assessment Practices for the Integration of AI, Education for Sustainable Development:

## Higher Education to Promote Education for Social Justice

**Doris Chasokela**
https://orcid.org/0009-0001-5983-8508
*National University of Science and Technology, Zimbabwe*

**Aleck Sithole**
*National University of Science and Technology, Zimbabwe*

## ABSTRACT

*In the context of the growing use of AI in education, this chapter explores the challenges and opportunities of integrating AI with education for sustainable development (ESD) in higher education (HE). It argues that equity, teaching, and assessment practices must be at the heart of this integration to promote social justice and to ensure that the benefits of AI are shared equally. The chapter outlines a vision for AI in ESD that is grounded in equity, pedagogy, and assessment. It explores the potential of AI in supporting the integration of ESD in Higher Education, and the need for innovative and inclusive practices that can help to address it. In the introduction, briefly explain the importance of ESD and the role of AI in supporting it. An overview of the challenges and opportunities associated with using AI in ESD*

DOI: 10.4018/979-8-3693-5623-4.ch004

*is examined. The role of equity in ESD, and how AI can be used to promote it are discussed. The chapter also highlights the importance of assessment in ESD, and how AI can be used to support it.*

## INTRODUCTION

As the world grapples with the complex challenges of sustainable development, higher education has a crucial role to play in equipping students with the knowledge, skills, and values necessary to address these issues. Education for Sustainable Development (ESD) has become a vital component of higher education, focusing on developing skills, knowledge, and values necessary for individuals to contribute to a more sustainable and equitable world. However, ESD is not just about teaching sustainable development; it is also about promoting Education for Social Justice (ESJ) by challenging dominant power structures, promoting equity, and addressing systemic inequalities. In this context, the integration of Artificial Intelligence (AI) with ESD in higher education presents a unique opportunity to promote ESJ by addressing the complex issues of equity, teaching, and assessment practices. AI can be used to create more personalized and inclusive learning experiences, provide additional support for students with disabilities, and promote equity and accessibility in higher education. However, AI adoption also requires careful consideration of the potential biases and inequalities that may arise from algorithmic decision-making. The integration of Artificial Intelligence (AI) with Education for Sustainable Development (ESD) in higher education presents a unique opportunity to promote Education for Social Justice (ESJ). However, this integration requires careful consideration of equity, teaching, and assessment practices to ensure that AI-enabled education is inclusive, equitable, and just. This overview provides a comprehensive overview of the key issues and considerations related to equity, teaching, and assessment practices in the context of AI-enabled ESD in higher education.

Equity considerations include addressing algorithmic bias where AI systems may perpetuate existing biases and inequalities if not designed with equity and inclusivity in mind. AI-enabled education should be designed to be accessible and inclusive for students with disabilities and marginalized groups. AI systems rely on high-quality data, which can be difficult to obtain, especially in developing countries. Educators may need to develop digital literacy skills to effectively integrate AI into their teaching practices. Teaching practices involve the personalised learning experiences created by AI adapted to individual students' needs and abilities. AI can facilitate collaborative learning by enabling students to work together on projects and assignments. With flipped classrooms, AI can be used to provide interactive learning experiences that supplement traditional teaching methods. Educators may need to develop new skills and competencies to effectively integrate AI into their teaching practices.

Assessment practices include AI-enabled assessment tools: AI can be used to develop assessment tools that are more accurate, efficient, and reliable. Alternative assessment methods: AI can be used to provide alternative assessment methods that are more inclusive and equitable. Feedback and formative assessment: AI can provide students with immediate feedback and support through formative assessment. Summative assessment: AI can be used to develop summative assessment tools that are more accurate and reliable. The integration of AI with ESD in higher education requires careful consideration of equity, teaching, and assessment practices. By addressing these issues, educators can promote ESJ and ensure that AI-enabled education is inclusive, equitable, and just.

## Overview of the Integration of AI with ESD in Higher Education to Promote ESJ

The integration of Artificial Intelligence (AI) with Education for Sustainable Development (ESD) in higher education is a rapidly emerging field that has the potential to transform the way we learn, teach, and promote sustainable development. ESD is a critical component of higher education, focusing on developing skills, knowledge, and values necessary for individuals to contribute to a more sustainable and equitable world (Arnold et al. 2024; Lorente-Echeverria, 2022). The integration of AI with ESD aims to leverage the potential of AI to enhance the quality, accessibility, and impact of ESD education. There are several benefits of the integration of AI such as:

- Personalised learning: AI can be used to create personalized learning experiences that adapt to individual students' needs and abilities.
- Enhanced student engagement: AI can be used to develop interactive and engaging learning experiences that increase student motivation and participation.
- Increased accessibility: AI can be used to provide access to education for students with disabilities and marginalised groups.
- Improved assessment and feedback: AI can be used to develop more accurate and reliable assessment tools, as well as provide immediate feedback and support (Al Samman, 2024; Amado-Salvatierra, 2024; Contreras, et al. 2024; Yusuf, 2024).

Strategies for integration of AI with ESD in higher education to promote ESJ are:

- Developing AI-enabled ESD curricula: Educational institutions can develop curricula that integrate AI with ESD concepts, such as sustainability, climate change, and social justice.
- Collaborative learning platforms: AI can be used to develop collaborative learning platforms that enable students to work together on projects and assignments.
- AI-enabled assessment tools: AI can be used to develop assessment tools that are more accurate, efficient, and reliable.
- Lecturer professional development: Educators may need to develop new skills and competencies to effectively integrate AI into their teaching practices.

Implications for Education for Social Justice (ESJ) include:

- Critical pedagogy: AI-enabled education must be designed with a critical pedagogy approach that challenges dominant power structures and promotes social justice.
- Inclusive design: AI-enabled education should be designed to be accessible and inclusive for students with disabilities and marginalised groups.
- Equitable access: AI-enabled education must provide equitable access to education for all students, regardless of their background or socioeconomic status.
- Social justice outcomes: AI-enabled education must be designed to promote social justice outcomes, such as addressing systemic inequalities and promoting environmental sustainability.

## UNDERSTANDING THE ROLE OF AI IN ESD

Artificial Intelligence (AI) is a rapidly evolving field that has the potential to transform the way we approach Education for Sustainable Development (ESD) (Goralski & Tan, 2020). As ESD seeks to address complex global challenges such as climate change, poverty, and inequality, AI can be leveraged to enhance the quality, accessibility, and impact of ESD education. AI can be used to personalise learning experiences, making education more effective and engaging for students (Chen, et al., 2020). For example, AI-powered adaptive learning systems can adjust the difficulty level of course materials based on a student's performance, providing a more tailored learning experience. Additionally, AI can help to identify and address learning gaps and misconceptions, ensuring that students have a solid understanding of complex concepts. Moreover, AI can be used to enhance the accessibility of ESD education. For instance, AI-powered language translation tools can enable students to access educational materials in their native language, regardless of their geographical location. Additionally, AI-powered virtual assistants can provide personalized support and guidance to students with disabilities, helping to bridge the gap between their abilities and the demands of ESD education (Neha, et al., 2024). Furthermore, AI can be used to analyse large datasets and provide insights on how to improve ESD education. For example, AI-powered analytics can help educators identify patterns and trends in student performance, allowing them to develop targeted interventions to improve learning outcomes. Additionally, AI-powered sentiment analysis can help educators gauge student attitudes and perceptions toward ESD education, enabling them to develop more effective strategies for engagement and motivation (Rahiman & Kodikal, 2024).

Incorporating AI into ESD education also has the potential to promote sustainable development outcomes by providing students with the skills and knowledge needed to address complex global challenges (Abulibdeh, et al., 2024; Kopnina, 2020). For example, AI-powered data analysis tools can enable students to analyze and visualize data on environmental sustainability, climate change, and social justice, empowering them to develop informed solutions to these problems. Overall, AI has the potential to revolutionize the way we approach ESD education by providing personalized learning experiences, enhancing accessibility, analyzing data, and promoting sustainable development outcomes. By understanding the role of AI in ESD education, we can better equip ourselves to address the complex challenges facing our world today. Roles of AI in ESD include:

- Data Analysis and Visualisation: AI can be used to analyse and visualise large datasets related to sustainable development, such as climate change, poverty, and inequality (Mhlanga, 2021). This can help educators and policymakers better understand the complex relationships between these variables and identify areas for intervention.
- Personalised Learning: AI can be used to create personalized learning experiences that adapt to individual students' needs and abilities Kaswan, et al., 2024). This can help students learn more effectively and efficiently and can be particularly beneficial for students with disabilities or those who are struggling in traditional learning environments.
- Simulation and Modelling: AI can be used to simulate real-world scenarios and model complex systems, allowing students to explore and experiment with sustainable development scenarios in a safe and controlled environment (De la Torre, et al., 2021).
- Virtual Fieldwork: AI can be used to create virtual fieldwork experiences that allow students to explore and interact with real-world environments without the need for physical travel. This can be particularly beneficial for stu-

dents who may not have access to resources or opportunities for traditional fieldwork.

- Natural Language Processing: AI can be used to analyse and process large amounts of natural language data, allowing educators to identify patterns and trends in language use related to sustainable development. This can help educators develop more effective teaching strategies and materials.
- Predictive Analytics: AI can be used to predict outcomes and identify potential risks and opportunities related to sustainable development. This can help educators and policymakers make more informed decisions about resource allocation and policy implementation.
- Collaborative Learning: AI can be used to facilitate collaborative learning experiences that bring together students from diverse backgrounds and locations. This can help students develop important skills such as communication, teamwork, and problem-solving.
- Gamification: AI can be used to create engaging and interactive learning experiences that incorporate elements of game design, such as rewards, leaderboards, and challenges. This can help students stay motivated and engaged in their learning (Bennani, et al., 2022).
- Mental Health Support: AI can be used to provide mental health support and wellness resources for students, particularly those who may be struggling with the emotional demands of sustainable development.
- Accessibility: AI can be used to provide accessibility features for students with disabilities, such as text-to-speech functionality, image recognition, and speech recognition (Abulibdeh et al. 2024; Amara, et al. 2024; Chemlal & Azzouazi, 2024; Hara, 2024).

## CHALLENGES AND LIMITATIONS OF THE INTEGRATION OF AI WITH ESD

Several challenges can be examined for the integration of AI such as:

- Data Quality: AI relies on high-quality data to function effectively, but data quality can be a challenge in ESD education.
- Data Bias: AI algorithms can perpetuate biases if they are not designed with inclusivity in mind and biased data can perpetuate existing inequalities.
- Cybersecurity: AI systems require robust cybersecurity measures to prevent unauthorised access or data breaches.
- Lecturer Training: Educators may not have the necessary skills or training to effectively integrate AI into their teaching practices.

- Equity: AI-enabled education must prioritize equity and ensure that all students have access to these resources.
- Access to technology: Not all students have equal access to technology, which can exacerbate existing inequalities.
- Curriculum design: AI-enabled education may perpetuate existing curriculum biases, reinforcing systemic inequalities.
- Student agency: AI-enabled education may inadvertently reduce student agency and autonomy, particularly for marginalised students (Abulibdeh et al. 2024; Tejedor, et al. 2022; Trevisan et al. 2024).

Recommendations for these challenges can be establishing data standards for ESD education to ensure high-quality data for AI analysis, designing AI-enabled education with inclusivity in mind, ensuring that all students have access to these resources, providing professional development opportunities for educators on how to effectively integrate AI into their teaching practices, implement robust cybersecurity measures to protect AI systems from unauthorised access or data breaches and monitoring equity outcomes in AI-enabled education to ensure that all students have equal access to these resources.

## BUILDING EQUITY INTO AI-ENABLED TEACHING AND LEARNING

As AI-enabled technologies become increasingly prevalent in education, it is crucial to prioritize equity in their design and implementation. Equity is not just a moral imperative, but also a critical factor in ensuring that AI-enabled teaching and learning can effectively promote inclusive and sustainable development outcomes (Roshanaei, et al., 2023). Strategies for building equity into AI-enabled teaching and learning include inclusive design, diverse data sets, lecturer training, curriculum design, student agency, accessibility features, feedback mechanisms, and monitoring and equity outcomes.

Design AI-enabled education with inclusivity in mind, considering diverse perspectives, experiences, and abilities. Using diverse data sets to train AI algorithms, ensures that the algorithms are not biased towards specific groups. Provide professional development opportunities for educators on how to effectively integrate AI into their teaching practices, focusing on equity and inclusivity. Design AI-enabled curricula that promote critical thinking, creativity, and problem-solving, rather than reinforcing existing biases. Design AI-enabled education that empowers students to take ownership of their learning, and make decisions about their education. Implement accessibility features in AI-enabled education to ensure that students with disabilities can participate fully. Establish feedback mechanisms that allow students to provide input on AI-enabled education, ensuring that it is responsive to their needs. Regularly monitor equity outcomes in AI-enabled education, addressing disparities and ensuring that all students have equal access to opportunities.

Several researchers cite the best practices for implementing AI-enabled assessment in educational settings (Alfredo et al. 2024; Muhabbat et al. 2024; Naseer et al. 2024; Onesi-Ozigagun et al. 2024). The best practices include: (1) piloting AI-powered tools with a small group of teachers and students to test functionality and identify potential issues, (2) developing clear guidelines for instructors on AI-generated feedback and grading, (3) providing ongoing training and support for educators on AI usage and interpretation, (4) ensuring alignment between AI-assessment criteria and existing curriculum standards, (5) incorporating human review and validation of AI-generated results to maintain accuracy and fairness, (6) establishing clear communication protocols for addressing student concerns and questions about AI-based assessments, (7) monitoring student progress and adapting AI algorithms to better meet diverse learning needs, and (8) fostering transparency about AI decision-making processes and limitations. By following these best practices, educators can harness the potential of AI-enabled assessments to personalize learning, improve student outcomes, and streamline administrative tasks. By implementing AI-enabled assessment thoughtfully and intentionally, organisations can promote diversity and inclusion in the hiring process, reduce biases, and create a more inclusive workforce.

## PROMOTING DIVERSITY AND INCLUSION THROUGH AI-ENABLED ASSESSMENT

Promoting diversity and inclusion through AI-enabled assessment is a critical aspect of ensuring that technology supports equity and fairness in education (Roscoe, et al., 2022). Traditional assessment methods often rely on biased language and cultural norms, which can lead to unfair outcomes for marginalised students. AI-enabled assessment offers a unique opportunity to address these biases by leveraging machine learning algorithms that can identify and mitigate biases, as well as provide personalized feedback and support. By incorporating AI-enabled assessment into education, we can create a more inclusive and equitable learning environment that recognizes and values diversity, empowering students from all backgrounds to reach their full potential (Roscoe, et al., 2022; Sumak, et al., 2024).

AI-enabled assessment is the use of artificial intelligence (AI) and machine learning algorithms to analyze and evaluate candidate responses, such as resumes, cover letters, and online assessments. This technology can help identify biases and provide more accurate and objective results. AI-enabled assessment is important for promoting diversity and inclusion as it:

- Reducing biases: AI-enabled assessment can help reduce biases in the hiring process by eliminating human judgment and bias. This ensures that all candidates are evaluated based on their skills, qualifications, and fit for the role, rather than their race, gender, age, or other demographic characteristics.
- Improves representation: AI-enabled assessment can help organizations increase diversity and inclusion by providing a more level playing field for candidates from underrepresented groups. This can help organizations tap into a broader pool of talent and create a more diverse and inclusive workforce.
- Enhances candidate experience: AI-enabled assessment can provide a more engaging and interactive experience for candidates, reducing the risk of bias and improving the overall hiring process.
- Enhances data-driven decision-making: AI-enabled assessment provides valuable insights into candidate performance, enabling organizations to make data-driven decisions about hiring and employee development.

AI-enabled assessment can also promote diversity and inclusion by:

- Using AI-powered screening tools: Implement AI-powered screening tools that can quickly sift through a large number of resumes and identify top candidates based on their skills and qualifications.
- Removing bias from evaluation criteria: Ensure that evaluation criteria are transparent, objective, and free from bias. AI-enabled assessment can help identify potential biases in evaluation criteria and provide recommendations for improvement.
- Using diverse training data: Train AI models with diverse training data to ensure that the algorithm is not biased towards a particular group or demographic.
- Monitoring and analyzing results: Monitor and analyze the results of AI-enabled assessment to identify areas where biases may be present and make adjustments to the algorithm as needed.
- Providing training and feedback: Provide training and feedback to hiring managers and assessors on how to identify and address biases in the hiring process.
- Encouraging diversity in candidate pools: Encourage diversity in candidate pools by targeting diverse sources, such as job fairs, internships, and mentorship programs.

- Using inclusive language: Use inclusive language in job descriptions, assessments, and other materials to ensure that all candidates feel welcome and included in the hiring process.

## Measuring the impact of AI on learning outcomes

As AI increasingly becomes an integral part of education, it is essential to measure the impact of AI on learning outcomes. With the potential to revolutionise teaching and learning, AI-powered tools and platforms can enhance student engagement, personalize learning, and provide real-time feedback (Rekha, et al., 2024). However, without a thorough understanding of the impact of AI on learning outcomes, educators and policymakers may struggle to make informed decisions about its adoption and implementation. By conducting rigorous research and evaluations, we can uncover the effects of AI on student achievement, motivation, and retention, as well as identify areas where AI can be most effective in improving learning outcomes. This knowledge will be critical in optimizing the use of AI to support education and drive positive change in the lives of students. Measuring the impact of AI on learning outcomes is crucial to understanding its effectiveness in education. Ways to measure the impact of AI on learning outcomes are:

- Learning Analytics: Collect and analyze data on student learning outcomes, such as grades, test scores, and completion rates. Use data visualization tools to identify patterns and trends.
- Assessment Scores: Use standardized assessment scores to compare student performance before and after using AI-powered learning tools. This can help identify whether AI has improved learning outcomes.
- Student Feedback: Collect feedback from students on their learning experience with AI-powered tools. This can help identify areas where AI has improved engagement, motivation, or understanding.
- Teacher Feedback: Collect feedback from teachers on their experience with AI-powered tools. This can help identify areas where AI has improved teacher workload, reduced grading burden, or enhanced teaching effectiveness.
- Surveys and Interviews: Conduct surveys and interviews with students, teachers, and administrators to gather qualitative feedback on the impact of AI on learning outcomes.
- Quasi-Experimental Designs: Conduct quasi-experimental designs, such as randomized controlled trials (RCTs), to compare the learning outcomes of students who use AI-powered tools with those who do not.

- Regression Analysis: Use regression analysis to control for other variables that may influence learning outcomes and isolate the impact of AI on learning outcomes.
- Correlation Analysis: Analyze the correlation between AI usage and learning outcomes to identify any relationships or trends.
- Longitudinal Studies: Conduct longitudinal studies to track student learning outcomes over time and analyze the impact of AI on long-term learning outcomes.
- Validation Studies: Conduct validation studies to ensure that the data collected is accurate and reliable and that the findings are generalizable to different populations.

Examples of metrics to measure the impact of AI on learning outcomes are grade point average, standardized test scores, student engagement, lecturer load, student satisfaction, learning gain, dropout rate, retention rate, graduation rate, and career readiness. Measure the average GPA of students who use AI-powered tools compared to those who do not. Standardized test scores measure the average scores of students who use AI-powered tools compared to those who do not. Student engagement levels are measured, such as time spent on tasks, participation rates, and attendance. Measure the reduction in teacher workload due to AI-powered tools. Student satisfaction is also measured by their learning experience using AI-powered tools. Measure the increase in learning gain (e.g., mastery of skills or knowledge) among students who use AI-powered tools. The dropout rate is measured among students who use AI-powered tools. Measure the improvement in retention rate among students who use AI-powered tools. Also, measure the improvement in graduation rate among students who use AI-powered tools. Above all measure the improvement in career readiness among students who use AI-powered tools.

Challenges in measuring the impact of AI on learning outcomes include data quality which ensures the accuracy and reliability of data collected. The complexity of education: education is a complex system, making it challenging to isolate the impact of AI on learning outcomes. Variability in student outcomes: Student outcomes can vary significantly due to individual differences, making it challenging to identify a clear impact of AI. Limited scalability: The limited scalability of AI-powered tools can make it challenging to measure their impact at a large scale. Contextual factors: contextual factors, such as socioeconomic status, can influence learning outcomes and make it challenging to isolate the impact of AI. By using these metrics and methods, educators can better understand the impact of AI on learning outcomes and make informed decisions about how to integrate AI into education effectively.

## RETHINKING LECTURER EDUCATION FOR THE AI-ENABLED CLASSROOM

Rethinking lecturer education for the AI-enabled classroom is crucial to ensure that educators are equipped to effectively integrate AI into their teaching practices. As AI continues to transform the way we teach and learn, lecturer education programs must evolve to prepare educators for the AI-enabled classroom. Traditional lecturer education models may not have adequately prepared teachers to integrate AI-powered tools and platforms into their instruction, leaving many educators feeling unprepared or overwhelmed. To address this gap, we must rethink teacher education to focus on developing the skills and competencies needed to effectively integrate AI into teaching and learning. This includes training educators on AI ethics, data analysis, and pedagogical strategies that leverage AI to support student learning. By rethinking lecturer education, we can ensure that educators are equipped to harness the potential of AI to improve student outcomes, enhance teaching practices, and drive innovation in education. The key considerations for rethinking lecturer education include:

- Focus on pedagogy: Emphasise pedagogical skills, such as lesson planning, classroom management, and assessment, to help lecturer adapt their teaching strategies to the AI-enabled classroom.
- AI literacy: Provide lecturers with AI literacy training, including understanding AI concepts, algorithms, and tools, to help them make informed decisions about integrating AI into their teaching practices.
- Technology integration: Offer training on technology integration, including how to use AI-powered tools, platforms, and software, to enhance teaching and learning.
- Data analysis: Teach lecturers how to analyze and interpret data generated by AI-powered tools, such as learning analytics, to inform instruction and improve student outcomes.
- Collaborative learning: Emphasize the importance of collaborative learning and teamwork in the AI-enabled classroom, highlighting the need for teachers to work together to design and implement effective AI-based instructional strategies.
- Professional development: Provide ongoing professional development opportunities for teachers to stay up-to-date with the latest developments in AI and its applications in education.
- Lecturer support: Offer teacher support services, such as coaching and mentoring, to help teachers overcome challenges and address concerns related to integrating AI into their teaching practices.

- Curriculum design: Develop curriculum design modules that incorporate AI-powered learning objects, simulations, and games, to help teachers create engaging and interactive lesson plans.
- Assessment and feedback: Teach Lecturers how to design and implement effective assessments and feedback mechanisms that utilize AI-powered tools to provide personalized feedback to students.
- Student-centered learning: Emphasize the importance of student-centered learning in the AI-enabled classroom, highlighting the need for lecturers to prioritize student autonomy, agency, and voice.
- Social-emotional learning: Incorporate social-emotional learning (SEL) into lecturer education programs to help educators develop students' emotional intelligence, empathy, and self-awareness.
- Lecturer well-being: Prioritize lecturer well-being by providing support services and resources that address burnout, stress, and compassion fatigue.
- Lecturer-student relationships: Emphasize the importance of lecturer-student relationships in the AI-enabled classroom, highlighting the need for lecturers to build trust, empathy, and understanding with students.
- Classroom management: Teach lecturers how to manage the AI-enabled classroom effectively, including strategies for managing student behavior, minimizing distractions, and promoting engagement.
- Continuous improvement: Encourage a culture of continuous improvement among lecturers by providing opportunities for reflection, feedback, and iteration in their teaching practices.

By incorporating these key considerations into lecturer education programs, educators can better prepare themselves for the AI-enabled classroom and provide high-quality learning experiences for their students.

## FUTURE RESEARCH DIRECTION ON EQUITY, TEACHING, AND ASSESSMENT PRACTICES FOR THE INTEGRATION OF AI ESD IN HIGHER EDUCATION TO PROMOTE ESJ

As AI continues to transform the way we learn and interact, it is essential to consider how it can be integrated into Education for Sustainable Development (ESD) to promote Education for Social Justice (ESJ). The rapid development and deployment of Artificial Intelligence (AI) technologies is transforming the way we learn, work, and interact. As AI becomes increasingly integrated into various aspects of our lives, it is essential to consider how it can be harnessed to promote ESD and ESJ (Tzotzou, et al., 2021). ESD is a critical component of education that focuses on developing the knowledge, skills, and values necessary to address the complex social, economic, and environmental challenges facing our world. ESD aims to promote sustainable development by fostering a culture of critical thinking, problem-solving, and collaboration. ESJ is a critical component of education that focuses on promoting social justice by addressing the systemic inequalities and injustices that perpetuate poverty, inequality, and marginalization. ESJ aims to promote social justice by empowering individuals and communities to take action against injustice and promoting human rights. The integration of AI into ESD and ESJ is crucial for several reasons as AI-powered learning platforms can increase accessibility to education, particularly for marginalized communities, by providing personalized learning experiences that cater to individual needs and abilities. AI can analyze large datasets related to ESD and ESJ issues, providing insights into complex problems and promoting data-driven decision-making. AI-powered tools can facilitate collaboration and communication among students, educators, and stakeholders, promoting global citizenship and collective action. AI-driven adaptive learning systems can provide personalized learning experiences that cater to individual learning styles, strengths, and weaknesses. AI-powered learning platforms can reduce costs associated with traditional education methods, such as infrastructure and labor costs.

As AI continues to transform the way we learn and interact, it is essential to consider how it can be integrated into ESD and ESJ to promote positive social change and sustainable development outcomes. As future directions, it is therefore crucial to examine:

- Equity in AI-enhanced ESD Education by investigating how AI can be used to identify and address systemic biases and inequalities in ESD education, particularly for marginalized groups. Develop strategies for incorporating diverse perspectives and experiences into AI-driven ESD education.
- Teaching practices for AI-integrated ESD Education: Explore the role of lecturer training and professional development in effectively integrating AI into ESD education. Investigate how teachers can adapt their teaching practices to incorporate AI-driven learning tools and simulations.
- Assessment practices for AI-integrated ESD Education: Develop new assessment methods that account for the potential biases and limitations of AI-driven learning tools. Investigate how AI can be used to provide personalized feedback and assessment to students, promoting deeper learning and engagement.
- Curriculum Development for AI-Integrated ESD Education: Develop curricula that integrate AI-driven learning tools and simulations into ESD education, focusing on critical thinking, problem-solving, and communication

skills. Investigate how AI can be used to develop interactive and immersive learning experiences that promote a deeper understanding of complex ESD issues.

- Student Engagement and Motivation in AI-integrated ESD Education: Investigate how AI-driven learning tools and simulations can be used to increase student engagement and motivation in ESD education. Develop strategies for using AI to provide personalized feedback and support to students, promoting a sense of autonomy and agency.
- Collaboration and Partnerships for AI-Integrated ESD Education: Investigate how collaborations between higher education institutions, NGOs, and industry partners can facilitate the development of innovative AI-driven ESD education initiatives. Develop strategies for fostering partnerships between educators, researchers, and industry experts to develop cutting-edge AI-driven learning tools and simulations.
- Ethical Considerations in AI-Integrated ESD Education: Investigate the ethical implications of using AI in ESD education, including issues related to data privacy, bias, and surveillance. Develop guidelines for educators and policymakers on how to address ethical concerns related to AI in ESD education.

By addressing these research directions, we can better understand the potential benefits and challenges of integrating AI with ESD education in higher education settings, ultimately promoting education for social justice (ESJ) and contributing to a more equitable and sustainable world.

## SUPPORTING EDUCATORS IN ADOPTING AI-ENABLED PRACTICES

In the dominion of education lecturers need to receive support in adopting AI-enabled practices can have a significant impact on education as this enhances teaching and learning experiences. According to Mohameid (2024), lecturers need professional development. Collaboration and networking, mentoring and coaching, and curriculum integration in adopting AI-enabled practices. Exposure to a comprehensive professional development program can help lecturers understand the potential of AI in education and its practical applications and this can be achieved through the provision of workshops, webinars, and training sessions that acquaint lecturers with AI technologies, tools, and platforms. Chen et al. (2020), avail educators with access to AI-enabled resources and tools meant for educational purposes like AI-powered learning platforms, virtual reality (VR) or augmented reality (AR) tools, adaptive learning systems, intelligent tutoring systems, and data analytics tools is great support lecturers in adopting AI-enabled practices. Collaboration, networking, mentoring, and coaching are key support lecturers in adopting AI-enabled practices (Shaheen, 2023).

To facilitate collaboration and networking opportunities as well as mentorship among teachers who have an interest in AI-enabled practices enhance both teaching and learning procedures that encourage them to share ideas, experiences, and best practices through online communities, forums, or professional learning networks. This can foster a supportive environment for lecturers to learn from each other and exchange innovative AI teaching methods. According to UNESCO (2019), a shift from traditional teaching methods to automatic and robotic AI-enabled technologies practices is tailored to meet individual student and lecturer needs in the classroom. This experience can guide lecturers in integrating AI technologies into their teaching practices. This transition aims to improve the effectiveness and gratification of learning, resulting in better academic outcomes. Mentors can provide individualized support, answer questions, offer feedback, and help lecturers troubleshoot any challenges they may encounter in their professional (Smith and Sanchez, (2022).

The above-mentioned support initiatives help lecturers integrate AI concepts and skills into the curriculum. Regular updates to the curriculum are needed to incorporate AI progressions, ensuring students are prepared to develop a digital landscape as well as the need to work with curriculum specialists to develop AI-focused lesson plans, projects, and activities that align with educational standards. The support initiatives will provide lecturers with resources and examples of how AI can be integrated across various subjects and grade levels. Lecturer empowerment through training gives the necessary technical support and assistance to teachers as they implement AI-enabled practices. This is achieved through AI integration in education via robust infrastructure, staff training, data protection, software development, financing, ethical controls, communication, and continuous evaluation. Al Husseiy (2023), outlined that the provision of dedicated help desks, online resources, and a knowledgeable support team address any technical issues or challenges lecturers may face. These challenges are generally research and evidence-based practice aligned with AI in education. To counter this lecturers, are encouraged to share relevant research studies, reports, and case studies that demonstrate the impact of AI on teaching and learning outcomes. This can help lecturers understand the potential benefits and limitations of AI and make informed decisions about its use. This can be achieved through data literacy training to equip teachers to develop data literacy skills to effectively collect, analyze, and interpret data generated by AI tools and platforms (Sheheen, 2023). The provision of training on data privacy, data ethics, and responsible AI use ensures lecturers make informed decisions when using AI-enabled technologies, AI tools, and platforms, and promotes responsible and equitable use of AI in the classroom (UNESCO, 2019).

## ESTABLISHING ETHICAL AND LEGAL FRAMEWORKS FOR AI IN EDUCATION

The establishment of ethical and legal frameworks for AI in education is essential to ensure that the use of artificial intelligence (AI) technologies in educational settings is responsible, and fair, and respects the rights and well-being of students and stakeholders involved. Privacy and data protection, equity and fairness, and transparency are some of the attentions for developing ethical and legal frameworks (Paraysta-Pomsta et al. 2023). These frameworks require collaboration among educators, policymakers, technologists, and other relevant stakeholders as it is important to engage in widespread public consultation and consider diverse perspectives to ensure that the frameworks are comprehensive, inclusive, and effective in addressing the ethical and legal challenges associated with AI in education. AI in education often involves the collection and analysis of large amounts of student data. It is important to have clear regulations and policies in place to safeguard the privacy and security of this data. Any data collection and processing should comply with relevant data protection laws, and explicit consent should be obtained when necessary. The AI systems used in education should be transparent and provide explanations for their decisions or recommendations (Holmes and Porayska-Pomsta, 2022). This is particularly important when AI is used for student assessment or personalized learning. Students, lecturers, and administrators should be able to understand how AI algorithms work and how they arrive at their conclusions. This calls for continuous close monitoring and evaluation. Ethical and legal frameworks for AI in education are dynamic and adaptable. They need continuous monitoring, evaluation, and updates to keep pace with technological advancements and address emerging ethical concerns. Ethical use of AI in education should be used ethically and within appropriate boundaries. It should not replace human lecturers or undermine the importance of human interaction in the learning process. AI is a tool to enhance education and support lecturers rather it is not a replacement for human expertise. Students and their parents or guardians should be adequately informed about the use of AI technologies in education. They should have the right to provide informed consent for the use of AI and should also have the option to opt-out if they choose not to participate (UNESCO, 2023). However, equity and fairness in AI use should not exacerbate existing educational inequalities. Efforts should be made to ensure that AI systems do not reinforce biases based on factors such as race, gender, or socioeconomic status (Henz, 2021). Regular audits and evaluations should be conducted to detect and mitigate any biases present in AI algorithms. Algorithmic Accountability mechanisms should be in place to hold developers and providers of AI systems accountable for their products. This includes regular auditing, testing, and validation of AI algorithms to ensure their accuracy, reliability, and safety. Clear responsibilities and liabilities should be established for all stakeholders involved.

## CHALLENGES WITH THE INTEGRATION OF ESD AND AI GLOBALLY NOWADAYS

The integration of Education for Sustainable Development (ESD) and AI presents several challenges on a global scale. Mahamed (2024) cites that many educational systems are actively integrating AI applications into teaching and learning processes to create innovative learning environments that help learners adapt to technologies and advancements. However, cognitive science, intelligent machines, and natural interfaces are the areas that need to be integrated into the school curriculum to promote learning experiences. Some of these challenges are access and infrastructure, technological divide, curriculum adaptation, and capacity building among other challenges. The major challenge in the integration of education for sustainable development and AI globally nowadays is ensuring equitable access and infrastructure to AI technologies and the necessary infrastructure for ESD. Al-Saidh et al. (2023) highlighted that to overcome these challenges AI adoption serves as a drive for sustainable development across various sectors by integrating modern technologies into individual and institutional management practices. Many regions, especially in developing countries, still lack basic access to technology and the Internet. UNESCO (2019) noted a technological divide between developed and developing countries, individuals in developed countries tend to have better access to AI resources, expertise, and funding, enabling them to advance ESD initiatives more rapidly than their counterparts in developing states. This difference does not ensure that all countries benefit from AI-driven ESD. Without access to AI tools and platforms, it becomes difficult to integrate ESD effectively. Limited funding and access to resources that enable the implementation of AI-driven ESD initiatives require significant financial resources, research and development investments, and infrastructure development. Securing funding and resources for such initiatives can be a challenge in resource-constrained settings such as Zimbabwe. UNESCO (2023) pleads for some global collaborative efforts between governments, international organizations, and the private sector to mobilize the necessary resources for capacity building meant to develop the necessary human capital that drives AI-driven ESD as this is a great challenge in education. It requires training and upskilling educators, policymakers, and other stakeholders to understand the potential of AI and its applications in sustainable development. Building capacity in AI technologies, data literacy, and AI ethics for AI towards ESD requires the integration of ESD and AI into the educational curricula through AI concepts, skills, and ethical considerations. However, the adaptation process can be a challenge, as it requires multi-stakeholder collaboration between education policymakers, curriculum developers, and AI experts. Training needs for educators to teach AI concepts to promote sustainable development goals.

When values and ethical principles are applied in education they dictate and guide the development and implementation of AI systems. Principles of values and ethics uphold human rights and values, minimizing negative outcomes and also maximizing benefits. According to Akagun and Greenhow (2022), values and ethics tailor-made toward the integration of AI and ESD need to be culturally and contextually relevant. Societies have diverse cultural, social, and economic contexts, and the implementation of AI-driven ESD should consider these variations. Customization of AI applications in educational content based on local needs and priorities is essential. These ethics aim to address bias and promote fairness, and transparency for all parties involved in education (education policymakers, curriculum developers, and educators). To ensure the successful and ethical integration of AI in education, ethical considerations related to data privacy, algorithmic bias, clear policies, and balancing human interaction are some of the issues to be employed. Integrating ESD with AI requires addressing these ethical considerations and ensuring that AI technologies are designed and deployed in a manner that aligns with sustainable development principles. This involves promoting transparency, accountability, and responsible AI practices. Addressing these challenges requires a multi-stakeholder approach, involving governments, educational institutions, AI experts, civil society organizations, and the private sector. Collaboration, knowledge sharing, and capacity building are key to overcoming these challenges and harnessing the potential of AI for sustainable development in higher education (Nguyen et al, 2023).

## THE CURRENT CHALLENGES FACED IN THE INTEGRATION OF ESD TO PROMOTE ESJ IN HIGHER EDUCATION

The integration of Education for Sustainable Development (ESD) with Education for Social Justice (ESJ) in higher education has come up on board with several challenges. The current challenges faced by educators in their attempt to promote ESJ in higher education include limited institutional support, curriculum design assessment and evaluation, training needs and development, résistance and relaxation, intersectionality, complexity, and inclusive pedagogies (Williamson et al, 2023). Lack of educational fund votes by governments led to many higher education institutions failing to prioritize or allocate sufficient resources towards the integration of ESJ into their curricula and educational practices. Thus lack of this essential support from institutional leadership can hinder efforts to promote ESJ effectively limited integration of ESJ into existing curricula and educational programs can be challenging as it requires a comprehensive review and restructuring of courses to incorporate ESJ principles, perspectives, and content. This process may face resistance from traditional disciplinary boundaries and established curriculum structures, making it difficult for educators to integrate ESJ effectively (Henz, 2021). To make social justice an integral part of Higher education educators need the necessary knowledge, skills, and pedagogical approaches to effectively incorporate ESJ into their teaching practices. The pedagogies should be inclusive to promote ESJ that is open for critical thinking, dialogue, and reflection although its implementations in large lecture-style classes or online learning environments can be challenging. Educators need support and guidance to develop and implement pedagogical approaches that actively engage teachers and students in ESJ learning across all facets of higher education (Holmes and Porayska-Pomsta, 2022).

Limited to lack of training and professional development opportunities among members in higher education with a focus on ESJ is the current challenges faced in the integration of ESD with Education for Social Justice (ESJ) in the educators' attempt to promote ESJ in Higher Education. Addressing this challenge and other after-aforementioned constraints requires providing educators with training programs, resources, and support to enhance their capacity to educate the learners on ESJ. The assessment and evaluation of issues of ESJ integration in higher education can be complex. This is because traditional assessment methods may not capture the multidimensional nature of ESJ learning outcomes. Thus the move to developing appropriate assessment tools and strategies to measure students' understanding of social justice issues and their ability to apply that knowledge in real-world contexts is fundamental but can be achieved with a significant number of challenges. However, resistance from existing power structures and social norms from various stakeholders, including students, educators, and administrators is a constraint. According to Roshanaei et al. (2023), some individuals view ESJ as politically biased or controversial, leading to relaxation towards its integration. Overcoming some of these challenges calls for fostering open dialogue, creating safe spaces for discussion, and addressing misconceptions about ESJ. ESJ recognizes the interconnectedness and networking of complex issues. Social justice is essential among educators in addressing multiple dimensions of social justice, including race, gender, class, and more, in a collaborative and all-inclusive manner (Emma et al, (2022). To address these challenges requires a collective effort from educators, administrators, policymakers, and students. This will effectively navigate the intersections of diverse perspectives that are included in ESJ education demands. The current challenges faced in terms of the integration of education for sustainable development with education for social justice (ESJ) in the educators' attempt to promote ESJ in Higher Education are achieved through the promotion of institutional commitment, providing professional development opportunities for institutions, reviewing and revising curricula, fostering inclusive learning environments, and creating spaces for dialogue and collaboration (McPhail, 2021). To achieve this higher education institutions, need to promote ESJ and prepare students to become socially responsible and engage among its global citizens.

## INTEGRATING ESD WITH AI EFFECTIVELY TO PROMOTE ESJ IN HIGHER EDUCATION BY EDUCATORS

The 21st century has perceived a transformation in the field of education, technology has become a game changer in all facets of the educational ecosystem as AI as it tries to make Sustainable Development Goals (SDGs) a reality. Thus, the integration of education for Sustainable Development (ESD) with AI effectively to promote Education for Social Justice (ESJ) in higher education requires a thoughtful and strategic approach. Educators need to integrate AI and ESJ by incorporating AI-related topics, applications, and ethical considerations into existing courses or developing new courses specifically focusing on the intersection of AI and social justice (Mahamed, 2024). This integration can explore how AI technologies can be upheld for social justice causes, and critically examine the potential ethical challenges and biases allied with AI. Educators should engage in continuous learning and professional development to stay updated on the latest advancements in AI and its intersection with social justice. This can involve attending workshops, and conferences, or participating in online courses related to AI ethics and social justice. Interdisciplinary collaboration among educators from different disciplines, such as computer science, social sciences, and humanities, can enrich the integration of AI and ESJ. Interdisciplinary teams can jointly design courses or collaborative projects that explore the social implications of AI and its potential to address social justice issues. Roshanaei et al. (2023) to promote social justice in Higher education ethical AI education consideration among educators should be accentuated as the ethical dimensions of AI in the context of ESJ. This includes exploring areas such as algorithmic bias, privacy concerns, and the impact of AI on marginalized communities. According to Emma et al. (2022), it is important to foster critical thinking and ethical decision-making skills among students when it comes to AI technologies and their role in promoting social justice.

Educators should identify practical applications and encourage students to apply AI technologies in real-world contexts to address social justice challenges. This can involve project-based learning, where students develop AI solutions or use AI tools to analyze and address social justice issues. For example, students can use AI for data analysis related to environmental justice, access to education, or equitable resource distribution. Through the integration of AI and ESJ in higher education, educators can empower learners to become critical thinkers, ethical AI practitioners, and advocates for social justice (Emma et al. 2022). This integration provides an opportunity to harness the potential of AI while addressing its challenges and ensuring that the development and deployment of AI technologies contribute to a more just and sustainable world. McPhail (2021), the provision of guest lectures, workshops, or joint research projects with AI professionals can provide students with insights into the latest AI developments, ethical considerations, and potential applications for social justice. The integration of AI collaborative efforts with education institutions, technology developers, and AI policymakers' experts. Educators need to engage with AI researchers and experts to bring their expertise into the classroom, these must devise robust frameworks that safeguard sensitive data from unauthorized access and misuse. This entails constructing stringent policies and regulations overseeing data collection and its subsequent use in academic contexts thereby preserving the privacy rights of the students.

Partnerships and experiential learning can nurture engagement with organisations working on social justice issues and AI. This nurturing arrangement provides students with opportunities for internships, research projects, or community-engaged learning experiences where they can apply their AI skills to address real-world challenges related to social justice. Inclusivity and participatory pedagogies that encourage diverse perspectives and active student engagement would also be encouraged. This can include group discussions, case studies, and incorporating examples and narratives that highlight the intersectionality of social justice issues and AI. Students' partnerships encourage them to critically analyze and question the social implications of AI as this will then develop appropriate assessment methods that capture students' understanding of AI's role in social justice and their ability to critically analyze AI applications. This may involve evaluating students' projects, presentations, or research papers that demonstrate their grasp of the subject matter and their ability to apply ethical considerations. Educators should engage in continuous learning and professional development to stay updated on the latest advancements in AI and its intersection with social justice. This is achieved through attending seminars, workshops, and conferences, or participating in online courses related to AI ethics and social justice.

## CONCLUSION

The integration of Artificial Intelligence in higher education enhances equity, teaching, and assessment practices for the integration of AI with education for sustainable development (ESD) in Higher Education to promote Education for Social Justice (ESJ). The efficacy of learning through the use of AI-powered learning platforms, instruction systems, and the adaption of automated assessment has created an active educational ecosystem that has equipped learners and lecturers with the needed skills and knowledge for the challenges of the 21st-century generation teaching and learning experiences. The overarching goal of fostering ethical considerations and a more inclusive and equitable educational landscape is drawn from the concerns explicated in the analysis and strengthening of private data measure issues that have emerged as persistent priorities. This impacts educational equity in the pedagogy toward the promotion of education for social justice. Collaboration among stakeholders including educators' policymakers, curriculum developers, and learners enhances accessibility and shapes the future of education. Transparency, accountability, and responsibility are guidelines to be enshrined integration of AI for education for sustainable development (ESD) in Higher Education. The integration of AI technologies opens up new opportunities for personalized responsibility that harness the potential drive to innovation, improve learning outcomes, and enhance education for sustenance in higher education and the promotion of social justice.

## REFERENCES


Abulibdeh, A., Zaidan, E., & Abulibdeh, R. (2024). Navigating the confluence of artificial intelligence and education for sustainable development in the era of industry 4.0: Challenges, opportunities, and ethical dimensions. *Journal of Cleaner Production*, *437*, 140527. DOI: 10.1016/j.jclepro.2023.140527

Abulibdeh, A., Zaidan, E., & Abulibdeh, R. (2024). Navigating the confluence of artificial intelligence and education for sustainable development in the era of industry 4.0: Challenges, opportunities, and ethical dimensions. *Journal of Cleaner Production*, *437*, 140527. DOI: 10.1016/j.jclepro.2023.140527

Akgun, S. and Greenhow, C. (2023). Artificial Intelligence in Education; addressing ethics Challenges in K-12 setting. AI ethic, 2(3): 431-440.

Al-Husseiy, F. (2023). Artificial Intelligence in Higher Education: A New Horizon. In Kaddaoura, S. (Ed.), *Handbook of Research of Artificial Intelligence Methods and Applications in Computer Engineering*. I.G.I. global.

Al Masry, N. O. (2022). The role of Artificial Intelligence technologies in improving the Jordan Students: A student Perspective. *Journal of the College of Education (Assiut)*, *30*(9), 265–290.

Al-Saidh, H. M. S., Al Balushi, F. A. M., & Al-Kaadbi, M. S. M. (2023). The availability of AI applications in Social Studies Curriculum in Basic Education Schools in the Sultanate of Oman. *Journal of Curriculum and Teaching Methods*, *2*(3), 1–14.

Al Samman, A. M. (2024, January). Harnessing Potential: Meta-Analysis of AI Integration in Higher Education. In *2024 ASU International Conference in Emerging Technologies for Sustainability and Intelligent Systems (ICETSIS)* (pp. 1-7). IEEE. DOI: 10.1109/ICETSIS61505.2024.10459420

Alfredo, R., Echeverria, V., Jin, Y., Yan, L., Swiecki, Z., Gasevic, D., & Martinez-Maldonado, R. (2024). Human-centered learning analytics and AI in education: A systematic literature review. *Computers and Education: Artificial Intelligence*, 100215.

Amado-Salvatierra, H. R., Morales-Chan, M., Hernandez-Rizzardini, R., & Rosales, M. (2024, March). Exploring Educators' Perceptions: Artificial Intelligence Integration in Higher Education. In *2024 IEEE World Engineering Education Conference (EDUNINE)* (pp. 1-5). IEEE. DOI: 10.1109/EDUNINE60625.2024.10500578

Amara, K., Altinay, F., Altinay, Z., & Dagli, G. (2024). Artificial intelligence and sustainable educational systems. In *Computational Intelligence and Blockchain in Complex Systems* (pp. 199–204). Morgan Kaufmann. DOI: 10.1016/B978-0-443-13268-1.00011-X

Arnold, P., Davids, J., & Reiser, M. (2024, June). Building Future Skills in Higher Education: An International Blended Project Seminar on Sustainable Development. In *Conference Proceedings. The Future of Education 2024.*

Bennani, S., Maalel, A., & Ben Ghezala, H. (2022). Adaptive gamification in E-learning: A literature review and future challenges. *Computer Applications in Engineering Education*, *30*(2), 628–642. DOI: 10.1002/cae.22477

Chemlal, Y., & Azzouazi, M. (2024). A Methodology for Evaluating and Reporting the Integration of Artificial Intelligence for Sustainability in Higher Education: New Insights and Opportunities. In *Engineering Applications of Artificial Intelligence* (pp. 113–130). Springer Nature Switzerland. DOI: 10.1007/978-3-031-50300-9_7

Chen, L., Chen, P., & Lin, Z. (2020). Artificial intelligence in education: A review. *IEEE Access : Practical Innovations, Open Solutions*, *8*, 75264–75278. DOI: 10.1109/ACCESS.2020.2988510

Contreras, J. R. I., Castillo, E. F. R., Verdezoto, M. K. S., & Liliana, C. L. (2024). Exploring the Implementation of Artificial Intelligence in Higher Education: Advantages and Hurdles. *Migration Letters : An International Journal of Migration Studies*, *21*(S2), 233–243. DOI: 10.59670/ml.v20i8.6496

De la Torre, R., Onggo, B. S., Corlu, C. G., Nogal, M., & Juan, A. A. (2021). The role of simulation and serious games in teaching concepts on circular economy and sustainable energy. *Energies*, *14*(4), 1138. DOI: 10.3390/en14041138

Emma, S., Daniela, D., Glansa, Y., Elglis, C., Mutize, T., Morales, D., & Jose, A. C. (2022). The right to Higher Education: A Social Justice Perspective. UNESCO, 7.

Goralski, M. A., & Tan, T. K. (2020). Artificial intelligence and sustainable development. *International Journal of Management Education*, *18*(1), 100330. DOI: 10.1016/j.ijme.2019.100330

Hara, M. (2024). Roles of Artificial Intelligence in Education for Sustainable Development in Asia-Pacific Contexts. *Global Journal of Business and Integral Security*, *1*(2).

Heinz, P. (2021). Ethical and Legal Responsibility for AI. *Discover AI.*, *1*, 2. DOI: 10. 1007/ 544163-021-00002-4

Holmes, W., & Porayska-Pomsta, K. (2022). *The Ethical of Artificial Intelligence in Education: Practice, Challenges and Debates*. Routledge.

Kaswan, K. S., Dhatterwal, J. S., & Ojha, R. P. (2024). AI in personalized learning. In *Advances in Technological Innovations in Higher Education* (pp. 103–117). CRC Press. DOI: 10.1201/9781003376699-9

Kopnina, H. (2020). Education for the future? Critical evaluation of education for sustainable development goals. *The Journal of Environmental Education, 51*(4), 280–291. DOI: 10.1080/00958964.2019.1710444

Lorente-Echeverria, S., Murillo-Pardo, B., & Canales-Lacruz, I. (2022). A systematic review of curriculum sustainability at university: A Key challenge for improving the professional development of teachers of the future. *Education Sciences, 12*(11), 753. DOI: 10.3390/educsci12110753

McPhail, C. J. (2021). Fostering Social Justice in Higher Education. Diverse: Issues in Higher Education. https://www.Diverseeducation.com./institutions-colleges/article/ 15108962/fostering-social-justice-in-higher-education

Mhlanga, D. (2021). Artificial intelligence in the industry 4.0, and its impact on Poverty, innovation, infrastructure development, and the sustainable development goals: Lessons from Emerging Economies? *Sustainability (Basel), 13*(11), 5788. DOI: 10.3390/su13115788

Muhabbat, H., Mukhiddin, K., Jalil, H., Dustnazar, K., Farxod, T., Shavkat, M., Khulkar, K., & Jakhongir, S. (2024). The digital frontier: AI-enabled transformations in higher education management. *Indonesian Journal of Educational Research and Technology, 4*(1), 71–88.

Muhamed, M. G. S. (2024). Artificial Intelligence and sustainability of educational services: An Overview. *World Journal of Social Sciences and Humanities, 10*(1), 8–17. DOI: 10.12691/wjssh-10-1-2

Naseer, F., Khalid, M. U., Ayub, N., Rasool, A., Abbas, T., & Afzal, M. W. (2024). Automated Assessment and Feedback in Higher Education Using Generative AI. In *Transforming Education with Generative AI: Prompt Engineering and Synthetic Content Creation* (pp. 433-461). IGI Global. DOI: 10.4018/979-8-3693-1351-0.ch021

Neha, K., Kumar, R., & Sankat, M. (2024). AI Wizards: Pioneering Assistive Technologies for Higher Education Inclusion of Students with Learning Disabilities. In *Applied Assistive Technologies and Informatics for Students with Disabilities* (pp. 59–70). Springer Nature Singapore. DOI: 10.1007/978-981-97-0914-4_4

Nguyen, A., Ngo, H. N., Hong, Y., Dang, B. and Nguyen, B. P. T. (2023). Ethical Principles for Artificial Intelligence in Education. Education, and Information Technologies, 28, 4221-4241, 10639-022-11316-w.DOI: <ALIGNMENT.qj></ ALIGNMENT>10.1007/s

Onesi-Ozigagun, O., Ololade, Y. J., Eyo-Udo, N. L., & Ogundipe, D. O. (2024). Revolutionizing education through AI: A comprehensive review of enhancing learning experiences. *International Journal of Applied Research in Social Sciences*, *6*(4), 589–607. DOI: 10.51594/ijarss.v6i4.1011

Porayska- Pomsta. K, Holmes, W. and Nemorin, S. (2023). The ethics of Artificial Intelligence in Education: In B. du Boulay, A. Mitrovic, and Yacet (Eds). The Handbook of AI in Education Edward Elgar Publishing Ltd.

Rahiman, H. U., & Kodikal, R. (2024). Revolutionizing education: Artificial intelligence empowered learning in higher education. *Cogent Education*, *11*(1), 2293431. DOI: 10.1080/2331186X.2023.2293431

Rekha, K., Gopal, K., Satheeskumar, D., Anand, U. A., Doss, D. S. S., & Elayaperumal, S. (2024, May). Ai-Powered Personalized Learning System Design: Student Engagement and Performance Tracking System. In *2024 4th International Conference on Advance Computing and Innovative Technologies in Engineering (ICACITE)* (pp. 1125-1130). IEEE.

Roscoe, R. D., Salehi, S., Nixon, N., Worsley, M., Piech, C., & Luckin, R. (2022). Inclusion and equity as a paradigm shift for artificial intelligence in education. In *Artificial Intelligence in STEM Education* (pp. 359–374). CRC Press. DOI: 10.1201/9781003181187-28

Roshanaei, M., Olivares, H., & Lopez, R. R. (2023). Harnessing AI to foster equity in education: Opportunities, challenges, and emerging strategies. *Journal of Intelligent Learning Systems and Applications*, *15*(04), 123–143. DOI: 10.4236/jilsa.2023.154009

Shaheen, H. A. M. (2023) Artificial Intelligence and the shift from Indoctrination to utilizing tools for sustainable education. Arab Journal for specific education. No26, 139-169. https:// search. Mandumad10.com/ Recrd/1355921

Sumak, B., Lopez-de-Ipria, D., Dziabenko, O., Correia, S. D., de Carvalho, L. M. S., Lopes, S., . . . Pusnik, M. (2024, May). AI-Based Education Tools for Enabling Inclusive Education: Challenges and Benefits. In *2024 47th MIPRO ICT and Electronics Convention (MIPRO)* (pp. 472-477). Institute of Electrical and Electronics Engineers.

Tejedor, G., Sanchez-Carracedo, F., & Segalas, J. (2022). Education for sustainable development in higher education: Introduction to a special issue. *Sustainability (Basel), 14*(17), 10530. DOI: 10.3390/su141710530

Trevisan, L. V., Eustachio, J. H. P. P., Dias, B. G., Filho, W. L., & Pedrozo, E. A. (2024). Digital transformation towards sustainability in higher education: State-of-the-art and future research insights. *Environment, Development and Sustainability, 26*(2), 2789–2810. DOI: 10.1007/s10668-022-02874-7 PMID: 36624732

Tzotzou, M., Poulou, M., Karalis, T., & Ifanti, A. (2021). *Reflecting upon the Greek state-school teacher's changing role in the 21st century: an 'ecosystemic' approach.* Preschool and Primary Education.

UNESCO. (2019). Artificial Intelligence in Education: Challenges and Opportunities for Sustainable Development. 0https:///unescdoc. Unesco.org/ark

UNESCO. (2023). Guidance for generative Artificial Intelligence in Education and Research, UNESCO Digital Literacy. https:///unescdoc. Unesco.org/ark

Williamson, B., Eynon, R., Knox, J., & Davies, H. (2023). Critical Perspectives on Artificial Intelligence in Education: Political Economy, Discrimination, Commercialisation, Governance and Ethics. In B, Du. Boulay. A Mitrovic and K. Yacet (Eds). The Handbook of AI in Education Edward Elgar Publishing Ltd.

Yusuf, A., Pervin, N., & Román-González, M. (2024). Generative AI and the future of higher education: A threat to academic integrity or reformation? Evidence from multicultural perspectives. *International Journal of Educational Technology in Higher Education, 21*(1), 21. DOI: 10.1186/s41239-024-00453-6

## KEY TERMS AND DEFINITIONS

**Artificial Intelligence (AI):** refers to the development of computer systems that can perform tasks that typically require human intelligence, such as learning, problem-solving, reasoning, perception, and language understanding

**Education for Sustainable Development (ESD):** is an approach to education that focuses on developing skills, knowledge, and values necessary for individuals to contribute to a more sustainable and equitable world. ESD aims to empower individuals to become active participants in creating positive change and promoting sustainable development.

**Equity:** refers to the state of fairness and justice in which all individuals have equal opportunities and access to resources, services, and opportunities. Equity is often used interchangeably with equality, but while equality focuses on treating everyone the same, equity recognizes that individuals may have different needs and circumstances.

**Higher education:** refers to post-secondary education that is typically provided at universities, colleges, and other institutions. Higher education is designed to provide students with advanced knowledge and skills in a specific field or discipline.

**Social justice:** refers to the fair and equal treatment of all individuals within a society. Social justice emphasizes the importance of addressing systemic inequalities and promoting equal access to resources, services, and opportunities.

# Chapter 5
# Examining Education for Sustainable Development in Higher Education to Promote Education for Social Justice in ChatGPT

**Özgül Keleş**
https://orcid.org/0000-0003-0812-2443
*Aksaray University, Turkey*

## ABSTRACT

*Generative AI can be employed as an effective instrument for the identification of the learning objectives that must be achieved in order to attain the Sustainable Development Goals (SDGs). Therefore, this research aims to answer these main research questions: (1) How does ChatGPT respond to issues (key competences, learning objectives, key pedagogical approaches, role of the artificial intelligence application ChatGPT) related to Education for Sustainable Development in higher education to promote Education for Social Justice?(2) Are the answers and suggestions provided by ChatGPT in line with the learning objectives of the UNESCO Education for Sustainable Development Goals (2017)? and (3) How was ChatGPT used in this study and what are the researcher's thoughts about its use as a research tool? An exploratory research method is used in this study. In this context, it aims to document experiences with ChatGPT and to discuss possible implications. In order to ascertain the results, the ChatGPT outputs were subjected to a detailed analysis.*

DOI: 10.4018/979-8-3693-5623-4.ch005

## INTRODUCTION

Artificial intelligence plays a crucial role in the digitalisation of societies. The emergence of productive AI offers transformative potential in the field of education The necessity for fundamental change in education systems is a central theme in United Nations Educational, Scientific and Cultural Organization's (UNESCO) recent and current policy documents, with the current "roadmap" for addressing the SDGs through education by 2030 representing a particularly pertinent example. In its 2020 publication, UNESCO emphasises the necessity for education to undergo a transformation that will enable individuals to comprehend sustainability issues, recognise their relevance to the realities around them and mobilise for change. This transformation must also trigger structural transformations in today's economic and social systems, address the new opportunities and risks to sustainable development posed by emerging technologies, and facilitate the understanding of the interconnectivity between these various factors.

Education can and must contribute to a new vision of sustainable global development (UNESCO, 2015). The well-known approach of Education for Sustainable Development (ESD) enables students to make informed decisions and take responsible actions for environmental integrity, economic viability and a just society for current and future generations. ESD aims to develop competences that enable individuals to reflect on their own actions, taking into account current and future social, cultural, economic and environmental impacts from a local and global perspective. Individuals should also be empowered to act sustainably in complex situations that may require them to move in new directions and to participate in socio-political processes by leading their communities towards sustainable development (United Nations Educational, Scientific and Cultural Organization [UNESCO], 2017). Generative artificial intelligence can be used as an effective tool in determining the learning objectives that need to be achieved in order to achieve sustainable development goals, in organising course content, in determining the teaching methods and techniques to be used.

Sustainable Development Goal-4 aims to ensure inclusive and equitable quality education and promote lifelong learning opportunities for all. AI technologies are being used to ensure equal and inclusive access to education. AI technologies provide access to appropriate learning opportunities for people with disabilities, refugees, out-of-school children and those living in isolated communities. AI can help personalize learning (UNESCO, 2019). AI can help teachers create a better professional environment for their students with learning difficulties. Bridging gaps in AI skills goes beyond the adoption of increasingly powerful technologies to facilitate learning. It also means rethinking the content and methods used to deliver education at all levels of education. Doing this effectively is not just a matter of funding, but also about monitoring and evaluating what works in education, and delivering it in ways that are meaningful for teachers and suitable for dissemination. (UNESCO, 2019). When used intelligently for projects and applications that promote sustainability, AI will enable more effective and efficient public policies for sustainability. More specifically, it will improve access, connectivity and efficiency in sectors ranging from health, sanitation and education to agriculture and transportation (Goralski & Tan, 2020).

The rise of AI tools such as ChatGPT has generated debates about how these innovative approaches can enhance teaching and learning in the context of sustainable development and social justice. The debate on the use of ChatGPT in education needs to go beyond purely technological considerations and examine deeper ethical and legal implications (Panagopoulou et al., 2023). As educators and policy makers navigate this evolving landscape, it is important to consider how reproductive AI can be used to promote sustainable development and social justice in higher education. An important aspect of this exploration is the potential for ChatGPT to support the integration of Sustainable Development Education (SDE) into higher education curricula.

The integration of AI into education for sustainable development is crucial to promote Education for Social Justice (ESJ) in higher education settings. The convergence of Education for Sustainable Development, Education for Social Justice and AI represents the power of higher education institutions to transform societies. By incorporating AI-driven tools and the methods and approaches it offers into ESD curricula, educators can prevent systemic inequalities and empower disadvantaged groups. For example, AI-enabled simulations and virtual reality experiences can provide opportunities for students to explore complex social issues and develop empathy towards different perspectives. AI-based assessment tools can reduce biases in assessment processes, creating fair and equitable outcomes for all students. Educators can foster a more inclusive, equitable and sustainable learning environment by adopting innovative teaching and assessment practices that harness the potential of AI.

This exploratory research aimed to critically examine the ChatGPT output of the integration of AI with sustainable development education in higher education to promote social justice education and compare it to the key themes in the research.

## Research Questions

The following are the key research aims of this paper;

1. What does the information in the ChatGPT and UNESCO (2017) document highlight about the key competencies related to education for sustainable development (ESD) in higher education to promote education for social justice?
2. What information in the ChatGPT and UNESCO (2017) document provides on specific learning objectives related to education for sustainable development (ESD) in higher education to promote education for social justice?"
3. What information in the ChatGPT and UNESCO (2017) document provides on key pedagogical approaches related to education for sustainable development (ESD) in higher education to promote education for social justice?
4. What is the role of the artificial intelligence application ChatGPT in the development of social justice education in the context of education for sustainable development in higher education?
5. What is the key objectives of the artificial intelligence application ChatGPT in the development of social justice education in the context of education for sustainable development in higher education?
6. How aligned is the information in the ChatGPT database with the information in the UNESCO 2017 document in enabling educators to provide education for sustainable development in higher education to promote education for social justice?
7. How was ChatGPT used in this study and what are the researcher's thoughts about its use as a research tool?

## BACKGROUND

### Artificial Intelligence in Education

Artificial intelligence (AI) has the power to change the world for good, Vinuesa et al. (2019) argue that any software technology we consider AI can be used for sensing - including audio, visual, text and haptic (e.g. face recognition), decision-making (e.g. medical diagnostic systems), prediction (e.g. weather forecasting), It emphasizes that it should have at least one of the following capabilities: automatic knowledge extraction and pattern recognition from data (e.g. discovery of fake news cycles in social media), interactive communication (e.g. social robots or chatbots), and logical reasoning (e.g. theorizing from premises).

In education, the use of AI tools is reshaping learning experiences, fostering innovation and preparing individuals for the digital age. AI chatbots such as ChatGPT are gaining widespread traction and have the potential to revolutionize various aspects of education. However, their integration into higher education systems raises ethical concerns, requires curriculum redesign, strategies for continuous learning, and alignment with industry standards (Ammar et.al., 2024).

While AI integration in education holds great promise, there is a lack of comprehensive examination of the ethical implications associated with its adoption (Rodríguez-Amigo et. al., 2022). Existing literature often focuses on technical and pedagogical aspects, ignoring the impact of AI on ESD. This includes ethical aspects related to AI-generated content, students' critical thinking, teacher and student competencies, data privacy concerns and potential biases.

In this dynamic context, the integration of AI tools into education has emerged as a key catalyst in reshaping learning experiences, fostering innovation and preparing individuals for the complexities of the digital age (Taecharungroj, 2023). AI tools such as ChatGPT have the potential to revolutionize various aspects of education, from content creation to personalization, beyond interactive engagement, and have had significant implications in both scientific and societal fields (Baidoo-Anu & Owusu Ansah, 2023).

The use of ChatGPT in education could provide several benefits. First, it can provide a more personalized learning experience for students. Second, ChatGPT can make it easier for teachers to answer students' questions. By using ChatGPT to generate answers to students' questions, teachers could save time and energy, which could be better spent on other tasks. Third, ChatGPT can provide a more engaging learning experience for students. ChatGPT can improve teaching models, assessment systems, and education ecology by empowering the teacher-student-technology triad structure. Fourth, ChatGPT can provide useful suggestions for teachers (Su & Yang, 2023).

Aligning education with AI tools to align with the requirements of Industry 4.0 requires a comprehensive approach that includes curriculum development, pedagogical strategies, collaboration with industry partners, and integration of emerging technologies (Brahma et al., 2021). To effectively harness the potential of AI in education, comprehensive policies and strategies are needed, including flexible curricula, faculty development, ethical AI integration, a culture of continuous learning, industry partnerships, inclusivity, innovative assessment methods, adequate resource allocation, and stakeholder engagement. It is also important to establish a well-defined regulatory framework to ensure the use of ethical AI (Ammar et al., 2024).

In the age of Industry 4.0, the integration of educational approaches with AI tools is emerging as the key to fundamentally change our approaches in education (Grimus, 2020). This alignment allows HEIs to offer more relevant and up-to-date curricula and strengthen the delivery of ESD content by providing personalized and adapted learning experiences (Grimus, 2020).

AI tools such as ChatGPT facilitate interdisciplinary collaboration, providing instant access to information from various fields, allowing students and educators to explore topics that cross disciplinary boundaries. AI tools can also facilitate interdisciplinary projects where students from different fields collaborate on real-world sustainability issues. Courses that combine elements of AI, sustainability, and other related disciplines can encourage students to think critically and creatively about complex global issues. Furthermore, institutions should establish interdisciplinary research centers and initiatives that bring together experts from various fields to address sustainability issues using AI and other advanced technologies (Ammar et al., 2024).

## Social Justice and Sustainability

Higher education institutions facilitate the development of the abilities and cultural understanding of the individuals and groups that comprise society. The concept of social justice is inextricably linked to the concepts of needs, rights and equality. Higher education institutions must be responsive to these demands. The most crucial elements in the creation of an education for social justice are the fostering of critical understanding and awareness, which are essential for the realisation of social change (Waghid, 2014). Higher education institutions are in a position to promote social justice, as they facilitate the creation of a just society, which in turn ensures the well-being of its members.

In his theories, Roland Martin (2013) defines social justice as an approach to higher education that emphasises both cultural transmission and individual learning, and the interaction of the two in the promotion of social justice (Roland Martin, 2013). According to Miller (2003), for a society to be just, the principles of needs, rights and equality must be respected; in this framework, institutional structures should ensure that an adequate share of social resources is allocated to individuals based on their needs. Thus, social justice requires that basic needs such as food, medical resources and housing be the criteria for the distribution of various resources (Miller, 2003).

Social justice in higher education is considered as an encounter between individuals' capacities and cultural backgrounds by increasing their sensitivity to needs, rights and equality. In his study, Waghid (2014) identified three main elements in the literature in which the realization of social justice in higher education on the basis of needs, rights and equity plays a significant role. These elements are sustainable development (SD), economic development and equity.

The issue of sustainability in higher education has been extensively debated as an exemplar of social justice. Fien (2002) posits in his research that SD can facilitate the development of more informed understandings of the principles of the 'Earth

Charter'. These principles include environmental protection, human rights, just human development and peace, and the achievement of justice through education. Stables (2002) argues that SD is an understanding of (environmental) education and that human beings should engage in a just dialog with the environment. Sauvé (2005) argues that SD reveals concerns about human development, sustaining life and promoting social justice.

Sustainable development is defined as measures taken to meet the developmental needs of current generations without endangering or limiting the ability of future generations to meet their own developmental needs (GHK, 2008). Furthermore, education for sustainable development is considered a continuous process from early childhood to higher education, where values, lifestyles and attitudes are formed from an early age. ESD is considered a "lifelong" process, during which learning takes place and individuals then assume different roles in society (Hargreaves, 2007; GHK, 2008). Furthermore, education is a prerequisite for promoting behavioral changes and providing all citizens with the competencies needed to achieve sustainable development; success in reversing unsustainable trends depends to a large extent on high quality education (GHK, 2008). Education and training should contribute to all social, economic and environmental aspects of sustainable development (GHK, 2008).

Social sustainability is about building sustainable and cohesive communities and involves the compilation of actions and efforts that promote development that does not endanger or deplete the stock of human and social resources, but enhances their potential (GHK, 2008). Thematic issues related to the social dimension of sustainable development include health, community cohesion, social justice, demography, migration management and cultural diversity, equal opportunities, resilient security, and human and capital skills development (GHK 2008). The term "economic sustainability" is defined as a way of achieving economic growth while respecting environmental limits, exploring new measures and developing new methods to minimize environmental degradation, protect and conserve natural resources effectively and efficiently (GHK, 2008; Scott & Gough 2003).

Bell (1997) emphasizes the importance of ESD as an example of social justice for (higher) education, arguing that the goal of such education is "the full and equal participation of all groups in a society in which they are jointly shaped to meet each other's needs". Given that the issue of need is fundamental to social justice, Bell's (1997) research suggests that ESD should be "democratic, participatory, inclusive and affirming of human agency and people's capacity to collaborate and create change" (as cited in Waghid, 2014).

Economic development considers the economic well-being, output, infrastructure, health, education, political and cultural aspects of people's lives. Economic development depends on good governance. The quality of education and universities can be broadly linked to development, and the impact of universities on the economy can be based in particular on the quality of educators. In particular, student performance should be evaluated in terms of creativity, the ability to work in teams, and personality traits. This is especially important when the focus is on the utilisation of basic cognitive skills, as educators should emphasise the key qualities that can lead to economic returns (Hanushek 2004; Hanushek & Woesmann 2008).

## Education for Sustainable Development and Artificial Intelligence

In 2015, the United Nations (UN) set 17 Sustainable Development Goals (SDGs) to be achieved by 2030 (UNESCO, 2015). These goals include environmental, social and economic dimensions. The SDGs offer a broad spectrum of human rights concerns, but are clearly distinct from them as they emphasize people, planet, prosperity, social justice, peace and partnership (UNESCO, 2015). One of the important shortcomings of this categorization in the literature is that the impact of policy is largely ignored in the areas where environmental, social and governance categories are created (UNESCO, 2015).

Emphasizing the political dimension of the sustainable development goals is both important and necessary to make real progress in achieving the sustainable development goals. It is also necessary to understand and limit the potential negative impacts of AI on these goals (Sætra, 2021).

In 1992, the United Nations Conference on Environment and Development in Rio de Janeiro emphasized the importance of higher education and pedagogy in realizing the principles of sustainability envisaged in the Sustainable Development Goals (SDGs). ESD has emerged as a new and dynamic paradigm that offers a comprehensive framework for instilling a sense of responsibility among citizens of all age groups, promoting pioneering engagement in shaping a sustainable future aligned with the SDGs. Such education is critical to the application of the principles of sustainable development, giving participants the ability to make informed choices and helping them understand their important role in driving future societal progress. At the same time, education equipped with SD principles encourages participants to act consciously in ways that ensure environmental stability, economic sustainability, and the creation of a safe environment for current and future generations (Ammar et.al., 2024).

AI, the Sustainable Development Goals provide a useful framework for analyzing and categorizing the potential benefits and harms generated by AI. The United Nations AI4Good initiative sees AI as a force for good (ITU, 2024).

Nevertheless, it can be argued that AI represents a technology that should be disseminated and made more widely accessible for almost all sustainable development goals, particularly with regard to capacity building in developing countries and the promotion of equity and justice. The fact that data-intensive AI is almost exclusively under the control of a small number of countries represents a significant obstacle to the achievement of sustainable development goals in general and is a major concern for those working on SDG17 (Sætra, 2021). Furthermore, an accurate interpretation of the SDGs must consider factors such as inclusivity, sustainability, universality, inequality and justice. Consequently, it becomes considerably more challenging to portray AI as a proponent of numerous SDG objectives. Another limitation is that the SDGs are underpinned by a broad technology-optimism. Many goals involve the use of technology to solve the problems we face. Indeed, technology is often at the heart of the problems we are trying to solve.

Furthermore, AI systems should focus on the problem to be solved, unless it serves the purpose of addressing a predefined sustainable development goal (Masanja & Mkumbo, 2020; Brock et al., 2019). The first issue to consolidate a sustainability-oriented AI is stakeholder engagement. In general, AI technologies are created solely by technology companies without any or much consultation with broader interest groups or stakeholders. A broad and inclusive range of stakeholders, especially during the development and deployment phases, would increase the caliber of AI's sustainability potential (Erskine, 2019; Loi et. al., 2019). At its core, this is a matter of inclusion and democracy. AI needs to be developed for social good and for the benefit of every member of society (Floridi et. al., 2020).

Another critical issue is ethics (Yigitcanlar & Cugurullo, 2020). We need to develop AI in a way that respects human rights, diversity and the autonomy of individuals. The European Commission's recent ethical guidelines for the development of AI offer a good starting point (Floridi, 2019).

However, as pointed out by Mittelstadt (2019) guidelines alone cannot guarantee the development of an ethical AI. Therefore, we need to develop a globally ethical AI-a multicultural system of moral principles that takes the risks of AI seriously - together with a mechanism to monitor ethical violations. Ethics should ensure that AI technologies are designed for human development worldwide (Jobin et al., 2019; Hagendorf, 2020).

AI can offer data-driven insights into the challenges of sustainable living through personalized learning experiences, real-time data analysis and industry trends. This can lead to more relevant and effective education programs that equip students with the skills and knowledge needed to solve sustainability problems in the context of Industry 4.0. Striking the right balance between harnessing AI's potentials for sustainable development and meeting these challenges is vital for AI-enabled education to promote an ethical, inclusive and just education while preparing students for the demands of Industry 4.0 (Ammar et al., 2024).

The use of AI tools can facilitate the interdisciplinary character of Sustainable Development in Education initiatives (Kubisch et al., 2020). Sustainability challenges often require interdisciplinary contributions. AI can help provide a more holistic and integrated approach to ESD by fostering collaboration among stakeholders both within and outside academia (Beynaghi et al., 2016; Fekih Zguir et al., 2021). Higher education institutions (HEIs) play a vital role in equipping future professionals with these skills, requiring curriculum updates and infrastructure improvements.

AI can play an important role in bringing together students from diverse academic backgrounds, encouraging them to collaborate on projects that address real-world sustainability challenges. This approach provides students with critical teamwork, problem-solving and communication skills, ensuring that they are well prepared for the collaborative nature of Industry 4.0 (Kar et al., 2022). The potential for Higher Education Institutions (HEIs) to foster an interdisciplinary approach through AI-enabled ESD not only enhances students' learning experiences but also equips them with the skills necessary to cope with the complex and interconnected challenges of the modern workforce (Klimova et al., 2016; Leal Filho et al., 2021).

The integration of AI tools within ESD promotes personalized learning experiences. Every student has unique learning styles, preferences and strengths. By analyzing individual data, AI algorithms can create customized learning paths and adjust content and progress accordingly (Leal Filho et al., 2021).

Nevertheless, there are also some significant challenges associated with the integration of AI tools in ESD in the context of Industry 4.0. One such challenge is the digital divide (Lambrechts et al., 2013). Not all students have equal access to technology and the internet, which can exacerbate existing educational inequalities. The over-reliance on AI tools can result in the exclusion of students who lack access to these resources, thereby perpetuating inequalities in learning opportunities (Dinca et al., 2007; Stephens et al., 2008).

The challenge of bridging the digital divide and ensuring fair access to AI-enabled education is a significant one that educational institutions and policy makers must address. Another challenge is the potential for bias and ethical concerns in AI (Klimova et al., 2016). It is possible that AI algorithms may lead to unfair and discriminatory outcomes. In the context of ESD, biased AI tools may provide distorted recommendations for sustainability initiatives or reinforce existing inequalities related to environmental justice (Leal Filho et al., 2021). In the context of ESD, a holistic and integrated approach is particularly necessary in education (Fekih Zguir et al., 2021; Sanchez-Carracedo et al., 2021).

The outdated content and tools may inadequately prepare graduates for the evolving sustainability challenges of the Industry 4.0 era (Sammalisto et al., 2015). Furthermore, there is the challenge of resistance to change within educational institutions.

The implementation of AI-enabled ESD necessitates a number of changes, including those pertaining to curriculum design, teaching methods, and institutional practices.

## MAIN FOCUS OF THE CHAPTER

### Methodology

This is an exploratory study; the aim is to document my experiences with ChatGPT and to reflect on the possible outcomes. This exploratory study supports the self-study methodology for investigating technology (Hamilton et al., 2009). As part of this research, to investigate the alignment, accuracy and reliability of scientific data in the UNESCO (2017) document by critically analyzing the ChatGPT output about education for sustainable development to achieve social justice in higher education is intended.

Qualitative research method was used in the study. The data were obtained from the responses of the ChatGPT artificial intelligence program to open-ended questions posed to it and the UNESCO (2017) Education for sustainable development goals-learning objectives document. The data obtained from ChatGPT were collected in May 2024 (OpenAI, 2024). It should be noted that since the ChatGPT artificial intelligence program constantly renews itself, the answers obtained are instantaneous and will change and evolve over time.

In this research, the comparison of the data obtained from ChatGPT was made with the UNESCO (2017) document. This is because UNESCO is the organization behind the current international policy document on Education for Sustainable Development (ESD). In this context, UNESCO strongly supports the global progress made to date on Education for Sustainable Development (ESD), reflecting both the urgency and the need for transformative change in education systems to achieve the Sustainable Development Goals (SDGs) (UNESCO, 2020).

NVivo 11.0 program, one of the qualitative research analysis software, was used to analyze the data obtained. The data were evaluated by content analysis, one of the qualitative data analysis techniques. First, open-ended questions prepared by the researcher within the scope of the research were asked to the ChatGPT program. The answers given to each question were coded under appropriate headings, and themes belonging to the relevant codes were created. Then, the answers to the questions directed to ChatGPT were searched in the UNESCO (2017) document. The answers to each question were coded and grouped under common themes. Then, the codes and themes were organized and maps were prepared with visualization tools that enable comparison of the data obtained from ChatGPT and UNESCO (2017) document. The findings obtained were analyzed in depth and presented.

## Findings

The objective of this study is to critically examine the integration of artificial intelligence with sustainable development education in higher education to promote social justice education. In order to achieve this, the output of ChatGPT was analysed in comparison with the UNESCO (2017) document. The following findings were reached:

*In the first sub-problem of the research, the data of ChatGPT and UNESCO (2017) document were analyzed in the categories of key competencies. The data obtained were presented under the relevant headings comparatively.* After collecting the data related to the responses of the related question, codes were determined under the key theme using the NVIVO 11 program. Comparison maps of the codes were drawn and presented in Figure 1.

*Figure 1. Comparison of key competencies for sustainability*

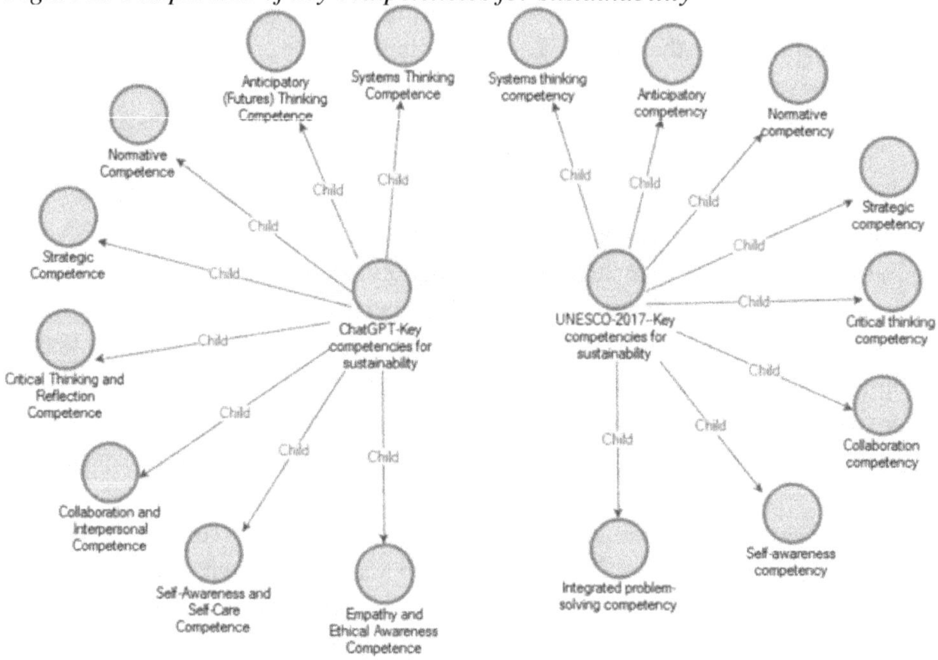


Upon examination of Figure 1, it becomes evident that eight codes related to fundamental competencies emerge as prominent in both the ChatGPT artificial intelligence program and the UNESCO (2017) document. While the seven codes are in coherence with each other, there is a difference in only one code. In the UNESCO (2017) document, the concept of integrated problem-solving competency, which is expressed as the ability to develop viable, inclusive and equitable solution options that promote sustainable development by integrating the competencies specified in the table, to apply different problem-solving frameworks to complex sustainability problems, comes to the forefront. The ChatGPT artificial intelligence application has presented the concept of empathy and ethical awareness competence within the framework of these competencies. It is evident that this dimension is of paramount importance in the teaching of the socio-emotional components of the 17 key goals of sustainable development, as outlined in the UNESCO (2017) document.

In the second sub-problem of the study, the answer to the question *"What information in the ChatGPT andUNESCO (2017)document provides on specific learning objectives related to education for sustainable development (ESD) in higher education to promote education for social justice?"* was sought. In line with the data obtained, comparison maps of the codes were drawn and presented in Figure 2 an Figure 3.

*Figure 2. Specific learning objectives in UNESCO (2017)*

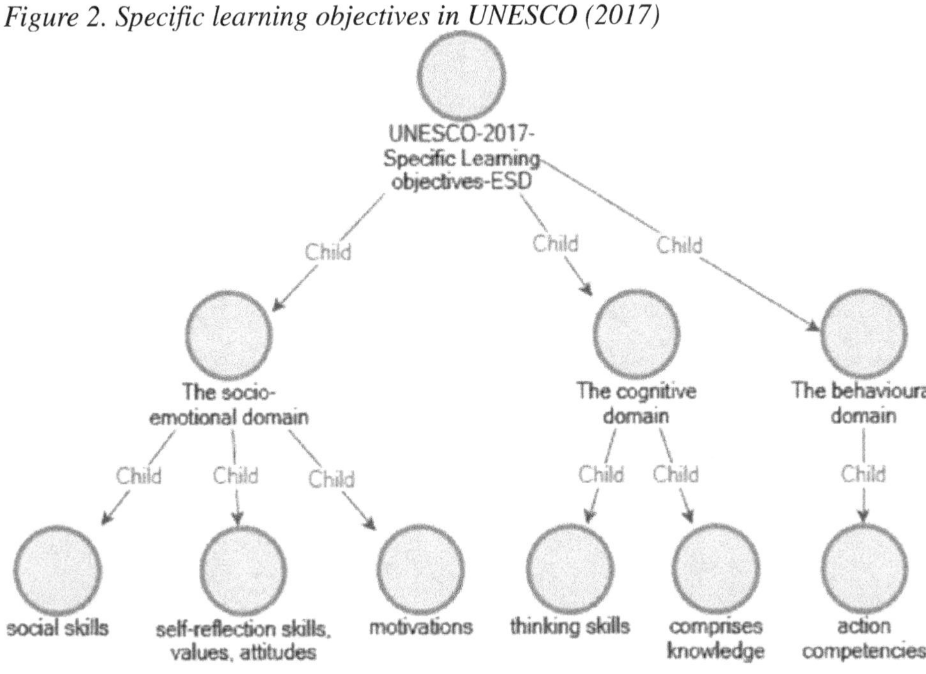


It is observed that the UNESCO (2017) document delineates specific learning objectives for each sustainable development goal across cognitive, socio-emotional, and behavioural dimensions. In the cognitive domain, knowledge and thinking are of particular importance, while in the socio-emotional domain, the ability to collaborate, negotiate and communicate, as well as the development of attitudes and motivation, are of significant relevance. In the behavioural domain, action competencies are of particular importance, as illustrated in Figure 2.

Figure 3 shows the matching map of the codes generated by the ChatGPT artificial intelligence application regarding the specific learning objectives in the UNESCO document. In the coding, it is seen that ChatGPT emphasizes the following topics: "Developing critical thinking and reflective skills, promoting interdisciplinary learning and systems thinking, developing ethical awareness and moral reasoning, promoting active citizenship and civic engagement, developing global awareness and local relevance, developing inclusion and respect for diversity, empowering students with knowledge and skills for action, promoting sustainable lifestyles and practices" (Figure 3).

*Figure 3. Comparison of special learning goals in education for sustainable development*

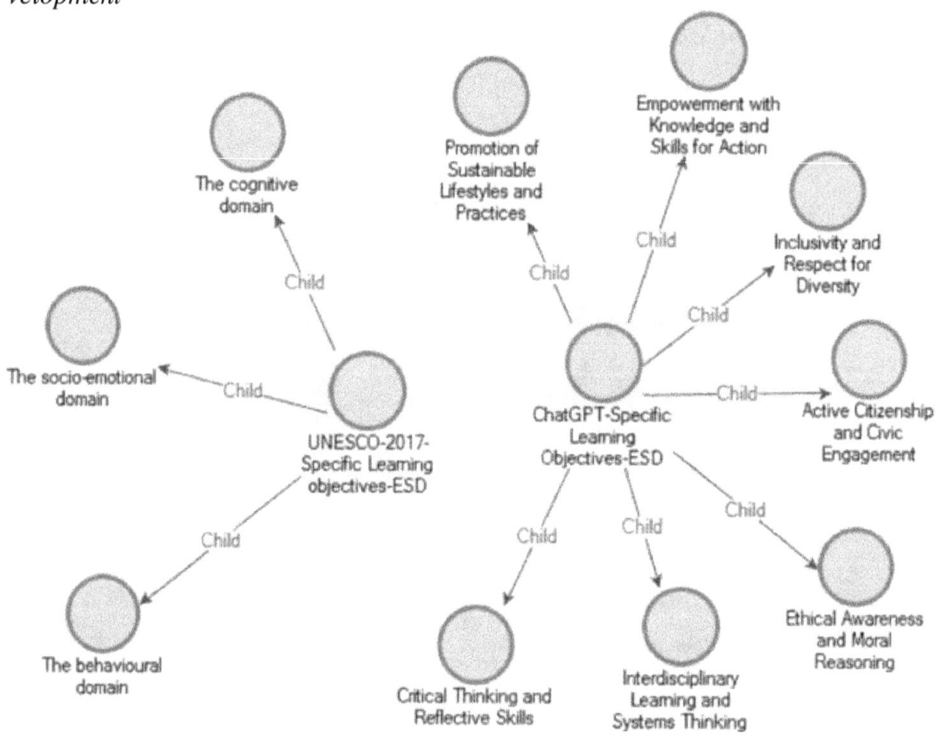


The responses of the ChatGPT AI program to this question indicate that students should not only learn to understand and address sustainability issues, but also to promote social justice through their actions. This would enable them to become multi-dimensional agents of change in their communities and beyond. In addition, while the concept of diversity is included in the UNESCO document as part of the qualified education goal, the concepts of critical thinking and the development of systems thinking are highlighted in the main text.

In the third sub-problem of the study, the answer to the question *"What information in the ChatGPT andUNESCO (2017)document provides on key pedagogical approaches related to education for sustainable development (ESD) in higher education to promote education for social justice?"* was sought. In line with the data obtained, comparison maps of the codes were drawn and presented in Figure 4. Figure 4 shows the benchmark map of the ChatGPT artificial intelligence application and the codes related to key pedagogical approaches in the UNESCO (2017) document.

When Figure 4 is examined, it is seen that the codes obtained are consistent with each other. Unlike the ChatGPT findings, problem-based learning and whole-institution approaches are also emphasized in the UNESCO (2017) document. Both maps show that they see student-centered, action-oriented transformative learning pedagogies as a driving force to ensure social justice in education for sustainable development in higher education. Action-oriented learning emphasizes providing opportunities for students to develop leadership skills through project-based learning, working collaboratively to address social injustices and promote sustainable solutions at local, national and global levels (ChatGPT).

*Figure 4. Comparison of key padogogical approaches in education for sustainable development*

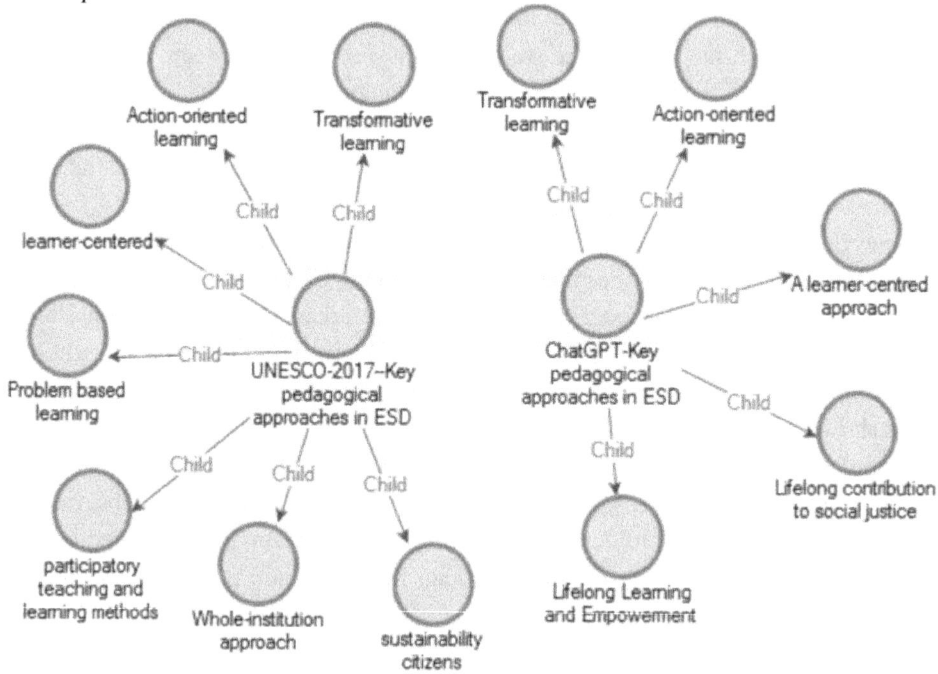


UNESCO (2017) states that education for sustainable development is a holistic and transformational education with learning content and outcomes, pedagogy and learning environment. It is emphasised that education for sustainable development not only incorporates content such as climate change, poverty, the prevention of injustice and equality into the curriculum, but also creates an interactive learning environment. It emphasizes the need for action-oriented, transformative pedagogy, self-learning, participation and collaboration, problem-orientation, inter- and trans-disciplinarity, and linking formal and non-formal education.

In the fourth sub-problem of the study, the answer to the question " *What is the role of the artificial intelligence application ChatGPT in the development of social justice education in the context of education for sustainable development in higher education?*" was sought. In line with the data obtained, comparison maps of the codes were drawn and presented in Figure 5.

As it seen Figure 5, ChatGPT and AI in general, can play several roles in integrating ESD in higher education to promote education for social justice:

*Figure 5. The role of AI in integrating ESD into higher education to promote education for social justice*

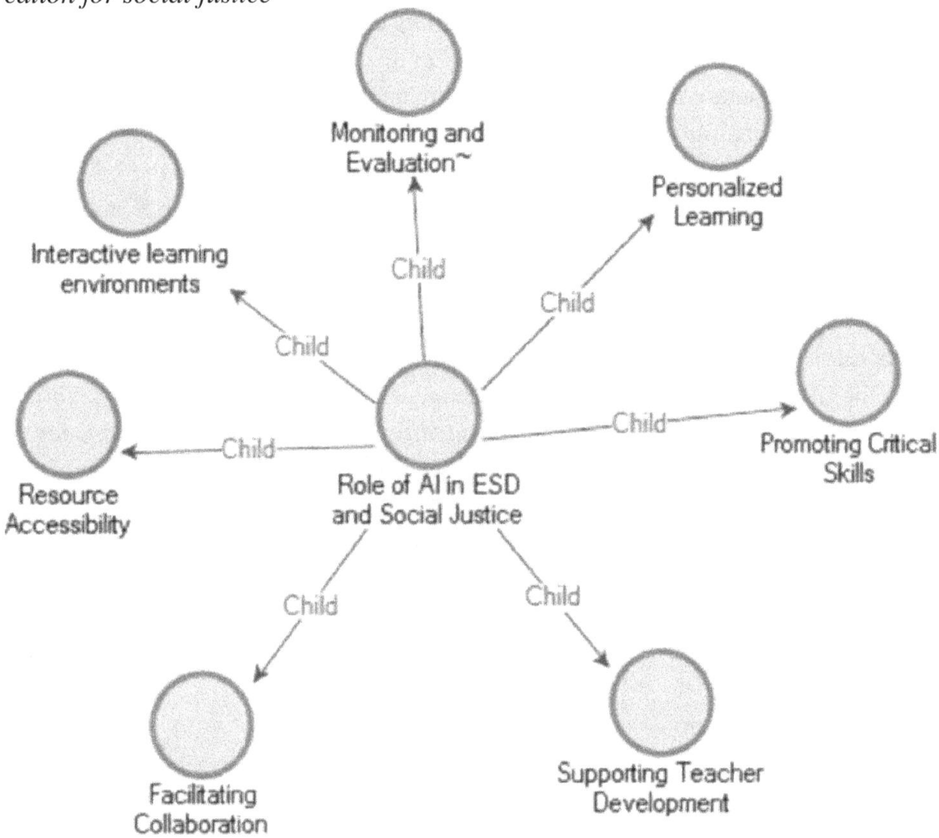


Figure 5 illustrates the potential of AI applications to enhance accessibility of educational resources to a diverse range of learners, facilitate access to high-quality ESD materials, and support students and educators, particularly in underserved areas. It is posited that AI can facilitate the provision of personalised learning experiences, which are tailored to the specific needs and learning styles of individual students. Furthermore, it can assist in the promotion of inclusive education practices, which are fundamental to the pursuit of social justice.

It is postulated that AI can facilitate interdisciplinary collaboration by connecting educators and researchers in different fields, thereby supporting the development and implementation of ESD. AI tools can be employed to monitor and evaluate the effectiveness of ESD programmes, analysing data on student learning outcomes and institutional practices to provide insights into what is working and what needs to be improved.

AI can support teacher professional development by providing customised training programmes, resources, and feedback. Artificial intelligence (AI) can be an effective tool in creating interactive and engaging learning environments that foster students' critical thinking and problem-solving skills. For instance, AI-driven simulations and virtual environments can provide students with hands-on experiences in addressing real-world sustainability issues.

When all these findings are evaluated in the light of the data in the UNESCO (2017) document, it is seen that the integration of artificial intelligence, including tools such as ChatGPT, with education for sustainable development in higher education has significant potential to improve learning experiences, support educators and promote social justice by making education more inclusive, personalized and effective.

In the fifth sub-problem of the study, the answer to the question *"What is the key objectives of the artificial intelligence application ChatGPT in the development of social justice education in the context of education for sustainable development in higher education?"* was sought. In line with the data obtained, maps of the codes were drawn and presented in Figure 6. Here are the key objectives set out by ChatGPT, an AI application related to Education for Sustainable Development (ESD) in higher education to promote education for social justice (Figure 6);

*Figure 6. The key objectives set out by the ChatGPT on ESD in higher education to promote education for social justice*

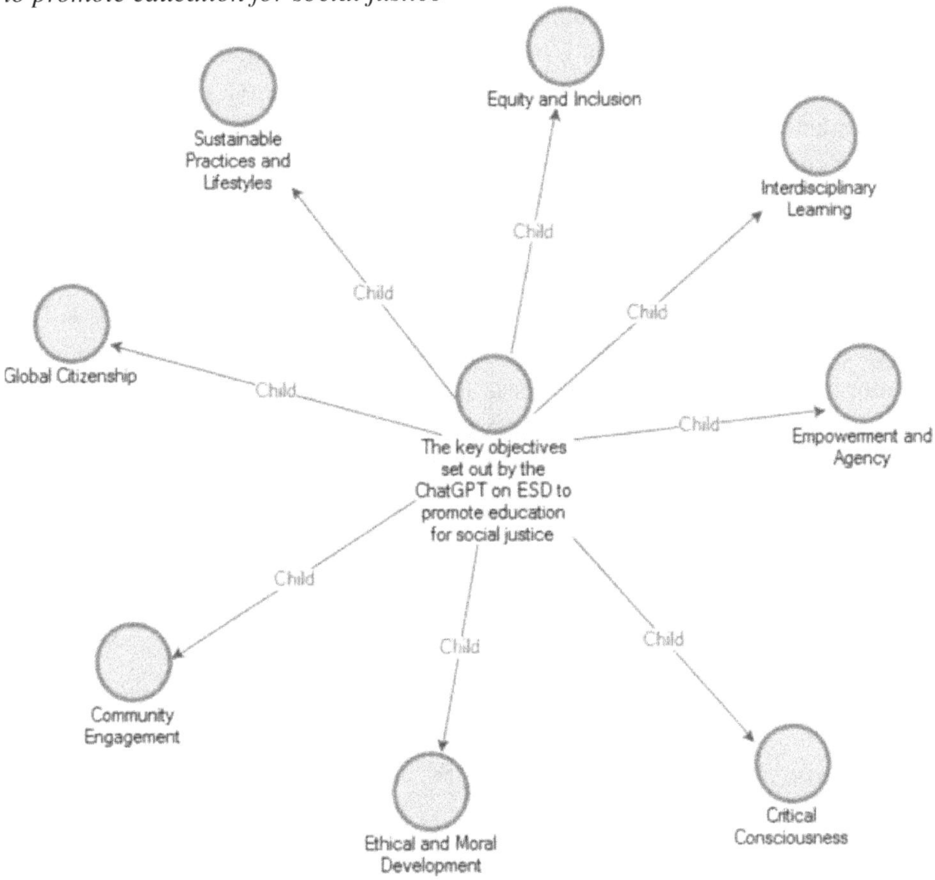


When Figure 6 is analyzed, it is seen that 8 codes are highlighted under this category. These codes are "Empowerment and Agency, Equity and Inclusion, Critical Consciousness, Interdisciplinary Learning, Ethical and Moral Development, Global Citizenship, Community Engagement and Sustainable Practices and Lifestyles". Empower students to become proactive agents of change who can address social injustices and contribute to sustainable development, promote equity and inclusion within the educational system and beyond, ensuring that all individuals, regardless of background, have equal access to opportunities and resources, develop students' critical consciousness about social, economic, and environmental injustices, enabling them to recognize and challenge systemic inequalities, encourage interdisciplinary learning approaches that integrate knowledge from various disciplines to address complex social justice and sustainability challenges, instill strong ethical and moral values that guide students in making decisions that promote social justice and sustainability, foster a sense of global citizenship, encouraging students to understand and engage with global issues while acting locally to create positive change, encourage students to participate in community engagement and service-learning activities that address local social justice issues and contribute to sustainable development and promote the adoption of sustainable practices and lifestyles among students, reducing their environmental footprint and fostering a culture of sustainability such processes constitute the detailed content of these objectives.

In light of the ChatGPT statements, these goals aim to integrate social justice principles into ESD in higher education, ensuring that students are equipped not only with the knowledge and skills to promote sustainability, but also with a deep commitment to equity and justice.

The sixth sub-problem of the study sought to determine the alignment between the information in the ChatGPT database and the information in the UNESCO 2017 document with regard to educators' capacity to provide education for sustainable development in higher education, with the objective of promoting education for social justice. In accordance with the data obtained, maps of the codes were constructed and presented in Figure 7.

*Figure 7. Alignment of ChatGPT Database Information with UNESCO (2017) Document on ESD*

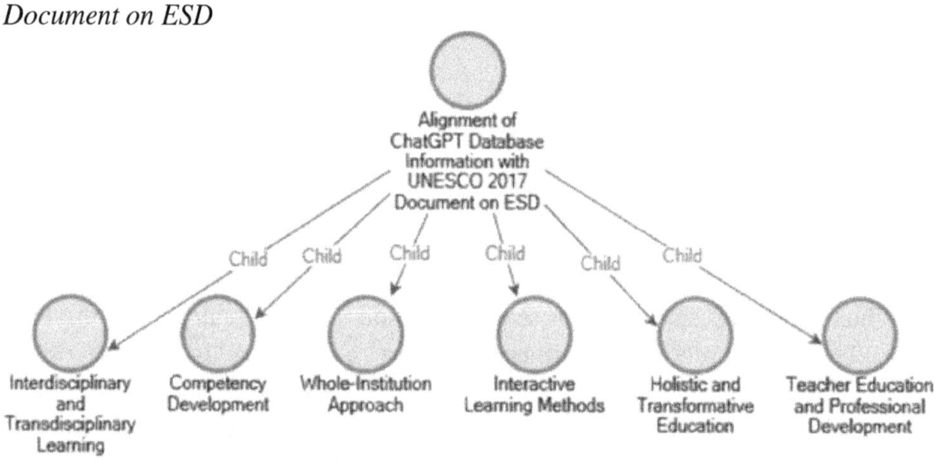


When these codes are examined in detail, it is seen that the information in the ChatGPT database is in line with UNESCO's 2017 document on Education for Sustainable Development (ESD) in many key areas.

The code on "Interdisciplinary and transdisciplinary learning" emphasises the integration of interdisciplinary and transdisciplinary perspectives, the understanding of complex sustainability issues and the promotion of cooperation with interdisciplinary and external partners to improve learning outcomes. The code on "Teacher education and professional development" emphasises the need for teacher education curricula to include ESD and the need for continuous professional development. The code on 'Holistic and transformative education' emphasises the need for a holistic approach to education and the move towards interactive, inclusive and student-centred methods. In the 'Whole institution approach', the concept of transforming all educational institutions to model sustainability practices emerges as a common theme. In the "Interactive Learning" code, the concepts of reflective practice, learning-centred approach and action-oriented learning come to the fore. In the "Competency Development" code, both the ChatGPT database and the learning objectives in the UNESCO (2017) document emphasise the importance of developing core competencies in students, such as critical thinking, problem solving and the ability to participate in socio-political processes.

## Discussion

Examining the results of the research, it is found that although both the ChatGPT artificial intelligence programme and the UNESCO (2017) document are compatible in terms of key concepts related to key competences, the concept of integrated problem solving competence related to key competences is addressed in the UNESCO (2017) learning objectives document. It has been observed that the ChatGPT artificial intelligence application includes the concept of empathy and ethical awareness competence within the framework of these competences. It has been observed that the concept of empathy and ethical awareness is included in the teaching of socio-emotional components of the 17 basic goals of sustainable development in the UNESCO (2017) document and supports ChatGPT in this context.

When examining the issue of specific learning objectives related to Education for Sustainable Development in higher education to promote education for social justice, it is seen that while the UNESCO (2017) document defines cognitive, socio-emotional and behavioural dimensions for each sustainable development goal, ChatGPT emphasises that students should not only understand and address sustainability issues, but also promote social justice through their actions, thus becoming multi-faceted change agents in their communities and beyond. In parallel with these findings, it can be seen that while the concept of diversity is included in the UNESCO document's goal of quality education, the concepts of critical thinking and the development of systems thinking come to the fore in the main text.

When analysed in terms of key pedagogical approaches, the codes obtained overlap. The comparison results show that both the ChatGPT artificial intelligence software and the UNESCO (2017) document data point to student-centred, action-oriented transformative learning pedagogies as a driving force for ensuring social justice in education for sustainable development in higher education.

Examining the role of the artificial intelligence application ChatGPT in the development of social justice education in the context of ESD in higher education, it is seen that artificial intelligence applications can help to make educational resources more accessible to a wider audience, thus reducing inequality; provide access to quality ESD materials and support students and educators, especially in underserved areas; provide personalised learning experiences; and promote inclusive educational practices, which is the key to social justice. These findings highlight that AI has significant potential to promote social justice in higher education by making ESD integration inclusive, personalised and effective.

ChatGPT, an artificial intelligence (AI) software application related to Education for Sustainable Development (ESD) in higher education to promote education for social justice, sets out the main goals of educating students who can address social injustices, who are egalitarian and inclusive, who have a critical perspective on social, economic and environmental injustices, and who have a sense of global citizenship with strong ethical and moral values. The ChatGPT data also highlighted that in order to achieve these goals, students need to be equipped not only with the knowledge and skills to promote sustainability, but also with a deep commitment to equity and justice, and that social justice principles need to be integrated into ESD in higher education.

As a result, this study, which was conducted with an exploratory research approach, concluded that the ChatGPT outputs examined in the integration of artificial intelligence with sustainable development education in higher education to promote social justice education are in line with the key themes of the UNESCO (2017) document, and the information obtained is mostly mutually supportive.

## CONCLUSION

In this study, the research questions used the ChatGPT artificial intelligence application under the headings of 'searching for answers to open-ended questions on the topic, organising the information obtained and getting support in creating codes and themes'. These exploratory research results show that artificial intelligence plays an important role in providing access to information. Artificial intelligence technologies have an important place in higher education to achieve the goals of both social justice education and education for sustainable development. This study contributes to a broader understanding of the relationship between AI in higher education and sustainability to achieve social justice. However, the data obtained shows that there is still much to be explored in this area. This study also highlights the need for the academic society to be prepared for an AI-enabled future.

By providing personalised and data-driven educational tools, AI can improve the quality and efficiency of education while contributing to education for sustainable development to ensure social equity. Through AI technologies tailored to the needs of higher education institutions, it can contribute to improving the quality of education in line with the SD-4 goal of quality education. In this way, the sustainability of education, the efficient use of resources, the prevention of waste (the reduction of the waste of resources, time, effort, materials, etc.) and the prevention of inequalities can come to the fore.

This transformation indicates that artificial intelligence (AI) applications are progressing towards a phase wherein they will supplant articles and theses utilized in scientific research with expedient and dependable responses to scientific queries. Despite the fact that the responses, recommendations, and data infrastructure generated by ChatGPT within the context of these research inquiries are aligned with scientific sources, the comparison of the data obtained is constrained to a pertinent document within the scope of the research.

The application of artificial intelligence (AI) in higher education institutions (HEIs) necessitates a critical examination of the data obtained from its use. This examination should be conducted by researchers from a scientific perspective. One of the key questions that needs to be answered is how to integrate AI applications into HEIs with a focus on sustainability to achieve the sustainable development goals (SDGs). In terms of social justice, while higher education institutions in developing countries are able to access AI-supported technologies more quickly, the issue of inequality faced by underdeveloped and developing countries still remains important in the social dimension of sustainable development.

In future studies, it is recommended that research be conducted on the means of enhancing the quality of education through the qualification of the learning outcomes of artificial intelligence in terms of both content and curriculum. This would facilitate the integration of artificial intelligence with sustainable development education (ESD) in higher education, thereby promoting social justice education (ESJ).

## REFERENCES


Ammar, A., Zaidan, E., & Abulibdeh, R. (2024). Navigating the confluence of artificial intelligence and education for sustainable development in the era of industry 4.0: Challenges, opportunities, and ethical dimensions. *Journal of Cleaner Production*, *437*, 140527. DOI: 10.1016/j.jclepro.2023.140527

Baidoo-Anu, D., & Owusu Ansah, L. (2023). Education in the era of generative artificial intelligence (AI): Understanding the potential benefits of ChatGPT in promoting teaching and learning. DOI: 10.2139/ssrn.4337484

Bell, L. A. (1997). Theoretical foundations for social justice education. In Adams, M., Bell, L., & Griffin, P. (Eds.), *Teaching for diversity and social justice: A sourcebook* (pp. 3–15). Routledge.

Beynaghi, A., Trencher, G., Moztarzadeh, F., Mozafari, M., Maknoon, R., & Leal Filho, W. (2016). Future sustainability scenarios for universities: Moving beyond the United Nations decade of education for sustainable development. *Journal of Cleaner Production*, *112*, 3464–3478. DOI: 10.1016/j.jclepro.2015.10.117

Brahma, M., Tripathi, S. S., & Sahay, A. (2021). Developing curriculum for industry 4.0: Digital workplaces. *Higher Education, Skills and Work-based Learning*, *11*(1), 144–163. DOI: 10.1108/HESWBL-08-2019-0103

Brock, J. K., & Von Wangenheim, F. (2019). Demystifying AI: What digital transformation leaders can teach you about realistic artificial intelligence. *California Management Review*, *61*(4), 110–134. DOI: 10.1177/1536504219865226

Dinca, C., Rousseaux, P., & Badea, A. (2007). A life cycle impact of the natural gas used in the energy sector in Romania. *Journal of Cleaner Production*, *15*(15), 1451–1462. DOI: 10.1016/j.jclepro.2006.03.011

Erskine, M. (2019). Artificial intelligence, the emerging needs for human factors engineering, risk management and stakeholder engagement. *InProceedings of the World Engineers Convention, Engineers Australia*, Melbourne, Australia.

Fekih Zguir, M., Dubis, S., & Koç, M. (2021). Embedding education for sustainable development (ESD) and SDGs values in curriculum: A comparative review on Qatar, Singapore and New Zealand. *Journal of Cleaner Production*, *319*, 128534. DOI: 10.1016/j.jclepro.2021.128534

Fien, J. (2002). Advancing sustainability in higher education: Issues and opportunities for research. *Higher Education Policy*, *15*(2), 143–152. DOI: 10.1016/S0952-8733(02)00005-3

Floridi, L. (2019). Establishing the rules for building trustworthy AI. *Nature Machine Intelligence*, *1*(6), 261–262. DOI: 10.1038/s42256-019-0055-y

Floridi, L., Cowls, J., King, T. C., & Taddeo, M. (2020). How to design AI for social good: Seven Essential factors. *Science and Engineering Ethics*, *26*(3), 1771–1796. DOI: 10.1007/s11948-020-00213-5 PMID: 32246245

GHK. (2008). Inventory of innovative practices in education for sustainable development [Brussels: GHK Consulting.]. *Order*, •••, 31.

Goralski, M. A., & Tan, T. K. (2020). Artificial intelligence and sustainable development. *International Journal of Management Education*, *18*(1), 100330. DOI: 10.1016/j.ijme.2019.100330

Grimus, M. (2020). Emerging technologies: Impacting learning, pedagogy and curriculum Development. In Yu, S., Ally, M., & Tsinakos, A. (Eds.), *Emerging Technologies and Pedagogies in the Curriculum (pp* (pp. 127–151). Springer., DOI: 10.1007/978-981-15-0618-5_8

Hagendorff, T. (2020). The ethics of AI ethics: An evaluation of guidelines. *Minds and Machines*, *30*(1), 1–22. DOI: 10.1007/s11023-020-09517-8

Hamilton, M. L., Smith, L., & Worthington, K. (2009). Fitting the methodology with the research: An exploration of narrative, self-study and auto-ethnography. *Studying Teacher Education*, *4*(1), 17–28. DOI: 10.1080/17425960801976321

Hanushek, E. A. (2005). The economic value of improving local schools. Proceedings, Federal Reserve Bank of Cleveland, 59-72.

Hargreaves, A. (2007). Sustainable leadership and development in education: Creating the future, conserving the past. *European Journal of Education*, *42*(2), 223–233. DOI: 10.1111/j.1465-3435.2007.00294.x

ITU. (2024). AI4Good global summit. Available online: https://aiforgood.itu.int (accessed on 27 May 2024).

Jobin, A., Ienca, M., & Vayena, E. (2019). The global landscape of AI ethics guidelines. *Nature Machine Intelligence*, *1*(9), 389–399. DOI: 10.1038/s42256-019-0088-2

Kar, A. K., Choudhary, S. K., & Singh, V. K. (2022). How can artificial intelligence impact sustainability: A systematic literature review. *Journal of Cleaner Production*, *376*, 134120. DOI: 10.1016/j.jclepro.2022.134120

Klimova, A., Rondeau, E., Andersson, K., Porras, J., Rybin, A., & Zaslavsky, A. (2016). An international Master's program in green ICT as a contribution to sustainable development. *Journal of Cleaner Production, 135*, 223-239. https://doi.org/. JCLEPRO.2016.06.032DOI: 10.1016/J

Lambrechts, W., Mulà, I., Ceulemans, K., Molderez, I., & Gaeremynck, V. (2013). The integration of competences for sustainable development in higher education: An analysis of bachelor programs in management. *Journal of Cleaner Production, 48*, 65–73. DOI: 10.1016/j.jclepro.2011.12.034

Leal Filho, F., Salvia, F., Azeiteiro, A. L., Alves, U., Castro, F., Will, P., Platje, M., Lovren, J., Brandli, V.O., Price, L., Doni, F., Mifsud, M., & Avila, L.V. (2021). A framework for the implementation of the Sustainable Development Goals in university programmes. *Journal of Cleaner Production, 299*, 126915. https://doi.org/. JCLEPRO.2021.126915DOI: 10.1016/J

Loi, D., Wolf, C. T., Blomberg, J. L., Arar, R., & Brereton, M. (2019). Co-designing AI futures: Integrating AI ethics, social computing, and design. *InProceedings of the 2019 on Designing Interactive Systems Conference*, San Diego, CA, USA. DOI: 10.1145/3301019.3320000

Masanja, N., & Mkumbo, H. (2020). The application of open source artificial intelligence as an approach to frugal innovation in Tanzania. *International Journal of Research and Innovation in Applied Science, 5*, 36–46.

Miller, D. (2003). *Principles of social justice*. Harvard University Press.

Mittelstadt, B. (2019). Principles alone cannot guarantee ethical AI. *Nature Machine Intelligence, 1*(11), 501–507. DOI: 10.1038/s42256-019-0114-4

Open, A. I. (2024). ChatGPT: Optimizing language models for dialogue. https://openai.com/blog/chatgpt/

Panagopoulou, F., Parpoula, C., & Karpouzis, Kostas. (2023). Legal and ethical considerations regarding the use of ChatGPT in education. arXiv preprint arXiv:2306.10037. .DOI: 10.31235/osf.io/c5hf3

Rodríguez-Amigo, A., Fernández-Alvarado, J. F., & Fernández-Rodríguez, S. (2022). Case of study on a sustainability building: Environmental risk assessment related with allergenicity from air quality considering meteorological and urban green infrastructure data on BIM. *The Science of the Total Environment, 838*, 155910. DOI: 10.1016/j.scitotenv.2022.155910 PMID: 35577081

Roland, M. J. (2013). *Education reconfigured: Culture, encounter, and change*. Routledge.

Sætra, H. S. (2021). AI in Context and the Sustainable Development Goals: Factoring in the Unsustainability of the Sociotechnical System. *Sustainability (Basel)*, *13*(4), 1738. DOI: 10.3390/su13041738

Sammalisto, K., Sundstrom, A., & Holm, T. (2015). Implementation of sustainability in universities as perceived by faculty and staff-a model from a Swedish university. *Journal of Cleaner Production*, *106*, 45–54. DOI: 10.1016/j.jclepro.2014.10.015

Sanchez-Carracedo, F., Sureda, B., Moreno-Pino, F. M., & Romero-Portillo, D. (2021). Education for Sustainable Development in Spanish engineering degrees. Case study. *Journal of Cleaner Production*, *294*, 126322. DOI: 10.1016/j.jclepro.2021.126322

Sauvé, L. (2005). Current in environmental education: Mapping a complex and evolving pedagogical field. *Canadian Journal of Environmental Education*, *10*, 12–37.

Scott, W., & Gough, S. (2003). *Sustainable development and learning: Framing the issues*. Routledge Falmer. DOI: 10.4324/9780203464625_chapter_4

Shen, Y., Heacock, L., Elias, J., Hentel, K. D., Reig, B., Shih, G., & Moy, L. (2023). ChatGPT and other large language models are double-edged swords. *Radiology*, *307*(2)230163. https://doi.org/. 230163DOI: 10.1148/radiol

Stables, A., & Scott, W. (2002). The quest of holism in education for sustainable development. *Environmental Education Research*, *8*(1), 53–60. DOI: 10.1080/13504620120109655

Stephens, J. C., Hernandez, M. E., Román, M., Graham, A. C., & Scholz, R. W. (2008). Higher education as a change agent for sustainability in different cultures and contexts. Higher education as a change agent for sustainability in different cultures and contexts. *International Journal of Sustainability in Higher Education*, *9*(3), 317–338. DOI: 10.1108/14676370810885916

Su, J., & Yang, W. (2023). Unlocking the power of ChatGPT: A framework for applying generative AI in education. *ECNU Review of Education*, *6*(3), 355–366. DOI: 10.1177/20965311231168423

Taecharungroj, V. (2023). What Can ChatGPT Do?" Analyzing early reactions to the innovative AI chatbot on Twitter. *Big Data and Cognitive Computing*, *7*(1), 35. DOI: 10.3390/bdcc7010035

Thorp, H. H. (2023). ChatGPT is fun, but not an author. *Science*, *379*(6630), 313–313. DOI: 10.1126/science.adg7879 PMID: 36701446

United Nations. (2015). Transforming our world: The 2030 Agenda for sustainable development; division for sustainable sevelopment goals. New York, NY, USA.

United Nations Educational, Scientific and Cultural Organization. (2012). *Education for sustainable development: source book*. Pars: UNESCO.

United Nations Educational, Scientific and Cultural Organization. (2017). *Education for sustainable development goals-learning objectives*. UNESCO.

United Nations Educational, Scientific and Cultural Organization. (2019). *Artificial Intelligence in education: challenges and opportunities for sustainable development*. UNESCO.

United Nations Educational, Scientific and Cultural Organization. (2020). *Education for sustainable development-roadmap: ESD for 2030*. UNESCO.

Vinuesa, R., Azizpour, H., Leite, I., Balaam, M., Dignum, V., Domisch, S., Felländer, A., Langhans, S. D., Tegmark, M., & Nerini, F. F. (2020). The role of artificial intelligence in achieving the sustainable development goals. *Nature Communications*, *11*(1), 1–10. DOI: 10.1038/s41467-019-14108-y PMID: 31932590

Waghid, Z. (2014). (Higher) Education for social justice through sustainable development, economic development and equity. *South African Journal of Higher Education*, *28*(4), 1448–1463.

Yigitcanlar, T., & Cugurullo, F. (2020). The sustainability of artificial intelligence: An urbanistic viewpoint from the lens of smart and sustainable cities. *Sustainability (Basel)*, *12*(20), 8548. DOI: 10.3390/su12208548

Zajda, J., Majhanovich, S., & Rust, V. (2006). Introduction: Education and Social Justice. *International Review of Education*, *52*(1/2), 9–22. DOI: 10.1007/s11159-005-5614-2

## ADDITIONAL READING

Keleş, Ö. (2011). Determination of the pre-service science teachers' views about sustainable development and sustainable schools. *European Journal of Social Sciences*, *22*(3), 382–392.

Keleş, Ö. (2015). Creative drama in the teaching of education for sustainable development: Sample activity about sustainability and sustainable production. *Journal of Environmental Sustainability*, *4*(4), 1–15.

Keleş, Ö. (2017). Investigation of pre-service science teachers' sustainable consumption behaviors in terms of some variables. *European Journal of Sustainable Development*, *6*(3), 321–332. DOI: 10.14207/ejsd.2017.v6n3p321

Keleş, Ö. (2017). Investigation of pre-service science teachers' attitudes towards sustainable environmental education. *Higher Education Studies*, *7*(3), 171–180. DOI: 10.5539/hes.v7n3p171

Keleş, Ö., Canbazoğlu Bilici, S., & Özer, İ. E. (2023). Sürdürülebilir kalkınma hedefleri ışığında ortaokulda STEM eğitimi. [STEM education in middle school within the context of sustainable development goals] In Çevik, U., & Şahin, E. (Eds.), *Sürdürülebilir kalkınma ve STEM eğitimi* [Sustainable development and STEM education]. (pp. 79–116). Nobel Publishing.

Keleş, Ö., Eriş, R., & Aydoğdu, M. (2017). 7th grade students' mental models about the concept of 'sustainable development'. *European Journal of Education Studies*, *3*(7), 12–37.

Serpa, S., Wang, F., Zhou, L., & Keleş, Ö. (2024). Artificial intelligence as author of scientific publications. *Science Insights*, *44*(1), 1215–1219. DOI: 10.15354/si.24.re866

## KEY TERMS AND DEFINITIONS

**ChatGPT:** ChatGPT is a type of language model developed by OpenAI (Thorp, 2023). ChatGPT is a type of large language model created to generate human-like text in NLP tasks (Shen et al., 2023). It is designed to generate human-like text based on a large corpus of text data and is trained to perform various language tasks, such as answering questions, writing stories, composing code, and generating essays.

**Education for Sustainable Development (ESD):** UNESCO (2012) defines Education for Sustainable Development (ESD) in its broadest sense as education for social transformation, with the goal of creating more sustainable societies. It emphasizes that ESD touches every aspect of education, including planning, policy development, program implementation, finance, curricula, teaching, learning, assessment, and administration. Furthermore, ESD aims to provide a coherent interaction between public awareness and education to foster a sustainable future.

**Education for Social Justice (ESJ):** As White and Talbert (2005:59) explain, education for social justice must transcend functionalist and vocationalist perspectives on schooling, which emphasize education for employment, and instead adopt a transformational pedagogy (cited in Zajda, Majhanovich, & Rust, 2006); ... we must prepare children for active participation as global citizens; and this means that we have a responsibility to teach for social justice ... Social justice education moves beyond traditionalist essentialist practice by suggesting that student and teachers are active and equal participants in all schooling ... Advocates for social jus tice education suggest that our schools are often demeaning and disempowering places where children and their teachers are either bored into submission or where the transmission and socialization techniques destroy any hope for critical-thinking.

**United Nations Educational, Scientific and Cultural Organization (UNESCO):** As UNESCO has played a leading role as the United Nations agency on Education for Sustainable Development (ESD) since the United Nations Decade of Education (2005-2014), this study utilizes the UNESCO (2017) document.

# Chapter 6
# Generative AI:
## Recent Advances and Their Impact on Education

**Sowmiya Baskar**
https://orcid.org/0000-0001-7043-8073
*S.I.V.E.T. College, India*

## ABSTRACT

*GenerativeAI (GenAI) is a buzz term in the field of Artificial Intelligence (AI). It is a branch of AI, which has the capability to create content in various forms such as text, audio and video, by leveraging patterns in existing data. GenAI utilizes variety of Machine Learning and Deep Learning algorithms. It offers an alternative to the traditional teaching-learning model by offering enhanced teaching and learning experiences. Learning is a challenge for special student categories like neurodiversity, where GenAI plays a vital role to achieve their academic goals by creating inclusive learning environments. Teachers can make lesson plans, customized learning content as per learner's individual characteristics and assessments for students with instant grading. Through technologies like Chatbot, the students can learn, even in the absence of teachers. GenAI is used in research for various activities like synthetic data generation, etc. This survey provides a comprehensive survey of the application of GenAI and the impact of GenAI in Education sector.*

## INTRODUCTION

Generative AI has a variety of applications in our day to day life. This technology is becoming so popular just as we use smart phones. Change is the only constant and adaptation to change is what we need. We should be prepared with the technological advancements which is a driving force for the growth and development of

DOI: 10.4018/979-8-3693-5623-4.ch006

the economy. Especially, there is a pressure out in educational sector to inculcate the skills of GenAI in the curriculum. After COVID-19, there is a massive shift towards the teaching and learning. To match the skills needed for the job market, there should be proper alignment towards the AI technologies. The research sector has been changed by AI tools, which assists the researchers, editors and reviewers. They help by skimming papers, writing the research papers, brainstorming formulating hypothesis and many more (Chan & Colloton, 2024, p. 287). It is interesting to know about the history of GenAI, which is possible after the advent of deep learning (Cao et al., 2023). GenAI tools are applied on experimental basis for authentic assessments and transformation of education sector is recorded, which is proven to open exciting opportunities (Salinas-Navarro et al., 2024, p. 83). By understanding what students think and their worries, policymakers can make better rules and plans for using GenAI tools. This helps improve teaching and learning in colleges (Chan & Hu, 2023). If GenAI is incorporated in academia, the scope and boundaries must be addressed (Yeralan & Lee, 2023). The challenges and opportunities of GenAI must be clearly understood, which the foundation for its future (Michel-Villarreal et al., 2023). Traditional teaching methods treat all students at equal level, which may fail to satisfy diverse needs of students (Karpouzis et al., 2024). Understanding Prompt Engineering and LLM is crucial because they help in efficiently using AI tools by crafting better instructions and knowing how the AI processes language. This ensures that AI can be used efficiently and responsibly (Marvin et al., 2023, pp. 387-402, Michel-Villarreal et al., 2023). However there is a darker side of AI exists, where AI possess serious threats to humanity and should be addressed (Ferrara, 2024). The awareness of GenAI, tools, techniques should be explored in a consistent manner (Prather et al., 2023, pp. 108-159). The synergy between GenAI and Learning Analytics will enhance the learning experiences (Yan et al., 2024, pp. 101-111). As AI is highly influential, it should be adapted by the academic industry after the proper reassessments in the existing framework (Hashmi & Bal, 2024). AI faces a lot of challenges such as biases, misuse, and nature of black box. So technologies like blockchain can be combined with AI, which helps addressing the aforementioned problems. Blockchain boosts transparency and decentralization (Brewer et al., 2024) and the duo (Blockchain and AI) provides best ground breaking opportunity for the business and organizations. GenAI policies and regulations are creating a broad gap, which needs to be addressed (Christodorescu et al., 2024).

The scope of this paper is to investigate the possible use of AI and its impact in education. This research is structured as follows. The paper begins with how GenAI works and the different techniques it uses, followed by how GenAI is changing education, especially how it can improve the way teachers teach and students learn. It also discusses about the GenAI usage and its experiences in classrooms, with its benefits and challenges. The paper then discusses some problems with AI in education, such as fairness, biases, and the risk of misuse. It also explore how prompt engineering and Large Language Models (LLMs) help improve AI tools. Ethical concerns like privacy and plagiarism are covered with focus on how they affect the education sector. How data can be used to personalize learning and help students succeed is briefly mentioned. The prompts and the results from experiments with ChatGPT are shared to show how well it works in education and where it falls short. Finally, the paper concludes by briefing how GenAI is changing education and what this means for the future of teaching and learning.

## GENERATIVE AI TECHNIQUES

This section elaborates latest generative AI techniques, such as GANs (Generative Adversarial Networks), VAEs (Variational Autoencoders), and Transformers, and their working. AI is designed to make machines think like human. AI uses algorithms and models where computers learn from data and make predictions on it. Advancements in hardware and electronics paved way to the development of AI with increased memory storage. The AI can be categorized into three types: Artificial Narrow Intelligence (ANI), Artificial General Intelligence (AGI) and Artificial Super Intelligence (ASI). ANI narrow down to one area and solves the problem. Fraud detection system is an example for ANI. AGI is designed to mimic human behavior and intelligence. A fair example is implementation of AI for teaching. ASI will surpass human intelligence in all aspects. ANI is said to be weak and AGI is said to be strong. Currently, we are in ANI and developments are ongoing in AGI and ASI.

## EVOLUTION OF GENERATIVE AI

Early generative models like hopfield networks laid foundation for understanding how neural networks could generate new patterns or sequences. Advanced systems including generative adversarial networks (GANs), variational autoencoders (VAEs), and transformer-based models like GPT-3 were developed. These models demonstrate a move towards more sophisticated systems that can generate new data resembling the training set. GenAI has two significant models namely: discriminative and generative models. (Chan & Colloton, 2024, p. 287). GAN has reached top miles, transformer architectures were introduced, which was applied in computer vision. Transformer architecure is a self-attention mechanism which includes an encoder and decoder and it analyses different parts in the input. The encoder and decoder are quite opposite to each other, yet both include multi-head attention and neural networks, which are feed-forward. Transformer architecture has revolutionized natural language processing and the Auto-reregressive Language Modeling (ARLM) and Masked Language Modeling (MLM) could handle advances NLP tasks like predicting the next sentence. (Cao et al., 2023)

## GENAI IN EDUCATION

AIGC is Artificial Intelligence Generated Content, where content is created with advanced Generative AI (GAI) techniques in lesser time. ChatGPT and DALL-E-2 are the significant examples of AIGC. It provides personalized content with multimodal data in various forms like research papers, videos, etc. The science and maths based dataset solves various topics including algebra, number theory, quantitaive problems, number theory, probability, physics, biology, chemistry, engineering and astronomy. It can solve mathematical problems in easy manner with simple steps. There are certain bots available with personalized content, self pace learning with online AI tutor, with continual improvement (Cao et al., 2023). Table1 depicts the examples of GenAI applications and the popular software applications.

*Table 1. Examples of GenAI applications and software*

| *Applications* | *Industries/Purposes* | *Popular Software Apps* |
|---|---|---|
| Image synthesis | Art and Design, Healthcare, Film, Advertising | Stable Diffusion, DALL-E, Runway ML, Midjourney, DeepAI, Fotor, Reface, SpeakPic, Syntegra, AlphaFold2 |
| Video generation | Film, Advertising, Customer Service for various industries | Pictory, Synthesia, VEED |
| Music and audio creation | Music Production, Healthcare, Customer Service for various industries | Amper Music, Jukebox, MuseTree, MuseNet, Musico, Vall-E, WaveNet, Flowtron |
| Text-to-speech, speech-to-speech | Customer Service for various industries, Electronics, Travel, Leisure | Siri, Alexa, Google Assistant |
| Text generation | Marketing, Advertising, Journalism, Script and Story Writing, Healthcare, Customer Service for various industries | ChatGPT, BARD, Bing, Quillbot, Jasper, Google Translate, Photomath |
| Code generation | All industries that require programming | Google's AutoML, OpenAI Codex, GitHub Copilot, Polycoder, Amazon CodeWhisperer |
| Text-to-speech, speech-to-speech | Customer Service for various industries, Electronics, Travel, Leisure | Siri, Alexa, Google Assistant |

(Chan & Colloton, 2024, p. 287)

## CHATGPT – A GAME CHANGER, HOW IT WORKS?

ChatGPT is Chat Generative Pretrained Transformer. It's a pretrained language processing model developed by OpenAI. ChatGPT is trained with various sources of data and learns to predict the successive word. It recognizes patterns and structures in sentences, what we call as Transformer, which weighs the significant parts in a question. GenAI generates content dynamically, helps researchers in doing research. It provides user centric design. It is customisable and scalable. Content is generated as per user requirement and is user-centric that's why. In ChatGPT, the user simply needs to prompt their requirement, just like a statement, the system immediately responds to the queries. It is simple like a conversation in messenger. One interesting research information is both Gen-Z and millennials prefer texting over talking, which can be compared to a conversation between the student (user) and the faculty (chatGPT). GenAI can provide varied responses with different styles as per user requirement but with consistency in data and variation in phrase (Chan & Colloton, 2024, p. 287).

## IMPACT OF GENERATIVE AI IN EDUCATION

This section explains the potential benefits of using GenAI in education, such as improving student engagement, enhancing learning outcomes, and facilitating accessibility.

ChatGPT provides real time responses continually 24/7 and provides personalized support. ChatGPT can assist in writing articles, assignments and solve complex problems. It provides ICT enabled pedagogical practices. It uses neural networks to predict and assess students' performance. GenAI tools like ChatGPT 3.5, Microsoft New Bing, and Anthropic Claude help understand pedagogical theories. They provide clear definitions, explanations, and practical applications from diverse perspectives. Teachers, researchers and students can use these insights to make learning experiences more meaningful and effective, focusing on the needs of the students. Each GenAI tool has its own unique strengths and perspectives. ChatGPT 3.5 mainly gives thorough explanations, including definitions, principles, and practical advice. Google Bard emphasizes practical aspects and real-world applications. New Bing focuses on clarifying theories and concepts, while Anthropic Claude highlights goals and principles (Salinas-Navarro et al., 2024, p. 83). GenAI based tool AI KAKU assist Japanese students to learn the concepts in English. AI chatbots improved students learning methodology and confidence level is improved (Chan & Hu, 2023).

## ENHANCING TEACHING AND LEARNING WITH GENERATIVE AI

This section explains how genAI technologies influence teaching practices, such as content creation, lesson planning, and assessment design. It also discusses the effects of using generative AI on student learning experiences. GenAI acts as a virtual teacher by providing personalized support and immediate responses. Work load of teachers can be reduced by providing personalized materials and lesson plans, according to students' needs. It helps in research with the latest AI-powered technologies by contributing to data collection and analysis. It helps in generating artworks in the form of slides, audios and videos with the given text. The repeated time consuming tasks in research can be handled by AI in an efficient manner, through which students can find more time to focus on the critical part of research and studies. Positive attitude is recorded with the use of AI in learning, research and career planning.

The studies report that conceptual understanding of students has been improved with GenAI. Some sort of personalized learning assistance, which is needed by the students, is provided at all the times (24/7). In terms of writing, the students need guidance to improve their content, writing style, spelling and grammar check. GenAI assists the students in terms of content improvement and does the brainstorming too by generating ideas and expanding them. The research activities are cumbersome process, where the literature survey plays a crucical role. It facilitates the students by searching for content, summarizing the literature and building on basic insights to develop their own research. GenAI tools therby improve the self learning capacity of the students. GenAI creates artworks with just a prompt, which provides great benefits to STEM students. The text is given as input and it produces images as outputs. Also with various forms including slides, audio and visual outputs are generated. The repetitive task is reduced, which are often non-creative and AI may provide greater time for their research and studies. (Chan & Hu, 2023)

AI can be used for enhanced online experiences. Unlike repetitive tasks like asking queries for answers and repeating same actions, chatGpt can be used as a co-pilot or co-worker similar to human communicate with each other. As chatGPT is more versatile, the online experiences can be enhanced. For instance, the chatGpt plug-in may be asked to summarize the information presented in different tabs, there the user gets rid of problem of switching between different tabs to read the information and to get the key points.Researchers struggle in the very beginnning, where they have no idea or very less idea, where AI helps in generating initial drafts, brainstorming and improve the thinking levels.AI Tools can be used by professors to generate quizzes or presentations. For students, based on their subjects, they may ask AI tools to prepare multiple choice questions and after getting their scores, if they want to improve their scores, they should be more expertise in their subjects. For which, they may use the AI tools to get suggestions for unfamiliar subject areas and get some sort of customised assistance, well focussed and targeted plan for study. Thereby GenAI acts as a smart tutor. GenAI can be used by students to generate essays based on their ideas and key points in to text rather than focusing on grammar and other stuff. It can be used as a writing assistance, where students can structure their thoughts and arguments in an effective manner (Yeralan & Lee, 2023). ChatGPT performs task like completion of given text, generation of a conversation. Students may come from versatile background. Language plays a vital role in the understanding of concepts. For non-English students, AI plays a good job in language editing and doing translations. It helps the educators in preparing lesson plans, preparing lesson notes, creating assessments and evaluating them. ChatGPT can be used as an additional resource to provide answers to theoretical questions and to help generate initial ideas for essays. ChatGPT can assist individuals with disabilities like dyslexia in several ways like reading assistance, writing support, round the clock support. For teachers, it reduces time by freeing them from doing repeated tasks and concentrate on higher-level tasks. They can use it as a valuable tool for lesson notes preparation, preparing course objectives and creating assessments and evaluation system for the same. Researchers spend a huge time in literature reviews. ChatGPT can be used as a research assistance tool and keeping in mind that it should not replace the role of researcher. (Michel-Villarreal et al., 2023)

It is an ongoing big argument that chatGpt may provide content which is plagiarized, so the academic policies are violated. Yet the thing is that, they are not at all new problems in education. The widespread absence of clear policies regarding AI tools like ChatGPT in contributes to increased academic dishonesty. To mitigate these challenges, institutions should update simple policies to clearly define AI tool usage guidelines, implement stringent penalties for violations, enhance detection methods for AI-generated content, and promote a strong social norm against AI-enabled cheating to uphold academic integrity effectively. From regular traditional learning, student may get benefitted by enriched teaching experiences and learn-by-doing activities with GenAI tools.

## CHALLENGES IN GENAI

This section elaborates the ethical implications of using generative AI in education and the challenges associated with implementing generative AI technologies in educational contexts, including technical barriers, teacher training, and acceptance by stakeholders.Though the GenAI has numerous benefits, it raises ethical and social issues including job replacement by AI, causing potential threats leading to privacy issues, etc. In some cases, the generated output may be unfair or biased. Human interaction is limited with use of AI (Chan & Hu, 2023). There is possibility of data leakage. There may be absence of emotional connection. AI may reduce jobs. Sometimes the results may be inappropriate or misleading. AI has a black-box nature due to its complexity for most of the end users, which makes the decision making process complicated. There are certain issues concerned with privacy and ethical. The private and sensitive information can be easily collected by the technology, which causes security threats. Plagiarism is an ethical concern, it's tricky to detect whether the content is human or AI-generated. As the technology improves, it is difficult to identify the plagiarised content which is developed by AI, which is a serious ethical issue. The human creativity and decision making skills may have detrimental effects, due to the relying on AI. Gradually, the thinking capacity is reduced. In experimental learning, students should build more constructive knowledge, which promotes a deep understanding of academic subjects through reflective and practical activities. Assessments that measure higher-level cognitive skills like analysis, creation, and evaluation can engage students in meaningful learning experiences and make it harder for GenAI tools to address them (Salinas-Navarro et al., 2024, p. 83). Though GenAI offers lot of faclilities to the students' community, it has some concern regarding accuracy, openness, confidentiality and ethics (Chan & Hu, 2023). There are chances for the AI to produce incorrect or outdated information. When it comes to Deep Neural Networks, there are potential issues with lack of transparency, which is often considered as a black box problem. The deep network architecture is highly complex and may be an issue for sorting out the problems behind the code even for the experts. (Chan & Hu, 2023). But still researchers are working on methods to improve the accuracy and eradicate the issues discussed above. There are several aspects are to be addressed. The balance between machine and man should be maintained. High quality content should be ensured before developing and implementing AI (Chan & Colloton, 2024, p. 287) .With the rise of AI tools, the ethical implications and preservation of integrity of scholars is a big question mark. There are many AI tools which can create research papers and generate research outputs; thereby academic integrity is violated (Yeralan & Lee, 2023). Students thinking capacity may be lost due to relying on chatGPT. Their problem solving skills may also be degraded. (Michel-Villarreal et al., 2023)

A tool called 'interactive mega-tool' is introduced in this study, which is proven to create effective lesson plans, which reduces time consumption for educators and improved learning experience for students. Not all students in a class have same level of knowledge and competency. Their level of knowledge is assessed before introducing a subject. With respect to students, based on their individual skills and learning potential, the course content is prepared. Thus, GenAI provides engaging and effective learning experience rather than just automating the process of education.

This study focuses on two aspects namely: adaptive lesson plan and peronalized education. Adaptive lesson plan focus on lesson planning based on the dataset of students. More refined and dynamic lesson plan is iteratively constructed based on students. Though this method provides to be efficient, relying on AI causes a diminishing threat to the role of creativity in teachers. Without AI tools, the teacher may think, analyze and prepup lesson plans and after AI tools usage, there are more chances for their declination of expertise knowledge. AI evaluates the assessments and provides feedback instantly, which improves the students to understand and re-learn the concepts correctly. But GenAI needs to carefully address the data privacy and bias in assessments. (Karpouzis et al., 2024)

## PROMPT ENGINEERING AND LLM

Simply put, LLM are programs which are trained on large amount of text to understand the text messages. They simply learn to read, write and interact with the users by predicting the next sentence. Popular examples for LLM include ChatGPT and GPT-4. With better prompts, the LLM performance is improved and will allow developers to adjust the content and find new uses that were not possible before. Prompt engineering will be important for making the best use of LLMs and can help make businesses more efficient and easier to run, making it a useful skill. New jobs will be created for people who are good at prompt engineering. Prompt engineering helps developers gain a deeper understanding of the behavior and capabilities of LLMs .It is important to understand about the contemporary digital competence popularly termed as ‘prompt engineering. Prompt Engineering is an art for effective communication with AI systems like ChatGPT. When the prompts are clear, AI systems provides accurate answers. This paper shares the techniques for optimizing the prompts. First understanding the capabilities of LLM is crucial. Test the results arrived and the prompt should be redefined. The prompt should be simple, not complex. There is a need to monitor and update the prompts consistently. By following the cyclic process of testing, refining prompts, the performance is optimized with expected results. Always make sure the instructions are clear and give examples of what you expect. Keep the task focused and watch the length and complexity to ensure it’s manageable. There are advanced prompt engineering concepts like Automatic Instruction Generation and Program Synthesis for Prompt Engineering. Automatic instruction generation is a broad term that includes many ways to create instructions automatically. In contrast, program synthesis for prompt engineering is a precise method that uses program synthesis techniques to create these instructions [8,9].

## Prompt engineering techniques and tools:

Prompt engineering improves the performance of NLP models. Several tools like LangChain, Dust.tt, OpenPrompt, BetterPrompt, Prompt Engine, Promptify, TextBox 2.0, ThoughtSource and GPT Index. Tthe Prompt Engineering tools and its usage are detailed in table 2.

*Table 2. Prompt Engineering tools and its usage.*

| Tool | Usage |
|---|---|
| LangChain | Assists in developing applications that integrate large language models with other computational sources. |
| Dust.tt | Helps build LLM applications through a series of prompted calls to external models. |
| OpenPrompt | A PyTorch-based library providing a flexible framework for implementing prompt learning. |
| BetterPrompt | A test suite for evaluating LLM prompts before production deployment. |
| Prompt Engine | An NPM utility for creating and managing LLM prompts. |
| Promptify | Aids in developing a pipeline for using LLM APIs in production. |
| TextBox 2.0 | A Python and PyTorch library for standardized text generation using pre-trained language models. |
| ThoughtSource | An open resource and community for chain-of-thought reasoning data and tools in LLMs. |
| GPT Index | Provides data structures to facilitate the use of large external knowledge bases with LLMs. |

Figure 1 depicts the various prompt engineering techniques.

*Figure 1. Prompt Engineering techniques*

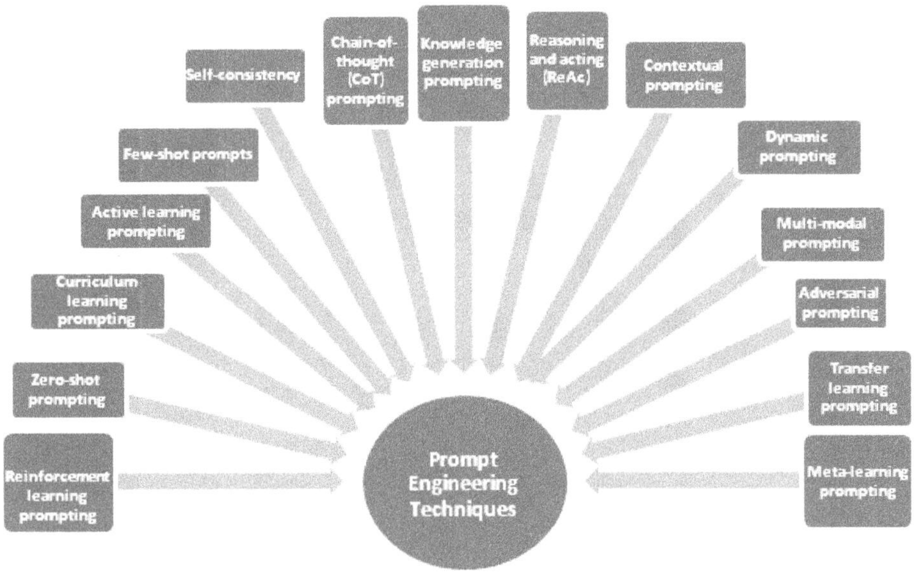


Figure 2 represents the word cloud of prompt engineering, where prompt engineering related terms are depicted. This word cloud serves as a visual summary, allowing readers to quickly grasp the core concepts and vocabulary involved in prompt engineering. The main ideas and common terms used in prompt engineering are depicted in the word cloud.

*Figure 2. Word cloud with regard to prompt engineering.*

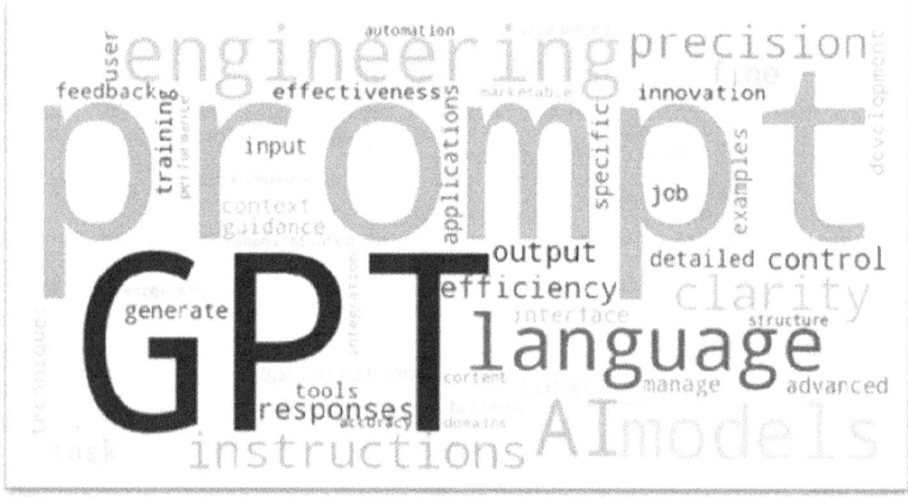


The instructional patterns are helpful in making prompts structured. The instructions should be direct.It should follow the sequence of steps. Based on the results, the prompt should be adjusted. The questions should be clear and precise. It may be open ended or closed ended questions. Zero-shot learning helps when you can't gather examples. For example, teaching a robot to recognize a dog by describing its features. Few-shot learning helps the model adapt with just a few examples. For example, the picture of dog is shown to identify the features and recognize in several situations. Refining few-shot learning is used to improve the accuracy of model by adjusting the parameters. For instance, in a dog classification task, if a robot confuses between two different varieties, the model can be trained with more pictures to identify the correct category of dog. There are certain drawbacks such as uncertainty in AI Responses, Complexity of Human Language, Ethical Concerns, Bias in AI Responses, Technology Limits, User Skill Differences, Consistency and Scalability, Privacy and Security Issues (Parmar & Patel, n.d.).

## ETHICAL CONSIDERATIONS OF GENAI AND RISK MITIGATION

The European Union (EU) and China are actively working together to set up regulations for Generative AI (GenAI) to ensure that its development and use adhere to ethical standards, safety protocols, and societal values. GenAI can create educational content for therapeutic experiences, but it can be misused to generate fake content. Medical images can be created for educational purposes but it can be misused by fabricating the images. They may be diagnosed wrongly. VR and AR images can be created by AI for educational purposes, but there are chances for false spread of information. There may be possibility of GenAI abuse. Authentication mechanisms such as Block chain-based authentication, token-based systems, or cryptographic methods should be followed to ensure the abuse of GenAI (Ferrara, 2024).

LLMs helps the instructor in improving productivity by reducing workload, student learning experiences and focus on problem-solving and suggesting new assessment practices If AI generated content has mistakes, they may have negative impact on learning. Also if the content is not up to the mark in case of programming languages, it may create poor programmers. If students are using GenAI, they need to spend time on prompt engineering, which may suck time and may leads to unproductivity. If GenAI students may wrongly think that they are making process, there are chances for them to reduce subect mastery. Educators using AI for assessments should not leave the students with the tool alone; they must find new resources to deal with LLM. AI should be introduced at the right time to the students; if introduced at the early stage, may create high reliance on it. Proper introduction of AI tools is essential. It is proved that socio-emotional competencies can be demonstrated by teacher alone and it is not the part of AI. Though AI tools exist, Teachers only can provide better guidance than AI tools. Research says AI tools are used by the students mostly for text generation largely than form code generation (Prather et al., 2023, pp. 108-159).

To bridge the gap between policies and technology in GenAI, a workshop was conducted which answered several queries regarding designing regulations and technological developments to be made to meet the regulatory requirements. This workshop focused on how the European Union (EU), the People's Republic of China (PRC), and the United States (US) are making rules for Generative AI, looking only at laws and proposals that directly involve it. The content creation plays a vital role and PRC's GenAI regulation focuses on controlling content creation from the beginning and prohibits violation the government sensorship rules. The providers must take responsinbility for the contents, which are illegal and should follow up their systems. The regulation aims to control online conversations, ensure that they match the values and rules of the Chinese Communist Party. The relaxation is provided as the regulation doesn't apply to systems used in private areas such as healthcare, public administration or industrial processes. The EU reached major milestone in AI regulation by categorizing AI's risk areas where sectors like education is considered to be of risk. AI providers must share information with respect to the models with training data. The risk associated with the model should meet certain standards like risk management, cybersecurity protection and the evaluations. The factors including computing power, number of parameters, and business users assess the risk status. The White House released the Blueprint for an AI Bill of Rights for ensuring fairness and transparency before ChatGPT. By October 2023, Congress held many AI hearings and introduced over 50 bills, released an Executive Order on AI primarily focused on the safety and national security, which prioritized AI-generated disinformation. It also monitored cyber threats.

## There are several conditions suggested for GenAI usage:

- GenAI should be utilized in higher level courses rather than in lower level courses.
- It can be utilized for minor assessments, not for major assessments.
- For learning complex tasks, GenAI can be allowed, not for simple tasks.
- Merely copying and pasting of content is not allowed.
- It is disallowed to use complete content generated by AI, rather parts of a generated solution can be used.
- GenAI can be used when there is a need for assistance and not as an entire tool from scratch to end.

## Suggestions for Educators:

- Acknowledge LLMs in the Class Rooms
- Discuss Institutional and Class Policy
- Assume LLM usage by Students
- Recognize LLM Capabilities
- Use LLMs for Course Material Generation
- Align Learning Objectives with Career Relevance
- Ensure Constructive Alignment of Objectives and Activities
- Examine Hidden or Implicit Learning Objectives
- Provide Feedback and Practice with LLMs
- Encourage Ethical Use of GAI
- Explicit Restrictions on GAI for Assessed Work
- Require Statement of GAI Usage
- Address Academic Misconduct and Consequences

Table 3 represents the evaluation of the three models: GPT-4, GPT-3.5-turbo, and GitHub Copilot.

*Table 3. Evaluation of the models: GPT-4, GPT-3.5-turbo, and GitHub Copilot.*

| Model | Description | Usage |
|---|---|---|
| GPT-4 | State-of-the-art LLM, powers the paid version of ChatGPT. | Used for solving problems. |
| GPT-3.5-turbo | Powers the free version of ChatGPT, likely to be used by many students. | Used for solving problems. |
| GitHub Copilot | Free for students and educators, embedded into the IDE, works slightly differently as it cannot be directly 'prompted'. | Used within Visual Studio Code Copilot plugin. |

To promote responsible use of AI in higher education, universities should conduct workshops, seminar or online courses that educate about the benefits, limitations, and potential risks associated with AI models (Michel-Villarreal et al., 2023).

Risk mitigation in GenAI is essential to ensure safety and security in the AI models, adhere to the regulations and foster innovation responsibly. There are several means of risk mitigation like model alignment, model inspection, provenance and watermarking, etc. In simpler terms, we can define alignment of AI models as providing them a good set of instructions and ensuring that they follow them, resulting in risk reduction. When AI systems are aligned in a right way, they are less likely to provide content which are biased or errored or harmful. Also the privacy is not violated. The AI models should be trained in such a way that the goals are clearly set, trained on diversified dataset and keeping an eye on the model frequently to check its behavior. AI model which performs the intended task is considered to be perfectly aligned and are safe and secured. Yet, they are still remaining a challenge. AI enabled chatbots are more common now and it is crucial to align them with human values and secure with robustness against the adversarial attacks. Certain key methods like Pre-deployment testing, Reinforcement Learning from Human Feedback (RLHF), and Red Teaming can be followed for discovering and mitigating vulnerabilities and the chatbots can be prevented from prompt injections. The key methods will test for vulnerabilities in cybersecurity, discrimination, content generation which are harmful or misleading, privacy violations and Large-scale societal impacts. On the other hand LLM can be fine-tuned, which can be at a greater risk of degrading model alignment. Figure 3 depicts the large scale societal impacts. (Christodorescu et al., 2024)

*Figure 3. Large Scale Societal impacts*

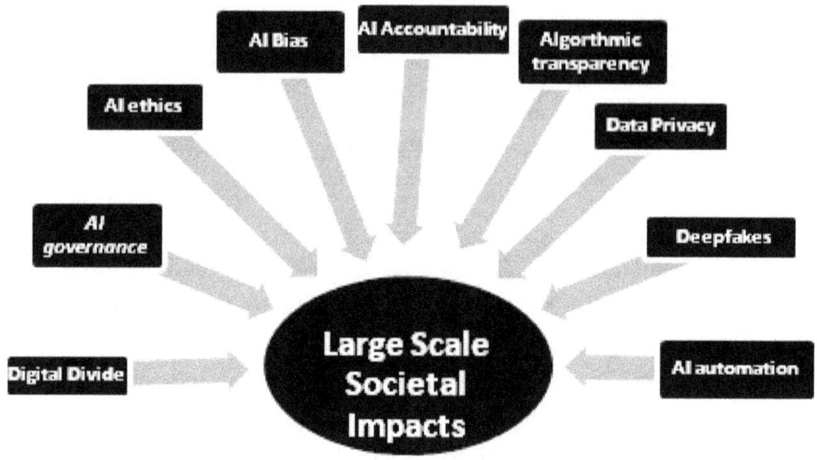


## GENERATIVE ARTIFICIAL INTELLIGENCE IN LEARNING ANALYTICS

This research explains the synergy between GenAI and LA. GenAI has extended scope beyond text-to-text generation, which includes image, video, and speech generation. Text-based GenAI includes chatbots and advanced AI agents like AgentGPT, which is based on models like GPT-4. They are capable of making decisions independently. LLMs are trained on code generation (e.g., OpenAI's Codex, Meta's Code Llama), which performs data analysis.

Though AI can help in the learning process like finding facts, summarizing the text, the deeper aspects of learning like understanding, motivation and using various strategies, still rely on human effort and experience. For research data capturing, GenAI tools like Whisper automate the transcription and streamline the process. The audio data is converted to text data, which is processed by LLMs. But more research is needed to validate GenAI's ability to transcribe speech data for its accuracy and reliability. As research improves, the need for manual transcription is reduced and analyzing students' verbal communication data is performed faster. Rather than using static text or images, with GenAI, animated sequences can be formed. With tools like Stable Diffusion, Midjourney, and Dall-E, the textual context can be converted to visual content, which would be of high use to educators and learners.

Tools such as Runway Gen-2 and Make-A-Video convert text into videos, which helps to analyze the reasoning and storytelling skills of students. It is especially helpful for students with disabilities like dyslexia and supports inclusive education. When there is such a reinforcement type of learning is introduced, the learners' choices should be considered. Synthetic data is a valuable intermediary for unavailable data. It offers researchers instant access. On during slow approval processes or data ownership issues, synthetic data allows researchers to refine their methods and test solutions quickly. AI agents like AgentGPT can simulate human behaviors, acting as learners, teachers or even patients for medical training, creating valuable data for future LA research and opening up new learning opportunities.

**Research Question:** How does the rise of GenAI affect capturing learner independence in Learning Analytics, and how can we keep learning focused on people?

The rise of GenAI can lead to biased learning data if we don't capture how learners make decisions and stay motivated. To prevent this, researchers need to create better ways to measure learner independence, ensuring that learning stays centered on human needs.

**Drawback:** For students with learning disabilities, instead of giving as text, graphical content could foster the learning process. However, caution should be taken when 'deepfake' technologies are used to create personalized content, as they may create ethical and cybersecurity risks, such as identity theft and the spread of false information. (Yan et al., 2024, pp. 101-111).

## Experiments with prompts and the results (arrived by ChatGPT)

This section depicts the results arrived by ChatGPT for some of the random questions related to GenAI.

**Question 1:** What type of tasks can ChatGPT assist with?

Answer: ChatGPT can help with a variety of tasks, including answering questions, providing explanations, offering writing and editing assistance, generating creative content, giving advice, and much more. It can assist with both simple and complex inquiries, making it a versatile tool for users.

**Question 2:** How does ChatGPT ensure the information it provides is accurate and reliable?

Answer: ChatGPT is trained on a vast dataset that includes diverse and reputable sources of information. While it strives to provide accurate and reliable responses, it's important for users to verify critical information from trusted sources. ChatGPT's answers are based on patterns in the data it was trained on, and it does not have real-time access to current events or databases.

**Question 3:** What are some ethical considerations regarding the use of GenAI?

Answer: Some ethical considerations regarding the use of GenAI include:

Bias and Fairness: Ensuring that the AI does not perpetuate or amplify existing biases present in the training data.

Privacy: Protecting users' personal data and ensuring it is not misused or exposed.Transparency: Being open about how the AI works, what data it uses, and how decisions are made.

Accountability: Establishing clear guidelines on who is responsible for the AI's actions and decisions.

Security: Safeguarding the AI systems from misuse or malicious attacks.

Impact on Employment: Considering the effects of automation on jobs and preparing for transitions in the workforce.

Misinformation: Preventing the AI from spreading false or misleading information.

**Question 4:** What are the ethical implications of incorporating ChatGPT in academic environments, particularly concerning issues of plagiarism and maintaining academic integrity?

The ethical implications of incorporating ChatGPT in academic environments primarily revolve around concerns related to plagiarism and maintaining academic integrity. Here are the key issues:

Plagiarism: ChatGPT can generate text that may be used by students without proper attribution, leading to unintentional or intentional plagiarism. Since the model produces content that isn't sourced from a specific author, students may misuse it as their own work, undermining the value of original thinking and proper citation practices in academia.

Academic Integrity: The easy access to AI-generated content raises concerns about students bypassing the learning process by using ChatGPT to complete assignments, essays, or projects. This could result in a diminished emphasis on critical thinking, creativity, and independent problem-solving, all of which are central to the educational process.

Over-reliance on AI: If students excessively depend on AI tools like ChatGPT for generating content, it may hinder the development of their own writing and analytical skills. This reliance can lead to shallow learning, where the focus shifts from deep understanding to quick results.

Assessment Challenges: Educators may face difficulty in distinguishing between AI-generated and student-written work, complicating the grading process and raising questions about fairness and authenticity in assessments.

To address these ethical concerns, institutions must implement clear guidelines on the appropriate use of AI tools, encourage academic honesty, and develop assessment methods that emphasize original student contributions.

**Question 5:** How can ChatGPT are utilized to support personalized learning and enhance student engagement in higher education?

ChatGPT can support personalized learning by providing tailored explanations, answering individual questions, and offering resources based on each student's needs and pace. It enhances student engagement by providing real-time, interactive feedback, encouraging active participation, and assisting with writing, research, and study planning. This makes learning more adaptive and interactive, helping students stay motivated and better understand difficult concepts.

**Question 6:** What impact does ChatGPT have on the development of critical thinking and problem-solving skills in students?

ChatGPT can influence the development of critical thinking and problem-solving skills in both positive and negative ways. On one hand, it encourages exploration by providing instant information and diverse perspectives, helping students think creatively and approach problems from different angles. However, over-reliance on ChatGPT may hinder students from developing independent critical thinking, as they might use it to generate answers without fully engaging in the analytical process. To foster these skills, students must balance AI assistance with active learning and personal problem-solving efforts.

Addressing these considerations is crucial for developing and deploying GenAI responsibly.

## CONCLUSION

The future of education is not just digital; it is smart, responsive, and tailored. Imagine classrooms that function like a high-tech ecosystem, adjusting to the needs of every student in real time. Imagine AI tools like ChatGPT, always ready to help, answering questions day or night. COVID-19 pushed us online, and now, tech like IoT and GenAI is taking us to the next level. The classroom of the future is innovative, flexible, and built on groundbreaking technology. As we ride this wave, one thing is clear: learning is about to get a whole lot more exciting .GenAI tools must not be used to make pedagogical human decisions, but should be used as supportive resources. GenAI can be used as a tool by the teachers to gear up students' creativity. It can be a great tool for competency development. The institutions should develop policies and frameworks on usage of GenAI technologies. AI development should focus on transparency, accuracy, and privacy to build trust and reduce potential risks. ChatGPT can enhance teaching practices by evaluating contemporary assessment methods to ensure they are comprehensive and effective and also to develop AI resistant assessments, leading to a more genuine evaluation of student learning. The limitations in the study is most of the findings are related to chatGPT, while other GenAI tools such as Bard or Gemini are of little use. The future research will try to compare the views of versatile GenAI tools. ChatGPT should be used as an assistant for active learning in our daily lives. Crucial understanding of ChatGPT is essential for making systems smarter. By better understanding of AI technologies, researchers can gain insights into how they think and make decisions for responsible use in variety of applications. Rather than seeing GenAI as a threat to learning integrity, we should view it as an opportunity to transform learning in the context of human-AI collaboration.

**Conflicts of Interest:** The authors declare no conflict of interest.

## REFERENCES


Brewer, J., Patel, D., Kim, D., & Murray, A. (2024). Navigating the challenges of generative technologies: Proposing the integration of artificial intelligence and blockchain. *Business Horizons*, *67*(5), 525–535. DOI: 10.1016/j.bushor.2024.04.011

Cao, Y., Li, S., Liu, Y., Yan, Z., Dai, Y., Yu, P. S., & Sun, L. (2023). A comprehensive survey of AI-generated content (AIGC): A history of generative AI from GAN to ChatGPT. *arXiv preprint*, arXiv:2303.04226.

Chan, C. K. Y., & Colloton, T. (2024). *Generative AI in Higher Education: The ChatGPT Effect*. Taylor & Francis. DOI: 10.4324/9781003459026

Chan, C. K. Y., & Hu, W. (2023). Students' voices on generative AI: Perceptions, benefits, and challenges in higher education. *International Journal of Educational Technology in Higher Education*, *20*(1), 43. DOI: 10.1186/s41239-023-00411-8

Christodorescu, M., Craven, R., Feizi, S., Gong, N., Hoffmann, M., Jha, S., & Turek, M. (2024). Securing the future of GenAI: Policy and technology. *Cryptology ePrint Archive*.

Ferrara, E. (2024). GenAI against humanity: Nefarious applications of generative artificial intelligence and large language models. *Journal of Computational Social Science*, *7*(1), 1–21. DOI: 10.1007/s42001-024-00250-1

Hashmi, N., & Bal, A. S. (2024). Generative AI in higher education and beyond. *Business Horizons*, *67*(5), 607–614. DOI: 10.1016/j.bushor.2024.05.005

Karpouzis, K., Pantazatos, D., Taouki, J., & Meli, K. (2024). Tailoring education with GenAI: A new horizon in lesson planning. *arXiv preprint*, arXiv:2403.12071. DOI: 10.1109/EDUCON60312.2024.10578690

Marvin, G., Hellen, N., Jjingo, D., & Nakatumba-Nabende, J. (2023, June). Prompt engineering in large language models. In *International Conference on Data Intelligence and Cognitive Informatics* (pp. 387-402). Singapore: Springer Nature Singapore.

Michel-Villarreal, R., Vilalta-Perdomo, E., Salinas-Navarro, D. E., Thierry-Aguilera, R., & Gerardou, F. S. (2023). Challenges and opportunities of generative AI for higher education as explained by ChatGPT. *Education Sciences*, *13*(9), 856. DOI: 10.3390/educsci13090856

Parmar, S., & Patel, H. (n.d.). *Prompt engineering for large language model*.

Prather, J., Denny, P., Leinonen, J., Becker, B. A., Albluwi, I., Craig, M., & Keuning, H. (2023). The robots are here: Navigating the generative AI revolution in computing education. In *Proceedings of the 2023 Working Group Reports on Innovation and Technology in Computer Science Education* (pp. 108-159). DOI: 10.1145/3623762.3633499

Salinas-Navarro, D. E., Vilalta-Perdomo, E., Michel-Villarreal, R., & Montesinos, L. (2024). Using generative artificial intelligence tools to explain and enhance experiential learning for authentic assessment. *Education Sciences*, *14*(1), 83. DOI: 10.3390/educsci14010083

Yan, L., Martinez-Maldonado, R., & Gasevic, D. (2024, March). Generative artificial intelligence in learning analytics: Contextualizing opportunities and challenges through the learning analytics cycle. In *Proceedings of the 14th Learning Analytics and Knowledge Conference* (pp. 101-111). DOI: 10.1145/3636555.3636856

Yeralan, S., & Lee, L. A. (2023). Generative AI: Challenges to higher education. *Sustainable Engineering and Innovation*, *5*(2), 107–116. DOI: 10.37868/sei.v5i2.id196

# Chapter 7
# Generative AI Is Changing Personalized Learning to Help Us Build a Sustainable Future

**Subhadip Kowar**
https://orcid.org/0009-0005-7758-4635
*Brainware University, India*

**Nilav Darsan Mukhopadhayay**
*Brainware University, India*

## ABSTRACT

*Generative artificial intelligence (GAI) is the process of analyzing a variety of inputs to produce new content, such as books, music, or artwork. GAI has the ability to create new opportunities in the creative industry. GAI might analyze data from different historical eras and civilizations to discover unique aesthetic combinations. Its well-reasoned arguments may even be able to forecast the number of distinct creative genres that will mix and have an influence on society before any art is created. GAI's storytelling skills about literary works that strike a balance are improving. Students may soon be able to practice reading novels produced by artificial intelligence (AI) thanks to individualized learning algorithms. The stories would be tailored to each learner's interests and understanding level, and the AI would improve its storytelling skills by analyzing feedback. Personalized learning based on GAI will demonstrate how it fosters creativity.*

DOI: 10.4018/979-8-3693-5623-4.ch007

## 1. INTRODUCTION

Production and dissemination of instructional material have undergone major changes as a result of the digital age's tremendous effects on education. With the abundance of tools and tactics available to them today, students can customize their educational experiences to fit their individual interests. It is their prerogative to choose which resources to employ, how to use them, and when to communicate with them. This change may be seen in the rising acceptance of AI-powered tutoring services and creative teaching strategies like flipped classes and collaborative learning approaches. Despite these advantages, technology has also brought up new distractions that can impair students' capacity to concentrate and process information.

Research on how technology affects learning and performance in the classroom has led to debate. Technology-enhanced learning (TEL) proponents claim that this approach can boost both teaching and learning. In agreement, Dror argues that technology provides a less taxing method of imparting knowledge, promoting greater student engagement and ultimately better learning. However, some researchers do draw attention to some potential drawbacks, such as a decline in students' reading and writing skills, a tendency for students to only use recorded materials rather than in-person instruction, and a general decrease in the amount of time dedicated to educational activities. Underachieving students without resources are disproportionately impacted by the detrimental effects of technology, it is a fact.

Students at both well-funded and underfunded schools have repeatedly said how much they value receiving individualized learning resources and face-to-face instruction from their teachers. Classrooms have not fully adopted customized instruction, despite evidence that it raises student achievement. Here's where technology, especially generative AI, may make a real difference. One potential application for it would be to deliver highly customized learning materials that are almost precisely matched to each student's needs.

Artificial intelligence has made it feasible for several innovative teaching and learning strategies that are either being tested or have already been put into use. This is an excellent opportunity to use these strategies to gather preliminary data and then progressively enhance them depending on feedback. As the concept of education for sustainable development (ESD), driven by initiatives like the Sustainable Development Goals (SDGs), gets popular, better, fairer, and higher-quality education for everyone will be substantially benefited by these activities. This aligns with the United Nations Sustainable Development Goal 4 (SDG 4), which aims to provide equitable access to high-quality education and opportunities for lifelong learning for all people by 2030. To achieve this, educational establishments need to impart sustainable

This field is being explored by researchers such as Abulibdeh and others, who have looked into how AI tools can be easily integrated into educational settings within the framework of ESD. Devy and Rroy have examined AI's potential to assist sustainable teaching, particularly in higher education. Meanwhile, a number of properties discovered by Klasnja-Milicevic and Ivanovic in e-learning systems could be used to enhance environmentally friendly teaching approaches using AI. This project aligns with the same long-term goal since it focuses on documenting, implementing, and assessing a plan for developing and distributing inclusive learning resources that can be customized for each student.

By the end of 2022, OpenAI's ChatGPT had shocked the artificial intelligence community. Because this technology can mimic human-like discourse on a wide range of topics, scientists and educators are interested in its potential educational uses. Some experts believe that the use of these advanced language models could significantly alter education by enabling the creation of questions and learning materials that are specifically tailored to each learner. Research is also being done on completely personalized learning environments; virtual mentors could be fictional or real-life individuals. This concept fits with Bill Gates's vision for education in the future: a personalized approach that allows children to use their love of video games, like Minecraft.

## Using Technology to Enhance Instruction

The notable rise in technology use in education over the past few decades can be attributed to a number of factors. First of all, more instruments than ever before are available than ever before. Furthermore, today's youth actually want technology to be used more in the classroom. A key element of this digital revolution is the learning management system (LMS), which is increasingly becoming a necessary tool in colleges and high schools. When it comes to online courses, LMSs are similar to the best multitaskers on the market. Discussion boards and the capacity to store content such as lesson plans, tests, and videos are some of its capabilities that enable them to be utilized for purposes other than just sending course materials.

Students are enthusiastic about utilizing technology in the classroom for purposes other than LMSs. For example, they have reacted well to technology innovations and augmented reality experiences, like Georgia Institute's AI-powered teaching assistant Jill Watson. Students have exhibited interest in and engagement with these strategies, even though they aren't as common as using LMSs (Pesovski et al.,2024).

Due to their clear advantages, information tools have been pushed in education, particularly in higher education contexts where they are used for administrative and intellectual goals.

## The Use of Generative AI in Education

Intelligent algorithms that are trained to learn from data and then generate new content in response to what they discover are known as generative AI models. They have come a long way from basic statistical methods such as the Naive Bayes classifier to these massive deep learning models with billions of small settings. You may be familiar with some of them, such as the Generative Pre-trained Transformer (GPT) and Meta's Llama-2. These algorithms may be able to generate new material on demand since they have access to so much textual data.

Large language models (LLMs) in education are still in their infancy and have not yet attained their full potential, but a growing body of research suggests that these methods.

Kasneci and colleagues provided numerous ways that large language models (LLMs) could support teachers during expert discussions regarding the possible advantages of LLMs in education. They concentrated on three main areas: keeping track of each student's progress, assisting students with their assignments, and assisting each student in having a unique learning experience. Under Zawacki-Richter's supervision, another team looked at potential applications of AI in higher education. With two minor additions—naming the characteristics of the pupils and projecting their future performance—they essentially reiterated Kasneci's theories.

Big language models (LLMs) can be useful in student evaluation in two key ways. The first is automatic question generation (AQG), in which the job of the LLM is to create difficult issues that students must solve. This is quite advantageous, particularly for large institutions. The long-term effectiveness of LLM-generated questions is still being studied, but initial testing in math, data science, and English shows promise. In general, experts and educators recommend them.

Another useful application of LLMs is the automated assessment of open-ended responses. For instance, Moore and associates examined a collection of chemistry students' succinct remarks using an updated Bloom taxonomy. They discovered that a human being matched the ideal LLM (Y. Lee et al., 2023).

## Customized Education and LLMs

Dialect models' (LMs') capacity to tailor learning encounters for each special understudy is generally decided by their instructing and assessment aptitudes. Learning module programming issue clarifications give understudies with individualized instruction and supportive criticism. Whereas criticism from learning directors

(LMs) helps in comprehension, ponders by the Bernius and Sailer groups appear that learners regularly appreciate and pick up from it.

For LLMs, there are some charming and comparatively unexplored chances to create lessons. Jauhiainen and Guerra's inquiry demonstrates that they empower course adjustments to oblige understudies of distinctive expertise levels. Besides, the alternative to plan customized courses presents the plausibility of having congenial virtual instructors that might provide the fabric in a more curiously way.

In reality, teachers might reduce their workload by utilizing LLMs to plan works out, examinations, and rubrics—all of which are dreary assignments within the instructive framework. Alqahtani et al. (2023) state that these imaginative devices may too offer assistance with lesson arrangement, which incorporates making learning destinations and appraisals as well as organizing the educational programs. It is said by Javaid et al. (2023) that "ChatGPT reactions are fast, totally free, and as often as possible a phenomenal beginning point."

Furthermore, LLMs have the alternative to review assignments and give personalized comments. Alqahtani et al. (2023) found that utilizing these approaches for reviewing contains a number of brilliant preferences and spares an extraordinary bargain of time and work for teachers (Y. Lee et al., 2023).

Since AI evaluation is so orderly and steady, it reduces personal predispositions and empowers instructors to comment more quickly and center more of their time on other vital obligations.

## LMSs Modified for AI

Fake insights (AI) is quickly making its way into instruction, and as a result, AI components are commonplace, in case not fundamental, in cutting edge learning frameworks. As already shown, these frameworks have as of late collected a critical sum of information, giving a solid establishment for applying machine learning and counterfeit insights strategies to completely realize the potential of generative AI within the field of instruction. But in light of progressions in AI, there are issues with the way these learning administration frameworks are advancing. Morze and others express concern approximately the sum of time required for execution and the prerequisite that instructors make alterations. They emphasize that education still requires academic preparation in order to move absent from conventional strategies of data transmission, indeed with built-in versatile learning capabilities.

There are a number of strategies for consolidating counterfeit insights (AI) into learning administration frameworks (LMSs). Fluffy rationale, choice trees, neural systems, Bayesian frameworks, developmental calculations, and hidden Markov systems are a couple of of these strategies. All things considered, putting these procedures into hone can be difficult and error-prone. Hence, a more direct strategy of getting to AI forms is required in order to move forward the different learning stages for understudies.

## 2. IMPORTANCE OF PERSONALIZED LEARNING FOR A SUSTAINABLE FUTURE

Faculty and students in postsecondary education are now confronting difficult circumstances. Since the autumn of 2019, the number of students enrolling in universities and colleges has decreased by around one million. Not much better are the percentages of degree completion: After six years of attendance, 45% of undergraduate students leave college. Students' tuition expenses are growing as a result of continuous state funding cuts, and many of them are uneasy or don't know how to apply for financial help. Numerous issues might potentially be resolved with the proper implementation and application of customized learning.

Personalized learning is now widely accepted in the educational community as a cutting-edge approach to teaching that takes into account each student's particular needs, interests, and learning style. Different from the conventional one-size-fits-all approach to education, individualized learning is one tactic to increase student engagement, motivation, and academic performance. Let's look at some of the key benefits of tailored learning:

### Customized Learning Paths

Envision a classroom setting where every learner has a sense of personalized teaching. That is what personalized learning supported by generative AI has to offer. Teachers utilize data on each student's areas of strength and need instead of creating courses specifically tailored to each student. These dynamic, constantly-evolving learning routes will keep youngsters interested and challenged as they grow and learn. Personalized learning may be advantageous for all students, regardless of how they prefer to absorb information—visually, auditorily, or slowly. By employing this tactic, teachers may help every student reach their full potential and increase understanding of the value and enjoyment of learning among all students (Zhen et al., 2024).

### Increased Student Engagement

Generative AI is revolutionizing tailored learning and dramatically increasing student engagement. Take into account enrolling in classes that are catered to your learning style and areas of interest. That's how powerful AI is. To keep students interested and motivated, the material provides tailored learning experiences that are directly relevant to their requirements (I. Pesovski,et al.,2024).

These AI-powered technologies provide realistic and captivating virtual reality environments, games, and simulations due to their real-time flexibility. Once this is accomplished, learning becomes interesting and pleasant instead of the traditional, one-size-fits-all approach. Additionally, generative AI provides fast feedback and support, allowing students to learn at their own pace and ensuring they fully understand the material before moving on.

AI makes it easier for students to collaborate on learning by matching them with others who share their goals or interests. This social component fosters a feeling of community and increases learner engagement. In the future, learning will be more interactive, socially linked, and individualized thanks to generative AI, which will improve education's efficacy, enjoyment, and accessibility for all.

## Targeted Instruction and Support

Generative AI is revolutionizing personalized learning by providing highly targeted support and advice. As opposed to the traditional one-size-fits-all approach to education, generative AI tailors content to the individual needs of every learner. To ensure that every learner has the resources they need to succeed, artificial intelligence (AI) creates individualized lesson plans and materials by analyzing data on a student's performance, preferences, and learning styles.

This technology also offers real-time support and feedback. Coaching programs powered by AI monitor students' development and quickly identify misunderstandings and knowledge gaps. Due to the prompt and customized assistance provided by these technologies, students are able to comprehend material more quickly. Additionally, AI is able to predict when a student might struggle and proactively offer extra resources or other explanations to help them remain on track (A. V. Y. Lee et al., 2023).

Thanks to the use of generative AI, we can now more successfully meet the learning objectives of students and build a more sustainable future in education. The best learning paths guarantee that students acquire the competencies needed for the quickly evolving job market of today, which can lower the dropout rate. Education becomes more effective and efficient with this focused teaching and assistance, enabling people to confidently confront present and future global concerns.

## Differentiated Instruction

Two cornerstones of differentiated education include acknowledging that every kid is different and needs a customized approach, as well as meeting students where they are. This idea is being revolutionized by generative artificial intelligence (AI), which builds customized learning environments that adjust to the demands of individual students. Envision a classroom in which every student receives a personalized lesson plan based on their interests, preferred method of learning, and pace of learning. By adopting AI-driven systems that analyze vast quantities of data to pinpoint each student's areas of strength and weakness, teachers may provide their students with more individualized instruction.

Our quest for a sustainable future depends on generative AI because it increases educational efficacy and inclusiveness. It ensures that all students, regardless of background or ability level, have access to an excellent education. Through the use of specialized tools and exercises, AI teaches kids how to think critically and solve problems—two skills required to address today's serious environmental concerns. Additionally, it promotes the efficient use of learning resources, which reduces waste and increases production.

In conclusion, reductive AI equips teachers with the resources they need to deliver individualized instruction and get pupils ready for rewarding postsecondary vocations that will support a sustainable society.

## Promotion of Critical Thinking and Problem-Solving Skills

Thanks to generative AI, the application of personalized learning has become possible which will help develop critical thinking and problem-solving skills that are crucial for the sustainability paradigm. A child or a learner under the traditional education system spends most of his/her time memorizing contents for examinations, and therefore less importance is given to creativity and critical thinking. On the other hand, generative AI provides individual, dynamic, and engaging learning that caters to the student's peculiarities.

For instance, in a class, there are real-life situations that students come across; this challenges them to use concepts learned in real-life situations and solve problems. Education based technologies are capable of preparing different problems in various courses such as math and science that would be new to the learners and would require them to think in a more creative manner to solve them. This way allows noting several possible ways to solve a given problem and makes student fully independent individuals who can respond to new situations.

Another advantage that makes generative AI attractive when it comes to providing feedback is that it is possible to obtain individualized feedback. Instead of general prompts, AI can show students their error and teach them about it. This constant feedback makes learning buoyant as everyone feels they are under a process of constant development and growth and this enhances the growth of a thriving culture of learning and innovation. Utilizing performance data AI is able to discern particular trends as well as prescribe particular operations to make certain that every student should develop at their own rate (M. Cardona et al., 2023).

Collaborative learning also being instigated by Generative AI in the sense that students are put together in groups to address problems and come up with solutions. AI can develop realistic simulations of the teamwork assignments that are usually performed in a working environment so that the students can learn how to organize and coordinate a team, assign duties, and integrate ideas. Such experiences are very useful for enhancing and polishing up critical analysis and problem sol-- solving skills practicable in resolving global challenges such as climate change and management of resources.

In other words, generative AI has brought a shift in the old traditional one-size-fits-all learning model by enhancing learners' critical thinking ability. Integrated with suitable elements such as personalization, interactivity, and collaboration, AI prepares students to meet the diverse issues of creating a sustainable society.

## Flexibility and Adaptability

The educational environment is rapidly developing these days, that is why it is crucial to be as versatile as possible. It must be noted here that the generative AI is leading this change and making differentiation in learning possible now. Learners need to be taught in the way that suits them best, and traditional education fails at this most times but not with generative AI. It can approach it as individual lessons with each child and give feedback instantly and develop lessons that help the child progress from their level of achievement.

Literally, this Plasticity is not about shifting between contents; it is about responsiveness. new educational standards and incorporate the latest research findings as well as integrate new technologies as and when needed. It offers an environmental strategy that development with the students, thereby making it easier for the students to learn and enhancing the interest in learning.

Flexibility is also indispensable when it comes to the training of students for the uncertainty of the future. Successful generative AI will enhance the development of skills such as reasoning, solving, and lifelong learning. It is those skills that are needed to effectively address the issues this world is facing and to construct a viable future. By doing so, we enhance education and at the same time prepare our students for the future world with the help of generative AI.

### Fostering a Growth Mindset

Similarly in the chapter, “Generative AI Is Changing Personalized Learning to Help Us Build a Sustainable Future,” a growth mindset could be for students as if you were planting seeds of confidence and perseverance into the students. It is the principles such as Ti, which states that one can try and become better as long as he or she will work hard. In particular, the cussedness in personalized learning supported by A. I is important. Mainly students realize how can they turn difficulties into opportunities, failures into lessons, efforts into progress.

Being built AI, the learning platforms respect every student and his or her learning rate and style. Stocks’ platforms provide feedback and support for clients that are positive and oriented toward progress. Thus, by cultivating this outlook through AI-based guidance, when students are learning subjects; they are also learning the concepts of how to solve problems, how to learn from failures, and how to develop skills that will enable them to build a more sustainable world in perpetuity.

## 3. CHALLENGES AND CONSIDERATIONS IN IMPLEMENTING GENERATIVE AI FOR PERSONALIZED LEARNING

While utilizing AI in education has clearly many advantages, it's also important to be aware of its drawbacks. Let's look into some specific challenges that generative AI applications in the education sector face:

*Figure 1. concerns and challenges*

## Quality Control

Making sure that the material provided to pupils is trustworthy and accurate might be difficult. You see, youngsters could be given incorrect information by AI systems due to their biases and weaknesses. It is also essential that we put robust controls in place to ensure the accuracy of data produced by artificial intelligence. We must ensure that it is in line with the objectives and information that children ought to be gaining.To ensure that everyone is treated equally, we should actively seek to eliminate any biases that could be present in the AI's thinking rather than just calling attention to errors after they occur. Teachers may maximize the benefits of AI technology while guaranteeing that students obtain a real education by routinely observing and making the required modifications.

## Originality of content

Students may find AI-generated content dull since it is frequently so formulaic and without individuality. To catch their attention and motivate them to keep exploring, they need an interesting object. If the material appears to have been generated mechanically, though,(P. Black & D. Wiliam,2009) it loses some of its attraction. It's quite possible that this dry material may hinder rather than aid in learning. In order to fully realize the potential of artificial intelligence in education, we need to make sure that it pushes boundaries, encourages students to think critically, and considers all of their preferred learning styles and ways to engage with the material.

## Ethical Concerns

With generative AI newly starting to rewrite the book on the concept of personalized learning, here are the ethical considerations that come with it. The privacy issue is probably the most important concern that can be raised regarding social media. Most AI systems are quite dependent on some personal details leading to compromise by hackers and various entities. The information has to be secured and there are severe privacy guidelines that must be obeyed in order to maintain trust of all the users.

Other problem is that AI algorithms are also biased. Since the AI algorithms used are trained from datasets which already contain bias, it is possible for the AI to perpetrate or even escalate such marginalization leading to unfairness in the education system. In response to this, there should be a blend of diverse and inclusion data as well as rigorous examinations in order to detect and eliminate bias within the AI systems.

Transparency in AI decision making is also a factor People must be able to inquire and know the thought pattern of the artificial intelligence systems in its decision making process. To minimize deception and boost confidence, everyone, from students to professors, must grasp how AI creates ideas. However, there is fear that an overreliance on AI would diminish the level of intelligence and decision-making in education.

Finally, one cannot ignore the digital divide as a factor that needs to be addressed in the dissemination of information in the current society. Any development employing the help of artificial intelligence should be made available to all with no consideration to their status in the society to prevent the widening gap in education. These ethical issues must be addressed in order to formulate an optimum approach for applying generative AI and creating a brand-new future for personalized learning that is efficient and fair for all consumers (İ. Çelik et al., 2022,pp. 616-630).

## Teacher Adaptation

The generative AI in KLT is advancing at the speed of light, thus opening opportunities that also pose difficulties to the instructors. Teacher adaptation is highly necessary in order to make changes for improving the learning-teaching process with the help of these technologies and implementing the development of a sustainable future. That is why, teachers can bring generative AI into their classroom to improve the quality of the approaches they use, providing students with the unique educational experience designed for every learner.

With generative AI in classrooms, teachers are able to design and deliver learning content based on students 'ability, individual learning ability or rate. It means students are able to get as much challenge as that can handle but also the level of support they need making it a more effective learning process. Further, the application of AI helps educators to monitor progress of students and predict the success rate through a set of intelligent algorithms to offer necessary feedback and correction at the appropriate time.

However, the use of generative AI in education requires the change of the traditional paradigms with regard to educating practices. Teachers need to learn how better to work with these various AI tools and circumnavigate them effectively. Another relevant aspect is the consistent learning to be in tune with innovations that must be practiced by any professional. There are certain ethical issues that must be appreciated by the educators as they incorporate the use of AI in their teaching and client interactions including privacy and fairness of the system in delivering services to every learner.

The former shows how stakeholder coalition in AI based educational context is important and the latter identifies the major policy and technology drivers in the use of AI in educational systems. One of the most critical stakeholders is the teachers since they are at the forefront of implementing these collaborations, and hence, they carry out formative assessments of AI systems. Only their flexibility and desire to change will define the level of AI integration in the learning process.

Thus, it can be stated that the adaptation of teachers is the primary factor in achieving optimal outcomes, given the use of generative artificial intelligence in the learning process. Incorporation of these technologies and constant improvement of practices allows educators to develop solutions for growing increase of personal, time, and cost-efficient learning experiences that would positively impact any student's education for a better future.

## Material originality

Vis Content Originality is the foundation of the generative AI adaptation that standards the personalized learning and Reforming of the educational material. Thanks to the development of the AI technologies in the modern society, people have a possibility to develop individualized learning material that can inspire each learner. This paradigm shift is truly revolutionizing education to become incredibly interactive and efficient than it has ever been (İ. Çelik et al., 2022,pp. 616-630).

Since generative AI can create materials unique and different from one another educators can develop lessons that are not only personalized but unique to each learner. This originality is necessary for setting a tone and seducing the audience into engaging in evaluative thought processes. Through the new paradigms and approaches of students, the essence of learning will be equivalent to understanding or appreciation of certain topics.

However, the opportuneness of the AI originating content in regard to creating the sustainable future is most important. Considering that the global context of the discipline is based upon the rapport with the emerging issue in today's society, utilizing these materials allows students to remain up to date. This makes the educational system dynamic and updated to face the rapidly growing growth of the advancements to enhance students with information in promoting sustainable practices and solutions.

Yet, to ensure that generated content does not infringe on the rights of creators or violate the law, precise supervision must be applied. To maintain work with little bias and errors in the content, it is critical to employ educators' input and AI systems in partnership. Therefore, educators are to supervise students and correct them constantly in order to achieve the necessary level of uniqueness and quality of AI calluses.

Therefore, one can conclude that the use of AI and methods of personalized learning depends on the availability of original materials necessary to create effective, relevant, and prospective learning environments. It enhances the learning process and prepares students for course to be responsible members in society especially in the area of environmental conservation.

## Technical Infrastructure

For Generative AI to be introduced into personalized learning as well as contribute to the creation of a lasting society, there is a need to establish a solid technical platform. This encompasses powerful computers to feed data, cloud services and storage hence requires a lot of space. Supercomputers as well as graphic processing units take much responsibility for complicated AI activities and the massive data from the individualized training instruments. To address the many requirements of learners all over the world, elasticity of cloud solutions is called for (V. J. Shute et al.,2013,pp.423-430).

Stable and fast connections as well as secure networks enable the students and faculties to use AI tools seamlessly. Maintaining this information properly is quite sensitive with the aim of presenting the privacy of the learner and meet legal requirements. That is why reliable mechanisms of information protection against threats are also important to maintain society's trust.

The sub-processes for updating and putting out the models also ensure learners get to use up to date AI models, more immediately. It also requires the cooperation of the schools, technology companies, and the government to provide a framework that sustains the concept's agility in the future. To solve the problems and provide methodologies for personalized knowledge acquisition as well as contribute to a sustainable future, we must apply technological advancements and keep a solid technical foundation of Generative AI.

## Training and Support

In order to properly integrate generative AI technology into the classroom, educators require extensive training as well as continuous support. This implies that the establishments will have to spend money and effort creating excellent training programs. After completing these courses, teachers must have the abilities and know-how required to incorporate AI technology into their lesson plans with ease. In addition, it is important to establish support networks to assist educators in resolving any problems that may arise during the implementation stage. Teachers need to be confident in their abilities to use these state-of-the-art resources if they want to enhance the educational experiences of their pupils.

**Financial considerations:** Using generative AI technologies could be costly. These expenses pay for ongoing maintenance and support fees in addition to the initial hardware, software, and training expenditure. Due to financial constraints, not all educational institutions might have access to the materials.

However, A comprehensive strategy involving legislators, technologists, educators, and other stakeholders is needed to get beyond these obstacles. By proactively addressing these difficulties, we can leverage the promise of generative AI to raise learning outcomes and transform the educational system (Z. Bahroun et al., 2023).

**Balancing Human Guidance with AI Assistance:** Consider yourself a teacher in a classroom that is changing quickly. Artificial intelligence (AI), despite its promise, is not a substitute for human intellect; rather, it is meant to support it. Using AI, educators can provide each student personalized education tailored to their specific learning styles. This frees up more time for you to focus on the important things, like building trusting relationships with your students and igniting a passion for learning.

One way to think of AI is as a super assistant. In addition to making assessments and ranking them, it could also suggest learning materials. But it can't make someone feel better on a bad day or make a complex concept easier to understand for everyone. Your creativity, kindness, and ability to hold students' attention.

Finding the right balance will be crucial for education in the future. Even if AI can do laborious tasks, teachers will always remain the focus of attention in the classroom. Together, they can create a classroom where every student can achieve. The key is that teachers should always be learning new things! Parents may choose what's best for their children if they are aware of the potential biases in AI. In this way, rather than taking the role of educators, AI begins to assist them.

## 4. FUTURE IMPLICATIONS AND POTENTIAL APPLICATIONS OF GENERATIVE AI IN PERSONALIZED EDUCATION

The application of generative AI in education is an indication of the evolving nature of teaching and learning, not just a fad. The possible uses of generative AI technology in higher education are discussed in this part, with a focus on the role of CIOs and the status of research and development at the moment.

*Figure 2. road to AI success*

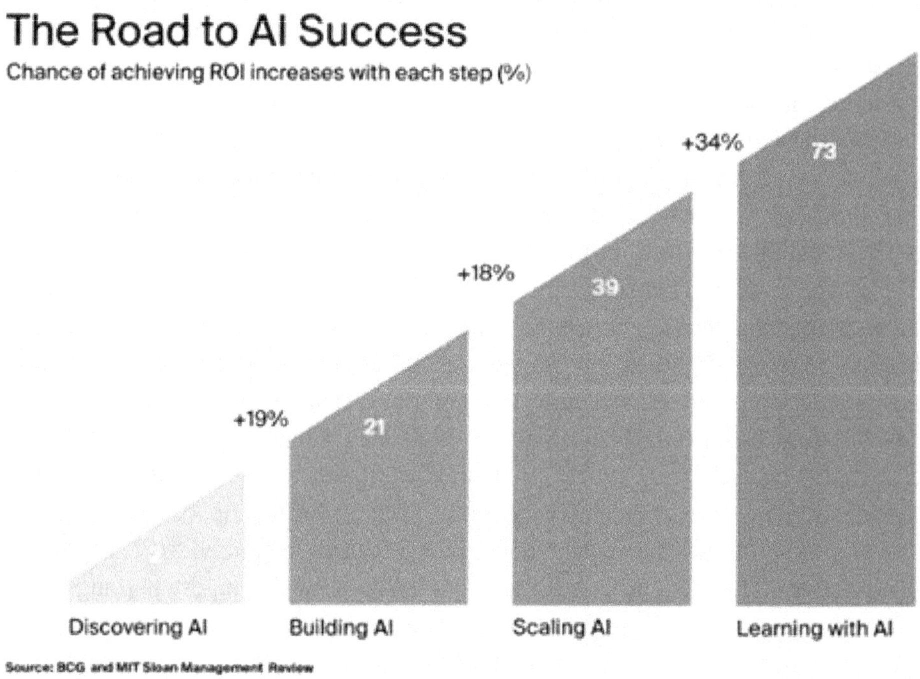

## Future-Ready

The Significance of Higher Education for Chief Information Officers (CIOs) Chief information officers (CIOs) are essential to the planning and preparation of the integration of generative AI into higher education since they are the guardians of technical innovation in their organizations. Their duties include helping educators and students foster a culture of lifelong learning and adaptability, as well as comprehending the potential and constraints of generative AI and guaranteeing its ethical application. In order to facilitate the smooth incorporation of generative AI technologies, they must also offer strong infrastructure frameworks.Career and Educational Advancement: Teachers need to continue their professional growth if they are to fully benefit from the potential that generative AI offers. This will facilitate acquisition (W. M. Lim et al.,2023).

## Continual Study and Improvement

We can learn a lot from the domains of generative artificial intelligence and education. To find new uses, enhance the tools already in place, and overcome the difficulties generative AI encounters, more research and development are required. This entails improving the approachability of user interfaces, lessening the biases present in AI systems, and better tailoring instructional materials.Collaborating Across Disciplines: Researchers in artificial intelligence, educators, psychologists, and other relevant stakeholders can collaborate across disciplines when generative AI and education interact. These collaborations may result in the creation of more advantageous and morally sound generative AI educational materials.

## Review and Assessment

Long-term integration of generative AI into education necessitates ongoing assessment of the technology's effects. This entails determining how much generative AI technologies improve learning outcomes, analyzing how they affect student-teacher interactions, and appreciating the long-term effects they have on the educational ecosystem.

There will probably be more creative applications and a change in the role of teachers, therefore the use of generative AI in education is far from over. If education is to effectively traverse the complex environment of generative AI and steer toward a future that augments the essence of teaching and learning, it must actively address the difficulties, grab the opportunities, and cultivate a culture of constant learning and collaboration.

## AI-generated Learning Resources and Materials

Knowledge from artificial intelligence (AI) works similarly to instruction from a human teacher who knows you well. These days, educational materials may be tailored to each student's unique learning preferences by utilizing sophisticated algorithms that evaluate vast quantities of data.

Imagine not feeling rushed or restricted while you explore subjects at your own pace. Because artificial intelligence (AI) adjusts content to your particular location, you are never overloaded with information or bored.

The interesting thing is that AI may consider your preferences. Imagine being able to communicate in a language that included all of your favorite topics, like sports or music. With the app, you seem to be able to maintain your motivation and interest.

It also extends beyond simple direction. AI is capable of acting as your virtual teacher, offering you individualized direction and training as you go. Engaging in interactive quizzes and simulations that adapt to your performance makes learning enjoyable.

Not just any kid will be able to get this customized instruction. For people who require a little additional assistance or have learning difficulties, it's revolutionary ("Using APA," 2021).

To put it briefly, AI-enabled learning allows you to receive just what you require at precisely the correct moment. It's like having a teacher who is more familiar with you than you are. Schools might be able to develop much more enjoyable learning environments for all students with the use of artificial intelligence.

## 5. CONCLUSION: HARNESSING THE WINDS OF CHANGE

This blog's investigation into the possibilities and challenges that arise in the field of generative AI and education warrants careful consideration. Here is a summary of the debate's major themes and some commentary on the idea that generative AI could pave the way for a radical overhaul of the educational system.

## Historical Development

Personalization has its base and starting point, which is based in the on learning and dates back as early as the Licensed Tutoring of ancient civilizations. It was in the 15th century that the advent of the printing press took place, this made education resources more available and made the world ready for personal teaching and learning.

The advancements in the 20th century were computer assisted instruction carrying with it new brighter prospects by initiating adaptive learning system, a system that can deliver content as per the capability of a student.

Currently, generative AI has turned the concept of learning into a revolution through personalization. Previous AI systems were simplistic and did not take into account the learner's identity; however, current machine learning, especially neural networks, allow the development of AI models that can generate highly individualized educational material. These models help in the evaluation of large amounts of data to imply each learner's preference, rhythm, and style and then provide them with a personalized educative experience which is quite impossible with normal models (T. T. Eapen et al., 2023).

Besides, this technological advancement not only improves the efficiency and declarative of the personalized learning but also better for the future environment. Thus, generative AI contributes to the improvement of educational models and making the learning process as effective and appealing as possible to shape a global-savvy, flexible-minded populace for the cause of sustainability.

## Application Spectrum

Moving ahead to the chapter entitled: Generative AI Is Changing Personalized Learning to Help build a Sustainable Future", the "Application Spectrum" presents a broad view of rather practical generative ways of AI in influencing personalized learning.

Think about new technologies that would help a child learn at their own pace and these developments could make learning easier and more pleasant. Imagine chatbots, smart devices and various software products that will generate individual lessons and materials including videos, games, individual tutoring based on the full understanding of the user's learning preferences.

Generative impels educators with intelligent feedback analyses that give insights of the students' performances in real time. This makes it possible for teachers to work out their strategies with improved efficiency and support students at proper occasions (H. Abunaseer et al., 2023).

By moving through the Application Spectrum of generative AI in learning, they not only enhance performance in education but also endorse sustainable utilization of educational solutions which guarantee compliance with the needs of learners all over the world.

## Community Engagement

In the chapter titled: "Generative AI Is Changing Personalized Learning to Help Us Build a Sustainable Future" the role of community engagement for sustainable development is emphasized. Here, it is possible to recognize generative AI as an instrument that makes people learn better in order to create their surroundings more actively. This participation enhances students' camaraderie, inter individuals, as well as inter-group inventiveness, all of which are vital for addressing problems with locales as well as on the international level sustainably. The results demonstrate that AI facilitates structured interactions and generates useful information that can help encourage people to engage in civil matters and find the solutions pertinent to their case. Finally, through effective collaboration with the communities, with help of Generative AI in Education, both the education process and the communities become more valuable and we, as people become more united.

## REFERENCES


Abunaseer, H. (2023). The use of generative AI in education: Applications, and impact. Technology and the Curriculum: Summer 2023.

Akgün, S., & Greenhow, C. (2021, September). Artificial intelligence in education: Addressing ethical challenges in K-12 settings. *AI and Ethics*, *2*(3), 431–440. DOI: 10.1007/s43681-021-00096-7 PMID: 34790956


Akgün, S., & Greenhow, C. (2021, September). Artificial intelligence in education: Addressing ethical challenges in K-12 settings. *AI and Ethics*, *2*(3), 431–440. DOI: 10.1007/s43681-021-00096-7 PMID: 34790956


Bahroun, Z., Anane, C., Ahmed, V., & Zacca, A. (2023, August). Transforming Education: A Comprehensive Review of Generative Artificial Intelligence in Educational Settings through Bibliometric and Content Analysis. *Sustainability (Basel)*, *15*(17), 12983. DOI: 10.3390/su151712983

Black, P., & Wiliam, D. (2009, January). Developing the theory of formative assessment. *Educational Assessment, Evaluation and Accountability*, *21*(1), 5–31. DOI: 10.1007/s11092-008-9068-5

"CC BY-SA 3.0 IGO Deed | Attribution-ShareAlike 3.0 Intergovernmental Organization | Creative Commons." https://creativecommons.org/licenses/by-sa/3.0/igo/

Çelik, İ., Dindar, M., Muukkonen, H., & Järvelä, S. (2022, March). The Promises and Challenges of Artificial Intelligence for Teachers: A Systematic Review of Research. *TechTrends*, *66*(4), 616–630. DOI: 10.1007/s11528-022-00715-y

Chui, M., Hazan, E., Roberts, R., Singla, A., & Smaje, K. (2023). The economic potential of generative AI.

Duong, M. T., Rauschecker, A. M., Rudie, J. D., Chen, P.-H., Cook, T. S., Bryan, R. N., & Mohan, S. (2019, November). "Artificial intelligence for precision education in radiology," *the British Journal of Radiology. The British Journal of Radiology*, *92*(1103), 20190389. DOI: 10.1259/bjr.20190389 PMID: 31322909

Eapen, T., Finkenstadt, D. J., Folk, J., & Venkataswamy, L. (2023). How generative AI can augment human creativity. *Harvard Business Review*, *101*(4).

Gardner, J., O'Leary, M., & Li, Y. (2021, July). Artificial intelligence in educational assessment: 'Breakthrough? Or buncombe and ballyhoo?'. *Journal of Computer Assisted Learning*, *37*(5), 1207–1216. DOI: 10.1111/jcal.12577

Lee, A. V. Y., Tan, S. C., & Teo, C. L. (2023, November). Designs and practices using generative AI for sustainable student discourse and knowledge creation. *Smart Learning Environments, 10*(1), 59. Advance online publication. DOI: 10.1186/s40561-023-00279-1

Lee, Y., Tan, S. C., & Teo, C. L. (2023, November). Seng Chee Tan, and Chew Lee Teo, "Designs and practices using generative AI for sustainable student discourse and knowledge creation,". *Smart Learning Environments, 10*(1), 59. Advance online publication. DOI: 10.1186/s40561-023-00279-1

Lim, W. M., Gunasekara, A., Pallant, J. L., Pallant, J., & Pechenkina, E. (2023, July). Generative AI and the future of education: Ragnarök or reformation? A paradoxical perspective from management educators. *International Journal of Management Education, 21*(2), 100790. DOI: 10.1016/j.ijme.2023.100790

M. Cardona, R. J. Rodríguez, K. Ishmael, and U.S. Department of Education, "Artificial intelligence and the future of teaching and learning," 2023. [Online]. Available: https://tech.ed.gov/files/2023/05/ai-future-of-teaching-and-learning-report.pdf

Pavlik, J. V. (2023, January). Collaborating with ChatGPT: Considering the implications of Generative Artificial intelligence for journalism and media education. *Journalism & Mass Communication Educator, 78*(1), 84–93. DOI: 10.1177/10776958221149577

Pesovski, I., Santos, R., Henriques, R., & Trajkovik, V. (2024). Generative AI for Customizable Learning Experiences. *Sustainability (Basel), 16*(7), 3034. DOI: 10.3390/su16073034

Pesovski, I., Santos, R., Henriques, R., & Trajkovik, V. (2024, April). Generative AI for customizable learning experiences. *Sustainability (Basel), 16*(7), 3034. DOI: 10.3390/su16073034

Pesovski, I., Santos, R., Henriques, R., & Trajkovik, V. (2024, April). Generative AI for customizable learning experiences. *Sustainability (Basel), 16*(7), 3034. DOI: 10.3390/su16073034

Shute, V. J., Ventura, M., & Kim, Y. J. (2013, November). "Assessment and learning of qualitative physics in Newton's playground," *the Journal of Educational Research. The Journal of Educational Research, 106*(6), 423–430. DOI: 10.1080/00220671.2013.832970

Zhen, H., & Yahaya, W. A. J. W. (2024). Use of Generative AI Tools to Facilitate Personalized Learning in the Flipped Classroom. In Transforming Education With Generative AI: Prompt Engineering and Synthetic Content Creation (pp. 327-349). IGI Global Scientific Publishing.

# Chapter 8
# Immersive Educational Pedagogy Development:
## Cloud-Based Adaptive System for Higher Education

**Ajibola Olaosebikan Waliu**
https://orcid.org/0009-0002-6857-3035
*Southampton Solent University, UK*

**Ugochukwu Okwudili Matthew**
https://orcid.org/0000-0003-0828-9710
*Hussaini Adamu Federal Polytechnic, Nigeria*

**Victoria Enemona Oseni**
https://orcid.org/0009-0007-3917-4840
*University of Salford, UK*

**David Oyewumi Oyekunle**
https://orcid.org/0009-0007-3994-1712
*University of Salford, UK*

**Matthew Abiola Oladipupo**
https://orcid.org/0000-0002-5984-6217
*University of Salford, UK*

**Temitope Samson Adekunle**
https://orcid.org/0000-0003-4828-6039
*Colorado State University, USA*

**Ejiofor Stanley Chukwuebuka**
https://orcid.org/0009-0005-2688-4910
*Arkansas Tech University, USA*

**Alain Claude Bah Esseme**
https://orcid.org/0009-0005-8086-4566
*Nexus Cloud Technologies, UK*

## ABSTRACT

*This work examines how immersive technologies, virtual reality (VR) and augmented reality (AR) in particular, can be used to improve educational outcomes by merging artificial intelligence (AI) in educational platform manageability. Immersive educational technology and AI working together to create a unique learning environment offers a rare chance to improve students' motivation, recall, and understanding of difficult material. In-depth investigation of the state of knowledge on VR and AR's efficacy in learning environments is conducted in this research, with a focus on*

DOI: 10.4018/979-8-3693-5623-4.ch008

*how these technologies are used in various pedagogical contexts. In this work, the authors provide a clinical simulation laboratory that is affordable for use by nursing students, practicing healthcare professionals, and midwives. The laboratory is designed to guarantee continuous learning and professional effectiveness by utilizing the technological pedagogical content knowledge (TPCK) model, which is centrally discussed and implemented in nursing education.*

## INTRODUCTION

The proliferation of information communication technologies (ICTs) hardware devices and software platforms have led to the growth of online learning, blended learning, mobile learning, electronic learning (e-learning) system and ubiquitous learning that have helped the modern education system to thrive(Ugochukwu Okwudili Matthew et al., 2022). These technologies have made it easier to share knowledge, promote continuous learning, facilitate distance learning, share study materials, and enable proper recording and video conferencing across Internet of Things (IoT) digital platforms(Ebong et al., 2024). It can be assumed that the application of a wide variety of the newest technology in education is conceivable in the identified environment since interactive education pedagogy has always been supported by the societal needs(Matthew, Kazaure, & Okafor, 2021). Teachers can create lesson plans using computer-based audio, video, and graphic aids by using immersive technologies, which are actively employed in education to enhance quality and learning outcomes. A number of researches on the efficacy of e-learning education have concluded that it can lead to positive results as long as it is supported by all-encompassing strategies that included appropriate policy, infrastructure enablement, professional development stream programme on adjusted curriculum accustomed for blended learners(Matthew, Kazaure, Kazaure, Onyedibe, & Okafor, 2022). Blended learning, often referred to as hybrid learning, web-enhanced learning, technology-mediated instruction, or mixed-mode instruction, is a teaching methodology that integrates virtual learning resources and online engagement with traditional classroom techniques(Matthew & Kazaure, 2020).

The twenty first century educational business will require big data science, cloud computing, artificial intelligence (AI), the IoT and integration of generative AI technologies into the classroom for students to understand how to use them safely, interactively and productively(Bucea-Manea- oniş et al., 2022). These technologies will reshape worldwide educational business while exemplifying today's society extreme automation and enterprise productivity. The manageability issues in e-learning environments will focus on what needs to be done to improve the return on investment in educational learning by enabling generative artificial intelligence(OpenAI) like ChatGPT to produce writing that resembles that of a human depending on the context using natural language processing(Matthew, Bakare, Ebong, Ndukwu, & Nwanakwaugwu, 2023). Students can receive individualized instruction and feedback through ChatGPT, which is based on each student's unique learning requirements and development through text generation enablement, virtual assistants, chatbots, and language translation offered by the natural language processing applications(Matthew et al., 2024). Integrating context-awareness and adaptive systems into the technologically advanced learning system that promotes student involvement with the course materials through immersive educational pedagogy like virtual reality, augmented reality simulation and mixed reality will be necessary for students constructive engagement(David Oyekunle, Ugochukwu, Rosa, Rodriguez, & Fatai, 2024),(D Oyekunle, Matthew, Waliu, & Fatai, 2024).

Education is an essential human entitlement, a driving force behind personal development, and one of the best ways to end poverty and promote equality in global health, peace, and stability in the modern society(Supriya et al., 2024). It is the most important factor in ensuring equity and inclusion that consistently yield substantial returns on human capital investments. The only way for girls and women to achieve gender equality and reap the many benefits of better maternal health and lower infant mortality rates is via education(Cheong, 2017). Gender equality in education means that all individuals, regardless of gender, can develop their skills and talents in an atmosphere where they are treated equally and have equal access to educational resources. This entails doing away with prejudice and stereotypes in the classroom and encouraging men and women to pursue education in all subject areas, including science, technology, the humanities, and the arts. Promoting gender equality concerns throughout all curriculum subjects and educational levels is UNESCO's central tenet for advancing gender equality through education(Wu, 2024). When human intellectual development are prioritized at the center of the educational system, people gain from it in terms of employment, income, health, and poverty reduction(Gumel, Abdullahi, & O, 2019). The majority of linked research contend that compared to women without formal education, women with formal education had higher advantages of using effective family planning techniques, delaying marriage and childbirth and having fewer healthier children. On the contrary, the offspring of educated women are better fed and have greater survival rates because these women are more likely to seek medical attention and are knowledgeable about best practices for themselves and their children(Menekaya, 2024). This is achieved by helping students find roles and talents that best fit their unique needs. The twenty-first educational learning theories underwent changes, progressing from instructivism, constructivism to social constructivism(Stapleford & Lee, 2024). Theories of learning are conceptual frameworks that explain how individuals take in, process and remember knowledge. Education systems integrate socio-constructivist theory to facilitate constructive processes of knowledge acquisition, as idea maps are utilized to help organize and synthesize newly learnt curriculum content.

In general, socio-constructivism gained popularity as a result of the ways in which education was evolving and the ways in which technology like virtual reality and augmented reality was used in the classroom to promote ICTs digital supremacy(Silva, Mendes, & Gomes, 2020). As a result of technological advancements, new paradigms in education and learning were produced, offering innovative pedagogical approaches that enables students to meet learning objectives through the adoption of synthetic settings and adaptive learning systems(Matthew, Kazaure, & Haruna, 2020). This virtually enabled ICTs environment improved students' comprehension by offering a level of realism not possible with a conventional two-dimensional interfaces, resulting in an interactive learning environment rich in senses with regards to pedagogical experiences. The modern immersive educational technology must be integrated with ICTs in order for government agencies and school administrators to carry out their duties in an efficient and successful manner(Hamraz & Hamidi, 2024). A pedagogical strategy known as immersive education uses immersive technologies to improve learning, including 360-degree video, augmented reality, virtual reality, and mixed reality(Chen, Xie, & Li, 2022). A system that makes use of cutting-edge ICT and information are combined to establish an electronic administration, or e-administration that promote educational supervision. E-administration embodies both technical improvements that makes it easier to deliver services and disseminate information to citizens (Sarai, Zockun, & Cabral, 2023). This paradigm change in favor of e-administration accelerates citizen educational service delivery while simultaneously improving organizational performances. The integration of cutting-edge technologies into administrative systems is needed in order to fully implement the e-administration framework for flexible education that addresses physical space, grouping of students for instruction and managing time of teaching within the learning environments(Cioca, Ivascu, Filip, & Doina, 2024).

*Figure 1. ICT Supported Educational Administration*

*(Hamraz & Hamidi, 2024).*

In health education for instance, nursing education frequently uses computer simulation-based learning, which includes virtual reality (VR) and augmented reality(AR) techniques that have become much more popular in the recent years to enhance the clinical study curriculum(Hung et al., 2021). With a focus on clinical practice, a critical component of healthcare disciplines, nursing education has incorporated theoretical and practical components to support the knowledge abilities, qualities and values that nursing students must acquire(Stenseth et al., 2022). Psychomotor cognitive and affective domains of learning are some of these components. Clinical psychomotor skills are acquired during nursing school and are essential to becoming a nurse and practicing safe nursing(Hernon, McSharry, MacLaren, & Carr, 2023). It could be difficult for nurse educators to find relevant clinical learning opportunities and procedural nursing skills for undergraduate nursing students without a computer based simulation. In order to effectively apply their knowledge to the practice of clinical medicine, students should have access to well-equipped laboratory sites where they can engage with patient care prior to working with real patients. These educational sites should also include game-based virtual reality and interactive learning strategies that help students strengthen their digital skills(Jibril et al., 2022). A safe and active learning digital environment, appropriate feedback and the opportunity for students to experience real-life scenarios without taking any risks are all provided by simulation, one of the interactive learning methodologies used in nursing education. A growing number of nations, including Australia, are depending more and more on educational institutions to offer realistic simulated learning experiences that sufficiently prepare nursing students for professional practice due to the fluctuating hours and competitive nature of obtaining quality industry work placements(Barlow et al., 2024). In spite of what you would think, there is growing pressure from the healthcare industry for recently graduated nurses to be work ready, which means they have to be able to use the skills they learned on their own through clinical simulations and practice within the dynamic healthcare environments in order to provide treatment(David Oyekunle et al., 2024).

The abilities required of nursing students to think about their future careers and get past challenges brought on by their work commitments should be instilled in them from their undergraduate courses(Squire, Gonzalez, & Shayan, 2024). The definition of VR as an immersive three-dimensional computer-generated environment is given by the healthcare simulation dictionary (com, 2021), empowering global medical laboratories into inventions of pedagogical and didactic models for educational and clinical training(Wilcox et al., 2018). In order to provide an affordable, portable, and realistic simulation that meets the wide range of user and technological preferences, maxSIMhealth leverages disruptive technologies (such as three dimensional (3D) printing, gaming, and new technologies like extended reality) as well as creative solutions(com, 2021),(Clarke, 2022). With the goal of producing future generations of academics with strong multidisciplinary competences to work together in unfamiliar settings and communicate professionally for successful medical-tech problem solving, maxSIMhealth's efforts will revolutionize the existing state of health professional education(Brooks, 2021). In order to increase proficiency and lower complications, healthcare trainees practice real-world skills on simulators before trying them on actual patients. Because, it is extremely expensive and frequently impractical to outfit large cohorts of learners with simulators, COVID-19 forced in-person learning to move online, which has prioritized clinical online-based simulation as essential pedagogic component in the nursing education(Tabbakhian Khaziran, 2021). VR simulation and 3D printing made it possible to produce precise, reasonably priced simulators that are easily tailored to the requirements of students educational engagement(Torrey, Woodruff, Matthew, & Jeromie, 2021).

The virtual reality simulation (VRS) provides an opportunity for students to engage in critical thinking, decision-making, performance optimization, efficient psychomotor control and communication, while assuming a vital role in an occupational setting (Liu et al., 2023). In addition to the unique information retention and skill acquisition that this analysis has highlighted, a systematic study has investigated the efficacy of VRS as a learning strategy in the development of clinical nursing skills in nursing and midwifery education(Goh, Ma, & Rizzo, 2024). Currently, the two main kinds of virtual worlds used in nursing education are desktop virtual simulation and immersive virtual reality simulation(Shorey & Ng, 2021). This research work will look at the outcomes of employing these two types of virtual worlds as teaching tools for nursing students and registered nurses. Virtual reality offers contactless, risk-free educational interaction(Cant, Ryan, & Kardong-Edgren, 2022). Examining existing researches on educational VR nursing simulations and evaluating techniques from both a didactic and technical perspective are the goals of this study. As new methods of teaching and learning have emerged in the educational field as a result of the paradigm change brought about by immersive technology(Ugochukwu Okwudili Matthew et al., 2022), intelligent technologies have led to the development of creative teaching strategies for students as well as opportunities to customize instruction in the classroom to meet the individual needs of every student. The rest of the paper is organized into background of the study, theoretical framework, the research design and methodology, the technological pedagogical content knowledge (TPCK) model of the system implementation, the design implementation and paper conclusion.

## RESEARCH BACKGROUND

The literature evaluation for the current study used a number of methods to find that VRS was found to boost skill performance and reinforce knowledge acquisition in most of the investigations(Al-Mugheed et al., 2022). VRS allows knowledge to be obtained through learning experiences, which is an important way for nursing students to learn while giving feedback on their actions. In order to develop knowledge in adaptive cloud-based learning systems in the contemporary high-tech educational environment and to promote access to them as tools for higher education pedagogical adoption, a variety of cognitive situations were investigated. Furthermore, it has been demonstrated that VRS enhances knowledge retention by incorporating virtual patients into case-based learning techniques and recreating actual settings into plausible scenarios at any time. VRS facilitates the transfer of knowledge by applying theoretical knowledge through a range of educational programs, also utilized in game-based virtual reality phone applications(Asad, Naz, Churi, & Tahanzadeh, 2021). The implementation of VRS in a range of learning methodologies, such as case studies, particular situations in safety education, pediatric courses, disaster training, and psychomotor skills showed improvements in the performance of a number of skills, was evidenced by the study's findings. VRS thus shown improved decision-making and the dissemination of safer behaviors that support experience learning.

Within the realm of computer-based environments, virtual reality encompasses a variety of settings that allow users to explore microworlds created by software and hardware technologies that are close to the subject matter(Tiwari, Agarwal, & Husain, 2023). In other hand, VR is a class of computer-controlled multimodal communication technologies that allows for more natural interactions with data and makes innovative, educationally engaging use of the senses(Souza, Manzolli, Campos, & Rennó-Costa, 2022). In essence, VR is a way to recreate or simulate an environment and give the user the sense that they are physically there, in control, and actively interacting with it on a personal level(Marougkas, Troussas, Krouska, & Sgouropoulou, 2024). With the use of 3D near-eye displays and location tracking, VR is a simulated technology experience that is utilized in business, education, and entertainment to give viewers an immersive impression of a virtual environment. The experience of being fully immersed in a digital environment that is conveyed to the senses through perceptual and psychological means is evoked by virtual reality(Kouijzer, Kip, Kelders, & Bouman, 2024). By using a virtual reality system, a user can escape the real world and enter a virtual environment where artificial intelligence is used to produce the sights, sounds, smells, and other senses instead of natural objects. Using VR approaches to create educational applications opens up new ways to teach subjects and makes understanding the technology and processes much more important. VR is categorized into three main forms that facilitate interactive pedagogical learning: (a) Immersive (Fully Immersive) VR systems; (b) Semi-Immersive VR systems; and (c) Non-Immersive VR systems. The least advanced VR technology implementation is found in non-immersive VR systems which entails putting VR software on a desktop personal computer(Onyesolu, Nwasor, Ositanwosu, & Iwegbuna, 2013).

The virtual environment can be accessed by desktop system users through an interactive clinical material library and a traditional high-resolution monitor. Users can engage with the virtual world using standard interfaces such as a keyboard, mouse, and joystick. Semi-immersive virtual reality systems consist of a relatively powerful graphics processing unit that can be connected to several television projection systems, a large screen monitor, or a large screen projection system. A wide field of view is offered by these systems, which can produce stereographic images with the use of shutter glasses, giving users an increased sense of presence or immersion. The most direct way to explore virtual surroundings is via an immersive (fully immersive) VR system(Wei & Yuan, 2023). Utilizing VR interaction, the technology combines a clinical soft tissue simulation visualization for engagement on cloud based adaptive e-learning platform. According to (Lougiakis, González, Ganias, Katifori, & Roussou, 2024), the semi-immersive virtual reality system has been effectively deployed and evaluated on two distinct computer platforms: an adaptable system that leverages the IoT cloud computing infrastructure, and a mobile device system for students engagements. These two platforms were selected because of their cost scalability and authenticity, offering flexibility to measure event-based timings and evaluated update loop timings of several software components to estimate latency and compare performance.

*Figure 2. Combined VR Simulation Implementation, Figure1(a) Fully Immersive VR System, Figure2(b) Semi- Immersive VR System(Ullrich, Rausch, & Kuhlen, 2011),Figure 2(c) Desktop VR Model*

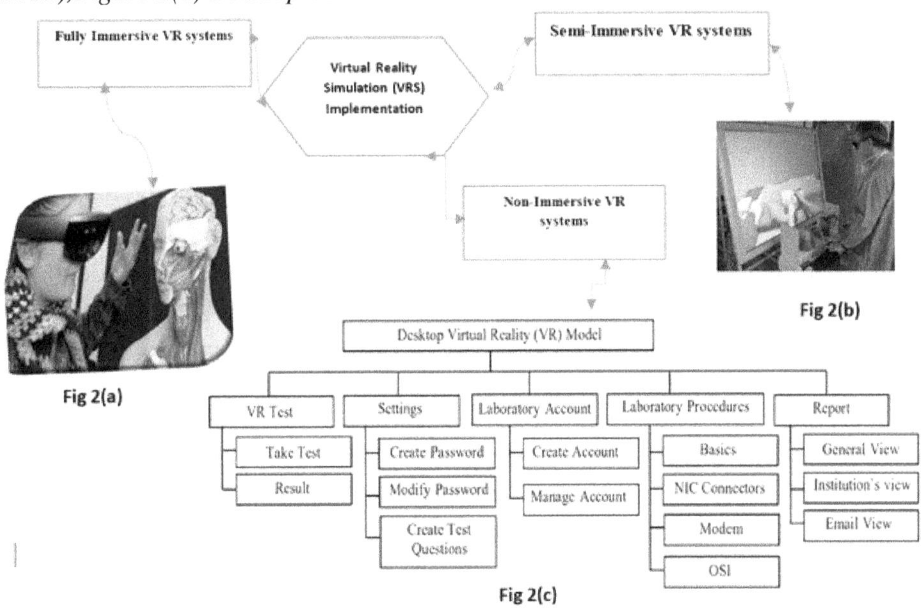


*(Onyesolu et al., 2013).*

## RESEARCH OBJECTIVE

The goal of this project is to create an adaptive e-learning system based on federated loops of information in cloud computing educational setting. Using cloud computing technologies, a tailored online learning environment was developed to fulfill the unique learning needs of clinical nursing students who need more learning sites for career and knowledge expansion. Finding out each student's individual preferences and structuring the course's learning activities around them was our key objective. We chose to utilize cloud computing technology since the adaptive system was created to handle the issues of tailored instruction and wide student access. Digital initiatives within the curriculum can consider the interactions between heterogeneous components and create interfaces for multiple purposes by employing a dynamic systems approach and game-like designs. Education uses simulators as an interactive teaching tool because they give students real-world experience without putting them in risk. Their sense of self-worth is boosted in addition to providing a safe and exciting learning environment, appropriate feedback, and content satisfaction. Individuals pursuing a bachelor's degree ought to have the abilities necessary to consider their future careers and overcome work-related obstacles. This paper successfully achieved the aforementioned goals.

## THEORETICAL FRAMEWORK

In education, immersive learning is a pedagogy that uses AI to enhance digital learning platforms and provide virtual or digital versions of real-world scenarios in a dynamic and engaging simulated environments for knowledge transfer(Dai & Ke, 2022). Synchronous learning stimulates lively debates and group problem-solving in addition to amplifying the effect of the course material. The importance of the course material therefore continues to be critical in asynchronous learning environments where they can work at their own pace. Students can use the adaptive learning system (ALS) to enhance their academic performance through customized synchronous and asynchronous self-study(Bolton & Emery, 2021). Through the integration of multimedia information and a range of learning opportunities, adaptive learning modifies the curriculum dynamically to meet the needs of each student(Matthew, 2019). Adaptive learning solutions are usually used to give different study groups access to a variety of information aggregations and varied learning habits(Sarshartehrani, Mohammadrezaei, Behravan, & Gracanin, 2024). An intelligent tutoring system can use technology-based personalization to address students' interests and tailor training to their background, experiences, and prior knowledge(Verma, Gupta, & Illinich, 2024), this is known as adaptive learning technologies, and they are becoming more and more common in educational settings at all level of digital interaction. An IoT-based distributed infrastructure for the distant sharing and use of different resources and services are provided by cloud computing systems for sharing of multimedia digital contents for educational engagement(Matthew et al., 2021). A big federated information system management is made possible by cloud computing services in education, which provide a way for the general public to participate in an Internet-based computing model(Onyebuchi, Matthew, Kazaure, Okafor, et al., 2022),(Ebong et al., 2024). These services offer a huge and dynamic resource pool with lots of virtual resources at their disposal. To increase the effectiveness of resource use, these virtual resources are dynamically distributed based on the cloud data warehouse workload for process synchronization(Onyebuchi et al., 2024).

After assigning a resource pool of computing jobs, the application system can then determine how much storage, processing power, and other services to be allocated based on the demands of the cloud workflow(Onyebuchi, Matthew, Kazaure, Nwanagwaugwu, et al., 2022). By combining information technology(IT) resources with a variety of centralized database repositories and IoT infrastructures, cloud computing is a technological advancement that expedites IT service operations to provide quick, safe and on-demand services(Onyebuchi et al., 2024). Cloud computing technology was used in the development of the cloud-based adaptive learning system to address several ALS-related educational requirements(Alam, 2021), such as the existence of a single point of information access, load balancing and the need for centralized access to resources. The software establishes the application priority as the application load grows. The re-allocation of resources to the virtual machines is determined by its priority evaluation, which is based on established resource allocation criteria. The two methods that are normally available are moving programs to a cloud server with higher resources and moving virtual machines to other applications on a cloud server that is inactive, which frees up additional resources on the local system. With the help of virtual integration server software, a virtual resource pool consisting of many virtual machines may be constructed and the system is built to be served both synchronously and asynchronously via an on-premise server(Weerasinghe & Perera, 2024). These virtual machines optimize resource utilization and resource allocation through policy-driven methods by pooling resources. The system leverages resource control capabilities that is provided by embedded software to maintain security. To enable dynamic resource allocation from the target aggregated resource pool, this program automatically uses a pre-allocation technique to control computing, networking, and storage resources in addition to additional specific client data and resources(Lee, Solat, Kim, & Poor, 2024).

Adoption of immersive AR, extensible reality (XR) and VR simulation environments will be necessary for the cloud IoT architecture for sustainable higher education e-learning in the healthcare industry(Hiran, Doshi, & Patel, 2024). This presents countless opportunities and is a highly intriguing and revolutionary technological advancement for teaching in the future. According to (Kayyali, 2024),VR and AR users can have immersive encounters using XR technology that take them to new virtual environment. Virtual worlds can be explored, virtual items can be interacted and digital content can be shown over real-world surroundings. Experiences become more effective and memorable when this degree of immersion is reached, which also increases constructive academic engagement due to generative imagination(Singh et al., 2024). When it comes to meaningful pedagogic interactive engagement, XR technology is revolutionizing the healthcare industry. Medical students can now practice difficult procedures in a secure setting, patients can receive immersive therapeutic treatments, and surgeons can conduct virtual surgery(Ryan et al., 2022). It will establish connections with interactive and collaborative resources which can achieve the targeted immersive learning environment, featuring professors and students in the virtual meeting rooms for educational planning. An integrated VR-based cyber-physical approach has the advantage of making collaborative knowledge frameworks more adaptable to changing students' academic needs(Paszkiewicz et al., 2021). To achieve learning targeted objectives, a number of partners may collaborate with virtual enterprise platforms, amalgamating their physical and digital resources into a federated learning paradigm. With the emphasis on interactive and collaborative methods of remote education, XR technology minimizes the need for travel by bringing educational services closer to students and learners in faraway locations(Newton, Annetta, & Bressler, 2024). According to(Jagatheesaperumal, Ahmad, Al-Fuqaha, & Qadir, 2024), the effectiveness of a federated learning education system can be demonstrated through interactive virtual reality services, virtual conference rooms and digital representations of teachers and students in an immersive learning environment. These practices support the growth of teacher's abilities by allowing them to work with students in a more genuine and immersive way and by offering training and chances for students to enhance their skills.

The creation of interactive experiences is also made easier by the virtual mainstreaming of the audio metaverse, which enables the synthesis of spatial sound in conjunction with XR-enabled video streaming services(Bibri & Jagatheesaperumal, 2023). The practices help teachers become more successful educators by giving them training and activities that help them develop their skills and by integrating them more authentically and fully into their field of work. A range of ICT tools and technologies for digital collaboration and interactive classroom participation have been made available to collaborative learning environments through the usage of the metaverse as a teaching tool in digital education(Bashir et al., 2023). Remote collaboration through the metaverse encourages cultural competence and teamwork while increasing student engagement through immersive learning(Damaševičius & Sidekerskienė, 2024). When students interact with and change 3-D products on the platform, their creativity and critical thinking are engaged. This improves their technology literacy and help them learn through problem-solving simulations. AI-driven virtual characters in the metaverse provide personalized education and emotional intelligence-boosting role-playing activities. As (Jagatheesaperumal et al., 2024), has demonstrated, it also makes extensive examination of historical and architectural places possible by offering interactive 3-D models that combine academic and practical learning. The introduction of XR and internet of everything (IoE) modules for integrated learning, supported by metaverse technology, opens the door for the integration of instructional materials into narratives and practical gamifications(Jibril et al., 2022). Although, immersive educational pedagogy services can be improved by the metaverse, XR, and IoT infrastructures, consumers still have difficulties in appropriately handling this technology. IoT devices and VR/AR gadgets are frequently abused, disregarding their intrinsic value, even with secure connection support(Bibri & Allam, 2022). Since simulations offer safe environments where students can repeat operations without risk in order to better understand concepts and theories, each metaverse-enabling technology has its own distinct qualities that make simulations extremely valuable in education(Lowell & Ilobinso, 2023). For students to gain practical experience, they also offer realistic models that they may interact with. Well known for its ability to create incredibly realistic 3D simulations with interactive and immersive elements, VR is a technological advancement that can help in learning accomplishment (Al-Ansi, Jaboob, Garad, & Al-Ansi, 2023).

On the other hand, (Familoni & Onyebuchi, 2024) provided a model of how VR technology can be applied to the development of instructional materials in the field of construction processes that stimulate educational importance. The authors created models of buildings in two common scenarios so that students could engage with the virtual representations in a way that would allow them to initiate the construction sequence required by real construction work. The methodology examined how various construction elements fit together and are integrated into the model. In order to simulate volumetric analysis studies,(Kalateh & Kheiry, 2024) established a brand-new Web-based virtual learning environment. Through the use of real-time interactive simulations of volumetric analysis experiments, their work enhanced learning by simulating real-world settings in a chemical laboratory using advancements in Web and VR technology. In addition to being a useful tool for distance learning and lifelong learning in chemistry, the virtual laboratory they described in their paper was also an affordable option for colleges and universities lacking the necessary infrastructure(Ndunagu, Ukhurebor, & Adesina, 2023). A Web-based multi-user 3D virtual world called Second Life, created by the San Francisco-based corporation Linden Lab, is the foundation for the simulated scenario(Kiong, 2024). Many instructors from around the world use Second Life, one of the most well-liked virtual reality platforms. It provides infinite possibilities for engagement, a feeling of belonging, and the ability for individuals to develop their own skills. Based on statistical data, more than 100 educational institutions have set up shop in Second Life and are operating in the virtual environment. As humans retain up to 90% of what they learn through active multimedia participation,(Tugtekin & Odabasi, 2022) proposed a model needed to incorporate VR into engineering curricula.

Nursing curricula that use simulated learning usually provide opportunities for students to learn and practice skills in safe environments that replicate a hospital or other healthcare setting(Fealy, Irwin, Tacgin, See, & Jones, 2023). These tools, which include mannikins and low-to-high fidelity task trainers, are often referred to as simulated learning environments (SLE)(Fealy et al., 2023). They are typically used in conjunction with roleplay and simulated patient scenarios to allow incremental learning from novice to expert without putting actual patients in danger(Fealy et al., 2023). According to(Heyn et al., 2023), the current nursing programs have gone beyond teaching and practicing psychomotor skills into creating contextual asynchronous and synchronous learning experiences that support the development of cognitive abilities such as facts, critical thinking, clinical reasoning and affective disposition which include beliefs, emotional intelligence, empathy skills requirements while maintaining the theoretical underpinnings of nursing education. Kolb's experiential learning theory (ELT) that supported the idea that knowledge is gained by learner through experience whether concrete or abstract (Chiu, 2019). The theory emphasized that reflection is required to generate new understandings and generalizations, which characterizes the foundation for nursing simulation education(Conner, 2022). Using technology-enabled approaches, such as the use of extended XR media, which includes immersive virtual reality (IVR), AR and mixed reality (MR), could be one way to give nursing students more realistic simulated learning experiences than can be gained with standard simulation media(Al Balushi et al., 2024). The variety of embedded media available in XR technology holds great potential for developing simulated learning environments that require active student interaction and participation, a factor that is widely believed to be critical for improved learning outcomes. One of the main advantages of XR technologies like IVR is their ability to immerse students in virtual settings through the use of head-mounted displays, simulating the contextual (physical and mental) experiences of being present and participating in the world around them in a virtual setting(Mallam, Nazir, & Renganayagalu, 2019). IVR and AR elements are combined in a method called MR to create a continuous interaction between virtual and real-world objects(Tadeja, Bohné, Godula, Cybulski, & Woźniak, 2024). Users can interact with digital and real-world objects, like lifelike mannequins, with ease by using MR.

## SYSTEM MODEL

Two well-known frameworks that can aid in the design process are the Technological Pedagogical Content Knowledge (TPCK) framework(Mohebi, 2021), and the Substitution, Augmentation, Modification, Redefinition (SAMR) models(Mafojane, 2021). The nursing educators can gain from utilizing these additional resources. The interplay between these three types of knowledge is referred to as technical pedagogical knowledge, technological knowledge, and content knowledge. It is stated that all three must be present for technology integration to be effective, necessitating expert collaboration. The various ways that technology can be incorporated into teaching and learning activities are categorized by the SAMR model(Ong & Annamalai, 2024). These strategies span from simple substitution to the utilization of various XR technology mediums to facilitate the creation of novel and unique learning experiences. As stressed by frameworks such as TPCK and SAMR, integrating learning theories into the design process is a guiding principle for developing effective XR educational experiences. Learning theory must be incorporated into the design process in order to successfully use these technologies in adaptive pedagogy and teaching. Learning theories constitute the basis for our comprehension of how students might acquire new skills, behaviors, and knowledge within the established educational curriculum.

As a result, incorporating these theories at every stage of the design ensures that educators are actively involved in creating XR experiences that successfully enhance students' learning(Drugova, Zhuravleva, Aiusheeva, & Grits, 2021). Teachers also need to identify and select the right technology tools to help students meet the learning objectives. Head-mounted displays can imitate learning, but not all students or teaching concepts will benefit equally from them, despite the well-established advantages of IVR systems. Learning designers, teachers, and subject matter experts should follow scientific methods and/or frameworks while creating classes to guarantee the best possible outcomes. A useful methodology that incorporates design-based research methods, like the scrum framework or stages of design, can help educators and producers of XR educational content(Fealy et al., 2023). The Figureure 3 provides a useful pathway for organizing and conceptualizing the creation of an XR learning environment. To be more precise, this roadmap could be a helpful resource to ensure that educational goals and learning theories are successfully integrated into the design process.

*Figure 3. Technological pedagogy content knowledge (TPCK) model*

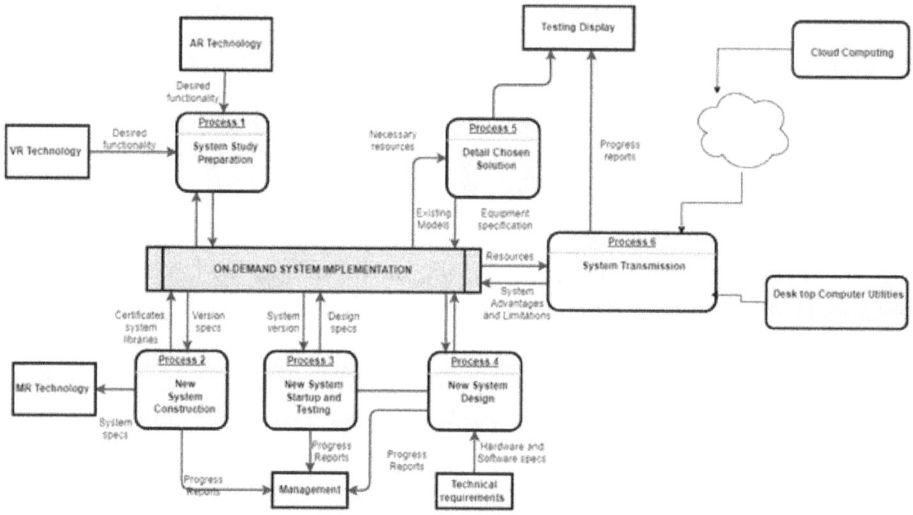


*Author Illustration.*

The Figureure 3 compares incremental process methodologies with the TPCK development pipelines. **Process 1:** System Study Preparation— selecting and loading VR or AR technology according to parameters that can be applied to technique or educational goals. **Process 2** New System — estimating the pedagogical project's effects or outcomes in a realistic manner, taking into account how likely or practical each outcome could be exemplified, do we have the necessary technical staff on hand?. **Process 3:** New System Startup and Testing —this entails comparing the results to the chosen criteria for the new system. **Process 4:** New System Design — the optimal method for addressing the pedagogy component transmission is ultimately decided upon based on the preceding processes. **Process 5:** Detail Chosen Solution- Communicating the process's outcomes in the last phase, where the carefully thought-out project process is presented to explain the reasoning behind the selected challenge, design, technology, results, and assessment techniques. **Process 6:** System Transmission - Transmission protocol establishes if the desktop protocol, cloud computing delivery, or both, has basic delivery capabilities. Educators and creators of XR materials can use these examples in addition to theoretical frameworks and concepts to ensure that their designs result in engaging and easily accessible learning experiences. It is crucial to acknowledge that learning is a complicated process. Effective integration of technology-enabled teaching methods requires an understanding of the distinctive characteristics of each student as well as the surrounding factors that may impact learning outcomes. Each case study was primarily flawed in that it was not intended or supported for a broad curriculum or for long-term integration with the university system.

## Design Implementation

*Figure 4. Cloud-Adaptive VR and AR Learning Environments*

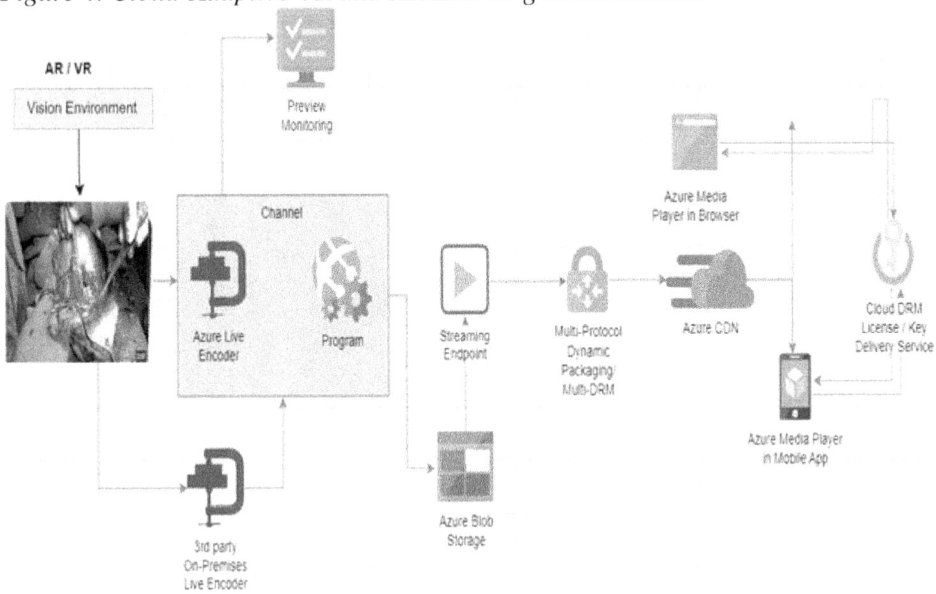


*Author Illustration*

The modernization of XR technology in nursing simulation education, as seen in Figureure 4 and Figureure 5, have been mainly led by small groups of technology and nursing experts who are enthusiastic about using XR to enhance student learning, with an emphasis on the Australian higher education context(Fealy et al., 2023). A cloud-based adaptive learning system was built as part of this research to help nursing educators and XR technology co-design synchronous and asynchronous learning experiences(Miao et al., 2022). This paper investigated VR and AR technology application in nursing education with the goal of better preparing students for the demands of real-world professional practice. In particular, it addressed the problems that postsecondary educational establishments with nursing programs faces. XR technology which includes AR, MR, and VR provided a range of media platforms for the creation of immersive, hands-on learning experiences set in virtual environments that can resemble some of the dynamic aspects of real healthcare settings. Through an examination and explanation of three actual situations, this document analysis explores the application of XR technology in nursing education,

Refer **to Figureure 2**. XR technology specialists work with nursing educators to offer synchronous and asynchronous learning experiences that go beyond traditional nursing simulation resources, better preparing clinical students for the rigors of real-world professional interaction.

*Figure 5. Model of Adaptive Learning Cloud Infrastructure*

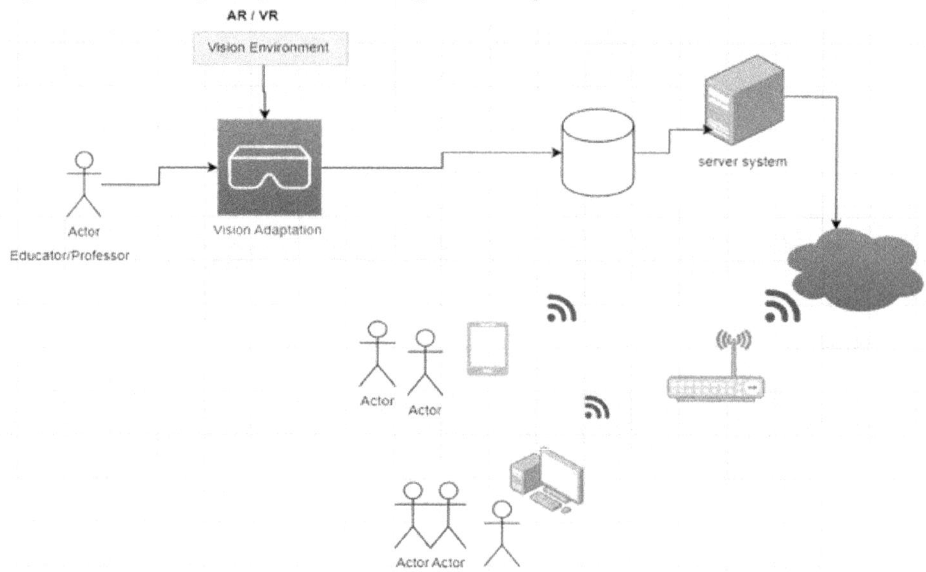


*(Matthew et al., 2021).*

Researchers studying virtual reality and learning theory have generally agreed that VR technology is fascinating and, when developed and used properly, offers a unique and effective way for students to learn since VR projects are very motivating to learners(Hou, Lai, & Wu, 2023). The application of VR to learning can be advantageous, as it has been shown that some students are capable of mastering subject and projecting their comprehension of the knowledge they have acquired. In order to visualize, manipulate, and interact with material that is necessary for learning, virtual reality offers a number of benefits. Some believe that the greatest benefit of this approach is that it allows students to demonstrate and interact with the material and surroundings. When teaching practice in the physical world provide a risk to students, teachers, equipment or the environment, adaptive learning approach can be a very effective substitute(Rapanta, Botturi, Goodyear, Guàrdia, & Koole, 2020). The advantages of this immersive technology have been emphasized by researchers and developers in a wide range of industries, including aviation inspection and maintenance, health sector, education, automobile and game industry for contextual engagement. Immersion technology, especially virtual reality, has sparked a paradigm change in the education industry by stimulating students' senses and immersing them in entirely new surroundings. This presents an intriguing alternative to traditional classroom training.

Technology has enabled the development of new instructional techniques which had prompted the adoption of VR in the classroom instruction to enable each student's needs to be met, utilizing state-of-the-art technology for educational engagement. The development of virtual reality-based educational apps creates new opportunities for the teaching of health-related courses, offering a promising method for experiential learning. The study and teaching of the physical sciences, engineering, and medicine, among other subjects, now have more options thanks to virtual reality. Virtual reality learning environments, or VLEs, help students meet diversified learning objectives. In the mainstream higher education like colleges and universities, VLE-based programs have gained popularity as an alternative to traditional teaching methods that lined to instructivism approach. VR learning environments have been discovered to have superior pedagogical impact on learners because they integrate constructivism, instructivism, and socio-constructivism within the higher education system.

## FUTURE RESEARCH FOCUS

As AI techniques and adaptive learning system come together to form a new trend, the cloud computing method offers fresh perspectives on the field of education. With enormous potential and promising futures for use in educational institutions, adaptive cloud-based learning systems represent a new phase in the development of adaptive systems. The intrinsic capacity of adaptive learning to customize the learning process for each student makes it an essential evolution in the field of education. The shift is propelled by the fundamental understanding that every student has a distinct set of abilities, limitations, and preferred learning styles. Since practically every career requires some combination of practical skills and creative thinking, education needs to shift its emphasis to skill-based learning. This goal of creating an effective learning environment is served by adaptive learning, which employs visual aids, an intuitive learning process, and hands-on subject study. Adaptive learning systems aim to provide a flexible and customized approach that caters to the varied requirements of students by breaking away from the inflexible structures of conventional education. A primary concern of contemporary educational pedagogical research is modernizing teaching and learning in higher education institutions to bring it into compliance with the latest advancements in science and technology.

In this paper and for future adaptive educational development consideration, the following key areas should be explored:

i. **Updates to the Curriculum and Instructional Strategies**: It is critically necessary to change the curriculum and teaching methods to take into account the realities of AR and VR in nursing education. The deliberate integration of technology into the curriculum is a step toward creating comprehensive and interesting learning experiences. As a result, developing instructional modules that leverage technology to enhance students' understanding of the material is essential.
ii. **Personalized Tutoring**: With ChatGPT, students can receive individualized instruction and feedback tailored to their unique learning requirements and advancement. Studies have shown that students can receive individualized math tutoring from a conversational agent called ChatGPT, which is built on a generative model(Baidoo-Anu & Ansah, 2023). This would lead to better learning outcomes as the results of the study demonstrated that the conversational agent could adjust its explanations to the students' comprehension levels and could be customized to address their misconceptions.
iii. **Language Translation:** A broader audience can access educational resources by translating them into multiple languages using ChatGPT. A generative model (ChatGPT) trained on a dataset of bilingual sentence pairs was shown in several studies used to translate between languages accurately and achieve state-of-the-art performance on various translation benchmarks(Matthew et al., 2023). The results of the investigation demonstrated that the model could provide precise translations into another language while also comprehending the meaning of sentences in the original language.
iv. **Adaptive Learning:** With ChatGPT, adaptive learning systems that modify their pedagogical approaches in response to a student's development and performance can be developed. An adaptive learning system built on a generative model (ChatGPT) may be able to support students learning programming more successfully, leading to better results on programming tests. The study demonstrated that the model could recognize what the students knew and modify the difficulty of the challenges it created accordingly. Personalized tutoring, automatic essay grading, language translation, interactive learning, and adaptive learning are just a few of the features that make ChatGPT a potentially effective tool for improving teaching and learning(Bahrami, Bahrami, Behboodi, & Pourrafie, 2023).
v. **Empowering Teachers as Agents of Change:** The core of the educational reform that is required to meet the demands of change in the age of augmented reality and virtual reality simulating ascendancy is expanding teacher professionalism. Since students will be working on real projects, innovative teaching strategies for the digital era will help them apply their newly gained skills and knowledge in real-world situations.

## RECOMMENDATION

The specific recommendation focuses on the following key results of how AR and VR contributes to student performance and engagement in higher education:

i. The utilization of AR technologies in medical and clinical settings has been observed to improve students' performance and engagement, as well as their attitudes toward nursing education.
ii. The performance and engagement levels increased when AR innovation was introduced into the classroom, indicating that these tools have the potential to greatly enhance learning and improve academic outcomes.
iii. Using VR to provide feedback on oral presenting skills improved performance, demonstrating VR's potential for skill-specific development.
iv. Higher engagement was observed when lectures were delivered using a virtual reality platform, demonstrating how well VR works to create immersive learning environments.
v. Improved education's adoption of mobile augmented reality was linked to improved levels of engagement, suggesting that AR can be leveraged on mobile devices to improve the learning process.
vi. When VR was introduced into a specially created clinical setting, many medical students' engagement levels significantly increased, demonstrating VR's scalability and potential to improve the learning environment.

## CONCLUSION

This study's overall significance in academic discussions is increased by the methodological combination, which allows for a thorough knowledge of how immersive technology affects learning results. This study lays the groundwork for future research and helpful applications as the educational landscape changes as a result of rapid technological advancements. It also provides insightful information on the current state of immersive technology in education. The findings highlight the critical role that immersive technology plays in transforming learners' educational experiences and creating new opportunities for innovative and effective teaching strategies in the future. As implied by this reality, remote learning may occur in semi-centralized labs equipped with VR/AR technologies in the future. Students may be able to physically access the necessary equipment at these locations, and teachers may engage and transfer knowledge remotely. This approach may be a more cost-effective and practical way to use immersive technologies in medical education, especially when it is not feasible for every student to purchase such a device. By offering educational benefits beyond those of conventional simulated learning media, XR technology could assist in preparing graduates who are ready for the workforce. XR technology integration offers a new and innovative approach to nursing education by enabling students to express their understanding of phenomena, see the dynamic relationships between variables in a system, see abstract concepts visualized in three dimensions, and experience events that may not be available due to time, money, safety, or availability constraints. Virtual worlds may be created to accurately reflect the complexities of real-world healthcare settings because to the inherent media diversity of XR technology, enabling students to actively engage in immersive and hands-on learning experiences.

## Conflict of Interest

There is no conflict of interest regarding this publication. The research was supported by U&J Digital Consult Limited, an IT and Educational Consulting Firm base in Nigeria.

## REFERENCES


Al-Ansi, A. M., Jaboob, M., Garad, A., & Al-Ansi, A. (2023). Analyzing augmented reality (AR) and virtual reality (VR) recent development in education. *Social Sciences & Humanities Open*, *8*(1), 100532. DOI: 10.1016/j.ssaho.2023.100532

Al Balushi, J. S. G., Al Jabri, M. I. A., Palarimath, S., Maran, P., Thenmozhi, K., & Balakumar, C. (2024). *Incorporating Artificial Intelligence Powered Immersive Realities to Improve Learning using Virtual Reality (VR) and Augmented Reality (AR) Technology*. Paper presented at the 2024 3rd International Conference on Applied Artificial Intelligence and Computing (ICAAIC).

Al-Mugheed, K., Bayraktar, N., Al-Bsheish, M., AlSyouf, A., Aldhmadi, B. K., Jarrar, M., & Alkhazali, M. (2022). Effectiveness of game-based virtual reality phone application and online education on knowledge, attitude and compliance of standard precautions among nursing students. *PLoS One*, *17*(11), e0275130. DOI: 10.1371/journal.pone.0275130 PMID: 36327261

Alam, A. (2021). *Cloud-based e-learning: development of conceptual model for adaptive e-learning ecosystem based on cloud computing infrastructure*. Paper presented at the International Conference on Artificial Intelligence and Data Science.

Asad, M. M., Naz, A., Churi, P., & Tahanzadeh, M. M. (2021). Virtual reality as pedagogical tool to enhance experiential learning: A systematic literature review. *Education Research International*, *2021*(1), 7061623. DOI: 10.1155/2021/7061623

Bahrami, M. R., Bahrami, B., Behboodi, F., & Pourrafie, S. (2023). *Teaching the future: the vision of AI/ChatGPT in education*. Paper presented at the KES International Symposium on Agent and Multi-Agent Systems: Technologies and Applications. DOI: 10.1007/978-981-99-3068-5_37

Baidoo-Anu, D., & Ansah, L. O. (2023). Education in the era of generative artificial intelligence (AI): Understanding the potential benefits of ChatGPT in promoting teaching and learning. *Journal of AI*, *7*(1), 52–62. DOI: 10.61969/jai.1337500

Barlow, M., Heaton, L., Ryan, C., Downer, T., Reid-Searl, K., Guinea, S., & Lamb, A. (2024). The Application and Integration of Evidence-Based Best Practice Standards to Healthcare Simulation Design: A Scoping Review. *Clinical Simulation in Nursing*, *87*, 101495. DOI: 10.1016/j.ecns.2023.101495

Bashir, A. K., Victor, N., Bhattacharya, S., Huynh-The, T., Chengoden, R., Yenduri, G., Maddikunta, P. K. R., Pham, Q.-V., Gadekallu, T. R., & Liyanage, M. (2023). Federated learning for the healthcare metaverse: Concepts, applications, challenges, and future directions. *IEEE Internet of Things Journal*, *10*(24), 21873–21891. DOI: 10.1109/JIOT.2023.3304790

Bibri, S. E., & Allam, Z. (2022). The Metaverse as a virtual form of data-driven smart cities: The ethics of the hyper-connectivity, datafication, algorithmization, and platformization of urban society. *Computational Urban Science*, *2*(1), 22. DOI: 10.1007/s43762-022-00050-1 PMID: 35915731

Bibri, S. E., & Jagatheesaperumal, S. K. (2023). Harnessing the potential of the metaverse and artificial intelligence for the internet of city things: Cost-effective XReality and synergistic AIoT technologies. *Smart Cities*, *6*(5), 2397–2429. DOI: 10.3390/smartcities6050109

Bolton, E., & Emery, R. (2021). Using educational technology to support students' real world learning. *Applied Pedagogies for Higher Education: Real World Learning and Innovation across the Curriculum*, 343-369.

Brooks, A. L. (2021). Gaming, VR, and Immersive Technologies for Education/ Training. *Recent Advances in Technologies for Inclusive Well-Being: Virtual Patients, Gamification and Simulation*, 17-29.

Bucea-Manea- oniş, R., Kuleto, V., Gudei, S. C. D., Lianu, C., Lianu, C., Ilić, M. P., & Păun, D. (2022). Artificial intelligence potential in higher education institutions enhanced learning environment in Romania and Serbia. *Sustainability (Basel)*, *14*(10), 5842. DOI: 10.3390/su14105842

Cant, R., Ryan, C., & Kardong-Edgren, S. (2022). Virtual simulation studies in nursing education: A bibliometric analysis of the top 100 cited studies, 2021. *Nurse Education Today*, *114*, 105385. DOI: 10.1016/j.nedt.2022.105385 PMID: 35569265

Chen, X., Xie, H., & Li, Q. (2022). *Vision, status, and topics of X Reality in Education* (Vol. 1). Elsevier.

Cheong, L. Y. (2017). Evidence Based Education and the UN Sustainable Development Goals (SDGs) 2016–2030. *Children and Sustainable Development: Ecological Education in a Globalized World*, 85-92.

Chiu, S. K., & Lee, J. (2019). Innovative experiential learning experience: Pedagogical adopting Kolb's learning cycle at higher education in Hong Kong. *Cogent Education*, *6*(1), 1644720. DOI: 10.1080/2331186X.2019.1644720

Cioca, L.-I., Ivascu, L., Filip, F. G., & Doina, B. (2024). *Digital Transformation: Technology, Tools, and Studies* (Vol. 253). Springer Nature. DOI: 10.1007/978-3-031-55952-5

Clarke, K. M. (2022). *Exploring the utility of crowdsourcing frameworks to inform the construction of a web-based 3D printing application (3DCrowdGo).* com, m. G. c. m. (2021). maxSIMhealth: An Interconnected Collective of Manufacturing, Design, and Simulation Labs to Advance Medical Simulation Training *Recent Advances in Technologies for Inclusive Well-Being: Virtual Patients, Gamification and Simulation* (pp. 141-176): Springer.

Conner, J. O. (2022). Applying experiential learning theory to student activism. *Journal of Further and Higher Education, 46*(9), 1229–1242. DOI: 10.1080/0309877X.2022.2061843

Dai, C.-P., & Ke, F. (2022). Educational applications of artificial intelligence in simulation-based learning: A systematic mapping review. *Computers and Education: Artificial Intelligence, 3*, 100087. DOI: 10.1016/j.caeai.2022.100087

Damaševičius, R., & Sidekerskienė, T. (2024). Virtual Worlds for Learning in Metaverse: A Narrative Review. *Sustainability (Basel), 16*(5), 2032. DOI: 10.3390/su16052032

Drugova, E., Zhuravleva, I., Aiusheeva, M., & Grits, D. (2021). Toward a model of learning innovation integration: TPACK-SAMR based analysis of the introduction of a digital learning environment in three Russian universities. *Education and Information Technologies, 26*(4), 4925–4942. DOI: 10.1007/s10639-021-10514-2 PMID: 33814955

Ebong, G. N., Matthew, U. O., Olofin, B., Andrew-Vitalis, N., Fatai, L. O., Waliu, A. O., & Oladipupo, M. A. (2024). *Multimedia Cloud Data Warehouse Design for Knowledge Sharing in the University Environment: A Proposed Digital Solution Implementing Interactive Learning Strategies in Higher Education.* IGI Global. DOI: 10.4018/979-8-3693-3559-8.ch010

Familoni, B. T., & Onyebuchi, N. C. (2024). Augmented and virtual reality in us education: a review: analyzing the impact, effectiveness, and future prospects of ar/vr tools in enhancing learning experiences. *International Journal of Applied Research in Social Sciences, 6*(4), 642–663. DOI: 10.51594/ijarss.v6i4.1043

Fealy, S., Irwin, P., Tacgin, Z., See, Z. S., & Jones, D. (2023). *Enhancing nursing simulation education: a case for extended reality innovation.* Paper presented at the Virtual Worlds. DOI: 10.3390/virtualworlds2030013

Goh, C., Ma, Y., & Rizzo, A. (2024). Normative performance data on visual attention in neurotypical children: Virtual reality assessment of cognitive and psychomotor development. *Frontiers in Virtual Reality*, *5*, 1309176. DOI: 10.3389/frvir.2024.1309176

Gumel, A. A., & Abdullahi, A. B., & O, U. M. (2019). *The Need for a Multimodal Means of Effective Digital Learning through Data Mining and Institutional Knowledge Repository: A Proposed System for Polytechnics in Northern Nigeria.* Paper presented at the Proceedings of the 2019 5th International Conference on Computer and Technology Applications. DOI: 10.1145/3323933.3324068

Hamraz, A. R., & Hamidi, A. (2024). Digitalizing Administration Systems in an Under-Resourced Context: Ministry of Higher Education's E-Readiness. *Science and Education*, *5*(6), 37–50.

Hernon, O., McSharry, E., MacLaren, I., & Carr, P. J. (2023). The use of educational technology in teaching and assessing clinical psychomotor skills in nursing and midwifery education: A state-of-the-art literature review. *Journal of Professional Nursing*, *45*, 35–50. DOI: 10.1016/j.profnurs.2023.01.005 PMID: 36889892

Heyn, L. G., Brembo, E. A., Byermoen, K. R., Cruaud, C., Eide, H., Flo, J., Nordstei-en, A., Overgaard, G., & Egilsdottir, H. Ö. (2023). Exploring facilitation in virtual simulation in nursing education: A scoping review. *PEC Innovation*, *3*, 100233. DOI: 10.1016/j.pecinn.2023.100233 PMID: 38033419

Hiran, K. K., Doshi, R., & Patel, M. (2024). Modern Technology in Healthcare and Medical Education: Blockchain, IoT, AR, and VR: Blockchain, IoT, AR, and VR: IGI Global.

Hou, H., Lai, J. H., & Wu, H. (2023). Project-based learning and pedagogies for virtual reality-aided green building education: Case study on a university course. *International Journal of Sustainability in Higher Education*, *24*(6), 1308–1327. DOI: 10.1108/IJSHE-06-2022-0197

Hung, C.-C., Kao, H.-F. S., Liu, H.-C., Liang, H.-F., Chu, T.-P., & Lee, B.-O. (2021). Effects of simulation-based learning on nursing students' perceived competence, self-efficacy, and learning satisfaction: A repeat measurement method. *Nurse Education Today*, *97*, 104725. DOI: 10.1016/j.nedt.2020.104725 PMID: 33373813

Jagatheesaperumal, S. K., Ahmad, K., Al-Fuqaha, A., & Qadir, J. (2024). Advancing education through extended reality and internet of everything enabled metaverses: Applications, challenges, and open issues. *IEEE Transactions on Learning Technologies*, *17*, 1120–1139. DOI: 10.1109/TLT.2024.3358859

Jibril, A. U., Abdullahi, N. M., Ali, A. S., Abdulkadir, H., Matthew, U. O., & Haruna, K. (2022). Motivational aspects of digital games in learning process. *Science in Information Technology Letters*, *3*(1), 1–9. DOI: 10.31763/sitech.v3i1.885

Kalateh, F., & Kheiry, M. (2024). A Review of Stochastic Analysis of the Seepage Through Earth Dams with a Focus on the Application of Monte Carlo Simulation. *Archives of Computational Methods in Engineering*, *31*(1), 47–72. DOI: 10.1007/s11831-023-09972-3

Kayyali, M. (2024). *Immersive Technologies: Virtual and Augmented Reality in Higher Education Reshaping Learning with Next Generation Educational Technologies*. IGI Global.

Kiong, L. V. (2024). *Metaverse Made Easy: A Beginner's Guide to the Metaverse: Everything you need to know about Metaverse, NFT and GameFi*. Liew Voon Kiong.

Kouijzer, M., Kip, H., Kelders, S. M., & Bouman, Y. (2024). The introduction of virtual reality in forensic mental healthcare–an interview study on the first impressions of patients and healthcare providers regarding VR in treatment. *Frontiers in Psychology*, *15*, 1284983. DOI: 10.3389/fpsyg.2024.1284983 PMID: 38746916

Lee, J., Solat, F., Kim, T. Y., & Poor, H. V. (2024). Federated learning-empowered mobile network management for 5G and beyond networks: From access to core. *IEEE Communications Surveys and Tutorials*, *26*(3), 2176–2212. DOI: 10.1109/COMST.2024.3352910

Liu, J. Y. W., Yin, Y.-H., Kor, P. P. K., Cheung, D. S. K., Zhao, I. Y., Wang, S., Su, J. J., Christensen, M., Tyrovolas, S., & Leung, A. Y. (2023). The effects of immersive virtual reality applications on enhancing the learning outcomes of undergraduate health care students: Systematic review with meta-synthesis. *Journal of Medical Internet Research*, *25*, e39989. DOI: 10.2196/39989 PMID: 36877550

Lougiakis, C., González, J. J., Ganias, G., Katifori, A., & Roussou, M. (2024). *Comparing Physics-based Hand Interaction in Virtual Reality: Custom Soft Body Simulation vs. Off-the-Shelf Integrated Solution.* Paper presented at the 2024 IEEE Conference Virtual Reality and 3D User Interfaces (VR). DOI: 10.1109/VR58804.2024.00094

Lowell, V. L., & Ilobinso, A. C. (2023). Virtual reality in online higher education for learner engagement, interaction, and experiential learning. *The SAGE handbook of online higher education*, 458.

Mafojane, M. A. J. (2021). *Changing perceptions regarding the use of information and communication technologies through subject-specific professional development: insights from a South African case study*. University of the Free State.

Mallam, S. C., Nazir, S., & Renganayagalu, S. K. (2019). Rethinking maritime education, training, and operations in the digital era: Applications for emerging immersive technologies. *Journal of Marine Science and Engineering*, *7*(12), 428. DOI: 10.3390/jmse7120428

Marougkas, A., Troussas, C., Krouska, A., & Sgouropoulou, C. (2024). How personalized and effective is immersive virtual reality in education? A systematic literature review for the last decade. *Multimedia Tools and Applications*, *83*(6), 18185–18233. DOI: 10.1007/s11042-023-15986-7

Matthew, U. O. (2019). Information System Management & Multimedia Applications in an E-Learning Environment. [IJICTHD]. *International Journal of Information Communication Technologies and Human Development*, *11*(3), 21–41. DOI: 10.4018/IJICTHD.2019070102

Matthew, U. O., Bakare, K. M., Ebong, G. N., Ndukwu, C. C., & Nwanakwaugwu, A. C. (2023). Generative Artificial Intelligence (AI) Educational Pedagogy Development: Conversational AI with User-Centric ChatGPT4. *Journal of Trends in Computer Science and Smart Technology*, *5*(4), 401–418. DOI: 10.36548/jtcsst.2023.4.003

Matthew, U. O., Kazaure, A. S., Kazaure, J. S., Hassan, I. M., Nwanakwaugwu, A. C., & Okafor, N. U. (2022). Educational Technology Adaptation & Implication for Media Technology Adoption in the Period of COVID-19. *Journal of Trends in Computer Science and Smart Technology*, *4*(4), 226–245. DOI: 10.36548/jtcsst.2022.4.002

Matthew, U. O., & Kazaure, J. S. (2020). Multimedia e-learning education in nigeria and developing countries of Africa for achieving SDG4. [IJICTHD]. *International Journal of Information Communication Technologies and Human Development*, *12*(1), 40–62. DOI: 10.4018/IJICTHD.2020010103

Matthew, U. O., Kazaure, J. S., & Haruna, K. (2020). Multimedia information system (MIS) for knowledge generation and ICT policy framework in education: Innovative sustainable educational investment. [IJICTHD]. *International Journal of Information Communication Technologies and Human Development*, *12*(3), 28–58. DOI: 10.4018/IJICTHD.2020070102

Matthew, U. O., Kazaure, J. S., Kazaure, A. S., Onyedibe, O. N., & Okafor, A. N. (2022). The Twenty First Century E-Learning Education Management & Implication for Media Technology Adoption in the Period of Pandemic. *EAI Endorsed Transactions on e-Learning, 8*(1).

Matthew, U. O., Kazaure, J. S., Ndukwu, C. C., Ebong, G. N., Nwanakwaugwu, A. C., & Nwamouh, U. C. (2024). *Artificial Intelligence Educational Pedagogy Development: ICT Pedagogy Development for Education 5.0 Educational Perspectives on Digital Technologies in Modeling and Management*. IGI Global. DOI: 10.4018/979-8-3693-2314-4.ch003

Matthew, U. O., Kazaure, J. S., & Okafor, N. U. (2021). Contemporary development in E-Learning education, cloud computing technology & internet of things. *EAI Endorsed Transactions on Cloud Systems*, *7*(20), e3–e3.

Menekaya, C. (2024). Gendered Innovations, and Skills for Societal Sustainability: Reflections on Today's Women and Women in the Bible. *International Journal of Gender Equity and Social Justice*, *1*(1), 1–15.

Miao, M., Rietdijk, R., Brunner, M., Debono, D., Togher, L., & Power, E. (2022). Implementation of web-based psychosocial interventions for adults with acquired brain injury and their caregivers: Systematic review. *Journal of Medical Internet Research*, *24*(7), e38100. DOI: 10.2196/38100 PMID: 35881432

Mohebi, L. (2021). Theoretical models of integration of interactive learning technologies into teaching: A systematic literature review. *International Journal of Learning. Teaching and Educational Research*, *20*(12), 232–254.

Ndunagu, J. N., Ukhurebor, K. E., & Adesina, A. (2023). *Virtual Laboratories for STEM in Nigerian Higher Education: The National Open University of Nigeria Learners' Perspective*. Paper presented at the Proceedings of the Technology-Enhanced Learning in Laboratories workshop (TELL 2023), CEUR Workshop Proceedings.

Newton, M. H., Annetta, L. A., & Bressler, D. M. (2024). Using Extended Reality Technology in Traditional and Place-Based Environments to Study Climate Change. *Journal of Science Education and Technology*, *33*(2), 208–227. DOI: 10.1007/s10956-023-10057-w

Ong, Q. K. L., & Annamalai, N. (2024). Technological pedagogical content knowledge for twenty-first century learning skills: The game changer for teachers of industrial revolution 5.0. *Education and Information Technologies*, *29*(2), 1939–1980. DOI: 10.1007/s10639-023-11852-z

Onyebuchi, A., Matthew, U. O., Kazaure, J. S., Ebong, G. N., Ndukwu, C. C., Nwanakwaugwu, A. C., & Okey, O. D. (2024). *Cloud-Based IoT Data Warehousing Technology for E-Healthcare: A Comprehensive Guide to E-Health Grids Pioneering Smart Healthcare 5.0 with IoT, Federated Learning, and Cloud Security*. IGI Global.

Onyebuchi, A., Matthew, U. O., Kazaure, J. S., Nwanagwaugwu, A. C., Nwamouh, U. C., & Adamu, U. A. (2022). Cloud based IoT Electronic Healthcare Data Warehouse Integration in emerging 5G Health Grid Ecosystem.

Onyebuchi, A., Matthew, U. O., Kazaure, J. S., Okafor, N. U., Okey, O. D., Okochi, P. I., Taiwo, J. F., & Matthew, A. O. (2022). Business demand for a cloud enterprise data warehouse in electronic healthcare computing: Issues and developments in e-healthcare cloud computing. [IJCAC]. *International Journal of Cloud Applications and Computing*, *12*(1), 1–22. DOI: 10.4018/IJCAC.297098

Onyesolu, M. O., Nwasor, V. C., Ositanwosu, O. E., & Iwegbuna, O. N. (2013). Pedagogy: Instructivism to socio-constructivism through virtual reality. *International Journal of Advanced Computer Science and Applications*, *4*(9).

Oyekunle, D., Matthew, U., Waliu, A., & Fatai, L. (2024). Healthcare applications of Augmented Reality (AR) and Virtual Real-ity (VR) simulation in clinical ceducation. *Journal of Clinical Images and Medical Case Reports*, *5*(6), 3141.

Oyekunle, D., Ugochukwu, O. M., Rosa, R. L., Rodriguez, D. Z., & Fatai, L. O. (2024). Novel Approaches in Clinical Simulation: Immersive Educational Technology to Enhance Nursing Education. *INFOCOMP Journal of Computer Science, 23*(1).

Paszkiewicz, A., Salach, M., Dymora, P., Bolanowski, M., Budzik, G., & Kubiak, P. (2021). Methodology of implementing virtual reality in education for industry 4.0. *Sustainability (Basel)*, *13*(9), 5049. DOI: 10.3390/su13095049

Rapanta, C., Botturi, L., Goodyear, P., Guàrdia, L., & Koole, M. (2020). Online university teaching during and after the Covid-19 crisis: Refocusing teacher presence and learning activity. *Postdigital science and education, 2*, 923-945.

Ryan, G. V., Callaghan, S., Rafferty, A., Higgins, M. F., Mangina, E., & McAuliffe, F. (2022). Learning outcomes of immersive technologies in health care student education: Systematic review of the literature. *Journal of Medical Internet Research*, *24*(2), e30082. DOI: 10.2196/30082 PMID: 35103607

Sarai, L., Zockun, C. Z., & Cabral, F. G. (2023). Public administration and innovation: E-government in the international perspective. *Beijing Law Review*, *14*(3), 1352–1371. DOI: 10.4236/blr.2023.143074

Sarshartehrani, F., Mohammadrezaei, E., Behravan, M., & Gracanin, D. (2024). *Enhancing E-Learning Experience Through Embodied AI Tutors in Immersive Virtual Environments: A Multifaceted Approach for Personalized Educational Adaptation.* Paper presented at the International Conference on Human-Computer Interaction. DOI: 10.1007/978-3-031-60609-0_20

Shorey, S., & Ng, E. D. (2021). The use of virtual reality simulation among nursing students and registered nurses: A systematic review. *Nurse Education Today*, *98*, 104662. DOI: 10.1016/j.nedt.2020.104662 PMID: 33203545

Silva, L., Mendes, A. J., & Gomes, A. (2020). *Computer-supported collaborative learning in programming education: A systematic literature review.* Paper presented at the 2020 IEEE Global Engineering Education Conference (EDUCON). DOI: 10.1109/EDUCON45650.2020.9125237

Singh, P., Pahuja, N., Kansal, M., Gurung, S., Shukla, U., & Gupta, S. (2024). *Enhancing Tourism Experiences and Preserving Cultural Heritage with AR and VR.* Paper presented at the 2024 2nd International Conference on Disruptive Technologies (ICDT). DOI: 10.1109/ICDT61202.2024.10489490

Souza, A. M. C., Manzolli, J., Campos, C. D. S., & Rennó-Costa, C. (2022). *Playing the Hypercube–Using Augmented Reality to Enhance a Multimodal Musical Performance.* Paper presented at the Proceedings of the 24th Symposium on Virtual and Augmented Reality. DOI: 10.1145/3604479.3604530

Squire, D., Gonzalez, L., & Shayan, C. (2024). Enhancing sense of belonging in nursing student clinical placements to advance learning and identity development. *Journal of Professional Nursing*, *51*, 109–114. DOI: 10.1016/j.profnurs.2024.01.007 PMID: 38614668

Stapleford, K., & Lee, K. (2024). *Online postgraduate education: Re-imagining openness, distance and interaction.* Taylor & Francis. DOI: 10.4324/9781003044048

Stenseth, H. V., Steindal, S. A., Solberg, M. T., Ølnes, M. A., Mohallem, A., Sørensen, A. L., & Riegel, F. (2022). Simulation-based learning supported by technology to enhance critical thinking in nursing students: Protocol for a scoping review. *JMIR Research Protocols*, *11*(4), e36725. DOI: 10.2196/36725 PMID: 35373777

Supriya, Y., Bhulakshmi, D., Bhattacharya, S., Gadekallu, T. R., Vyas, P., Kaluri, R., Sumathy, S., Koppu, S., Brown, D. J., & Mahmud, M. (2024). Industry 5.0 in Smart Education: Concepts, Applications, Challenges, Opportunities, and Future Directions. *IEEE Access : Practical Innovations, Open Solutions*, *12*, 81938–81967. DOI: 10.1109/ACCESS.2024.3401473

Tabbakhian Khaziran, M. (2021). *The impact of the COVID-19 pandemic on nursing simulation use and the influence of simulation use on future admissions.* UCLA.

Tadeja, S. K., Bohné, T., Godula, K., Cybulski, A., & Woźniak, M. M. (2024). Immersive presentations of real-world medical equipment through interactive VR environment populated with the high-fidelity 3D model of mobile MRI unit. *Computers & Graphics*, *120*, 103919. DOI: 10.1016/j.cag.2024.103919

Tiwari, R. G., Agarwal, A. K., & Husain, M. (2023). 13 Integration of virtual reality in the e-learning environment. *Augmented and Virtual Reality in Industry 5.0*, *2*, 253.

Torrey, T., Woodruff, N., Matthew, C., & Jeromie, W. (2021). Educators' Interests, Prior Knowledge and Questions Regarding Augmented Reality, Virtual Reality and 3D Printing and Modeling. *TechTrends*, *65*(4), 548–561. DOI: 10.1007/s11528-021-00594-9

Tugtekin, U., & Odabasi, H. F. (2022). Do interactive learning environments have an effect on learning outcomes, cognitive load and metacognitive judgments? *Education and Information Technologies*, *27*(5), 7019–7058. DOI: 10.1007/s10639-022-10912-0

Ullrich, S., Rausch, D., & Kuhlen, T. W. (2011). *Bimanual Haptic Simulator for Medical Training: System Architecture and Performance Measurements.* Paper presented at the EGVE/EuroVR.

Verma, R. K., Gupta, S., & Illinich, S. (2024). *Technology-enhanced personalized learning in higher education Advances in Technological Innovations in Higher Education*. CRC Press.

Weerasinghe, S., & Perera, I. (2024). Optimized Strategy in Cloud-Native Environment for Inter-Service Communication in Microservices. *International Journal of Online & Biomedical Engineering*, *20*(1), 40–57. DOI: 10.3991/ijoe.v20i01.44021

Wei, Z., & Yuan, M. (2023). Research on the current situation and future development trend of immersive virtual reality in the field of education. *Sustainability (Basel)*, *15*(9), 7531. DOI: 10.3390/su15097531

Wilcox, R. L., Adem, P. V., Afshinnekoo, E., Atkinson, J. B., Burke, L. W., Cheung, H., & LeGallo, R. (2018). The Undergraduate Training in Genomics (UTRIG) Initiative: Early & active training for physicians in the genomic medicine era. *Personalized Medicine*, *15*(03), 199–208. DOI: 10.2217/pme-2017-0077 PMID: 29843583

Wu, J. (2024). Enhancing Policies on Promoting Gender-inclusive and Equitable Quality STEM in Higher Education. Directions and challenges from a comparative analysis between Italy and China.

Chapter 9

# Inclusive Integration of Generative AI–ChatGPT With Education for Sustainable Development (ESD) in Higher Education

**Ayush Kumar Shukla**
*Bidhan Chandra College, Rishra, India*

**Unmesh Mandal**
https://orcid.org/0000-0003-4065-8264
*Bidhan Chandra College, Rishra, India*

## ABSTRACT

*This book chapter aims to establish the generative AI ChatGPT (GPT 3.5) as a valid source for active learning in higher education settings, based on fundamental educational and learning theories that describe efficient active learning methodologies and techniques. The research methodology aims to perform qualitative comparisons of ChatGPT and its various functionalities with the principles of the discussed learning theories. The prompts given to ChatGPT play an important role in how well the AI acts as a learning resource, the quality of the prompt is directly related to the quality of the response given by the AI. Various Prompt Experiments have been included in our case studies that showcase prompts given to the AI and the response received. These experiments will help in consolidating the comparisons between the working of the AI and the principles of the learning theories. Lastly, the chapter discusses the various deficiencies of ChatGPT (GPT 3.5) that need to be taken cautiously when using it as a tool for higher education.*

DOI: 10.4018/979-8-3693-5623-4.ch009

## 1. INTRODUCTION

Generative AI, in a formal sense, refers to a subset of artificial intelligence (AI) models designed to generate new content or data that is analogous to the patterns observed in the training data. Unlike discriminative models, which aim to classify input data into predefined categories, generative models focus on creating new instances that resemble the input data distribution. These models leverage techniques such as neural networks to learn complex patterns and generate novel outputs.

Within the realm of generative AI, ChatGPT, developed by OpenAI, represents a significant milestone. Built upon the foundations of natural language processing (NLP), ChatGPT embodies the capabilities of a sophisticated generative model tailored specifically for text-based interactions. Through its architecture, ChatGPT possesses the ability to comprehend and respond to natural language prompts with a level of coherence and relevance that mirrors human conversation. This proficiency enables ChatGPT to not only provide factual answers but also engage in nuanced analyses and logical reasoning, thereby facilitating interactions akin to human discourse. Leveraging its extensive training on vast textual datasets spanning diverse subjects, ChatGPT stands as a testament to the advancements in generative AI, exemplifying the potential of such models in transforming various domains.

In the context of education, the integration of AI models like ChatGPT holds immense promise. By harnessing the capabilities of these models as catalysts for active learning, educators can revolutionize traditional pedagogical approaches. Through personalized interactions and tailored feedback, ChatGPT can stimulate intellectual curiosity, foster critical thinking, and deepen engagement with educational content. Thus, within the broader framework of generative AI, the utilization of models like ChatGPT represents a paradigm shift in education. By augmenting human intellect with AI-driven capabilities, we pave the way for a more dynamic and effective learning environment, wherein individuals can explore, learn, and grow with unprecedented depth and breadth.

### 1.1 Active Learning Versus Passive Learning

*"Neurons that fire together, wire together." - Donald Hebb on Neural Plasticity*

Human learning, from a traditional perspective, is construed as a dynamic process characterized by the progressive formation of synaptic connections within the brain. As individuals engage in iterative learning and practice, these synaptic connections strengthen, facilitating the encoding and interpretation of information. This phenomenon, known as long-term potentiation, underscores the pivotal role of neural plasticity in cognitive development. Central to this concept is the notion that active engagement in learning tasks fosters the consolidation of neural pathways.

When individuals actively participate in tasks requiring problem-solving, critical thinking, and knowledge application, neural circuits associated with these activities are reinforced. This active involvement not only enhances cognitive proficiency but also promotes deeper understanding and retention of information.

In contrast, passive learning modalities, typified by passive reception of information through activities like reading, listening, or observing, lack the cognitive engagement necessary for robust neural development. While these methods may facilitate initial exposure to information, they often fall short in promoting durable learning outcomes. Without active participation and deliberate practice, synaptic connections remain relatively weak, impeding comprehensive understanding and retention of learned material.

Active learning methodologies, on the other hand, advocate for deliberate practice and engagement in learning activities that necessitate cognitive effort. Techniques such as active recall, wherein learners actively retrieve information from memory, and spaced repetition, which involves revisiting learned material at intervals to enhance retention, exemplify strategies that capitalize on neural plasticity. By actively engaging learners in meaningful tasks and challenges, active learning methodologies foster the formation of robust neural connections conducive to comprehensive understanding and long-term retention of knowledge.

In essence, the dichotomy between active and passive learning underscores the critical role of cognitive engagement in shaping neural development and learning outcomes. By embracing active learning methodologies that leverage the brain's innate plasticity, educators can optimize learning experiences and empower learners to achieve deeper levels of understanding and mastery.

## 1.2 The Role of Computers in Learning

The evolution of computers has played a pivotal role in shaping the landscape of education across different epochs marked by technological progress.

### Pre-Internet Era:

In the pre-internet era, computers emerged as essential tools primarily employed for text processing, document management, and programming tasks. However, their utility in learning was somewhat limited due to the absence of online repositories of information. Information retrieval relied heavily on physical storage media, necessitating cumbersome processes for data exchange. Despite these limitations, computers laid the groundwork for digital literacy and computational skills, serving as precursors to more advanced educational technologies.

## Internet Era:

The advent of the internet ushered in a new era of connectivity and information accessibility. Computers gained the ability to access vast online repositories of information, facilitating unprecedented opportunities for learning and research. While this development revolutionized information retrieval, it predominantly involved accessing pre-existing data rather than fostering the generation of novel insights. Furthermore, the internet lacked sophisticated natural language processing capabilities, constraining its ability to analyze and respond to natural language prompts in a meaningful manner.

## Generative AI Era:

However, the contemporary landscape witnesses the emergence of the generative AI era, epitomized by transformative innovations such as ChatGPT. Equipped with advanced natural language processing capabilities, ChatGPT transcends the limitations of previous technologies by adeptly interpreting natural language prompts and generating contextually appropriate responses. This paradigm shift heralds a new era in learning methodologies, particularly in higher education settings. In this generative AI era, ChatGPT serves as a virtual tutor, revolutionizing the traditional model of education. By harnessing the power of AI-driven insights and personalized feedback, ChatGPT facilitates enhanced comprehension, elucidates complex concepts, and resolves queries with unparalleled efficacy. Its ability to engage in meaningful dialogue and provide tailored assistance empowers learners to navigate complex subject matter with confidence and proficiency.

Overall, the role of computers in learning has evolved significantly over time, culminating in the advent of generative AI technologies like ChatGPT. As we continue to embrace these innovations, we pave the way for a more dynamic and personalized educational experience, redefining the boundaries of knowledge acquisition and intellectual exploration. Table 1 provides a historical evaluation of different versions of ChatGPT along with their corresponding abilities. It is evident from the table that with each successive iteration, the capabilities of ChatGPT have grown exponentially, enabling it to fulfill increasingly complex tasks and engage in more sophisticated interactions.

*Table 1. Evolution of GPT*

| Model Name | Abilities |
|---|---|
| GPT – 1 | • Capable of answering general inquiries, paraphrasing text, and performing language translation.<br>• Responsive to relatively brief input or extracts. |
| GPT – 2 | • Underwent 'Modified Objective Training' to enhance coherence and relevance in responses.<br>• Incorporates additional contextual elements such as Parts of Speech, including verbs and nouns, as well as identifying subjects and objects. |
| GPT – 3 | • Demonstrates enhanced depth and realism in generated text.<br>• Represents a refined iteration of the GPT-2 model. |
| GPT – 3.5 | • Adheres to guidelines designed with human values in mind.<br>• Implements Reinforcement Learning with Human Feedback (RLHF) techniques. |
| GPT – 4 | • Proficient in generating contextually appropriate text from visual data.<br>• Trained on both textual and visual datasets.<br>• Capable of interpreting documents containing images, schematics, and diagrams. |

## 1.2 Research Objectives

Our research endeavours encompass the following objectives:

a. **Provide Empirical Evidence for Establishing ChatGPT as a Learning Resource:**

Generative AI, exemplified by ChatGPT, is increasingly recognized as a valuable adjunct to learning processes, aiding in tasks ranging from factual inquiries to logical analyses and automation of educational workflows. This objective seeks to furnish empirical evidence, drawing upon established theories in educational psychology and pertinent case studies, to substantiate the efficacy of ChatGPT as a legitimate learning resource. Furthermore, insights gleaned from this investigation will inform the refinement of AI functionalities to optimize its utility as an efficient learning aid.

b. **Exemplify Proper Framing of Prompts to Elicit Efficient Responses from AI:**

The efficacy of interactions with AI systems is contingent upon the quality and specificity of prompts issued by users. The emerging discipline of 'Prompt Engineering' addresses the optimization of prompts to elicit desirable responses from AI models. Through a series of meticulously designed 'Prompt Experiments', this objective aims to elucidate the characteristics of effective prompts for ChatGPT, thereby enhancing the efficacy and relevance of AI-generated responses.

c. **Illustrate the Deficiencies of AI as a Learning Resource:**

Despite advancements, generative AI technologies such as ChatGPT exhibit certain limitations and performance gaps that warrant consideration when utilized as learning resources. While these deficiencies are not prohibitive, they necessitate prudent user handling to mitigate their impact effectively. This objective aims to identify and elucidate these limitations, fostering a nuanced understanding of AI's role in the educational landscape.

d. **Demonstrate the Use of AI in Learning:**

This objective entails the deployment of case studies and 'Prompt Experiments' to showcase diverse scenarios wherein ChatGPT can serve as a potent learning tool. These scenarios span from factual inquiries to analytical tasks and may include tasks such as elucidating complex concepts through conversational interactions or generating essay ideas and formats. By exemplifying the multifaceted utility of AI in learning contexts, this objective underscores its potential to augment and enrich educational experiences.

## 1.3 Unique Contributions

Plenty of studies have explored various aspects of ChatGPT's utilization in educational settings, ranging from its performance and benefits to its drawbacks and potential risks. However, empirical studies that delve into the nuanced functioning of ChatGPT within the framework of established learning theories, particularly in higher education contexts, are noticeably scarce. Our research attempt seek to fill this gap by providing empirical evidence and assessing the validity of incorporating AI, specifically ChatGPT, in higher education. To achieve this, we undertake a comprehensive examination that juxtaposes the functionality of ChatGPT with several prominent learning theories. Our research makes distinctive contributions to the intersection of education psychology and artificial intelligence, fostering advancements that directly impact the higher education sector:

a. Promote Unification of Educational Psychology and AI:

By integrating principles from educational psychology with AI methodologies, our work aims to illuminate techniques that can significantly enhance the efficacy of higher education practices. This interdisciplinary approach facilitates the development of tailored interventions and learning strategies that leverage AI technologies to optimize learning outcomes.

b. Provide an Approach to Prompt Engineering from an Educational Psychology Perspective:

Our research offers a novel perspective on Prompt Engineering by synthesizing insights from educational psychology. By considering cognitive and behavioral factors that influence human-AI interactions, we delineate approaches to crafting prompts that elicit optimal responses from AI systems. This approach not only enhances the effectiveness of AI-mediated learning experiences but also fosters a deeper understanding of human-computer interaction dynamics.

c. Highlight Shortcomings of AI in Higher Education:

Recognizing that no technology is without limitations, our research endeavors to identify and elucidate the shortcomings of AI, particularly in the context of higher education. By delineating these limitations, ranging from algorithmic biases to contextual constraints, we provide critical insights that inform judicious utilization of AI as a tool for enhancing higher education practices.

d. Spreading Awareness and Understanding of ChatGPT and Generative AI:

Our efforts extend to disseminating awareness among scholars, educators, and learners regarding the effectiveness and deficiencies of ChatGPT and generative AI as learning resources. Through empirical evidence and critical analysis, we seek to foster a nuanced understanding of the potential benefits and limitations of AI-mediated learning experiences, empowering stakeholders to make informed decisions regarding its integration into educational practices.

## 2 REVIEW OF LITERATURE

ChatGPT, a Large Language Model (LLM) Chatbot developed by OpenAI, exhibits the capability to respond naturally to queries of diverse nature (OpenAI, 2022). Existing literature reveals a plethora of studies exploring the utility of ChatGPT across various academic settings.

Cooper (2023) demonstrated how ChatGPT serves as a valuable source for generating study materials conducive to science education. Findings indicate that ChatGPT not only delivers proficient answers reflecting human-like thought processes but also generates quizzes, teaching units, and rubrics, enriching the learning experience.

Numerous studies have underscored ChatGPT's efficacy in addressing technical and application-based inquiries. Wang et al. (2023) presented college-level engineering physics questions, revealing that ChatGPT successfully tackled over 60% of the problems when prompts were well-specified. Additionally, Waseem et al. (2023) employed ChatGPT to support novice developers in a software engineering project, with developers reporting a consensus on the positive influence of AI during project completion.

Montenegro-Rueda et al. (2023) conducted a systematic review of 12 research articles following PRISMA guidelines, highlighting ChatGPT as a significant catalyst in learning across various contexts. The importance of training educators and students to effectively utilize the tool was also emphasized.

Dwivedi (2023) discussed multidisciplinary contributions describing ChatGPT's potential in enhancing productivity across fields such as tourism and banking. Ethical considerations surrounding AI usage were also addressed, underscoring the need for further investigation.

Javaid et al. (2023) outlined major use cases of ChatGPT in education and business settings, including study material generation and virtual tutoring. However, shortcomings in prompt specification and the current stage of GPT 3.5 LLM were identified, calling for refinement to ensure efficacy and safety in educational environments (Tlili et al., 2023).

Strzelecki (2023) utilized an extended version of the UTAUT2 theoretical model by Venkatesh et al. (2003) to investigate the behavioral motivation of a group of 503 students. The study found that the primary factors driving students to use AI were “habit” and “performance expectancy.” This indicates that the majority of students in higher education view AI and chatbots as integral parts of their study routines, directly influencing their learning processes. The research suggests that ChatGPT can serve as a catalyst for the adoption of AI in higher education and assist with personalized learning.

Boueterra et al. (2024) conducted a similar analysis using a hybrid UTAUT-SCT model to understand students' behaviors regarding the inclusion of ChatGPT in their study routines. They found that ChatGPT can help reduce academic-related anxiety by providing various forms of assistance. However, students with higher academic integrity tended to avoid using ChatGPT due to concerns about academic dishonesty. This highlights that the misuse of ChatGPT and AI for educational dishonesty is more of a social issue than a technological one and should be addressed through awareness rather than prohibition.

Bhullar et al. (2024) examined 47 research papers from the Scopus database to identify the most influential articles and journals related to the use of ChatGPT in higher education. Their findings suggest that the topic of AI in higher education is of significant interest to the research community.

Gill et al. (2024) studied the transformative effects of ChatGPT on education. Their article raises important concerns about integrating AI with contemporary pedagogical norms, pointing out inconsistencies such as the production of erroneous or false information and the potential for plagiarism. These issues must be resolved before AI can be fully integrated into mainstream education.

Nazari (2024) elaborates on prompt engineering, discussing how effective communication can be established with ChatGPT using well-crafted prompts. They provide examples of how university instructors can use ChatGPT in several key areas, including planning course structures, implementing pedagogical processes, and assessing students.

Despite the wealth of existing research on ChatGPT's applications and effects, there remains a dearth of literature exploring the psychological underpinnings of its functionality. A critical analysis of why ChatGPT serves as a learning resource and the educational theories supporting its efficacy is warranted.

## 2.1 Research Gap

Our study aims to address the following research gaps:

a. **Understanding the Rationale Behind ChatGPT's Efficacy in Higher Education:** There is a lack of background understanding regarding why ChatGPT serves as an effective learning resource in higher education contexts.
b. **Establishing a Psychological Justification for ChatGPT's Role in Higher Education:** A psychological perspective is needed to justify ChatGPT's utilization as a tool for aiding higher education, yet this perspective remains largely unexplored in existing literature.
c. **Providing Evidence for AI-Assisted Active Learning Techniques:** Existing literature lacks sufficient evidence, grounded in foundational educational and learning theories, to support the use of AI-based techniques that promote active learning. Our study aims to fill this gap by providing empirical evidence for the effectiveness of such techniques in personalized learning contexts.

Our work attempts to establish a coherent link between educational psychology and the functionality of generative AI, such as ChatGPT, in personalized learning within higher education settings.

## 3 METHODOLOGY

Our methodology entails a multifaceted approach aimed at thoroughly examining the integration of ChatGPT into higher education through the lens of fundamental educational and learning theories. By systematically evaluating the alignment between ChatGPT's functionality and the principles advocated by these theories, we aim to provide a robust justification for its role as an active learning resource. The flowchart of the research methodology (Figure 1) visually represents the iterative process of how ChatGPT enhances learning through various types of user prompts. This process can be broken down into several key stages, starting with the user's natural language prompt and resulting in one of three significant learning phenomena. Here's a detailed breakdown of each component:

A. User's Natural Language Prompt
    - **Initiation:** The process begins when a user inputs a natural language prompt into ChatGPT. This prompt is essentially a question or command phrased in everyday language.

B. Processing by Chatbot
    - **Classification:** Once the prompt is received, ChatGPT processes it and classifies it into one of three categories based on the nature of the query:
        - o **Directive:** Prompts that ask the chatbot to generate new content or modify existing content.
        - o **Instructive:** Prompts that request the chatbot to provide instructions or steps necessary to complete a task.
        - o **Explanatory:** Prompts that seek explanations or clarifications on specific topics or concepts.

C. Mapping to Learning Phenomena

Each prompt category is mapped to a specific learning phenomenon:

- **Directive Prompts:**
    - o **Example:** "Write an essay on climate change" or "Edit the following paragraph for clarity."
    - o **Learning Phenomenon:** This typically results in the reduction of cognitive load, as the chatbot automates content generation and modification tasks that might otherwise be time-consuming or challenging for the learner.
- **Instructive Prompts:**
    - o **Example:** "Provide the steps to solve a quadratic equation" or "How do I set up a database?"

- o **Learning Phenomenon:** These prompts align with the Zone of Proximal Development (ZPD). The chatbot acts as the "more knowledgeable other," guiding the learner through tasks that they can perform with assistance but might struggle with independently.
- **Explanatory Prompts:**
  - o **Example:** "Explain the theory of relativity" or "What are the causes of World War II?"
  - o **Learning Phenomenon:** These prompts foster Experiential Learning. The chatbot provides detailed explanations and resolves doubts, allowing the learner to construct knowledge based on these interactions.

D. Iterative Process

- **Feedback Loop:** This process is iterative, meaning that after receiving and processing a prompt, the results help the learner, which may lead them to ask further questions or refine their learning goals. This creates a continuous feedback loop where each interaction builds upon the previous one, leading to progressive learning and understanding.

The flowchart sets the stage for the "prompt experiments" section further in the chapter, where specific examples of each prompt category and their respective learning outcomes are discussed. These examples illustrate how ChatGPT's responses can effectively enhance learning by reducing cognitive load, assisting within the learner's ZPD, and promoting experiential learning. This systematic approach demonstrates how AI can be leveraged to support educational processes, making learning more efficient and tailored to individual needs.

## 3.1 Case Study of Various Learning Theories:

In this section, we delve into the core tenets of select learning theories, highlighting their significance in educational contexts and elucidating their potential implications for the integration of AI technologies like ChatGPT. We have chosen three prominent learning theories for detailed examination:

A. Experiential Learning Theory (David A. Kolb, 1984)

According to Kolb, learning is a cyclical process involving concrete experiences, reflective observation, abstract conceptualization, and active experimentation. We explore how ChatGPT can facilitate each stage of this iterative cycle, from providing insights into real-world experiences to assisting learners in conceptualizing and experimenting with new ideas. Through interactive engagement with ChatGPT, learners can reinforce their understanding through experiential learning activities.

B. Zone of Proximal Development (Lev Vygotsky, 1962; 1978)

This theory underscores the importance of scaffolding and guided instruction in facilitating learning. Through our prompt experiments, we position ChatGPT as a "more knowledgeable other," capable of providing guidance and support to learners as they navigate complex subject matter. By leveraging ChatGPT's capabilities, learners can engage in scaffolded learning experiences, gradually advancing their understanding with the aid of the AI's responses.

C. Cognitive Load Theory (John Sweller, 1988)

Sweller's theory emphasizes the role of cognitive load in learning and advocates for strategies to manage cognitive resources effectively. Our prompt experiments investigate how ChatGPT can mitigate extraneous cognitive load by streamlining information retrieval processes and optimizing learning environments. By leveraging ChatGPT's capabilities, learners can allocate their cognitive resources more efficiently, focusing on active learning tasks without being overwhelmed by irrelevant information

## 3.2 Prompt Experiments for Comparative Analysis:

In this section, we conduct prompt experiments to compare ChatGPT's responses with the key principles of the learning theories discussed above. By analyzing the correspondence between ChatGPT's functionality and the theoretical frameworks, we aim to demonstrate its efficacy as a personalized learning resource for higher education. Through a qualitative comparative analysis, we seek to highlight the ways in which ChatGPT aligns with established educational theories, thereby reinforcing its suitability for facilitating active learning experiences.

Through our comprehensive case study, we aim to provide empirical evidence and theoretical justification for the integration of ChatGPT into higher education settings. By elucidating the alignment between ChatGPT's functionality and fundamental learning theories, we seek to establish its credibility as a valuable tool for promoting active learning and enhancing educational outcomes.

*Figure 1. Iterative Process of Learning Enhancement through ChatGPT*

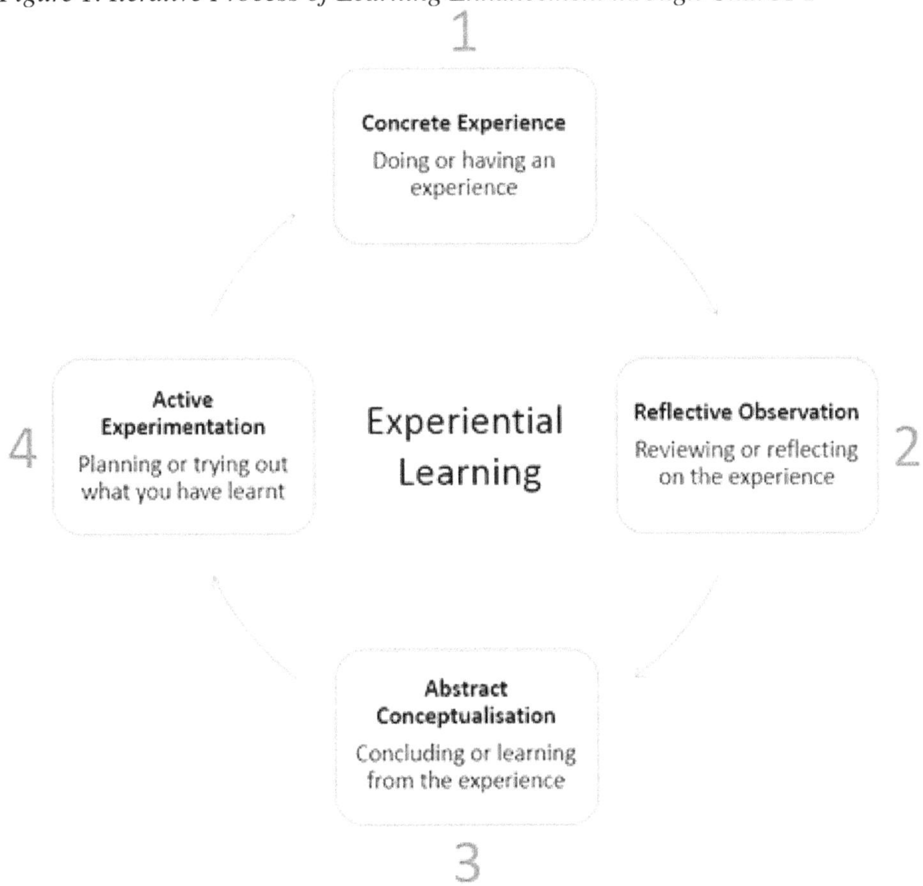


## 4 CASE STUDY WITH EXPERIMENTAL RESULTS

In the forthcoming sections, we delve into the viability of ChatGPT as an active learning resource by juxtaposing its functionality with the foundational principles of cognitive theories. To conduct this case study, we utilize the web version of ChatGPT running on the default GPT-3.5 model. Various prompts are administered to the model, and its responses are evaluated in comparison with the tenets of the specified cognitive theories. Additionally, this case study serves as a practical guide on leveraging ChatGPT to obtain desired answers across diverse topics.

## 4.1 David Kolb's Experiential Learning Model (ELM)

David A. Kolb's Experiential Learning Model (ELM) posits that experiential engagement is pivotal in fostering deep understanding and meaningful learning experiences. The model emphasizes hands-on experiences as catalysts for active cognition, wherein learners engage in reflective observation, abstract conceptualization, and active experimentation. This iterative process facilitates a comprehensive understanding of the subject matter, transcending mere passive reception of information.

This case study serves as a testament to the versatility and utility of ChatGPT as a tool for promoting active learning experiences, echoing the sentiment of Aristotle's timeless wisdom on the centrality of experiential engagement in the learning process. The ELM illustrates an iterative process inherent in experiential learning. This model depicts a cyclical journey individuals embark upon when engaging in experiential learning practices. Each stage of the process builds upon the preceding one, fostering a dynamic and continuous cycle of learning and development. Figure 2 represents the visual representation of the ELM process.

*Figure 2. The Experiential Learning Model*

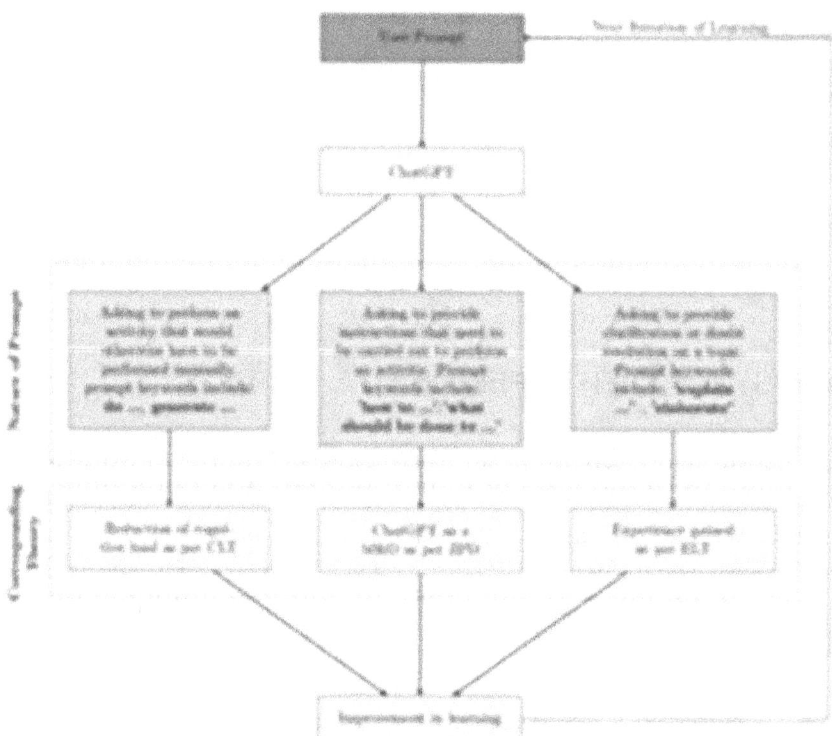

In the Experiential Learning Model (ELM), each stage of the learning process contributes to the overall cycle of learning and growth:

a. Concrete Experience

At this stage, the learner engages in direct, hands-on experiences with the subject matter. This could involve problem-solving, seeking efficient solutions, or identifying errors in solutions. The learner actively interacts with the material, gaining firsthand knowledge and experience.

b. Reflective Observation

Following the concrete experience, the learner engages in reflective observation. This entails critically analyzing and reflecting on the experience and its outcomes. Whether successful or unsuccessful, the learner contemplates their approach, identifies errors or areas for improvement, and gains insights into the subject matter.

c. Abstract Conceptualization

Building on the insights gained through reflection, the learner proceeds to abstract conceptualization. Here, the learner synthesizes their observations and experiences into a broader understanding of the subject matter. They create mental models or conceptual frameworks that encapsulate the essence of the concept, forming connections between various elements and developing a deeper understanding.

d. Active Experimentation

Armed with their refined understanding, the learner engages in active experimentation. This involves applying their new insights and conceptualizations to real-world scenarios or problems. The learner tests alternative approaches, explores different perspectives, and evaluates the outcomes of their actions. The results of this experimentation feed back into the cycle, prompting further reflection, conceptualization, and experimentation.

By applying Kolb's ELM framework to our examination of ChatGPT, we aim to assess the extent to which the model's responses align with the iterative learning process delineated by this theory. Through this comparative analysis, we seek to elucidate ChatGPT's efficacy as a facilitator of experiential learning, empowering learners to engage in active cognition and construct meaningful understandings of complex concepts.

### 4.1.1 Applying the ELM Theory with ChatGPT

In the following scenarios, we explore how ChatGPT can serve as a valuable tool to enhance learning using the ELM.

A. Scenario 1:

**Problem Description:***A student encounters a compound interest problem: "You borrow \$6500 for a car. The bank loans the money at a 7.25% annual interest rate compounded annually. If you aim to repay the loan in 5 years, what will be your total payoff?"*

The student carefully reads the problem and formulates a prompt to seek guidance from ChatGPT. The prompt and the answer from Chat GPT are depicted in Table 2.

*Table 2. The Learner asks for the formula for calculating compound interest.*

| **User Prompt:**<br>*What is the formula for compound interest?* |
|---|
| **Response:**<br>Compound interest is calculated using the following formula:<br>$A = P \times (1 + \frac{r}{n})^{n \times t}$<br>Where:<br>$A$ is the amount of money accumulated after $t$ years, including interest.<br>$P$ is the principal amount (the initial amount of money).<br>$r$ is the annual interest rate (expressed as a decimal).<br>$n$ is the number of times that interest is compounded per year.<br>$t$ is the time the money is invested for, in years.<br><br>This formula computes the total amount $A$ after a specified time $t$ when the principal amount $P$ is compounded at an interest rate $r$ per period, compounded $n$ times per year.<br><br>Compound interest allows for exponential growth of an investment or loan, as the interest is calculated not only on the initial principal but also on the accumulated interest from previous periods. This compounding effect can significantly increase the total amount over time. |

The student attempts to solve the problem using a specific formula but discovers that her textbook presents a different formula. Perplexed by this inconsistency, the student decides to inquire about it from the AI(Table 3):

*Table 3. ChatGPT explains the difference between the general formula and specific formula for calculating compound interest*

| **Follow-up Prompt:**<br>*But in my book, the formula is a bit different, it states* $A = P \times (1 + r)^t$ |
|---|
| **Response**<br>The formula you mentioned, $A = P \times (1 + r)^t$, represents the formula for calculating compound interest when it's compounded annually. This formula assumes that the interest is compounded once per year.<br><br>It's a simplified version of the compound interest formula, specifically for annual compounding, where:<br><br>$A$ is the amount of money accumulated after t years, including interest.<br>$P$ is the principal amount (the initial amount of money).<br>$r$ is the annual interest rate (expressed as a decimal).<br>$t$ is the time the money is invested for, in years.<br><br>This formula is a basic representation of compound interest without considering more frequent compounding periods within a year. If compounding happens more frequently (such as quarterly, monthly, daily, etc.), the first formula I mentioned with n for the number of times interest is compounded per year would be more accurate for calculation.<br><br>Both formulas essentially convey the same principle of compound interest but differ with n accounts for more frequent compounding which can lead to slightly higher accumulated amount due to the effect of compounding multiple times within a year. |

The student discerns that the formula provided in the textbook represents a specific case applicable when the interest is compounded annually. However, she realizes that the general formula is designed to accommodate any arbitrary frequency of compounding.

## B. Scenario 2

**Problem Description:** "*A student has learnt about the way planet Earth orbits around the Sun and believes that the primary reason for change in seasons is due to the changing distance between the Earth and the Sun in orbit. The student approaches ChatGPT while in the reflective observation phase.*"

The student asks ChatGPT to clarify the primary cause for the change in seasons on Earth. (Table 4).

*Table 4. ChatGPT clarifies the primary cause for change in seasons on the Earth*

| **User Prompt:**<br>*I learnt that the Earth has a elliptical orbit, which means that the Earth is closer to the Sun at a certain point in the orbit and further away from it at another point. I believe that this changing distance between the Earth and the Sun causes change in seasons and the temperature. Is my reasoning correct?* |
|---|
| **Response:**<br>Absolutely! Your understanding is spot on. The Earth's orbit around the Sun is indeed elliptical, meaning it's not a perfect circle but rather an elongated, slightly flattened shape. This elliptical orbit causes variations in the Earth-Sun distance throughout the year.<br><br>However, it's important to note that while the changing distance between the Earth and the Sun does have some effect on the planet's temperature, it's not the primary reason for the seasons. The primary cause of the seasons is actually the tilt of the Earth's axis.<br><br>The Earth's axis is tilted at an angle of approximately 23.5 degrees relative to its orbit around the Sun. This tilt is responsible for the varying amounts of sunlight that different parts of the Earth receive during different times of the year.<br><br>During summer in the Northern Hemisphere, that part of the Earth is tilted more toward the Sun, receiving more direct sunlight and longer days, leading to warmer temperatures. Meanwhile, during winter, the Northern Hemisphere is tilted away from the Sun, receiving less direct sunlight and shorter days, resulting in colder temperatures.<br><br>Conversely, when it's summer in the Southern Hemisphere, it's winter in the Northern Hemisphere, and vice versa, due to the opposite tilt and position relative to the Sun.<br>So, while the elliptical orbit does cause minor variations in the Earth-Sun distance, the tilt of the Earth's axis is the primary reason for the changing seasons. Both factors-elliptical orbit and axial tilt-work together to create the climate variations experienced across different parts of the world throughout the year. |

*Application of ELM in the above scenarios:*

By providing specific details about the problem and its objective, the student ensures ChatGPT has the necessary information to offer tailored assistance. ChatGPT can respond with step-by-step instructions on solving the problem, including relevant formulas and explanations. This interaction mirrors the concrete experience phase of the ELM.

- **Concrete Experience:** The student encounters the problem and seeks assistance from ChatGPT.
- **Reflective Observation:** ChatGPT provides guidance, and the student reflects on the solution process.
- **Abstract Conceptualization:** Armed with insights from ChatGPT, the student develops a conceptual understanding of compound interest calculations.
- **Active Experimentation**: The student applies the knowledge gained to solve similar problems independently, closing the learning loop.

*Key Takeaways and Practical Applications:*

- David Kolb's ELM can be colloquially called the 'try-fail-fix-repeat' method, in which the learner forms nascent ideas and concepts about a topic and, after consulting a source of information, identifies the flaws in their reasoning and strengthens them incrementally until reaching mastery or unaided performance.
- For example, ChatGPT, trained on a large amount of factual data, can elucidate the relations between various concepts and their contexts. It can effectively resolve doubts and flaws in understanding across a range of subjects, much like consulting another human for clarification and guidance. However, for more analytical questions involving logical or mathematical reasoning, ChatGPT's performance may vary depending on the nature of the question. It may struggle with intricate series of equations, analyses, or questions requiring mathematical rigor.

## 4.2 Zone of Proximal Development

The zone of proximal development (ZPD), introduced by Lev Vygotsky, delineates the space between what a learner can accomplish independently and what she cannot achieve even with considerable guidance. In this concept, the learner interacts with a "more knowledgeable other" (MKO), such as a teacher or peer, who possesses a higher level of understanding and proficiency in the subject the learner is studying. With the assistance of the MKO, the learner can perform tasks that would otherwise be beyond her capability.

A typical application of ZPD involves the following steps:

a. **Task Assignment:** The learner is assigned a task beyond her current abilities.
b. **Interaction with MKO:** The learner engages in ongoing interaction with the MKO, who provides guidance on task completion.
c. **Skill Development:** Through this interaction, the learner gradually improves her proficiency in the task, requiring less assistance over time.
d. **Independent Performance:** Eventually, the learner achieves proficiency and can complete the task independently.
e. **Iterative Process:** The cycle repeats with new tasks as the learner progresses.

As the learner's proficiency increases, the level of support needed diminishes, ultimately leading to independent task performance. This approach is preferred over simply presenting a study plan to learners and allowing them full control, as it ensures they receive appropriate guidance and instruction tailored to their abilities. However, the potential drawback is that learners may lack the necessary skills to progress on their own, underscoring the importance of mentorship in facilitating advancement.

ZPD employs scaffolding, allowing learners to start at their current ability level and progressively move towards proficiency. Through heavy interaction with the MKO, learners benefit from the instructor's experiences and knowledge, fostering collaboration and social interaction, which can enhance the learning experience, particularly in moderately sized groups.4.2.1: How ChatGPT can be used to apply this theory.

### 4.2.1 Applying the ZPD Theory with ChatGPT

ChatGPT can be used as a tool to enhance the steps discussed above. We now present some prompt experiments that explain our idea.

A. Scenario 1

**Problem Description:** "*A student has been assigned to write a scientific paper using LaTeX, since the student does not know how to use LaTeX, she consults ChatGPT for it.*"

The prompt and its corresponding answer are as follows:

*Table 5. ChatGPT instructs the student on how to get started with using LaTeX for scientific writing*

**User Prompt:**
*How to use LaTeX to write mathematical expressions?*

**Response:**
Certainly! LaTeX is a powerful typesetting system widely used for writing mathematical expressions. Here's a basic guide to get you started:

**Setting up a LaTeX Document:**
Start your document with \documentclass{article}.
Use \begin{document} and \end{document} to enclose the content.

**Inline Math Mode:**
For inline math, use $...$ or \(...\):
The quadratic formula is $x = \frac{-b \pm \sqrt{b^2-4ac}}{2a}$.

**Display Math Mode:**
For standalone equations, use \[...\] or $$...$$:
\[ F = ma \]
$$ E = mc^2 $$

**Symbols and Operators:**
Use ^ for superscripts, _ for subscripts.
Basic symbols like +, -, *, / work as expected.

**Fractions:**

Use \frac{numerator}{denominator}:
The fraction $\frac{1}{2}$ is a basic example.

**Greek Letters:**
Greek letters are written with a backslash, e.g., \alpha, \beta, \gamma.

**Square Roots and Exponents:**
Use \sqrt{} for square roots:

The square root of $x$ is denoted as $\sqrt{x}$.
**Matrices:**

continued on following page

*Table 5. Continued*

| **User Prompt:**<br>*How to use LaTeX to write mathematical expressions?* |
|---|
| Use bmatrix environment for matrices:<br>\[<br>A = \begin{bmatrix}<br>1 & 2 \\<br>3 & 4 \\<br>\end{bmatrix}<br>\]<br><br>**Functions:**<br>Standard functions like \sin, \cos, \tan, \log, \exp are available:<br>$\sin(\theta) + \cos(\theta) = 1$<br><br>**Brackets and Parentheses:**<br>Use \left(and \right) for dynamically sized parentheses.<br><br>**Equation Numbering and Alignment:**<br>Use equation environment for single equations:<br>\begin{equation}<br>a^2 + b^2 = c^2<br>\end{equation}<br>Use align environment for aligning multiple equations:<br>\begin{align}<br>x + y &= 10 \\<br>2x - y &= 5<br>\end{align |

The student further faces challenges in writing integrals, which leads to the following prompt.

*Table 6. ChatGPT answers follow-up question regarding writing integrals in LaTeX*

**Follow-up Prompt:**
*How do I write Integrals?*

**Response:**
In LaTeX, you can write integrals using the \int command. Here are some examples:

**Basic Integral:**
Use \int for a basic integral:
\[ \int f(x) \, dx \]
The \, adds a small space for better formatting.

**Definite Integral:**
For definite integrals, use the underscore _ and caret ^ for limits:
\[ \int_{a}^{b} f(x) \, dx \]
Replace a and b with your lower and upper limits.

**Multiple Integrals:**
For double integrals, triple integrals, etc., use \iint and \iiint:
\[ \iint_{D} f(x, y) \, dxdy \]
\[ \iiint_{V} g(x, y, z) \, dxdydz \]
Adjust the number of integral signs accordingly.

**Limits:**
You can add limits using the \limits command:
\[ \int\limits_{a}^{b} f(x) \, dx \]
This places the limits above and below the integral sign.

**Other Integral Symbols:**
For contour integrals, line integrals, etc., use specific symbols like \oint, \ointclockwise, \ointctrclockwise.

Here's a simple example in a complete LaTeX document:

```
\documentclass{article}
\begin{document}
Basic integral: \(\int f(x) \, dx \)
Definite integral: \(\int_{a}^{b} f(x) \, dx \)
Double integral: \(\iint_{D} f(x, y) \, dxdy \)
Triple integral: \(\iiint_{V} g(x, y, z) \, dxdydz \)
Limit with integral: \(\int\limits_{a}^{b} f(x) \, dx \)
\end{document}
```

Feel free to customize the expressions based on your specific integrals and limits. If you encounter more complex integrals, LaTeX provides additional packages and commands for advanced mathematical notation.

## B. Scenario 2

**Problem Description:** "*A student is trying to learn to use the Microsoft Office Suite Software which includes MS Word, MS Excel, MS Powerpoint etc.*"

To solve specific problems, the student prompts ChatGPT about how to solve them, for example: The student wants to know how she can quickly calculate the sum of cells in MS Excel.

*Table 7. ChatGPT resolves the student's query about MS Excel*

| **User Prompt:**<br>*How to calculate the sum of a large number of cells in MS Excel?* |
|---|
| **Response:**<br>In Excel, if you want to sum a large number of cells, you can use the SUM function. Here's how you can do it:<br>**Using the SUM function**: The SUM function allows you to add up values in multiple cells.<br>Syntax: `=SUM(cell1, cel12, cel13,..)`<br>For example, to sum the values in cells A1 to A10, you can enter: `=SUM(A1:A10)`.<br><br>**Manually selecting cells**: If the range of cells is extensive and not continuous, you can select them manually. To do this:·<br>Click on the first cell you want to include in the sum.<br>Hold down the Shift key on your keyboard.<br>• Click on the last cell you want to include in the sum. This selects all the cells between the first and last cell.<br>• Type `Alt + =` to automatically create a SUM formula for the selected cells.<br><br>**Using AutoSum**: You can use the AutoSum feature to quickly add up a column or row of numbers.<br>• Click on the cell where you want the sum to appear.<br>• Click on the "AutoSum" button (Σ) in the "Editing" group on the "Home" tab.<br>Excel will try to guess the range to be summed, usually selecting the adjacent cells. Press<br>Enter to accept the suggested range or adjust it manually by dragging through the cells you want to include.<br><br>These methods should help you efficiently calculate the sum of a large number of cells in Excel. |

The student prompts ChatGPT on how to remove table borders in MS Word.

*Table 8. ChatGPT resolves the student's query about MS Word*

| **Follow-up Prompt:**<br>*How to make the borders of a table invisible in MS word?* |
|---|
| **Response:**<br>To make the borders of a table invisible in Microsoft Word, you can follow these steps:<br>1. **Select the table**: Click inside the table you want to modify. This action will display the "Table Tools" tab in the toolbar.<br>2. **Go to the Design tab**: Click on the "Design" tab under "Table Tools".<br>3. **Modify border options**:<br>**Borders drop-down menu**: Look for the "Borders" drop-down menu in the "Table Styles" group.<br>**Select "No Border"**: Click on the drop-down menu and choose "No Border". This will remove all borders from the table cells, making them invisible.<br>Alternatively, if you want to remove specific borders from the table:<br><br>1. **Select the table**: Click inside the table to activate the "Table Tools" tab.<br>2. **Go to the Layout tab**: Click on the "Layout" tab under "Table Tools". 3. Select the borders to remove:<br>**Borders button**: Locate the "Borders" button in the "Table" group.<br>**Choose "No Border" or customize**: Click on the drop-down menu and select "No Border" to remove all borders from the entire table. If you want to remove specific borders, choose "Borders and Shading" from the menu. In the dialog box that opens, select the border lines you want to remove and click "OK". |

*Key Takeaways and Practical Applications:*

The ZPD theory can be likened to the "learn by doing" method, where learners progress from a state of limited understanding to mastery through the guidance of a "more knowledgeable other." ChatGPT can effectively act as this knowledgeable guide, facilitating skill-based tasks and providing step-by-step instructions.

For instance, ChatGPT can assist users in learning how to navigate and utilize specific software by offering guidance on where to find features and how to apply them effectively. Similarly, it can provide detailed steps and formulas for solving mathematical problems, as well as offer prerequisite information necessary for understanding complex concepts or undertaking certain tasks.

## 4.3 The Cognitive Load Theory

The Cognitive Load Theory, as formulated by John Sweller, provides insights into how the human mind processes information during learning, particularly focusing on the role of working memory. Here's an elaboration on the key concepts:

a. Working Memory:

This refers to the temporary storage system in the human mind that holds information currently being processed. When a learner is actively engaged in learning a topic, the relevant information is stored in working memory for cognitive processing.

b. Types of Cognitive Load:
- **Intrinsic Load:** This is the inherent difficulty or complexity associated with understanding a topic. It depends on factors such as the complexity of the subject matter and the learner's prior knowledge or experience. Intrinsic load is fixed for a specific learner and cannot be altered.
- **Extraneous Load:** Extraneous load refers to the cognitive burden imposed on the learner by the learning material and the learning environment. Factors such as poorly organized instructional material or distracting learning environments contribute to extraneous load, making it more challenging for learners to process information effectively.
- **Germane Load:** Germane load arises from active learning techniques such as problem-solving, information retrieval, and collaborative learning. While germane load adds to the overall cognitive load, it is beneficial for learning as it enhances comprehension and retention by actively engaging the learner's working memory.

c. Significance of Cognitive Load:

Exceeding the working memory capacity can lead to cognitive overload, resulting in reduced learning effectiveness. Therefore, it's essential to manage cognitive load effectively to optimize learning outcomes. Minimizing extraneous load while maximizing germane load ensures that the learning process remains efficient and conducive to effective knowledge acquisition.

d. Optimal Learning Environment:

Creating an optimal learning environment involves designing instructional materials and activities that minimize extraneous load and maximize germane load. This may include providing well-organized learning materials, reducing distractions, and incorporating active learning strategies that engage learners' working memory effectively. By balancing cognitive load, educators can create learning experiences that facilitate deeper understanding and long-term retention of knowledge.

### 4.3.1 How ChatGPT complies with the theory

Now let's consider some scenarios in which ChatGPT can be used to decrease the amount of extraneous cognitive load for students.

A. Scenario 1

**Problem Statement:** "*A student has been assigned with writing an essay on endangered rodent species. The deadline being strict, the student prompts ChatGPT to provide her a list of such species so that the research effort is reduced*". The following are the prompts given to the ChatGPT along with the corresponding responses:

*Table 9. Learner asks ChatGPT to generate a list of endangered rodent species*

| **User Prompt:**<br>*I have been assigned to write about 10 endangered rodent species, can you list them with a brief description so that I can use that information to do further research and write my essay?* |
|---|
| **Response:**<br>Certainly! Here are descriptions of 10 endangered rodent species:<br>1. **Amargosa Vole (Microtus californicus scirpensis)**:<br>• Habitat: Found in the wetlands of the Amargosa River Basin in California.<br>• Threats: Habitat destruction due to human activities, water depletion, and invasive species.<br>2. **Ilin Island Cloud Rat (Crateromys paulus)**:<br>Habitat: Endemic to Ilin Island in the Philippines.<br>Threats: Deforestation, habitat degradation, and hunting have severely impacted its population.<br>3. **Cotton Deermouse (Peromyscus gossypinus allapaticola)**:<br>Habitat: Native to the southeastern United States, particularly Florida.<br>Threats: Loss of habitat due to urbanization, agriculture, and changes in land use patterns.<br>4. **Santa Cruz Island Harvest Mouse (Reithrodontomys megalotis santacruzae):**<br>Habitat: Endemic to Santa Cruz Island in California.<br>Threats: Predation by invasive species and habitat alteration due to human activities.<br>5. **San Quintin Kangaroo Rat (Dipodomys gravipes)**:<br>Habitat: Found in the San Quintin area of Baja California, Mexico.<br>Threats: Habitat destruction caused by agricultural expansion and invasive species.<br>6. **Black-footed Tree-rat (Mesembriomys gouldii)**:<br>Habitat: Native to rainforests in Australia, particularly in Queensland.<br>Threats: Habitat loss due to deforestation, logging, and land clearance for agriculture.<br>7. **Sumatran Giant Sunda Rat (Sundamys infraluteus)**:<br>Habitat: Found in the rainforests of Sumatra, Indonesia.<br>Threats: Deforestation, habitat fragmentation, and hunting for consumption.<br>8. **Panay Bushy-tailed Cloud Rat (Crateromys heaneyi)**:<br>Habitat: Endemic to Panay Island in the Philippines.<br>Threats: Habitat destruction from logging, agriculture, and mining activities.<br>9. **Mexican Hairy-tailed Bat (Baiomys mexicanus)**:<br>Habitat: Occupies grasslands and shrublands in Mexico.<br>Threats: Habitat loss due to agriculture, urbanization, and conversion of land for human use.<br>10. **Laotian Rock Rat (Laonastes aenigmamus)**:<br>Habitat: Found in limestone cliffs in Laos and Vietnam.<br>Threats: Habitat disturbance caused by quarrying and deforestation.<br><br>These species face endangerment due to a variety of factors such as habitat destruction, fragmentation, invasive species, and human activities. Further research into these species will offer deeper insights into their conservation needs and the challenges faced in preserving them. |

B Scenario 2

**Problem Statement:** "*A student has been assigned to give a presentation on the events that lead to the outbreak of the second world war, even though the first world war had ended. The student approches ChatGPT to gain information about such an event*".

*Table 10. ChatGPT summaries the events that lead to the outbreak of the second world war*

| **User Prompt:**<br>*"I have to give a presentation on the events that lead to the second world war even though the first world war had ended. Describe the events in brief and important facts about them."* |
|---|
| **ChatGPT Response:**<br>The events leading to World War II were complex and multifaceted, arising from a culmination of factors following the aftermath of World War I. Here's a brief overview of some key events and factors that contributed to the outbreak of World War II:<br><br>**Treaty of Versailles (1919)**: The Treaty of Versailles, signed in 1919, formally ended World War I. However, its terms placed heavy reparations and blame on Germany, causing resentment and economic hardship within the country. This created a fertile ground for future conflict.<br><br>**Rise of Totalitarian Regimes**: In the 1920s and 1930s, dictatorial regimes emerged in several countries. Adolf Hitler's Nazi Party gained power in Germany in the 1930s, promising to overturn the Treaty of Versailles and restore Germany's former glory. Similarly, Mussolini's fascist rule in Italy and militaristic expansion in Japan added to global tensions.<br><br>**Expansionist Policies**: Germany, under Hitler, pursued an aggressive expansionist policy. He violated the Treaty of Versailles by rearming the military and annexing territories such as Austria and Czechoslovakia, aiming to create a "Greater Germany."<br><br>**Appeasement and Policy of Non-Intervention**: Some European powers initially followed a policy of appeasement, hoping to prevent conflict by conceding to Hitler's demands. The Munich Agreement of 1938 allowed Germany to annex the Sudetenland from Czechoslovakia but failed to prevent further aggression. |
| **Invasion of Poland (1939)**: The event that triggered the outbreak of World War II was Germany's invasion of Poland on September 1, 1939. This action prompted Britain and France to declare war on Germany, marking the official beginning of the war.<br><br>**Axis and Allies**: Following the invasion of Poland, alliances formed. Germany, Italy, and Japan formed the Axis Powers, while Britain, France, the Soviet Union, and later the United States formed the Allies.<br><br>These events represent just a fraction of the numerous political, economic, and social complexities that led to World War II. The war itself would go on to become one of the most catastrophic global conflicts in history, lasting from 1939 to 1945 and resulting in significant geopolitical, social, and economic changes worldwide.<br><br>To delve deeper into these topics, you might explore:<br><br>Books: "The Second World War" by Antony Beevor, "The Rise and Fall of the Third Reich" by William L. Shirer.<br>Documentaries/Films: "The World at War," "WWII in HD," "The Nazis: A Warning from History."<br>Historical Figures: Winston Churchill, Adolf Hitler, Benito Mussolini, Joseph Stalin, Franklin D. Roosevelt, Hideki Tojo.<br>Important Battles: Battle of Stalingrad, Battle of Normandy (D-Day), Battle of Britain, Pearl Harbor.<br><br>Studying these resources and figures will provide you with a comprehensive understanding of the events leading to World War II and the significant figures and moments associated with this global conflict. |

The student further asks ChatGPT to deliberate the reasons that prevented a third world war from happening

*Table 11. ChatGPT deliberates important measures that curbed the possibility of a third world war*

| **Follow-up Prompt:** **What prevented the third world war from happening?** |
|---|
| **Response:** Preventing a third world war has been a primary concern for global leaders since the end of World War II. Several key factors and developments have contributed to averting a large-scale global conflict:<br><br>1. **Nuclear Deterrence**: The development and proliferation of nuclear weapons during the Cold War led to the concept of mutually assured destruction (MAD). This idea suggested that any large- scale conflict between nuclear-armed superpowers (like the United States and the Soviet Union) would result in catastrophic consequences for both sides. The fear of the devastating impact of nuclear war acted as a deterrent and discouraged direct confrontation between major powers.<br><br>2. **Formation of International Organizations**: The establishment of international organizations like the United Nations (UN) aimed to promote cooperation, diplomacy, and conflict resolution among nations. The UN's creation provided a platform for dialogue, negotiation, and peaceful resolution of disputes, reducing the likelihood of large-scale conflicts.<br><br>3. **Global Interconnectedness and Economic Interdependence**: The increasing interconnectedness of economies and the rise of globalization have tied countries' economic interests together. Nations became more interdependent, making the costs of war economically prohibitive. Economic ties and shared interests incentivized countries to resolve conflicts through diplomatic means rather than resorting to warfare. |
| 4. **Diplomacy and Conflict Resolution**: Diplomatic efforts, negotiations, and treaties have played crucial roles in preventing conflicts from escalating. Various crises and conflicts throughout the latter half of the 20th century were diffused or resolved through diplomatic channels, preventing them from spiraling into global conflicts.<br><br>5. **Evolution of Alliances and Security Pacts**: The formation of alliances and security pacts, such as NATO (North Atlantic Treaty Organization) and other regional defense alliances, aimed to deter aggression by providing collective defense against potential aggressors. These alliances served as deterrents and fostered stability in their respective regions.<br><br>6. **Global Consciousness and Lessons from History**: The collective memory of the devastation caused by past world wars and conflicts serves as a reminder of the catastrophic consequences of large-scale warfare. This awareness has contributed to a global consciousness that emphasizes the importance of diplomacy, cooperation, and conflict resolution to prevent future conflicts.<br><br>While these factors have been instrumental in preventing a third world war so far, global geopolitics remains complex and volatile. Ongoing efforts in diplomacy, multilateral cooperation, and the continued commitment to conflict resolution and peacekeeping are crucial in maintaining global stability and preventing large-scale conflicts in the future. |

## *Key Takeaways and Practical Applications:*

One of the key benefits of using ChatGPT is its ability to handle tasks that are otherwise time-consuming, require excessive effort, or are impractical to complete manually. This significantly reduces the cognitive load on learners.

*Reducing Cognitive Load:*

As demonstrated, ChatGPT can provide detailed and reliable factual information on various topics and concepts. Normally, gathering this information would require extensive manual searching on the internet, which consumes both time and effort. By using ChatGPT, learners can access comprehensive information directly, allowing them to focus on applying this knowledge to their specific needs.

*Practical Applications:*

1. Information Retrieval:

ChatGPT excels at retrieving and summarizing information from its vast knowledge base. Whether a learner needs detailed explanations of historical events, scientific theories, or literary analysis, ChatGPT can deliver thorough and accurate descriptions. This eliminates the need to sift through multiple sources, enabling deeper learning and application.

2. Formula Provision and Problem Solving:

For subjects like mathematics, physics, and chemistry, ChatGPT can quickly provide necessary formulas and explain their usage. Learners can ask ChatGPT to solve specific problems, verify solutions, or understand the steps involved in complex calculations. This saves time and reinforces conceptual understanding.

3. Data Generation and Analysis:

ChatGPT can generate tables, lists, and structured data based on user requirements. For example, it can create a table of periodic elements with specific properties instantly. This capability is particularly useful for assignments, research projects, and data analysis tasks.

4. Instruction Following and Custom Tasks:

ChatGPT's proficiency in understanding and following user instructions makes it a versatile tool for various tasks. Whether drafting emails, creating study guides, or providing programming assistance, learners can use ChatGPT for virtually any task involving text input and output. This adaptability allows learners to customize their interactions with ChatGPT according to their unique academic and personal needs.

*Enhanced Learning Experience:*

Integrating ChatGPT into their study routines provides learners with a more efficient and enriched learning experience. As an accessible resource, ChatGPT can answer questions, provide explanations, and assist with various academic tasks. This reduces extraneous cognitive load, allowing learners to allocate more mental resources to germane load activities such as critical thinking, problem-solving, and practical application of knowledge.

## 5 RESULTS

This study reveals two major inferences regarding the performance of ChatGPT in educational settings:

a. Strengths in Handling Factual and Common Queries:

ChatGPT excels in responding to factual or information-based queries, particularly those that are frequently discussed within the community. This strength stems from its extensive training on a large corpus of text data, which includes commonly discussed problems and concepts. For instance:

- **Technical Queries:** Issues like specific bugs in computer programs or commonly encountered errors can be swiftly addressed by ChatGPT due to the widespread discussion of such problems in online forums and documentation.
- **Scientific Theories:** Information related to well-established scientific theories and principles is readily available and accurate because these topics are thoroughly covered in the training data.
- **Historical Events:** Details about significant historical events and phenomena are accurately provided, reflecting the comprehensive historical content available in its training set.

These examples demonstrate ChatGPT's capability to handle queries efficiently when the topics are well-represented in its training data, making it a reliable source for widely acknowledged and factual information.

b. Challenges with Analytical and Niche Queries:

ChatGPT shows limitations when dealing with queries that require non-linear thinking, complex analytical or mathematical reasoning, or when the questions pertain to unique and less commonly discussed topics. Such limitations arise due to:

- **Analytical and Mathematical Reasoning**: While ChatGPT can provide basic explanations and solutions, it struggles with intricate mathematical problems or advanced analytical tasks that require step-by-step logical processing.
- **Niche Topics:** Questions revolving around specialized or niche subjects may not be as well-represented in the training data, leading to a higher likelihood of incorrect or incomplete responses. This is particularly evident in areas where community discussions are sparse or highly specialized knowledge is required.

## 5.1 Implications for Learning Theories:

From the case studies, it is evident that ChatGPT aligns well with the principles of three major learning theories—David Kolb's Experiential Learning Model (ELM), Lev Vygotsky's Zone of Proximal Development (ZPD), and John Sweller's Cognitive Load Theory (CLT). Here's how ChatGPT supports these theories:

- **Experiential Learning Model (ELM):** ChatGPT facilitates the 'try-fail-fix-repeat' cycle by providing immediate feedback and corrective information, allowing learners to refine their understanding through iterative interaction.
- **Zone of Proximal Development (ZPD):** ChatGPT acts as a 'more knowledgeable other' (MKO), offering guidance and support that helps learners perform tasks they cannot complete independently, thus bridging the gap between their current abilities and potential capabilities.
- **Cognitive Load Theory (CLT):** ChatGPT helps manage cognitive load by providing clear, structured information and reducing the need for extensive independent research, thus minimizing extraneous load and allowing learners to focus on the intrinsic and germane aspects of learning.

## 5.2 Mitigating Shortcomings:

Despite the identified deficiencies, particularly with analytical and niche queries, users can still leverage ChatGPT effectively by:

- **Scrutinizing Responses:** Critical evaluation of the AI's output ensures that users can identify and correct any errors or inaccuracies. This involves cross-referencing information with other reliable sources.
- **Validating Information:** Before relying on the AI's responses, especially for high-stakes decisions or complex problems, users should validate the provided information through additional research or expert consultation.

- **Iterative Questioning:** Engaging in an iterative dialogue with ChatGPT, where follow-up questions and clarifications are sought, can help refine the responses and provide a deeper understanding of the topic.

The findings of this study establish ChatGPT as a viable resource for promoting active learning among higher education students. By leveraging its strengths in handling factual and well-documented queries and mitigating its shortcomings through careful validation and critical assessment, ChatGPT can significantly enhance the learning experience. It serves as a dependable tool for students, aiding them in efficiently acquiring, processing, and applying knowledge, thereby supporting their academic growth and development.

# 6 CONCLUSION

## 6.1 Key Findings

This study demonstrates that AI chatbots like ChatGPT align well with fundamental educational theories, providing a scientific and comprehensive rationale for their use in higher educational settings. The key behaviors of the chatbot observed across various prompt experiments include:

- **Detailed Explanation of Concepts:** ChatGPT consistently provides thorough explanations of concepts and detailed solutions to specific problems, aiding in the understanding and application of knowledge.
- **Human-like Interaction:** The chatbot engages in interactive dialogue with users, including follow-up questions and responses, creating a dynamic and engaging learning environment.
- **Error Correction:** ChatGPT assists users by identifying and correcting mistakes in their reasoning or logic, facilitating a deeper comprehension of the subject matter.

These capabilities highlight ChatGPT's potential to enhance learning by providing immediate, accurate, and contextually relevant information, supporting students in their academic pursuits and promoting active learning.

## 6.2 Shortcomings in the Functionality of ChatGPT

While ChatGPT performs well in aligning with educational theories, its effectiveness is limited by the complexity of the information it handles. The following points highlight its shortcomings:

- **Fact-based and General Concept Queries**: ChatGPT excels when responding to fact-based questions or general concept explanations. It performs well with definitions, historical information, and well-known problems—essentially, information present in its training data.
- **Complex Analytical and Critical Thinking Tasks:** The AI struggles with prompts requiring deep critical thinking, such as high-level science problems involving complex mathematical calculations or reasoning that demands non-linear thinking. When faced with questions outside its training data, ChatGPT often provides unsatisfactory or incorrect responses.

Given these limitations, ChatGPT is best suited for beginner to intermediate levels in higher education. It is effective when learners are being introduced to new topics and the complexity level is manageable. For more advanced and complex topics, human supervision remains essential to ensure accurate understanding and problem-solving.Ethical Use of AI in Higher Education: The functionality of ChatGPT has been proven to be beneficial as a learning resource. But just like the internet, generative AI also faces the problem of being misused and used for academic dishonesty. The very same qualities that make ChatGPT a viable learning resource can be misused and cause mass disruption of academic processes.

Already, there has been a consensus among the academic community about the vulnerability of online tests and tests that contain questions that can be easily answered by ChatGPT. Some suggestions include replacing the traditional way of academic testing with tests that explicitly test the reasoning capabilities of the students. These questions fall under point 2 of the results section and pose a difficulty to AI models, including ChatGPT, this causes the threat of AI being used to cheat on tests to be greatly reduced. The students using ChatGPT for their higher education must be aware that the capabilities of the model must only be used for the purpose of self-study or doubt-resolution

## 6.3 Jailbreaking ChatGPT as a Major Threat to Its Integrity

The term "jailbreaking" typically refers to bypassing restrictions imposed by system creators to gain unauthorized access. In the context of ChatGPT, jailbreaking involves using specific prompt engineering techniques to manipulate the AI into providing responses that violate its content policy. This policy is designed to prevent the AI from generating answers to malicious or harmful queries. Jailbreaking undermines the integrity of ChatGPT by enabling the creation of content that could be used for unethical or dangerous purposes, posing a significant threat to the responsible use of AI technology.

## 6.4 Use of Adversarial Training to Prevent Jailbreaking

Adversarial training is a technique employed to mitigate the risk of jailbreaking AI models like ChatGPT. In this approach, one chatbot is designed to act as an adversary, attempting to jailbreak another chatbot by prompting it with questions that could lead to violations of the content policy.

When the adversary successfully manipulates the target chatbot into providing inappropriate or harmful responses, these instances are logged and added to the training dataset as "filters." These filters instruct the AI to completely reject such prompts in the future. By continually updating the training data with these adversarial examples, the AI becomes increasingly robust against jailbreaking attempts. This ongoing process helps to enhance the integrity and safety of the AI, significantly reducing the likelihood of it being used for malicious purposes.

# 7 FUTURE SCOPE

The work presented in this book chapter lays a solid foundation for the development of large language models (LLMs) that are fine-tuned specifically for instructing higher education students. These tailored LLMs have the potential to revolutionize the way education is delivered and can significantly enhance active learning among students. As AI continues to evolve rapidly, there is a growing need to refine AI models to undertake specific tasks with greater efficiency and accuracy. From software development to image generation, from grammar correction to voice recognition, AI is increasingly becoming integrated into various domains.

Moving forward, there is a pressing need to build AI models that address the shortcomings identified in this study. Specifically, AI models tailored for educational instruction should focus on:

a. **Addressing Cognitive Load:** Future AI models should aim to reduce cognitive load on learners by providing clear and concise explanations, minimizing extraneous information, and offering interactive learning experiences tailored to individual student needs.

b. **Enhancing Critical Thinking Skills:** AI models should be developed to facilitate higher-order thinking skills such as critical thinking, problem-solving, and analytical reasoning. This can be achieved through the incorporation of interactive problem-solving tasks, simulations, and real-world case studies.
c. **Customizing Learning Experiences:** Personalized learning experiences are essential for catering to diverse student needs and learning styles. AI models should be designed to adapt and customize learning content and delivery methods based on individual student preferences, abilities, and learning goals.
d. **Ensuring Ethical and Responsible Use:** It is crucial to prioritize ethical considerations and responsible use of AI in education. Future AI models should be equipped with robust mechanisms for filtering inappropriate or harmful content, safeguarding student privacy, and promoting digital literacy and responsible online behavior. By focusing on these areas, future AI models can overcome existing limitations and fulfill their potential as powerful tools for enhancing education and promoting active learning among students in higher education settings.

## 8 DECLARATIONS

### 8.1 Conflict of Interests

The authors declare that they have no known competing financial interests or personal relationships that could have appeared to influence the work reported in this chapter.

### 8.2 Funding

No funding was received from any sources for this work.

### 8.3 Acknowledgement

We are grateful to the reviewers and facilitators whose constructive comments were useful in improving the content of this document. This work was supported by Bidhan Chandra College, Rishra by providing the platforms and means.

## REFERENCES


Bhullar, P. S., Joshi, M., & Chugh, R. (2024). ChatGPT in higher education - a synthesis of the literature and a future research agenda. *Education and Information Technologies*, *29*(16), 21501–21522. Advance online publication. DOI: 10.1007/s10639-024-12723-x

Bouteraa, M., Bin-Nashwan, S. A., Al-Daihani, M., Dirie, K. A., Benlahcene, A., Sadallah, M., Zaki, H. O., Lada, S., Ansar, R., Fook, L. M., & Chekima, B. (2024). Understanding the diffusion of AI-generative (ChatGPT) in higher education: Does students' integrity matter? *Computers in Human Behavior Reports*, *14*, 100402. DOI: 10.1016/j.chbr.2024.100402

Cooper, G. (2023). Examining Science Education in ChatGPT An Exploratory Study of Generative Artificial Intelligence. *Journal of Science Education and Technology*, *32*(3), 444–452. Advance online publication. DOI: 10.1007/s10956-023-10039-y

Dwivedi, Y. K., Kshetri, N., Hughes, L., Slade, E. L., Jeyaraj, A., Kar, A. K., Baabdullah, A. M., Koohang, A., Raghavan, V., Ahuja, M., Albanna, H., Albashrawi, M. A., Al-Busaidi, A. S., Balakrishnan, J., Barlette, Y., Basu, S., Bose, I., Brooks, L., Buhalis, D., & Wright, R. (2023). "So what if ChatGPT wrote it?" Multidisciplinary perspectives on opportunities, challenges and implications of generative conversational AI for research, practice and policy. *International Journal of Information Management*, *71*, 102642. Advance online publication. DOI: 10.1016/j.ijinfomgt.2023.102642

Gill, S. S., Xu, M., Patros, P., Wu, H., Kaur, R., Kaur, K., Fuller, S., Singh, M., Arora, P., Parlikad, A. K., Stankovski, V., Abraham, A., Ghosh, S. K., Lutfiyya, H., Kanhere, S. S., Bahsoon, R., Rana, O., Dustdar, S., Sakellariou, R., . . . Buyya, R. Transformative effects of ChatGPT on modern education: Emerging Era of AI Chatbots, Internet of Things and Cyber-Physical Systems, Volume 4, 2024, Pages 19-23, ISSN 2667-3452, https://doi.org/DOI: 10.1016/j.iotcps.2023.06.002

Javaid, M., Haleem, A., & Singh, R. P.. (2023). An era of ChatGPT as a significant futuristic support tool: A study on features, abilities, and challenges. *Benchcouncil Transactions on Benchmarks. Standards and Evaluations, 100089.* Advance online publication. DOI: 10.1016/j.tbench

Javaid, M., Haleem, A., & Singh, R. P.. (2023). Unlocking the opportunities through ChatGPT Tool towards ameliorating the education system. *Benchcouncil Transactions on Benchmarks. Standards and Evaluations, 100115.* Advance online publication. DOI: 10.1016/j.tbench.2023

Karen, D. Wang, Eric Burkholder, Carl Wieman, Shima Salehi, & Nick Haber. (2023). *Examining the Potential and Pitfalls of ChatGPT in Science and Engineering Problem Solving*. https://arxiv.org/abs/2310.08773

Kolb, D. A. (1984). *Experiential learning: experience as the source of learning and develop- ment*. Prentice Hall.

Montenegro-Rueda, M., Fernández-Cerero, J., Fernández-Batanero, J. M., & López-Meneses, E. (2023). Impact of the Implementation of ChatGPT in Education A Systematic Review. *Computers*, *12*(8), 153. Advance online publication. DOI: 10.3390/computers12080153

Nazari, M., & Saadi, G. (2024). Developing effective prompts to improve communication with ChatGPT: A formula for higher education stakeholders. *Discover Education*, *3*(1), 45. DOI: 10.1007/s44217-024-00122-w

Open, A. I. (2022). *OpenAI Blog Introducing ChatGPT*. https://openai.com/blog/chatgpt

Page, M. J., McKenzie, J. E., Bossuyt, P. M., Boutron, I., Hoffmann, T. C., Mulrow, C. D., ... & Moher, D. (2021). The PRISMA 2020 statement: an updated guideline for reporting systematic reviews. bmj, 372.

Strzelecki, A. (2024). Students' Acceptance of ChatGPT in Higher Education: An Extended Unified Theory of Acceptance and Use of Technology. *Innovative Higher Education*, *49*(2), 223–245. DOI: 10.1007/s10755-023-09686-1

Sweller, J. (1988). Cognitive Load During Problem Solving: Effects on Learning. *Cognitive Science*, *12*(2), 257–285. Advance online publication. DOI: 10.1207/s15516709cog1202_4

Tlili, A., Shehata, B., Adarkwah, M. A., Bozkurt, A., Hickey, D. T., Huang, R., & Agyemang, B. (2023). *What if the devil is my guardian angel ChatGPT as a case study of using chatbots in education*. Smart Learning Environments., DOI: 10.1186/s40561-023-00237-x

Venkatesh, V., Morris, M. G., Davis, G. B., & Davis, F. D. (2003). User acceptance of information technology: Toward a unifed view. *Management Information Systems Quarterly*, *27*(3), 425–478. DOI: 10.2307/30036540

Vygotsky, L. (1962). *Thought and language*. MIT Press. DOI: 10.1037/11193-000

Vygotsky, L. (1978). *Mind in Society: The Development of Higher Psychological Processes*. Harvard University Press.

Waseem, M., Das, T., Ahmad, A., Fehmideh, M., Liang, P., & Mikkonen, T. (2023). ChatGPT as a Software Development Bot: A Project-based Study. https://arxiv.org/abs/2310.13648

## KEY TERMS AND DEFINITIONS

**Generative AI:** Artificial intelligence models that can generate textual or multimedia data in response to a human query.

**Prompt:** A natural language instruction given to a generative AI.

**Large Language Model (LLM):** Artificial neural networks with a capability to understand and generate human languages.

**Natural Language Processing (NLP):** A branch of computation that deals with processing information presented in natural (human) languages.

**Neural pathways:** A connection between several neurons in the brain.

**Working memory:** The amount of memory used when performing a cognitive task.

**Cognitive schema:** The unique way of structuring information in a human brain.

**Non-linear thinking:** Thinking that requires several different perspectives and thought processes to be merged together to solve a problem.

**MKO:** "More Knowledgeable Other" – an entity in ZPD that is capable of guiding the learner.

**Jailbreaking:** Gaining unauthorized access to a system.

**Adversarial Training:** Voluntary attempts to break into a system in order to identify vulnerabilities, followed by modifications made to the system to prevent harmful use in real-life scenarios.

**Cognitive Load:** Amount of working memory needed to undertake an activity.

**AI Integrity:** A state of AI systems where no unethical responses must be produced against any prompt.

**Hallucination:** Response given by AI that is erroneous or contains misleading information presented as a fact.

Chapter 10

# Intercultural Communication and Assessment Practices in the Integration of AI With Education

**C. Santhini**
https://orcid.org/0000-0002-6161-049X
*Velalar College of Engineering and Technology, India*

**M. Ruba**
https://orcid.org/0000-0002-1614-7096
*Velalar College of Engineering and Technology, India*

**V. Sakthi Priya**
*Velalar College of Engineering and Technology, India*

**R. Hemalatha**
https://orcid.org/0000-0002-5535-7184
*Velalar College of Engineering and Technology, India*

## ABSTRACT

*Assessment practices play a crucial role in AI-integrated Education for Sustainable Development (ESD), serving to evaluate student learning outcomes, guide instructional practices, and inform decision-making processes. By leveraging AI technologies, educators can enhance the efficiency, scalability, and effectiveness of assessment practices in sustainable development education. However, it is essential to address the*

DOI: 10.4018/979-8-3693-5623-4.ch010

*challenges and considerations associated with AI-integrated assessment, including concerns about reliability, validity, bias, ethics, and pedagogy. As we navigate the complexities of the digital age, it is essential to ensure that assessment practices in AI-integrated ESD are aligned with the principles of equity, inclusivity, and social justice, empowering students to become informed, engaged, and responsible global citizens committed to building a more sustainable future.*

# 1. UNDERSTANDING INTERCULTURAL COMMUNICATION: BRIDGING DIVIDES IN A GLOBALIZED WORLD

## 1.1 Introduction

In an increasingly interconnected world, intercultural communication has emerged as a crucial skill for individuals and organizations alike. As societies become more diverse and globalized, the ability to effectively navigate cultural differences and communicate across linguistic and cultural boundaries is essential for building meaningful relationships, fostering cooperation, and addressing complex global challenges. This comprehensive exploration will delve into the fundamental principles of intercultural communication, examining its importance, challenges, and strategies for success in diverse cultural contexts. (Bennett, 2013)

## 1.2 Understanding Culture

At the heart of intercultural communication lies the concept of culture, which encompasses shared beliefs, values, norms, customs, and behaviors that characterize a particular group of people. Culture shapes individuals' perceptions, communication styles, and social interactions, influencing how they interpret and respond to verbal and nonverbal cues. It is important to recognize that culture is not static but rather dynamic and evolving, shaped by historical, social, economic, and political factors. Moreover, individuals often belong to multiple cultural groups simultaneously, leading to complex and multifaceted identities. (Ting-Toomey & Chung, 2012)

## 1.3 Key Components of Intercultural Communication

Intercultural communication involves the exchange of messages between individuals or groups from different cultural backgrounds. It encompasses both verbal and nonverbal communication, including language, gestures, facial expressions, body language, and social customs. Effective intercultural communication requires sensitivity to cultural differences and a willingness to adapt one's communication style to accommodate diverse cultural norms and expectations. Moreover, it involves active listening, empathy, and the ability to suspend judgment in order to understand others' perspectives and experiences. (Ting-Toomey & Chung, 2012)

### 1.3.1 Introduction

Intercultural communication is a complex process that involves the exchange of messages between individuals or groups from different cultural backgrounds. In today's globalized world, intercultural communication has become increasingly important as people from diverse cultural, ethnic, and linguistic backgrounds interact and collaborate in various contexts, including education, business, healthcare, and diplomacy. This exploration will delve into the key components of intercultural communication, examining the factors that shape communication across cultural boundaries and strategies for navigating diversity effectively.

### 1.3.2 Cultural Awareness and Sensitivity

Cultural awareness and sensitivity are fundamental components of intercultural communication. It involves recognizing and understanding cultural differences in values, beliefs, norms, and communication styles. Cultural awareness requires openness to learning about other cultures, suspending judgment, and approaching interactions with curiosity and respect. Sensitivity to cultural differences involves empathy, the ability to adapt one's communication style to accommodate diverse cultural norms, and an awareness of how cultural factors may influence perceptions and behaviors. Culturally aware individuals are able to navigate intercultural interactions more effectively, building rapport and fostering mutual understanding with people from diverse backgrounds. (Bennett, 2013)(Ting-Toomey & Chung, 2012) (Spitzberg & Changnon, 2009).

### 1.3.3 Language and Verbal Communication

Language plays a central role in intercultural communication, serving as a medium through which individuals express ideas, convey information, and build relationships. In multicultural settings, language differences can pose challenges to effective communication, leading to misunderstandings, misinterpretations, and conflicts. Therefore, proficiency in a common language or the use of translation and interpretation services may be necessary to facilitate communication across linguistic barriers. Moreover, awareness of linguistic diversity and the use of clear, simple language can enhance comprehension and minimize communication breakdowns. Additionally, verbal communication involves more than just words; tone of voice, intonation, volume, and pace of speech also convey meaning and can vary across cultures. Therefore, attentiveness to paralinguistic cues and the ability to interpret nuances in verbal communication are essential for effective intercultural communication. (Ting-Toomey & Chung, 2012)(Bennett, 2013)(Spitzberg & Changnon, 2009)

### 1.3.4 Nonverbal Communication and Body Language

Nonverbal communication, including body language, gestures, facial expressions, and eye contact, also plays a significant role in intercultural communication. Nonverbal cues often convey emotions, attitudes, and intentions more powerfully than words alone and can vary widely across cultures. For example, while direct eye contact may be interpreted as a sign of confidence and sincerity in some cultures, it may be perceived as disrespectful or confrontational in others. Similarly, gestures that are considered appropriate and meaningful in one culture may be misinterpreted or offensive in another. Therefore, cultural sensitivity and awareness of nonverbal cues are essential for avoiding miscommunication and building positive relationships across cultural boundaries.

### 1.3.5 Cultural Context and Contextual Understanding

Cultural context shapes the way communication is interpreted and understood in intercultural interactions. Contextual factors, such as social norms, cultural values, historical background, and situational context, influence the meaning of messages and the expectations for appropriate behavior. Therefore, understanding the cultural context is essential for interpreting communication accurately and responding appropriately. Moreover, cultural context extends beyond individual interactions to broader societal and institutional norms and practices. For example, cultural differences in power distance, collectivism vs. individualism, and attitudes toward authority can influence communication dynamics in organizational settings. Therefore, awareness of cultural context and sensitivity to cultural nuances are essential for navigating intercultural interactions effectively.

### 1.3.6 Adaptability and Flexibility

Adaptability and flexibility are key attributes of effective intercultural communicators. It involves the ability to adjust one's communication style, behavior, and expectations to accommodate diverse cultural norms and preferences. Adaptability requires openness to new experiences, a willingness to learn from others, and the ability to embrace uncertainty and ambiguity. Moreover, flexibility involves the capacity to respond to unexpected challenges and navigate cultural differences creatively and resourcefully. By being adaptable and flexible, individuals can build rapport, establish trust, and foster meaningful connections with people from diverse cultural backgrounds.

### 1.3.7 Empathy and Perspective-taking

Empathy and perspective-taking are essential for building rapport and fostering mutual understanding in intercultural communication. Empathy involves the ability to understand and share the feelings, thoughts, and experiences of others, while perspective-taking involves seeing the world from another person's point of view. By empathizing with others and adopting their perspective, individuals can develop deeper connections and bridge cultural divides. Moreover, empathy facilitates active listening, validation of others' experiences, and acknowledgement of cultural differences, fostering trust and respect in intercultural interactions.

## 1.4 Challenges in Intercultural Communication

Despite its importance, intercultural communication is fraught with challenges and complexities. Cultural differences in communication styles, language proficiency, and nonverbal cues can lead to misunderstandings, misinterpretations, and conflicts. Moreover, stereotypes, prejudices, and ethnocentrism can hinder intercultural understanding and perpetuate intergroup tensions. In addition, power dynamics, inequalities, and historical tensions may exacerbate communication barriers and reinforce social divides. Overcoming these challenges requires awareness, empathy, and a commitment to building trust and mutual respect across cultural boundaries.

- Challenges in intercultural communication arise due to differences in cultural norms, values, communication styles, and worldviews among individuals or groups from diverse cultural backgrounds. (Ting-Toomey & Chung, 2012) These challenges can include:
- Language Barriers: Differences in language proficiency and fluency can lead to misunderstandings, misinterpretations, and communication breakdowns. Translation and interpretation services may be needed to facilitate communication across linguistic barriers. (Bennett, 2013
- Nonverbal Communication Differences: Variations in body language, gestures, facial expressions, and eye contact can convey different meanings and interpretations across cultures, leading to confusion or misinterpretation of intentions. (Spitzberg & Changnon, 2009)
- Cultural Norms and Expectations: Different cultural norms regarding politeness, hierarchy, personal space, and social etiquette can influence communi-

cation dynamics and expectations for appropriate behavior, leading to cultural misunderstandings or offense.

- Stereotypes and Prejudices: Stereotypes, prejudices, and biases based on cultural or ethnic backgrounds can hinder effective communication and perpetuate intergroup tensions, affecting the quality of relationships and interactions. (Ting-Toomey & Chung, 2012)
- Ethnocentrism: Ethnocentrism, or the tendency to view one's own cultural group as superior to others, can lead to judgmental attitudes, dismissiveness, and lack of appreciation for cultural diversity, inhibiting open-mindedness and empathy in intercultural interactions. (Bennett, 2013)
- Cultural Sensitivity and Awareness: Lack of awareness or sensitivity to cultural differences and nuances can result in unintentional disrespect or insensitivity, undermining trust and rapport in intercultural relationships.
- Power Dynamics: Power imbalances based on factors such as race, gender, socioeconomic status, or nationality can influence communication dynamics and the distribution of voice and influence in intercultural interactions, affecting the fairness and inclusivity of communication processes.
- Conflict Resolution: Cultural differences in conflict management styles, negotiation strategies, and resolution mechanisms can complicate efforts to address conflicts or disagreements in intercultural contexts, requiring cultural sensitivity and adaptive strategies for effective resolution.
- Addressing these challenges requires cultural competence, empathy, open-mindedness, and willingness to learn and adapt to diverse cultural norms and perspectives. Strategies for overcoming intercultural communication challenges include enhancing language proficiency, developing cultural awareness and sensitivity, practicing active listening and empathy, fostering mutual respect and understanding, and promoting inclusive communication practices that recognize and value cultural diversity. (Bennett, 2013)

## 1.5 Strategies for Effective Intercultural Communication

Several strategies can enhance intercultural communication and promote mutual understanding in diverse cultural contexts. First and foremost, individuals must cultivate cultural competence, which involves developing an awareness of one's own cultural biases and assumptions, as well as a willingness to learn about and respect other cultures. Active listening, open-mindedness, and curiosity are essential for bridging cultural divides and building meaningful relationships. Moreover, language proficiency, intercultural training, and cultural immersion experiences can enhance communication skills and foster intercultural competence. Finally, building rapport, establishing common ground, and practicing empathy are critical for overcoming cultural barriers and fostering collaboration and cooperation in multicultural settings. Effective intercultural communication requires strategies that promote understanding, respect, and collaboration across diverse cultural backgrounds. Here are some key strategies (Ting-Toomey & Chung, 2012)(Bennett, 2013)(Spitzberg & Changnon, 2009)(Adams, Bell, & Griffin, 2007):

- Cultural Awareness and Sensitivity: Develop an awareness of your own cultural biases, assumptions, and values, and strive to understand and respect the cultural norms, beliefs, and perspectives of others. Avoid making assumptions or judgments based on stereotypes, and approach intercultural interactions with openness, curiosity, and respect.
- Active Listening: Practice active listening by focusing on what the other person is saying without interrupting or imposing your own assumptions. Pay attention to both verbal and nonverbal cues, and ask clarifying questions to ensure understanding. Demonstrate empathy and validate the other person's experiences and perspectives.
- Adaptability and Flexibility: Be adaptable and flexible in your communication style, behavior, and expectations to accommodate diverse cultural norms and preferences. Be willing to adjust your approach based on the cultural context and the needs of the situation, and be open to learning from others.
- Clear and Simple Communication: Use clear, simple language and avoid jargon or complex terminology that may be difficult for non-native speakers to understand. Be mindful of differences in language proficiency and adjust your communication style accordingly to ensure clarity and comprehension.
- Respect for Differences: Embrace cultural differences as opportunities for learning and growth, and approach intercultural interactions with a mindset of curiosity and respect. Recognize that diversity enriches our perspectives and enhances creativity, innovation, and problem-solving.
- Nonverbal Communication: Pay attention to nonverbal cues, such as body language, gestures, facial expressions, and eye contact, as these can convey important messages and meanings across cultures. Be mindful of cultural differences in nonverbal communication and adapt your behavior accordingly.
- Seek Feedback and Clarification: If you are unsure about something or if there is a potential misunderstanding, don't hesitate to seek feedback or clarification from the other person. Ask open-ended questions and encourage them to share their perspective and concerns to facilitate mutual understanding and resolution of any communication challenges.
- Cultural Immersion and Learning: Take opportunities to immerse yourself in different cultures, whether through travel, cultural events, or interactions with diverse communities. Engage in cross-cultural learning experiences and

seek out resources, such as books, articles, and workshops, to deepen your understanding of different cultures and perspectives.

- Building Trust and Rapport: Invest time and effort in building trust and rapport with individuals from diverse cultural backgrounds. Show genuine interest in their culture, experiences, and perspectives, and demonstrate empathy, integrity, and authenticity in your interactions. Building trust is essential for fostering open communication and collaboration in intercultural relationships.
- Conflict Resolution Skills: Develop effective conflict resolution skills that are sensitive to cultural differences and respectful of diverse perspectives. Approach conflicts or disagreements with empathy, patience, and a willingness to listen and compromise, and seek mutually beneficial solutions that respect the needs and interests of all parties involved.

By implementing these strategies, individuals can enhance their ability to communicate effectively across cultural boundaries, foster mutual understanding and respect, and build inclusive and collaborative relationships in diverse cultural contexts.

## 1.6 Applications of Intercultural Communication

Intercultural communication has broad applications across various domains, including business, education, diplomacy, healthcare, and international development. In the business world, effective intercultural communication is essential for building successful partnerships, negotiating deals, and navigating global markets. In education, intercultural communication skills are critical for promoting diversity, equity, and inclusion in the classroom and preparing students for success in a multicultural society. In diplomacy, intercultural communication plays a vital role in building trust, resolving conflicts, and fostering peace and cooperation among nations. In healthcare, intercultural communication is essential for delivering culturally competent care and addressing the unique needs of diverse patient populations. Finally, in international development, intercultural communication is crucial for promoting cross-cultural understanding, empowering marginalized communities, and advancing social justice and human rights. Intercultural communication has diverse applications across various domains and contexts, including:

- Business and International Trade: In the globalized economy, intercultural communication is essential for conducting business transactions, negotiating deals, and building partnerships across borders. Understanding cultural nuances, etiquette, and communication styles is critical for establishing trust, fostering positive relationships, and navigating cultural differences in business settings.

- Diplomacy and International Relations: Intercultural communication plays a crucial role in diplomacy and international relations, where representatives from different countries interact to address global issues, negotiate treaties, and resolve conflicts. Effective intercultural communication skills are essential for building diplomatic rapport, bridging cultural divides, and fostering cooperation and collaboration among nations.
- Education and Academic Exchange: In educational settings, intercultural communication is vital for promoting diversity, equity, and inclusion, both within classrooms and across campuses. Intercultural communication skills enable educators to create inclusive learning environments, facilitate cross-cultural dialogue, and support the academic success of students from diverse cultural backgrounds. Moreover, intercultural exchange programs provide opportunities for students and scholars to learn from different cultures, perspectives, and academic traditions.
- Healthcare and Cross-Cultural Medicine: In healthcare settings, intercultural communication is essential for delivering culturally competent care and addressing the unique needs of diverse patient populations. Healthcare providers must be sensitive to cultural differences in health beliefs, practices, and communication styles to effectively communicate with patients from diverse cultural backgrounds, build trust, and provide quality care.
- Humanitarian Aid and Development Work: Intercultural communication is critical for humanitarian aid and development organizations working in culturally diverse communities around the world. Understanding local customs, traditions, and social norms is essential for designing culturally appropriate interventions, building community trust, and fostering sustainable development outcomes.
- Media and Cross-Cultural Representation: In the media and entertainment industry, intercultural communication plays a significant role in shaping representations of diverse cultures and identities. Media professionals must be sensitive to cultural stereotypes, biases, and misrepresentations and strive to promote accurate, respectful, and inclusive portrayals of diverse communities.
- Travel and Tourism: Intercultural communication skills are essential for travelers and tourism professionals navigating diverse cultural landscapes and interacting with people from different cultural backgrounds. Understanding cultural norms, customs, and taboos can enhance travelers' experiences, facilitate cross-cultural exchanges, and promote positive interactions with locals.
- Community and Social Services: Intercultural communication is vital for community organizations and social service providers working with diverse

populations in multicultural communities. Culturally competent communication enables organizations to effectively engage with community members, address their needs, and develop programs and services that are responsive to cultural diversity.

- Technology and Virtual Collaboration: In an increasingly digital world, intercultural communication is also relevant in virtual environments, where individuals from different cultural backgrounds collaborate and communicate remotely. Understanding cultural differences in virtual communication styles, technology use, and digital etiquette is essential for fostering productive virtual collaborations and overcoming communication barriers in global teams.
- Conflict Resolution and Peacebuilding: Intercultural communication skills are valuable in conflict resolution and peacebuilding efforts, where individuals from conflicting groups seek to understand each other's perspectives, address grievances, and negotiate peaceful resolutions. Effective intercultural communication promotes empathy, dialogue, and reconciliation, contributing to the resolution of conflicts and the promotion of social harmony.

Overall, intercultural communication is a fundamental skill with wide-ranging applications in diverse contexts, enabling individuals and organizations to navigate cultural diversity, build relationships, and foster mutual understanding and cooperation across cultural boundaries.

## 1.7 Conclusion

In conclusion, intercultural communication is a multifaceted and dynamic process that plays a central role in bridging divides and fostering mutual understanding in an increasingly diverse and interconnected world. By cultivating cultural competence, practicing empathy, and embracing diversity, individuals and organizations can overcome communication barriers, build meaningful relationships, and work together to address pressing global challenges. As we navigate the complexities of a rapidly changing world, the principles of intercultural communication will continue to be essential for promoting harmony, cooperation, and social justice across cultural boundaries.

# 2. ASSESSMENT PRACTICES IN AI-INTEGRATED EDUCATION FOR SUSTAINABLE DEVELOPMENT (ESD): PROMOTING MEANINGFUL LEARNING AND EVALUATION IN THE DIGITAL AGE

## 2.1 Introduction

Assessment is a fundamental component of education, serving to evaluate student learning outcomes, guide instructional practices, and inform decision-making processes. In the context of Education for Sustainable Development (ESD), assessment plays a critical role in evaluating students' understanding of sustainability concepts, fostering critical thinking skills, and promoting active engagement with real-world sustainability issues. With the integration of Artificial Intelligence (AI) into education, assessment practices are undergoing transformation, offering new opportunities to enhance teaching, learning, and evaluation processes. This comprehensive exploration will delve into the significance of assessment practices in AI-integrated ESD, examining their benefits, challenges, and implications for promoting meaningful learning and evaluation in the digital age.

## 2.2 Understanding AI-Integrated ESD

Education for Sustainable Development (ESD) aims to equip students with the knowledge, skills, and values necessary to address pressing socio-environmental challenges and promote a more sustainable future. AI-integrated ESD leverages artificial intelligence technologies, such as machine learning algorithms, natural language processing, and data analytics, to enhance teaching, learning, and assessment practices in sustainable development education. AI tools can analyze large datasets, identify patterns and trends, and provide personalized feedback to students, thereby facilitating more targeted instruction and assessment strategies. Moreover, AI-integrated ESD offers opportunities for immersive learning experiences, simulations, and virtual reality environments, enabling students to explore complex sustainability issues in interactive and engaging ways.

AI-integrated ESD encompasses various applications of AI technologies, including machine learning algorithms, natural language processing, data analytics, virtual reality, and augmented reality, to support teaching, learning, and assessment processes. These technologies can analyze large datasets, personalize learning experiences, provide real-time feedback, simulate complex environmental scenarios, and facilitate immersive learning experiences, thereby enhancing engagement, motivation, and learning outcomes in sustainability education. Key aspects of AI-integrated ESD include:

- Personalized Learning: AI technologies can analyze students' learning preferences, strengths, and weaknesses to tailor instruction and resources to individual needs, interests, and learning styles. Personalized learning approaches can enhance engagement, motivation, and retention in sustainability education by providing learners with relevant and adaptive learning experiences.
- Data-driven Decision-making: AI technologies can analyze educational data, such as student performance metrics, learning trajectories, and assessment results, to inform instructional planning, curriculum design, and policy decisions in sustainability education. Data-driven approaches enable educators and policymakers to identify trends, patterns, and areas for improvement, leading to more effective and evidence-based practices.
- Predictive Analytics: AI technologies can use predictive analytics to forecast future trends, outcomes, and challenges in sustainability education, enabling proactive interventions and targeted support for at-risk learners. Predictive models can identify early warning signs of academic difficulties, dropout risk, or disengagement, allowing educators to implement timely interventions to support student success.
- Simulation and Virtual Reality: AI-powered simulations and virtual reality environments can provide immersive and interactive learning experiences in sustainability education, allowing learners to explore complex environmental scenarios, simulate decision-making processes, and experiment with innovative solutions to real-world sustainability challenges. Virtual reality technologies can enhance experiential learning, critical thinking, and problem-solving skills in sustainability education.
- Natural Language Processing: AI technologies such as natural language processing (NLP) can analyze text-based resources, educational materials, and student-generated content to extract insights, assess comprehension, and provide personalized feedback. NLP algorithms can support language learning, reading comprehension, and writing skills development in sustainability education by identifying language patterns, vocabulary usage, and grammatical errors.
- Assessment and Feedback: AI technologies can automate assessment processes, providing instant feedback on student performance, progress, and mastery of sustainability concepts and competencies. Automated assessment tools can reduce educators' workload, enhance the efficiency and scalability of assessment practices, and provide timely and targeted feedback to support student learning and improvement.

## 2.3 Benefits of AI-Integrated Assessment Practices

The integration of AI into assessment practices offers several benefits for education for sustainable development. Firstly, AI algorithms can analyze student data to identify learning gaps, personalize instruction, and provide targeted feedback, thereby promoting individualized learning and supporting students' diverse learning needs. Additionally, AI-powered assessment tools can facilitate the assessment of complex skills and competencies, such as critical thinking, problem-solving, and systems thinking, which are essential for addressing sustainability challenges. Moreover, AI-integrated assessment practices can enhance the efficiency and scalability of assessment processes, enabling educators to assess student learning outcomes more effectively and efficiently. Finally, AI technologies can provide insights into student learning behaviors and preferences, enabling educators to optimize instructional strategies and interventions to support student success.

AI-integrated assessment practices offer a range of benefits that enhance the effectiveness, efficiency, and fairness of assessment processes in education. Some of the key benefits include:

- Personalization: AI technologies can analyze large datasets of student performance and behavior to provide personalized assessments tailored to individual learning needs, preferences, and abilities. By adapting assessment tasks, questions, and feedback to each student's unique profile, AI-integrated assessments can support differentiated instruction and promote student engagement and achievement.
- Immediate Feedback: AI-powered assessment tools can provide immediate feedback to students on their performance, highlighting areas of strength and areas for improvement. Instant feedback enables students to identify misconceptions, correct errors, and adjust their learning strategies in real time, leading to more effective learning outcomes and greater self-regulation.
- Adaptive Assessment: AI algorithms can dynamically adjust assessment difficulty and complexity based on students' responses, ensuring that assessment tasks are appropriately challenging and aligned with learners' skill levels. Adaptive assessments can optimize learning progression, minimize frustration, and maximize student motivation and achievement by providing tailored experiences that meet individual learning needs.
- Efficiency and Scalability: AI technologies automate time-consuming tasks such as test scoring, item analysis, and data interpretation, reducing educators' workload and administrative burden associated with assessment. Automated assessment processes improve efficiency, accuracy, and scalability, allowing

educators to focus more time and resources on instructional planning, student support, and personalized learning interventions.

- Data-driven Decision-making: AI-integrated assessment tools generate rich educational data on student performance, learning trajectories, and instructional effectiveness, enabling data-driven decision-making at the classroom, school, and system levels. Educators can analyze assessment data to identify trends, patterns, and areas for improvement, inform instructional planning, and personalize learning experiences to better meet students' needs and goals.
- Validity and Reliability: AI algorithms can enhance the validity and reliability of assessment instruments by minimizing bias, errors, and inconsistencies in scoring and evaluation. AI-powered assessments can standardize scoring criteria, ensure objectivity and consistency in grading, and reduce human subjectivity and variability, leading to more accurate and reliable assessment results.
- Accessibility and Inclusivity: AI-integrated assessment practices can accommodate diverse learning needs, preferences, and abilities, making assessments more accessible and inclusive for all students, including those with disabilities or special educational needs. AI technologies can provide alternative formats, accommodations, and supports to ensure that assessments are fair, equitable, and accessible to learners with diverse backgrounds and learning profiles.
- Innovative Assessment Formats: AI technologies enable the development of innovative assessment formats and modalities, such as interactive simulations, virtual reality environments, and game-based assessments, that engage students in authentic, real-world tasks and problem-solving activities. These immersive and interactive assessment experiences enhance student motivation, creativity, and critical thinking skills, while also providing rich, authentic performance data for evaluation and feedback.

## 2.4 Challenges and Considerations

Despite their potential benefits, AI-integrated assessment practices also pose several challenges and considerations. Firstly, there are concerns about the reliability and validity of AI algorithms in assessing complex skills and competencies, as well as the potential for algorithmic bias and discrimination. Moreover, there are ethical considerations related to data privacy, security, and student consent in the collection and analysis of student data. Additionally, there may be challenges in integrating AI technologies into existing assessment practices and workflows, as well as the need for professional development and training for educators to effectively use AI-powered assessment tools. Finally, there are questions about the role of human judgment and expertise in assessment processes and the potential for AI to replace or augment traditional forms of assessment.

## 2.5 Promoting Meaningful Learning and Evaluation

To promote meaningful learning and evaluation in AI-integrated ESD, educators must adopt a pedagogically sound approach to assessment that prioritizes authentic, contextually relevant, and socially meaningful tasks and activities. Assessment tasks should align with the goals and objectives of ESD, focusing on real-world sustainability issues and challenges. Moreover, assessment practices should be designed to promote higher-order thinking skills, such as critical thinking, creativity, and problem-solving, rather than rote memorization or regurgitation of facts. Additionally, educators should employ a variety of assessment methods and tools, including performance-based assessments, project-based learning, portfolios, and self-assessment, to provide multiple opportunities for students to demonstrate their understanding and skills.

## 2.6 Conclusion

In conclusion, assessment practices play a crucial role in AI-integrated Education for Sustainable Development (ESD), serving to evaluate student learning outcomes, guide instructional practices, and inform decision-making processes. By leveraging AI technologies, educators can enhance the efficiency, scalability, and effectiveness of assessment practices in sustainable development education. However, it is essential to address the challenges and considerations associated with AI-integrated assessment, including concerns about reliability, validity, bias, ethics, and pedagogy. By adopting a pedagogically sound approach to assessment and prioritizing meaningful learning and evaluation, educators can harness the potential of AI to promote student engagement, critical thinking, and active participation in addressing pressing sustainability challenges. As we navigate the complexities of the digital age, it is essential to ensure that assessment practices in AI-integrated ESD are aligned with the principles of equity, inclusivity, and social justice, empowering students to become informed, engaged, and responsible global citizens committed to building a more sustainable future.

# 3. POLICIES FOR ETHICAL AI INTEGRATION IN EDUCATION: SAFEGUARDING STUDENTS' RIGHTS AND PROMOTING RESPONSIBLE USE OF TECHNOLOGY

## 3.1 Introduction

Artificial Intelligence (AI) is increasingly being integrated into educational settings, offering new opportunities to enhance teaching, learning, and assessment practices. However, the adoption of AI in education raises ethical concerns related to data privacy, algorithmic bias, transparency, and equity. To address these challenges and promote ethical AI integration, policymakers, educators, and stakeholders must collaborate to develop comprehensive policies and guidelines. This comprehensive exploration will delve into the significance of policies for ethical AI integration in education, examining their objectives, principles, and implications for safeguarding students' rights and promoting responsible use of technology.

## 3.2 Understanding Ethical AI Integration

Ethical AI integration in education involves the responsible and transparent deployment of AI technologies to enhance teaching, learning, and assessment practices while safeguarding students' rights, privacy, and well-being. Ethical AI integration requires adherence to principles of fairness, transparency, accountability, and inclusivity throughout the AI lifecycle, from data collection and algorithm development to deployment and evaluation. Moreover, ethical AI integration involves promoting digital literacy, critical thinking, and ethical reasoning skills among students to empower them to navigate the complexities of AI-enabled technologies responsibly. Key components of Ethical AI Integration include:

- Transparency: Ethical AI integration entails transparency in the development, deployment, and use of AI systems, including disclosing information about algorithms, data sources, decision-making processes, and potential biases. Transparency enables accountability, fosters trust among stakeholders, and promotes informed decision-making about AI technologies.
- Fairness and Equity: Ethical AI integration requires ensuring fairness and equity in AI systems to prevent discrimination, bias, and disparities in outcomes. This involves designing AI algorithms and models that are unbiased, equitable, and inclusive, and implementing mechanisms to detect and mitigate algorithmic biases and unfair outcomes.
- Accountability and Responsibility: Ethical AI integration involves establishing clear lines of accountability and responsibility for AI systems and their

impacts. This includes defining roles and responsibilities for developers, users, and stakeholders, establishing mechanisms for oversight and governance, and holding individuals and organizations accountable for the ethical use of AI technologies.

- Privacy and Data Protection: Ethical AI integration prioritizes privacy and data protection by safeguarding sensitive information and respecting individuals' rights to privacy, autonomy, and consent. This entails implementing robust data governance frameworks, anonymizing and securing data, and ensuring compliance with relevant privacy regulations and standards.
- Beneficence and Non-maleficence: Ethical AI integration requires prioritizing the well-being and safety of individuals and communities by maximizing benefits and minimizing harms associated with AI technologies. This involves conducting risk assessments, considering potential societal impacts, and prioritizing ethical considerations in AI design, development, and deployment.
- Explainability and Interpretability: Ethical AI integration involves ensuring that AI systems are explainable and interpretable, enabling users to understand how decisions are made, interpret algorithmic outputs, and assess the reliability and trustworthiness of AI technologies. Explainable AI promotes transparency, accountability, and user trust in AI systems.
- Social and Environmental Impact: Ethical AI integration considers the broader social, environmental, and ethical implications of AI technologies, beyond individual use cases or applications. This includes assessing the potential socio-economic consequences, environmental sustainability, and ethical implications of AI deployment, and promoting responsible AI innovation that aligns with societal values and goals.
- Stakeholder Engagement and Participation: Ethical AI integration involves engaging stakeholders, including affected communities, users, experts, policymakers, and civil society organizations, in decision-making processes related to AI development, deployment, and governance. Stakeholder engagement promotes inclusivity, diversity of perspectives, and democratic participation in shaping AI policies and practices.
- Continuous Learning and Improvement: Ethical AI integration requires a commitment to continuous learning, adaptation, and improvement to address emerging ethical challenges, technological developments, and societal concerns. This includes fostering a culture of ethical reflection, interdisciplinary collaboration, and knowledge sharing among AI developers, researchers, practitioners, and policymakers.

## 3.3 Objectives of Policies for Ethical AI Integration

### 3.3.1 Policies for ethical AI integration in education aim to achieve several objectives

- Protecting Student Privacy: Policies should establish clear guidelines for the collection, storage, and use of student data, ensuring compliance with data protection laws and regulations. Moreover, policies should address issues related to data security, consent, and data ownership, safeguarding students' privacy rights and preventing unauthorized access or misuse of personal data.
- Mitigating Algorithmic Bias: Policies should require transparency and accountability in algorithmic decision-making processes, addressing issues of bias, discrimination, and fairness. Moreover, policies should promote the use of diverse and representative datasets and algorithmic auditing practices to mitigate bias and ensure equitable outcomes for all students, regardless of race, gender, ethnicity, or socio-economic status.
- Promoting Transparency and Accountability: Policies should mandate transparency in AI systems and algorithms used in education, ensuring that stakeholders understand how AI technologies work, their limitations, and potential implications for teaching and learning. Moreover, policies should establish mechanisms for accountability and oversight, enabling stakeholders to challenge algorithmic decisions and hold responsible parties accountable for any adverse impacts or ethical violations.
- Fostering Digital Literacy and Ethical Awareness: Policies should prioritize the integration of digital literacy and ethical education into the curriculum, equipping students with the knowledge, skills, and values necessary to critically evaluate and ethically engage with AI-enabled technologies. Moreover, policies should support professional development opportunities for educators to enhance their digital literacy and ethical competence in using AI technologies in teaching and assessment practices.

### 3.3.2 Policies for ethical AI integration in education should be guided by several key principles

- Human-Centered Design: AI technologies should be designed with the needs, values, and preferences of students and educators in mind, prioritizing user-centered approaches that enhance usability, accessibility, and inclusivity.
- Transparency and Explainability: AI systems and algorithms used in education should be transparent, explainable, and accountable, enabling stakehold-

ers to understand how decisions are made, identify potential biases or errors, and challenge algorithmic outcomes.

- Fairness and Equity: AI technologies should be designed and deployed in a manner that promotes fairness, equity, and inclusivity, ensuring that all students have equal access to educational opportunities and resources, regardless of background or identity.
- Data Privacy and Security: Student data should be collected, stored, and used in accordance with applicable laws, regulations, and ethical standards, prioritizing data privacy, security, and confidentiality to protect students' rights and interests.
- Ethical Use of Technology: AI technologies should be used in ethically responsible and socially beneficial ways, promoting the ethical use of technology for educational purposes and minimizing potential harms or risks to students' well-being and development.

## 3.4 Implementation and Evaluation

To effectively implement and evaluate policies for ethical AI integration in education, stakeholders must collaborate to develop clear guidelines, protocols, and procedures for compliance and enforcement. Moreover, ongoing monitoring, evaluation, and refinement of policies are essential to ensure their effectiveness, relevance, and responsiveness to evolving ethical and technological challenges. Stakeholder engagement, transparency, and accountability are critical for fostering trust and confidence in AI-enabled educational technologies and promoting a culture of ethical responsibility and innovation in education. Implementing and evaluating policies for ethical AI integration in education involves a systematic approach to address ethical considerations, promote responsible use of AI technologies, and ensure positive outcomes for learners, educators, and stakeholders. Here's a framework for implementing and evaluating such policies:

- Policy Development and Governance: Establish a multidisciplinary task force or committee comprising educators, researchers, policymakers, AI experts, and stakeholders to develop ethical AI integration policies.
- Conduct a comprehensive review of existing AI ethics frameworks, guidelines, and best practices in education to inform policy development.
- Ethical Guidelines and Standards: Develop clear and comprehensive ethical guidelines and standards for AI integration in education, addressing issues such as algorithmic bias, data privacy, transparency, accountability, and human rights.

- Risk Assessment and Mitigation: Conduct a thorough risk assessment to identify potential ethical risks, biases, and unintended consequences associated with AI technologies in education.
- Transparency and Accountability: Promote transparency and accountability in AI integration by requiring developers and vendors to disclose information about algorithms, data sources, decision-making processes, and potential biases.
- Data Privacy and Security: Implement robust data governance policies and practices to protect student privacy, confidentiality, and data security in accordance with relevant privacy laws and regulations.
- Educator Training and Capacity Building: Provide professional development opportunities and training programs for educators to build their capacity in understanding and implementing ethical AI practices in teaching and learning.
- Stakeholder Engagement and Community Outreach: Engage stakeholders, including students, parents, community members, and advocacy groups, in the policy development process to ensure diverse perspectives and input.
- Monitoring and Evaluation: Establish mechanisms for ongoing monitoring, evaluation, and continuous improvement of the ethical AI integration policy.
- Feedback and Iteration: Solicit feedback from stakeholders, including educators, students, and administrators, on their experiences with AI integration and the effectiveness of ethical policies and practices.
- Dissemination and Communication: Communicate the ethical AI integration policy, guidelines, and resources to all stakeholders through clear, accessible, and culturally responsive channels.

By following this framework, education policymakers can implement and evaluate policies for ethical AI integration that prioritize the well-being, dignity, and rights of all stakeholders, uphold ethical principles, and promote positive educational outcomes in the digital age.

## 3.5 Conclusion

In conclusion, policies for ethical AI integration in education play a crucial role in safeguarding students' rights, promoting responsible use of technology, and ensuring equitable and inclusive access to educational opportunities. By adhering to principles of fairness, transparency, accountability, and inclusivity, policymakers, educators, and stakeholders can address ethical concerns related to AI-enabled technologies and harness their potential to enhance teaching, learning, and assessment practices. As we navigate the complexities of the digital age, it is essential to prioritize ethical considerations and human values in the design, deployment, and evaluation of AI technologies in education, fostering a culture of ethical responsibility, innovation, and equity in educational settings.

## 4. PROMOTING EDUCATION FOR SOCIAL JUSTICE THROUGH AI-INTEGRATED EDUCATION FOR SUSTAINABLE DEVELOPMENT (ESD): EMPOWERING STUDENTS FOR A JUST AND EQUITABLE SOCIETY

### 4.1 Introduction

Education for Sustainable Development (ESD) and Education for Social Justice (ESJ) are integral components of contemporary education, aiming to empower students with the knowledge, skills, and values necessary to address pressing socio-environmental challenges and promote a more just and equitable society. With the integration of Artificial Intelligence (AI) into education, new opportunities emerge to advance ESJ objectives and foster transformative learning experiences. This comprehensive exploration will delve into the significance of promoting education for social justice through AI-integrated ESD, examining its potential benefits, challenges, and implications for empowering students for a just and equitable society.

### 4.2 Understanding Education for Social Justice

Education for Social Justice (ESJ) encompasses efforts to promote equity, diversity, inclusion, and human rights within educational systems and society at large. It seeks to address systemic inequalities, discrimination, and social injustices by fostering critical consciousness, empathy, and a commitment to social change among students. ESJ aims to empower individuals to recognize and challenge injustice, advocate for marginalized communities, and work towards creating a more equitable and inclusive world. Key components of Education for Social Justice include:

- Critical Inquiry and Reflection: ESJ encourages learners to critically examine social, economic, and political structures that perpetuate inequality and injustice. Through critical inquiry and reflection, students analyze power dynamics, privilege, and marginalization in society, question dominant narratives, and develop a deeper understanding of social justice issues.
- Empowerment and Agency: ESJ empowers individuals to recognize their agency and capacity to effect positive change in their communities and society. By providing opportunities for civic engagement, advocacy, and activ-

ism, ESJ enables learners to become active agents of social transformation and contribute to building a more just and equitable world.

- Equity and Inclusion: ESJ promotes equity and inclusion by addressing systemic barriers to education, advocating for the rights and needs of marginalized and underserved populations, and creating inclusive learning environments that honor diversity and celebrate cultural differences. ESJ recognizes the interconnectedness of social identities and experiences and seeks to dismantle structures of oppression that perpetuate inequality and exclusion.
- Human Rights and Social Responsibility: ESJ emphasizes the importance of human rights, social responsibility, and ethical citizenship in fostering a culture of respect, dignity, and justice. By promoting awareness of human rights violations, historical injustices, and global challenges, ESJ encourages learners to take action to uphold human rights, defend social justice, and promote solidarity with marginalized communities.
- Intersectionality and Interconnectedness: ESJ recognizes the intersectionality of social identities, experiences, and systems of oppression, acknowledging that individuals may face multiple forms of discrimination and marginalization based on factors such as race, gender, class, sexuality, and ability. ESJ emphasizes the interconnectedness of social justice issues and encourages intersectional approaches to advocacy and activism that address the root causes of inequality and oppression.
- Community Engagement and Collaboration: ESJ fosters collaboration, dialogue, and collective action among learners, educators, community members, and stakeholders to address social justice issues and promote positive change. By engaging with diverse perspectives, building coalitions, and mobilizing resources, ESJ initiatives create opportunities for collaboration and solidarity in advancing social justice goals.
- Transformative Learning and Praxis: ESJ aims to facilitate transformative learning experiences that challenge learners' assumptions, beliefs, and worldviews, leading to personal and social transformation. Through praxis, or the integration of theory and action, ESJ encourages learners to apply their knowledge and skills to real-world contexts, engage in meaningful social action, and reflect on their roles as agents of change in society.

## 4.3 Integration of AI into Education for Sustainable Development

The integration of Artificial Intelligence (AI) into Education for Sustainable Development (ESD) offers new opportunities to enhance teaching, learning, and assessment practices in ways that promote social justice objectives. AI technologies, such as machine learning algorithms, natural language processing, and data analytics, can analyze large datasets, identify patterns and trends, and provide personalized feedback to students, thereby facilitating more targeted instruction and assessment strategies. Moreover, AI-integrated ESD offers opportunities for immersive learning experiences, simulations, and virtual reality environments, enabling students to explore complex socio-environmental issues from diverse perspectives and engage in critical reflection and dialogue.

### 4.3.1 Benefits of Promoting Education for Social Justice through AI-Integrated ESD

Promoting education for social justice through AI-integrated ESD offers several potential benefits:

- Enhanced Access and Inclusivity: AI technologies can personalize learning experiences to accommodate diverse learning styles, abilities, and backgrounds, thereby promoting inclusivity and equitable access to educational opportunities for all students.
- Empowering Student Voice and Agency: AI-integrated ESD can empower students to actively participate in their own learning process, exercise agency, and contribute to addressing real-world social justice issues through project-based learning, collaborative problem-solving, and civic engagement activities.
- Fostering Critical Consciousness and Empathy: AI technologies can facilitate the exploration of complex social justice issues, helping students develop critical thinking skills, empathy, and a deeper understanding of systemic injustices and inequalities.
- Promoting Collaborative Action and Social Change: AI-integrated ESD can foster collaboration, dialogue, and collective action among students, educators, and community members to address pressing social justice issues and advocate for positive change in their local and global communities.

### 4.3.2 Challenges and Considerations

Despite its potential benefits, promoting education for social justice through AI-integrated ESD also poses several challenges and considerations:

- Ethical and Privacy Concerns: There are ethical concerns related to the collection, storage, and use of student data in AI-powered educational technologies, as well as the potential for algorithmic bias and discrimination.

- Digital Divide and Access Inequities: There is a risk of exacerbating existing inequities in access to technology and digital literacy skills, particularly for marginalized and underserved communities who may lack access to reliable internet connectivity, devices, or technical support.
- Cultural and Contextual Sensitivity: AI-integrated ESD must be sensitive to cultural, social, and linguistic diversity, recognizing the unique needs, perspectives, and experiences of students from different cultural backgrounds and communities.
- Teacher Professional Development: Educators require training and support to effectively integrate AI technologies into their teaching practices and promote education for social justice objectives, including digital literacy, critical pedagogy, and culturally responsive teaching strategies.

### 4.3.3 Strategies for Promoting Education for Social Justice through AI-Integrated ESD

To effectively promote education for social justice through AI-integrated ESD, several strategies can be employed:

- Equitable Access and Digital Inclusion: Policies and initiatives should be implemented to ensure equitable access to technology and digital literacy skills for all students, regardless of socio-economic status, geographic location, or cultural background.
- Culturally Responsive Pedagogy: Educators should adopt culturally responsive teaching strategies that acknowledge and incorporate students' cultural identities, experiences, and perspectives into the learning process, fostering a sense of belonging and empowerment.
- Critical Inquiry and Dialogue: AI-integrated ESD should encourage critical inquiry, dialogue, and reflection on social justice issues, enabling students to interrogate power dynamics, challenge dominant narratives, and envision alternative futures.
- Community Engagement and Partnership: Collaboration with community organizations, advocacy groups, and social justice activists can enrich students' learning experiences and provide opportunities for real-world application of social justice principles through service-learning projects, internships, and community-based research initiatives.

## 4.4 Conclusion

In conclusion, promoting education for social justice through AI-integrated Education for Sustainable Development (ESD) offers significant potential to empower students for a just and equitable society. By leveraging AI technologies to enhance teaching, learning, and assessment practices, educators can foster critical consciousness, empathy, and collective action among students to address pressing social justice issues and advocate for positive change in their communities. However, it is essential to address ethical, cultural, and contextual considerations and ensure equitable access to technology and digital literacy skills for all students. Through collaborative efforts and a commitment to social justice principles, AI-integrated ESD can play a transformative role in preparing students to become informed, engaged, and responsible global citizens committed to building a more just and sustainable world

## REFERENCES


Adams, M., Bell, L. A., & Griffin, P. (Eds.). (2007). *Teaching for Diversity and Social Justice*. Routledge. DOI: 10.4324/9780203940822

Baker, R. S., & Inventado, P. S. (2014). Educational data mining and learning analytics. In Larusson, J. A., & White, B. (Eds.), *Learning Analytics: From Research to Practice* (pp. 61–75). Springer. DOI: 10.1007/978-1-4614-3305-7_4

Bengio, Y., LeCun, Y., & Hinton, G. (2015). Deep learning. *Nature, 521*(7553), 436–444. DOI: 10.1038/nature14539 PMID: 26017442

Bennett, M. J. (2013). *Basic Concepts of Intercultural Communication: Paradigms, Principles, & Practices*. Intercultural Press.

Brown, S., & Glasner, A. (Eds.). (1999). *Assessment Matters in Higher Education: Choosing and Using Diverse Approaches*. Open University Press.

Dörnyei, Z., & Al-Hoorie, A. H. (2017). The motivational foundation of learning languages other than global English: Theoretical issues and research directions. *Modern Language Journal, 101*(3), 455–468. DOI: 10.1111/modl.12408

European Commission. (2018). Artificial Intelligence for Europe. *European Union.*

European Commission. (2020). White Paper on Artificial Intelligence: A European Approach to Excellence and Trust. European Union.

Freire, P. (1970). Pedagogy of the Oppressed. *Continuum : an Interdisciplinary Journal on Continuity of Care.*

Holmes, W., Bialik, M., & Fadel, C. (2019). *Artificial Intelligence in Education: Promises and Implications for Teaching and Learning*. Center for Curriculum Redesign.

Leicht, A., Heiss, J., & Byun, W. J. (Eds.). (2018). *Issues and Trends in Education for Sustainable Development.* UNESCO Publishing.

Luckin, R., Holmes, W., Griffiths, M., & Forcier, L. B. (2016). *Intelligence Unleashed: An Argument for AI in Education*. Pearson.

Nicol, D., & Macfarlane-Dick, D. (2006). Formative assessment and self-regulated learning: A model and seven principles of good feedback practice. *Studies in Higher Education, 31*(2), 199–218. DOI: 10.1080/03075070600572090

Nieto, S. (2010). *The Light in Their Eyes: Creating Multicultural Learning Communities*. Teachers College Press.

OECD. (2019). *AI in Education: Challenges and Opportunities for Sustainable Development*. OECD Publishing.

OECD. (2021). *Education for Sustainable Development: Learning for the Future*. OECD Publishing.

Spitzberg, B. H., & Changnon, G. (2009). Conceptualizing intercultural competence. In Deardorff, D. K. (Ed.), *The SAGE Handbook of Intercultural Competence* (pp. 2–52). SAGE Publications. DOI: 10.4135/9781071872987.n1

Sterling, S. (2001). *Sustainable Education: Re-visioning Learning and Change*. Green Books.

Sterling, S. (2010). Transformative learning and sustainability: Sketching the conceptual ground. *Learning and Teaching in Higher Education*, *5*, 17–33.

Ting-Toomey, S., & Chung, L. C. (2012). *Understanding Intercultural Communication*. Oxford University Press.

UNESCO. (2014). Shaping the Future We Want: UN Decade of Education for Sustainable Development (2005-2014) Final Report. UNESCO Publishing.

UNESCO. (2017). *Education for Sustainable Development Goals: Learning Objectives*. UNESCO Publishing.

# Chapter 11
# Navigating the Digital Economy:
## Crowd Work, AI Integration, Sustainability, and Higher Education's Response

**Teuta Hazizi**
https://orcid.org/0000-0003-0907-0112
*University of Elbasan "Aleksandër Xhuvani", Albania*

**Imelda Scjdini**
https://orcid.org/0000-0002-9067-1259
*University of Elbasan "Aleksandër Xhuvani", Albania*

## ABSTRACT

*This chapter explores the transformative impact of digital platforms on work, centring on crowd work as a task-based, online labour model. Through a comprehensive literature review, it examines crowd work's characteristics, benefits such as flexibility and skill development, and challenges like job precarity and algorithmic management powered by artificial intelligence (AI). While AI enhances efficiency in task allocation, it raises ethical concerns about transparency and worker rights. The chapter also addresses how higher education can adapt to the digital economy through curriculum changes, policy advocacy, and collaborative learning spaces to prepare students for digital work. It concludes with future research recommendations, highlighting the need for sustainable labour practices and cross-cultural studies to better understand the evolving gig economy.*

DOI: 10.4018/979-8-3693-5623-4.ch011

## INTRODUCTION

The rise of digital platforms and the gig economy has fundamentally transformed the nature of work, leading to the emergence of crowd work as a significant alternative to traditional employment models (Fieseler et al., 2019). Characterised by short, task-based jobs facilitated through online platforms, crowd work provides flexibility and autonomy, enabling workers to manage their own schedules. However, this transformation is not without challenges: job insecurity, income instability, limited access to conventional employment benefits, and ethical dilemmas related to platform control mechanisms are prevalent (Bucher & Fieseler, 2016).

This shift represents more than a reorganisation of existing labour practices; it marks a fundamental change in the structure, management, and valuation of work in the digital age. Crowd work is redefining the boundaries between formal and informal labour and reshaping relationships between workers, employers, and platforms. As crowd work expands, critical questions arise regarding workers' rights, the legal status of gig workers, and the broader social and environmental consequences of this labour model. This chapter explores the theoretical frameworks that underpin crowd work, such as platform capitalism and algorithmic management, while applying empirical findings to examine worker motivations, experiences, and the sustainability of work conditions. It also addresses how higher education can adapt to prepare students for participation in the digital economy.

By synthesising these perspectives, the chapter seeks to provide a comprehensive analysis of crowd work's key characteristics, with a focus on the sustainability of its practices. The areas to be analysed include workers' motivations and experiences, exploring what drives individuals to engage in crowd work and how these motivations align with sustainable career development, financial stability, and work-life balance. Additionally, the chapter examines platform management and algorithmic control, focusing on how platforms use algorithmic systems to manage workers and the social, psychological, and ethical implications of these practices. It also addresses challenges and sustainability of work conditions by identifying the legal, economic, and social challenges faced by crowd workers and exploring potential policy measures to create fair and sustainable working conditions. Finally, the chapter considers higher education's response to the digital economy shift, analysing how higher education can adapt to equip students with the skills needed for sustainable engagement in crowd work and foster readiness for the digital economy.

This chapter reviews current research on crowd work, highlighting its dual nature. While it offers benefits such as flexibility and greater access to work for marginalised groups, it also raises significant ethical challenges, particularly concerning workers' rights, protections, and long-term sustainability. The chapter concludes with policy recommendations and proposes areas for future research to ensure that crowd work remains a viable, fair, and sustainable option in the evolving gig economy.

## BACKGROUND

The rise of the gig economy has redefined employment structures, leading to the prominence of crowd work, characterised by remote, task-based jobs facilitated through digital platforms. As a flexible and accessible form of work, crowd work appeals to a broad spectrum of individuals seeking alternative income sources or supplementary employment. The theoretical frameworks of platform capitalism and algorithmic management provide valuable lenses for understanding the dynamics of crowd work. Platform capitalism critiques how platforms commodify labour, creating power imbalances between workers and platform operators. Algorithmic management, meanwhile, highlights the role of technology in overseeing and influencing workers' tasks and compensation, often at the expense of transparency and worker autonomy.

Crowd work presents both opportunities and challenges. On the one hand, it allows for financial independence and skill development, particularly in underdeveloped regions. On the other, income variability and the lack of social protections pose significant threats to economic stability. The COVID-19 pandemic further underscored these vulnerabilities, demonstrating how gig workers, classified as independent contractors, were left without support during economic downturns.

Understanding these elements is essential for assessing the sustainability of crowd work. Existing literature provides valuable insights into worker experiences, economic impacts, and technological and ethical considerations. This literature review aims to synthesise these perspectives, exploring how economic, technological, and sustainability dimensions intersect with crowd work and how higher education can respond to these trends.

## MAIN FOCUS OF THE CHAPTER

### Methodology

This qualitative literature review synthesizes existing theoretical and empirical studies on crowd work. The goal is to identify, analyse, and integrate key themes, theories, and findings, offering a comprehensive understanding of crowd work's characteristics, challenges, and future trends, especially in the context of digital platforms (J. W. Creswell & J. D. Creswell, 2017, Chapter 2). A systematic search was conducted using NOVA University of Lisboa's digital databases, including Web of Science, JSTOR, and Scopus, focusing on peer-reviewed sources published between 2010 and 2024. Keywords such as "crowd work," "gig economy," "digital labour," "sustainability," "algorithmic management," and "workforce preparation" were used to capture a wide range of perspectives (Booth et al., 2016, pp.92-96). Non-peer-reviewed articles and those not specifically addressing crowd works were excluded.

The selection process involved three stages:

- Initial Screening: Titles and abstracts were reviewed to exclude irrelevant studies. Only those directly addressing crowd work aspects like worker motivations and platform management were considered.
- Full-Text Review: Relevant articles were fully assessed for their contribution to key themes, prioritizing empirical data and new theoretical insights.
- Thematic Categorization: Studies were categorized by themes such as work conditions, platform dynamics, trainings and learning, and gender diversity to facilitate synthesis and identify literature gaps (Booth et al., 2021, Chapter 6).

Key findings, theories, and methodologies from the selected studies were coded and analysed using a narrative synthesis approach. This method integrated and compared findings across studies, identifying recurring themes, contradictions, and gaps, leading to the development of a conceptual framework on crowd work. The rigor of the review was ensured by evaluating each study's methodological soundness, relevance, and impact on the field, focusing on the robustness of design, theoretical clarity, and validity of findings (Stern et al., 2020).

## Integrated Review of Theoretical and Empirical Perspectives on Crowd Work

This review provides a comprehensive analysis of crowd work by examining key theoretical frameworks such as platform capitalism, algorithmic management, and Self-Determination Theory (SDT), alongside empirical research on worker experiences and practices. These perspectives are critical for informing both academic research and policy development, ensuring that the gig economy evolves equitably and sustainably.

The rise of crowd work can be linked to the broader framework of platform capitalism, a term that describes the economic system where digital platforms act as intermediaries in labour and commerce (Langley & Leyshon, 2017; Srnicek, 2017). Platforms such as Upwork, Uber, and Amazon Mechanical Turk have centralised control over the gig economy by determining the terms of engagement between workers and clients. This shift represents a new form of capitalist accumulation, where value is extracted not through traditional employment structures but by connecting independent workers with tasks, often at the expense of workers' rights and protections. In platform capitalism, digital intermediaries play a pivotal role in controlling access to work, determining pay scales, and managing work distribution. Platforms accumulate wealth by facilitating these connections while shifting the risks and responsibilities onto the workers themselves. Classified as independent contractors, gig workers face a significant power imbalance as they are denied the legal protections typically afforded to employees, such as minimum wage guarantees, health benefits, and the right to unionise (Patterson, 2020). This has led to concerns about the widespread exploitation of gig workers, particularly those in low-paying sectors.

Algorithmic management adds another layer of complexity to crowd work. Digital platforms frequently employ AI-driven systems to monitor, evaluate, and allocate tasks based on algorithms prioritising efficiency and profitability (Zaggl et al., 2023). Although this technology streamlines platform operations, it often undermines worker autonomy and job satisfaction. The opaque nature of these algorithms leaves workers uncertain about task allocation and performance evaluations, fostering feelings of powerlessness and deprivation (Tegtmeier et al., 2022). The lack of transparency complicates workers' efforts to improve performance or optimise earnings, leading to stress and dissatisfaction. High-pressure environments driven by algorithmic management can demand rapid task completion, intensifying workloads and contributing to adverse health outcomes, such as stress and fatigue (Tegtmeier et al., 2022). The continuous surveillance embedded in these systems exacerbates these pressures, diminishing job satisfaction and posing mental health risks. The disconnect between platform expectations and worker capacity further compounds these negative outcomes, creating a cycle where workers struggle to keep pace without clear feedback or recourse.

While the frameworks of platform capitalism and algorithmic management illustrate the structural and systemic challenges faced by crowd workers, it is also important to understand what drives individuals to participate in this form of work despite its complexities. The motivations for participating in crowd work are varied and encompass both internal and external factors. SDT proposes that individuals are driven by fundamental needs for autonomy, competence, and relatedness (Howard et al., 2020). The flexibility and autonomy that crowd work offers align closely with these internal motivations, allowing workers to manage their work around personal commitments such as caregiving, education, or other freelance projects (Blyth et al., 2022). This adaptability is particularly appealing for those seeking a work-life balance that is difficult to achieve in conventional employment settings. For skilled professionals such as designers, developers, and writers, crowd work provides an opportunity to pursue skill enhancement and competence, which is essential for professional satisfaction and growth. Platforms like Upwork enable individuals to refine their skills, build their portfolios, and strengthen their career prospects, contributing to the attractiveness of crowd work as an alternative or complementary form of employment (Lehdonvirta et al., 2019).

Although motivations such as flexibility, autonomy, and skill development are strong incentives for engaging in crowd work, these benefits are often accompanied by significant challenges that shape the overall experience for workers. Chief among these is income variability. Unlike traditional employment, where wages are stable and predictable, crowd workers are compensated on a per-task basis. This structure results in fluctuating earnings, which complicates financial planning and poses challenges to long-term economic security (Kang et al., 2012; McDonald, 2023). The issue of inconsistent earnings is particularly acute for those in low-wage sectors, such as delivery services and microwork, where task availability can be irregular and highly dependent on demand (McDonald, 2023). This economic instability often forces workers to take on multiple platforms or work longer hours, impacting their well-being and work-life balance.

Beyond income variability and job insecurity, other aspects of crowd work, such as social isolation, further complicate the worker experience and highlight the nuanced implications of remote digital labour. Unlike traditional workplaces that offer built-in opportunities for interaction and camaraderie, crowd work is often conducted in isolation, which can have a detrimental effect on mental health. While some workers find limited connection through online communities and forums, these virtual interactions do not fully replicate the benefits of face-to-face communication and collaboration (Choi & Cho, 2018). The resulting feelings of loneliness and disconnection can impact not only mental health but also productivity and job satisfaction, underscoring the complex nature of crowd work's impact on well-being.

Moreover, the pressure to perform under algorithmic management can further exacerbate these challenges. Many platforms use algorithms to assign tasks and evaluate worker performance, creating a system where workers must adhere to opaque standards that can feel dehumanising (Tegtmeier et al., 2022). The uncertainty surrounding task allocation and performance evaluation adds to the stress of maintaining a consistent income and can create a sense of disenfranchisement among workers. This lack of transparency makes it difficult for workers to improve their performance, optimise their earnings, or challenge unfair evaluations, impacting job satisfaction and financial stability.

The empirical findings on worker experiences, combined with theoretical perspectives, underscore the dual nature of crowd work and call for policy interventions that can bridge these gaps and enhance worker protections. The integration of theoretical frameworks with empirical findings provides a nuanced understanding of the dual-edged nature of crowd work. Theories such as platform capitalism and algorithmic management (Srnicek, 2017; Zaggl et al., 2023) offer critical perspectives on how digital platforms exert control over workers, often leading to the depersonalisation and commodification of labour. These insights are supported by empirical studies that highlight the ways in which algorithmic management leads to diminished worker autonomy, increased surveillance, and greater precariousness (Floros, 2024; Patterson, 2020).

At the same time, SDT (Howard et al., 2020) and the concept of self-branding (Bucher & Fieseler, 2016) provide valuable frameworks for understanding the motivations of crowd workers. Empirical research emphasises the importance of internal motivations, such as autonomy, skill development, and job satisfaction, in driving workers to engage in crowd work (Blyth et al., 2022). However, these motivations are often undermined by the precarious nature of gig work, which is characterised by significant income instability, lack of benefits, and poor working conditions (McDonald, 2023). Bringing together these theoretical and empirical insights highlights both the opportunities and constraints of crowd work, pointing towards essential considerations for future research and policy development to create a balanced, sustainable gig economy.

## Economic and Technological Impacts

The expansion of crowd work within the gig economy has significantly influenced economic structures and technological practices. This section examines the economic opportunities and disparities of crowd work, the role of technology in shaping work processes, and the ethical challenges it presents. By analysing these dimensions, a comprehensive understanding of how crowd work reshapes modern employment can be achieved.

Crowd work, as an essential part of the gig economy, offers significant economic opportunities, especially for individuals facing barriers to traditional employment. Its global accessibility and minimal training requirements open new pathways for workers from diverse backgrounds (Jacques & Kristensson, 2019). This inclusivity has been transformative in many contexts. For instance, Schriner and Oerther's (2014) pilot project in rural Kenya showed that income earned from crowd work was used for essential expenses, including education and small business investments, which in turn promoted local economic growth and self-sufficiency. Such examples underscore the role of crowd work as both an alternative and a supplementary income source, particularly in regions with limited formal employment options.

While these economic benefits are significant, it is important to examine the disparities that come with them. Crowd work incentivises productivity by enabling workers to choose tasks that match their skills, creating a competitive environment that rewards merit (Mrass et al., 2020). This model benefits workers by allowing them to optimise their work and maximise earnings while providing employers with a flexible, cost-effective labour solution. Empirical data from Germany indicates that many crowd workers rely on this income to meet essential expenses, illustrating the economic dependence on crowd work when task availability is sufficient (Mrass et al., 2020). Additionally, crowd work supports income diversification, acting as a buffer for workers during periods of economic transition or downturns. This productivity-focused approach supports short-term economic gains and, when managed well, can contribute to personal and community development.

However, despite these opportunities, crowd work presents significant challenges. The task-based payment system can lead to considerable income variability, which creates financial instability for workers (Huđek & Širec, 2023). This financial unpredictability often compels workers to modify their schedules and workloads frequently to sustain their earnings, perpetuating a cycle of economic precarity. Moreover, the disparities in economic opportunities between developed and developing regions further exacerbate these challenges. Workers in high-income countries generally have access to more stable and higher-paying tasks, while those in developing regions often face lower earnings and more insecure conditions. These inequalities highlight a critical issue within the global gig economy: monopsony-like conditions that enable platforms to control wage structures and limit workers' bargaining power (Cantarella & Strozzi, 2021). Such conditions contribute to the underutilisation of human capital, as workers may be limited to low-paying tasks that do not fully utilise their skills or education.

The lack of social protections compounds these economic difficulties. The classification of crowd workers as independent contractors excludes them from benefits typically associated with formal employment, such as health insurance, pensions, and paid leave, leaving them financially vulnerable (Jacques & Kristensson, 2019; Mrass et al., 2020). This vulnerability became particularly evident during the COVID-19 pandemic when many gig workers faced reduced opportunities without access to social safety nets (Kozar & Bolimowski, 2024). These limitations underscore the need for policies that promote equitable treatment, including transparent wage structures and fair working conditions. Effective policy measures could help mitigate these economic vulnerabilities and support the long-term sustainability of crowd work as a viable employment option.

Transitioning to technological aspects, it is clear that technology plays an essential role in shaping the crowd work experience, particularly through algorithmic management systems. These systems monitor worker performance, allocate tasks, and determine compensation, creating a controlled and often depersonalised work environment where worker autonomy is severely restricted (Connelly et al., 2021). While such systems enhance efficiency and reduce platform operational costs, they raise significant ethical concerns related to transparency, fairness, and worker rights (Elbanna & Idowu, 2022). One of the primary issues with algorithmic management is the opacity of decision-making processes. Platforms frequently employ proprietary algorithms to make critical decisions, leaving workers uncertain about how their performance is assessed or how their compensation is determined, fostering power imbalances (Fieseler et al., 2019).

The ethical challenges extend beyond transparency and encompass data privacy, worker exploitation, and biased decision-making. Bhalla et al. (2024) emphasise the need for platforms using AI to implement comprehensive ethical frameworks to prevent discriminatory practices, ensure fair pay, and protect workers' data. Without such transparency, workers are vulnerable to potentially unjust evaluations and decisions influenced by biased algorithms. This can exacerbate existing inequalities within the gig economy, further disadvantaging workers who lack the means to understand or challenge the algorithms that dictate their work experience (Bhalla et al., 2024). Ensuring fairness requires platforms to communicate clearly how AI systems function, providing workers with some insight and agency in their interactions with platform management.

Concerns about worker exploitation are especially pertinent in sectors where workers are treated as interchangeable units of labour. In microwork, for instance, tasks are often repetitive and low-skill, offering minimal pay and little recognition for the value contributed by workers. This depersonalised treatment can undermine worker morale and raises questions about the long-term sustainability of such labour practices. Environments that prioritise efficiency over human well-being challenge platforms' ethical responsibility to uphold fair labour standards and acknowledge the human element behind digital work.

The use of crowd workers in academic research further highlights ethical considerations. Researchers frequently employ crowd workers for tasks like surveys and data collection, often providing minimal compensation. This practice has drawn criticism for potentially exploiting vulnerable workers who may be treated as data sources rather than individuals with rights (Rea et al., 2021). Aligning academic and commercial uses of crowd work with ethical standards requires oversight and a commitment to fair compensation and treatment.

Ensuring the long-term sustainability of crowd work necessitates collaborative efforts from policymakers and platforms to implement transparent practices, uphold worker rights, and support fair compensation. Technological advancements and algorithmic management shape the work environment and influence skill development and career progression. Crowd work offers significant opportunities for skill development and career progression, though these benefits are unevenly distributed. Freelancers and professionals in fields like graphic design, software development, and writing often leverage platforms like Upwork or Fiverr to build their portfolios, gain practical experience, and secure higher-paying projects that can lead to stable employment (Bucher & Fieseler, 2016). By showcasing their skills and expanding professional networks, these workers strengthen their reputations and access better work. One designer noted, "Working on platforms like Upwork helped me showcase my skills and eventually led to a full-time role in an international firm," exemplifying how crowd work can bridge the gap between freelance and traditional employment (Upwork Community, 2024).

However, for microworkers involved in repetitive, low-skill tasks, the experience is markedly different. Limited opportunities for meaningful skill acquisition or career progression can lead to frustration. One worker described their experience as "being stuck in a cycle of low-paying tasks with no chance of advancement," illustrating the challenge of upward mobility in the gig economy (Bucher & Fieseler, 2016). The structural divide within gig platforms perpetuates these inequalities, making it difficult for lower-skilled workers to move into higher-paying roles.

Self-branding has become a critical component of career progression in the gig economy, demanding significant investment of time and effort from workers to refine their online presence and remain competitive (Bucher & Fieseler, 2016). While effective self-branding can lead to higher earnings and better opportunities, maintaining a professional profile is time-consuming and stressful, highlighting the precarious nature of crowd work and its uncertain economic stability. Moreover, while platforms facilitate global connections between workers and clients, career growth potential is influenced by sustainable work practices. Economic sustainability ensures workers can depend on crowd work as a stable source of income, while environmentally sustainable practices impact the long-term viability of the infrastructure supporting the gig economy.

## Sustainability in Crowd Work

The sustainability of crowd work is a multifaceted issue, encompassing economic and environmental dimensions as well as the legal and regulatory frameworks that shape these aspects. While crowd work has introduced new avenues for income and flexibility, ensuring its long-term viability requires addressing its economic vulnerabilities and environmental impacts. The rapid expansion of the gig economy has illuminated disparities in earnings, working conditions, and concerns about the ecological footprint of digital labour. Sustainability challenges in this sector often resonate with those seen in other emerging industries. For example, entrepreneurs in nature-based tourism have emphasised the importance of tackling both macro-

and micro-environmental challenges to ensure long-term growth and sustainability (Sinanaj et al., 2024). Similarly, creating a sustainable future for crowd work necessitates a comprehensive evaluation of its economic and environmental impacts, alongside policy and regulatory solutions to support fair and stable working conditions.

Crowd work presents a nuanced landscape in terms of economic sustainability. It provides essential income opportunities, particularly for individuals who face barriers to securing traditional full-time employment. The flexibility to engage in short-term tasks and micro-entrepreneurship boosts workforce participation, especially in areas where formal jobs are scarce (Bhalla et al., 2024). This capacity for economic participation enables individuals to achieve a degree of self-sufficiency, which is crucial in underdeveloped regions where employment options are limited. However, despite these benefits, significant challenges threaten the long-term sustainability of this model. Persistent wage disparities and income instability are central issues. Workers in developed regions generally access better-paying, more complex tasks, whereas those in developing areas are often confined to lower-skill, lower-paying jobs. This disparity reinforces social and economic hierarchies and raises questions about whether crowd work can serve as a viable, long-term employment solution for a diverse, global workforce.

Worker perspectives further exemplify these economic challenges. The unpredictability of income and the lack of traditional employment benefits are common concerns. One gig worker from a developing region remarked, "I value the flexibility that crowd work offers, but I never know how much I will make each week, which makes budgeting almost impossible." This economic precarity pushes workers to navigate financial uncertainty without the safety nets and stability typical in traditional employment settings (Margaryan et al., 2022). The absence of job security, health insurance, pensions, and paid leave compounds their vulnerability, complicating long-term financial planning. To counteract these issues, policy interventions that address wage disparities and introduce fair pay and basic protections are essential to making gig work a sustainable employment option.

Turning to environmental sustainability, crowd work presents both challenges and opportunities. On one hand, services such as Uber and Lyft have been linked to increased traffic congestion and higher carbon emissions, particularly in urban centres. Research by Diao et al. (2021) shows that these services can significantly increase vehicle miles travelled, contributing to environmental strain. On the other hand, workers engaged in remote digital tasks can have a positive environmental impact by eliminating the need for commuting, which reduces emissions (Tegtmeier et al., 2022). A remote IT worker commented, "Being able to work from home means I don't contribute to daily pollution from commuting, which makes me feel like I'm playing a small part in reducing emissions." These contrasting examples illustrate that the environmental impact of crowd work varies depending on the type of work being performed.

The interplay between economic and environmental sustainability in crowd work underscores their interconnected nature. Addressing income instability and economic disparities can create a more supportive gig economy that encourages environmentally conscious practices. For instance, promoting remote work and sustainable task allocation can help reduce emissions while supporting workers' economic stability. Achieving sustainability in crowd work requires comprehensive policy reforms that align economic resilience with environmental responsibility. Policies integrating economic and environmental goals will contribute to a resilient gig economy that benefits both workers and society.

A significant challenge in realising sustainability in crowd work is the absence of basic worker protections, particularly regarding minimum wage and social security. Many gig workers earn wages below traditional employment standards, exacerbating economic vulnerability. This instability is compounded by the absence of essential benefits like health insurance and paid leave, leaving workers exposed during economic downturns and making long-term financial planning difficult (Huđek & Širec, 2023). The reality for many gig workers is one of economic uncertainty, where the lack of protections fuels both financial and social precarity.

Policymakers play a crucial role in addressing these regulatory gaps. Legislative measures like California's Assembly Bill 5 aimed to reclassify certain gig workers as employees, thus granting them rights to minimum wage, health benefits, and collective bargaining (Floros, 2024). Spain's 'Riders Law' similarly reclassified food delivery workers as employees, ensuring their access to social security and paid leave (Waeyaert et al., 2022). Such initiatives reflect a global movement towards extending labour protections to gig workers while maintaining the valued flexibility of gig work. Although these policies are not without controversy, they set an important precedent for balancing workers' rights with platform operational needs.

Algorithmic management adds further complexity to regulatory challenges. Platforms often use proprietary algorithms to allocate tasks and evaluate worker performance, typically operating with limited transparency (Elbanna & Idowu, 2022). This opacity leaves workers uncertain about the decision-making processes affecting their work and constrains their ability to challenge unfair practices. Implementing regulatory frameworks that require algorithmic transparency could empower workers, enabling them to understand and contest decisions impacting their work (Bhalla et al., 2024). Such measures would promote a more equitable relationship between platforms and workers, fostering trust and fairer practices.

Beyond immediate protections, policy should also promote sustainable and ethical platform practices. Cooperative models, where workers have a say in decision-making and a share in profits, offer a promising way forward (Tandon & Rathi, 2022). By aligning platform success with worker well-being, these models could create a more balanced and sustainable gig economy, fostering ownership and collective responsibility. Such approaches ensure that economic growth and worker rights are prioritised alongside platform efficiency.

## Higher Education's Response to the Digital Economy Shift

The expansion of the digital economy and the rise of platform-based work have significantly altered the employment landscape, presenting both challenges and opportunities for higher education. This shift necessitates that universities reassess their approaches to preparing students for a job market increasingly defined by digital technologies. Crowd work, characterised by tasks completed through online platforms, has emerged as an essential element of this new employment model (Lehdonvirta et al., 2019). To respond effectively, higher education institutions must ensure students acquire relevant skills, foster adaptability in digital contexts, and promote sustainable practices aligned with these evolving demands (Alenezi & Faisal, 2020; Elbanna & Idowu, 2021).

Integrating competencies related to crowd work into university curricula is a fundamental step. Evidence suggests that participation in crowd work helps students develop a broad range of skills, including technical capabilities, platform-specific expertise, and business acumen (Lehdonvirta et al., 2019). Embedding these elements into educational programmes equips students to handle the complexities of modern work, where adaptability and self-directed learning are paramount (Margaryan et al., 2022). This approach bridges the gap between academic knowledge and practical experience, aiding students in making smoother transitions into the workforce (Elbanna & Idowu, 2021). Research by Balliu et al. (2024) on start-ups in Elbasan, Albania, highlights that skills such as strategic planning, coping with uncertainty, collaboration, and experiential learning are instrumental in fostering business growth. Integrating such competencies into educational frameworks can further strengthen students' abilities to thrive in digital work environments.

Moreover, the establishment of collaborative learning environments, such as co-working spaces and entrepreneurial hubs, plays a crucial role in helping higher education adapt to the digital economy. These spaces encourage partnerships among students, academics, and industry practitioners, thereby fostering project-based learning and innovation (Sterev et al., 2023). Such initiatives enhance problem-solving abilities and entrepreneurial skills, preparing students for active participation in real-world digital projects (Alenezi & Faisal, 2020). This type of experiential learning is essential for students to gain practical insights and develop a proactive approach to problem-solving in a dynamic job market.

Crowd work also supports continuous skill development, which requires self-regulation and learning adaptability (Lehdonvirta et al., 2019). To address this, universities should emphasise teaching self-directed learning techniques and nurturing proficiencies that enhance platform navigation. This includes developing technical knowledge alongside essential soft skills such as communication, time management, and resilience (Margaryan et al., 2022). Equipping students with these versatile skills ensures they are prepared for lifelong learning, allowing them to stay adaptable and competitive in their careers (Elbanna & Idowu, 2021; Lehdonvirta et al., 2019). Such an approach reinforces the value of self-sufficiency and proactive career management, which are crucial in an ever-changing digital landscape.

Beyond curriculum integration, policy advocacy remains a critical role for higher education institutions. Universities should support and promote policies that foster digital inclusion and ensure equitable access to digital opportunities for students from diverse backgrounds (Alenezi & Faisal, 2020). This commitment includes supporting initiatives aimed at bridging the digital divide and embedding ethical considerations regarding workers' rights and fair practices into the curriculum (Lehdonvirta et al., 2019; Margaryan et al., 2022). By embedding these ethical considerations, higher education can prepare students not just to engage in digital work, but to do so ethically and responsibly. This contributes to building a fairer and more sustainable digital economy where students are not only equipped to thrive but also to champion practices that prioritise fairness and integrity.

## Discussion

The comprehensive review of theoretical and empirical literature on crowd work reveals a nuanced picture of its impact on the modern employment landscape. The integration of theories such as platform capitalism (Srnicek, 2017) and algorithmic management (Zaggl et al., 2023) highlights how digital platforms shape the experience of crowd work, underscoring economic and ethical challenges. Empirical studies further illustrate the precarious nature of gig work, characterised by income variability, limited social protections, and algorithmic oversight (Margaryan et al., 2022; Tegtmeier et al., 2022). This discussion synthesises these insights, drawing implications for stakeholders and suggesting directions for future research.

A central theme emerging from the literature is the dual nature of crowd work. On one hand, it provides flexibility, opportunities for supplementary income, and skill development, especially for individuals in regions where traditional employment is limited (Lehdonvirta et al., 2019; Schriner & Oerther, 2014). On the other hand, significant disparities persist between developed and developing regions, where workers often face lower pay and less secure conditions (Bhalla et al., 2024; Cantarella & Strozzi, 2021). The economic sustainability of crowd work remains uncertain, calling for policy measures that address wage equity and worker protections while maintaining the flexibility that workers value (Huđek & Širec, 2023; Jacques & Kristensson, 2019).

Technological advancements, particularly algorithmic management, play a pivotal role in shaping the work environment. While these systems enhance efficiency, they present challenges related to transparency, fairness, and the psychological well-being of workers (Connelly et al., 2021; Elbanna & Idowu, 2022). The reviewed literature points to the need for regulatory frameworks that mandate algorithmic transparency and protect against biased decision-making (Bhalla et al., 2024; Fieseler et al., 2019). Such measures would empower workers by providing them with insights and the ability to contest unfair practices, fostering a fairer relationship between platforms and labourers (Tegtmeier et al., 2022).

Higher education's response to these challenges is equally significant. Universities play a crucial role in equipping students with the skills needed for the gig economy, bridging academic knowledge with practical experience (Lehdonvirta et al., 2019; Margaryan et al., 2022). The integration of crowd work competencies into curricula, the promotion of collaborative learning environments, and the teaching of self-directed learning techniques have been shown to be effective strategies (Alenezi & Faisal, 2020; Elbanna & Idowu, 2021). However, more empirical research is needed to assess the long-term effectiveness of these educational adaptations and how well they prepare students for sustainable careers in the gig economy (Sterev et al., 2023).

The reviewed literature highlights the critical balance that must be struck between economic opportunity and sustainability. While crowd work can contribute positively to workforce participation and skill development, the accompanying economic and technological challenges must be carefully managed. This discussion has synthesised these findings to provide a nuanced understanding of how economic structures, technological advancements, and higher education intersect within the context of the gig economy.

## Implications, Recommendations, and Future Research Directions

The building on the analysis of crowd work and its multifaceted impacts outlined earlier, this section provides targeted recommendations and explores future trends to ensure the sustainable development of the gig economy. Higher education institutions, policymakers, and platform developers have pivotal roles to play in fostering an environment where crowd work is both equitable and viable for all participants. While previous sections highlighted how universities must integrate crowd work competencies into their curricula, it is crucial to delve deeper into practical solutions. Universities should not only equip students with technical skills and digital literacy but also foster adaptability and resilience. Establishing partnerships with gig platforms and industry stakeholders to create collaborative learning programmes can provide students with hands-on experience that bridges academic learning and real-world practice (Sterev et al., 2023). By incorporating platform-based projects supervised by mentors, higher education can better prepare graduates for the evolving job market.

As discussed, regulatory frameworks are necessary to protect workers and promote fair conditions within the gig economy. Building on this foundation, policymakers should prioritise creating laws that balance the need for flexibility with essential protections such as fair wages, transparent algorithmic processes, and the right to contest platform decisions (Bhalla et al., 2024; Elbanna & Idowu, 2022). Examples like California's Assembly Bill 5 and Spain's 'Riders Law' provide valuable starting points for crafting policies that support both workers and platforms (Floros, 2024; Waeyaert et al., 2022). To avoid repetition, this section focuses on the implementation challenges and scalability of such measures in various socio-economic contexts. Policymakers must assess the practicality of alternative platform models, such as cooperatives, and adapt frameworks to local conditions to ensure equitable outcomes (Langley & Leyshon, 2017).

To complement policy interventions, education and training must address current gaps in worker readiness. Training organisations and universities should develop practical workshops on negotiation skills, financial planning, and strategic task management. Unlike previous sections that highlighted the necessity of these skills, this part emphasises implementation. Online learning modules and accessible resources, such as video tutorials and webinars, can ensure continuous support for both students and current gig workers (Wheelahan & Moodie, 2022). These tools should be tailored to address the varying needs of workers across regions and skill levels, promoting a more inclusive approach.

While earlier discussions noted the gaps in existing research, this section underscores the importance of cross-cultural and longitudinal studies to understand crowd work's impact more comprehensively. Future research should focus on how regional economic and social contexts influence crowd work practices, particularly in the Global South, to inform policy adjustments that are culturally and economically sensitive. Longitudinal research is also needed to track the progression of crowd work over time, examining how workers adapt to evolving platform policies and technological changes. This will help policymakers and educators foresee potential shifts in the gig economy and respond proactively.

The review has touched on the influence of technology and alternative models within the gig economy. This section elaborates on how emerging technologies, such as AI and blockchain, could redefine work practices by promoting transparency and decentralisation. However, these advancements must be implemented carefully to avoid exacerbating existing inequalities. Investigating the feasibility of cooperative and worker-owned platforms can provide insights into creating fairer work environments. Research should assess the long-term viability of these models and their potential to foster a more inclusive digital labour market.

While much has been discussed about the current challenges and strategies related to crowd work, continued collaboration between academia, industry, and policy bodies is essential. By integrating academic training, targeted policy efforts, and innovative platform models, the gig economy can evolve into a sustainable and equitable landscape. Future empirical studies and strategic partnerships will be vital for ensuring that crowd work supports workers' well-being and contributes positively to the global workforce.

## CONCLUSION

This chapter has provided a comprehensive analysis of the key characteristics of crowd work, focusing on the sustainability of its practices. By examining the motivations and experiences of workers, the discussion has highlighted how intrinsic and extrinsic factors drive participation in the gig economy. While flexibility and autonomy are primary motivators, the pursuit of sustainable career development, financial stability, and a balanced work-life dynamic often encounters challenges such as income variability and job precarity.

The analysis of platform management and algorithmic control has revealed the significant role that digital systems play in shaping the work environment. These algorithmic practices, while optimising efficiency and reducing operational costs for platforms, often lead to reduced worker autonomy and increased psychological and ethical concerns. The opaque nature of algorithmic decision-making creates power imbalances and limits workers' ability to fully engage in or challenge their work conditions.

Addressing the challenges and sustainability of work conditions, this chapter has identified the pressing economic, social, and legal vulnerabilities faced by crowd workers. The lack of job security, social protections, and consistent income highlights the urgent need for policies that protect worker rights, ensure fair compensation, and promote transparency in algorithmic management. Sustainable practices are essential for fostering a fairer environment, including cooperative platform models that empower workers by distributing power and profits more equitably.

Higher education's response to the digital economy shift was explored, emphasising the role of universities in preparing students for participation in platform-based work. Integrating crowd work competencies into curricula and fostering critical thinking, adaptability, and digital literacy are key to enabling future workers to engage sustainably in the gig economy. Collaborative learning spaces and partnerships with industry can bridge the gap between academic theory and practical experience, equipping graduates with the skills needed to navigate this evolving landscape effectively.

As the gig economy continues to grow and evolve, ensuring that crowd work remains a viable and equitable employment option requires a coordinated effort among policymakers, educational institutions, platform developers, and workers themselves. By fostering inclusive, transparent, and fair practices, the potential of crowd work can be harnessed while addressing its ethical, economic, and social challenges. The findings and discussions in this chapter contribute to a better understanding of crowd work and set the stage for further research and policy development aimed at making this model of digital labour sustainable and socially responsible.

## REFERENCES


Alenezi, H. S., & Faisal, M. H. (2020). Utilizing crowdsourcing and machine learning in education: Literature review. *Education and Information Technologies*, *25*(4), 2971–2986. DOI: 10.1007/s10639-020-10102-w

Balliu, T. H., Sinanaj, X. A., Tapija, N. K., Durmishi, A., & Madhi, D. (2024). Analyzing the impact of entrepreneurial traits on business growth: A study of start-ups in Elbasan, Albania. *Multidisciplinary Reviews*, *7*(7), 2024152. DOI: 10.31893/multirev.2024152

Bhalla, R., Vidyasree, A., Chotai, N. A., Mahendher, S., & Agrawal, A. (2024). The gig economy and sustainable work practices in startups. *European Economic Letters*, *14*(2), 1914–1915. DOI: 10.52783/eel.v14i2.1520

Blyth, R., Chia, A., & Warner, J. (2022). Self-branding strategies of online freelancers on Upwork. *Journal of Management Inquiry*, *31*(4), 410–424. DOI: 10.1177/10564926211035699

Booth, A., Martyn-St James, M., Clowes, M., & Sutton, A. (2021). *Systematic approaches to a successful literature review* (3rd ed.). SAGE Publications.

Booth, A., Sutton, A., & Papaioannou, D. (2016). *Systematic approaches to a successful literature review* (2nd ed.). SAGE.

Bucher, E., & Fieseler, C. (2016). The flow of digital labor: Microworkers' strategies for skill development. *Media and Communication*, *4*(3), 12–24. DOI: 10.17645/mac.v4i3.547

Cantarella, M., & Strozzi, C. (2021). Workers in the crowd: The labour market impact of the online platform economy. *Industrial and Corporate Change*, *30*(6), 1429–1458. DOI: 10.1093/icc/dtab022

Choi, O. K., & Cho, E. (2018). The mechanism of trust affecting collaboration in virtual teams and the moderating roles of the culture of autonomy and task complexity. *Computers in Human Behavior*, *91*, 305–316. DOI: 10.1016/j.chb.2018.09.032

Connelly, C. E., Fieseler, C., Černe, M., Giessner, S. R., & Wong, S. I. (2021). Working in the digitized economy: HRM theory & practice. *Human Resource Management Review*, *31*(1), 100762. Advance online publication. DOI: 10.1016/j.hrmr.2020.100762

Creswell, J. W., & Creswell, J. D. (2017). *Research design: Qualitative, quantitative, and mixed methods approaches* (5th ed.). SAGE.

Diao, M., Kong, H., & Zhao, J. (2021). Impacts of ride-hailing on vehicle miles traveled and greenhouse gas emissions: The case of San Francisco. *Journal of Transpersonal Research, 153*, 56–67. DOI: 10.1088/1748-9326/ad3285

Elbanna, A., & Idowu, A. (2021). Crowdwork as an elevator of human capital: A sustainable human development perspective. *Scandinavian Journal of Information Systems, 33*(2), 4. https://aisel.aisnet.org/sjis/vol33/iss2/4

Elbanna, A., & Idowu, A. (2022). Crowd work, digital liminality, and the enactment of culturally recognised alternatives to Western precarity: Beyond epistemological terra nullius. *European Journal of Information Systems, 31*(1), 128–144. DOI: 10.1080/0960085X.2021.1981779

Fieseler, C., Bucher, E., & Hoffmann, C. P. (2019). Unfairness by design? The perceived fairness of digital labor on crowd working platforms. *Journal of Business Ethics, 156*(4), 987–1005. DOI: 10.1007/s10551-017-3607-2

Floros, C. (2024). Rethinking algorithmic management in minor key: The case of housecleaning platform labour in Denmark. *Work, Employment and Society, 38*(1), 67–84. DOI: 10.1177/09500170231112893

Howard, J. L., Gagné, M., & Morin, A. J. S. (2020). Putting the pieces together: Reviewing the structural conceptualization of motivation within SDT. *Motivation and Emotion, 44*(6), 846–861. https://www.oii.ox.ac.uk/research/projects/crowdlearn/?publications. DOI: 10.1007/s11031-020-09838-2

Huđek, I., & Širec, K. (2023). Unveiling the impact of the gig economy on sustainable development. In V. Bevanda (Ed.), *ERAZ Conference – Knowledge Based Sustainable Development: Vol. 9. Selected papers* (pp. 125–133). Association of Economists and Managers of the Balkans. DOI: 10.31410/ERAZ.S.P.2023.125

Jacques, J. T., & Kristensson, P. O. (2019). Crowdworker economics in the gig economy. *CHI Conference on Human Factors in Computing Systems Proceedings (CHI 2019),* May 4–9, 2019, Glasgow, Scotland, UK. DOI: 10.1145/3290605.3300621

Kang, M., Yoo, Y., & Park, Y. (2012). Analyzing online mentoring process and facilitation strategies. *Procedia: Social and Behavioral Sciences, 46*, 5158–5162. DOI: 10.1016/j.sbspro.2012.06.400

Kozar, L. J., & Bolimowski, S. (2024). Gig economy and sustainable development: Bibliometric analyses and identification of future research directions. *Scientific Papers of Silesian University of Technology. Organization & Management/Zeszyty Naukowe Politechniki Slaskiej.Seria Organizacji i Zarzadzanie*, (194). Advance online publication. DOI: 10.29119/1641-3466.2024.194.11

Langley, P., & Leyshon, A. (2017). Platform capitalism: The intermediation and capitalisation of digital economic circulation. *Finance and Stochastics*, *3*(1), 11–31. DOI: 10.2218/finsoc.v3i1.1936

Lehdonvirta, V., Margaryan, A., & Davies, H. (2019). *Skills formation and skills matching in online platform work: Policies and practices for promoting crowdworkers' continuous learning (CrowdLearn)*. Moray House School of Education and Sport, Centre for Research in Digital Education. Commissioned report.

Margaryan, A., Albert, J., & Charlton-Czaplicki, T. (2022). Workplace learning in Crowdwork Questionnaire (WLCQ): Measuring self-regulated learning and skill development in online platform work. *International Journal of Training and Development*, *26*(3), 495–515. DOI: 10.1111/ijtd.12268

McDonald, P. (2023). Income generation on care work digital labour platforms. *British Journal of Industrial Relations*, *61*(1), 142–162. DOI: 10.1111/bjir.12625

Mrass, V., Peters, C., & Leimeister, J. M. (2020). Crowdworking platforms in Germany: Business insights from a study & implications for society. In *82. Jahrestagung des Verbands der Hochschullehrer für Betriebswirtschaft (VHB)*, Frankfurt am Main, Germany. https://ssrn.com/abstract=3926265

Patterson, C. A. (2020). Maintaining transmission: DIRECTV's work-at-home technical support, virtual surveillance, and the gendered division of labor. *Feminist Media Studies*, *20*(4), 561–578. DOI: 10.1080/14680777.2020.1748947

Rea, M., Lundmark, L., & Björk, M. (2021). Crowdsourcing as a tool for research: Methodological, fair, and political considerations. *Research Policy*, *50*(4), 104155. Advance online publication. DOI: 10.1016/j.respol.2020.104155

Schriner, A., & Oerther, D. (2014). No really, (crowd) work is the silver bullet. *Procedia Engineering*, *78*, 224–228. DOI: 10.1016/j.proeng.2014.07.060

Sinanaj, X. A., Hazizi, T. B., Durmishi, L., Tapija, N. K., & Durmishi, A. (2024). Albanian challenges for sustainable development: Nature-based tourism sector evidence from entrepreneurs' point of view. *Multidisciplinary Reviews*, *7*(7), 2024153. Advance online publication. DOI: 10.31893/multirev.2024153

Srnicek, N. (2017). The challenges of platform capitalism: Understanding the logic of a new business model. *Juncture*, *23*(4), 254–257. DOI: 10.1111/newe.12023

Sterev, N., Kostadinov, K., Yordanov, D., & Yorgova, T. (2023). Open entrepreneurial academic centres. [Ikonomicheski Izsledvania]. *Economic Studies Journal*, *32*(4), 116–134.

Stern, C., Lizarondo, L., Carrier, J., Godfrey, C., Rieger, K., Salmond, S., Apóstolo, J., Kirkpatrick, P., & Loveday, H. (2020). Methodological guidance for the conduct of mixed methods systematic reviews. *JBI Evidence Synthesis*, *18*(10), 2108–2118. DOI: 10.11124/JBISRIR-D-19-00169 PMID: 32813460

Tandon, A., & Rathi, S. (2022). Sustaining urban labour markets: Situating migration and domestic work in India's gig economy. *Journal of South Asian Development*, *17*(2), 135–157. DOI: 10.1177/09731741221118787

Tegtmeier, P., Weber, C., Sommer, S., & Tisch, A. (2022). Criteria and guidelines for human-centred work design in a digitally transformed world of work. *International Journal of Environmental Research and Public Health*, *19*(23), 15506. DOI: 10.3390/ijerph192315506 PMID: 36497580

Upwork Community. (2024). From decades of traditional work to freelancing: Share your experience. *Upwork*. https://community.upwork.com/t5/Freelancers/From-decades-of-traditional-work-to-freelancing-Share-your/m-p/1115097

Waeyaert, W., Lenaerts, K., & Gillis, D. (2022). Spain's 'Riders Law': New regulation on digital platform work. *European Agency for Safety and Health at Work (EU-OSHA)*. https://osha.europa.eu/en/publications/spain-riders-law-new-regulation-digital-platorm-work

Wheelahan, L., & Moodie, G. (2022). Gig qualifications for the gig economy: Micro-credentials and the 'hungry mile'. *Higher Education*, *83*(6), 1279–1295. DOI: 10.1007/s10734-021-00742-3 PMID: 34366441

Zaggl, M. A., Malhotra, A., Alexy, O., & Majchrzak, A. (2023). Governing crowdsourcing for unconstrained innovation problems. *Strategic Management Journal*, *44*(11), 2783–2817. DOI: 10.1002/smj.3505

## ADDITIONAL READING

Bonacini, L., Gallo, G., & Scicchitano, S. (2021). Working from home and income inequality: Risks of a "new normal" with COVID-19. *Journal of Population Economics*, *34*(1), 303–360. DOI: 10.1007/s00148-020-00800-7 PMID: 32952308

Graham, M., Hjorth, I., & Lehdonvirta, V. (2017). Digital labour and development: Impacts of global digital labour platforms and the gig economy on worker livelihoods. *Transfer: European Review of Labour and Research*, *23*(2), 135–162. DOI: 10.1177/1024258916687250 PMID: 28781494

Howcroft, D., & Bergvall-Kåreborn, B. (2020). A typology of crowd work platforms. *Work, Employment and Society*, *34*(1), 21–38. DOI: 10.1177/0950017018760136

Huws, U. (2021). *Reinventing the welfare state: Digital platforms and public policies*. Pluto Press.

Kuek, S. C., Paradi-Guilford, C., Fayomi, T., Imaizumi, S., Ipeirotis, P., Pina, P., & Singh, M. (2020). *The global opportunity in online outsourcing*. World Bank Publications. https://hdl.handle.net/10986/22284

McDonnell, A., Carbery, R., Burgess, J., & Sherman, U. (2021). Technologically mediated human resource management in the gig economy. *International Journal of Human Resource Management*, *32*(19), 3995–4015. DOI: 10.1080/09585192.2021.1986109

Myhill, K., Richards, J., & Sang, K. (2021). Job quality, fair work and gig work: The lived experience of gig workers. *International Journal of Human Resource Management*, *32*(19), 4110–4135. DOI: 10.1080/09585192.2020.1867612

Norlander, P., Jukic, N., Varma, A., & Nestorov, S. (2021). The effects of technological supervision on gig workers: Organizational control and motivation of Uber, taxi, and limousine drivers. *International Journal of Human Resource Management*, *32*(19), 4053–4077. DOI: 10.1080/09585192.2020.1867614

Schor, J. B., & Attwood-Charles, W. (2017). The "sharing" economy: Labor, inequality, and social connection on for-profit platforms. *Sociology Compass*, *11*(8), e12493. DOI: 10.1111/soc4.12493

Vallas, S., & Schor, J. B. (2020). What do platforms do? Understanding the gig economy. *Annual Review of Sociology*, *46*(1), 273–294. DOI: 10.1146/annurev-soc-121919-054857

Wood, A. J., Lehdonvirta, V., & Graham, M. (2018). Workers of the internet unite? Online freelancer organization against digital platform practices. *New Technology, Work and Employment*, *34*(2), 99–115. DOI: 10.1111/ntwe.12112

## KEY TERMS AND DEFINITIONS

**Algorithmic Management:** The application of AI-driven systems to monitor, allocate, and evaluate work within digital platforms, prioritising efficiency and profit but often at the expense of worker autonomy and job satisfaction.

**Crowd Work:** A type of employment facilitated through digital platforms, where individuals undertake tasks remotely. While offering flexibility and global accessibility, it is often characterised by income instability and limited worker protections.

**Digital Economy:** An economic system grounded in digital technologies and platforms, transforming how goods and services are produced, distributed, and consumed.

**Economic Sustainability:** The capability of a labour model, such as crowd work, to provide fair and reliable income over time, ensuring the long-term financial security of workers.

**Gig Economy:** A labour market dominated by short-term, flexible work arrangements facilitated through digital platforms. While promoting adaptability, it often lacks the security and benefits of traditional employment.

**Higher Education Adaptation:** The strategic response of universities to the changing job market, involving the incorporation of digital skills, self-directed learning, and platform-based competencies into academic curricula.

**Platform Capitalism:** An economic system wherein digital platforms serve as intermediaries for labour and commerce, extracting value by connecting independent workers to tasks and shifting risks onto them, which impacts labour rights and protections.

**Task-Based Compensation:** A remuneration model where workers are paid per completed task, contributing to economic precarity due to income variability and uncertainty.

**Transparency in Algorithmic Systems:** The extent to which digital platforms disclose the operation of their algorithmic management systems, affecting workers' understanding and ability to contest task allocation and performance assessments.

Chapter 12

# Professional Development and Assessment, Teaching and Learning Practices, Polices in Higher Education:

## Promoting the Integration of AI With Education for Sustainable Development

**Doris Chasokela**
https://orcid.org/0009-0001-5983-8508
*National University of Science and Technology, Zimbabwe*

**Joseph Hlongwane**
https://orcid.org/0009-0001-2482-4659
*National University of Science and Technology, Zimbabwe*

## ABSTRACT

*This chapter examines the potential of integrating artificial intelligence (AI) in higher education to enhance professional development, assessment, and teaching and learning practices while promoting education for sustainable development (ESD). It explores the latest research, policies, and initiatives that are shaping the future of higher education in the era of AI. The chapter highlights the need for*

DOI: 10.4018/979-8-3693-5623-4.ch012

*continuous professional development of educators to keep pace with technological advancements and provides insights into the potential uses of AI in assessment and feedback processes to improve student learning outcomes. Additionally, it discusses the integration of AI into teaching and learning practices, including personalised learning, adaptive instruction, and interactive simulations.*

## INTRODUCTION

Artificial Intelligence (AI) is revolutionising how we live, work, and learn. In higher education, AI has the potential to transform the way students learn, educators teach, and institutions operate. As AI continues to evolve, it is essential to understand its applications, benefits, and challenges in higher education. AI in higher education refers to the use of artificial intelligence and machine learning technologies to enhance teaching, learning, and administrative processes. AI applications can be used to: Personalise learning: AI-powered adaptive learning systems can tailor educational content to individual students' needs, abilities, and learning styles. Enhance teaching: AI can assist teachers in grading, providing feedback, and identifying areas where students need additional support. Improve student engagement: AI-powered chatbots and virtual assistants can help students stay connected with educators and peers, fostering a sense of community and social interaction. Streamline administrative tasks: AI can automate routine administrative tasks, such as student registration, course scheduling, and financial aid processing. Facilitate research: AI-powered analytics tools can help researchers analyse large datasets, identify patterns, and make predictions. Benefits of AI in higher education include improved student outcomes where AI can help students achieve better grades, reduce dropout rates, and increase retention. There are enhanced teaching practices and AI can provide educators with valuable insights into student learning styles, needs, and preferences. There is also increased efficiency and AI can automate administrative tasks, freeing up educators to focus on teaching and research. AI can help reduce costs by streamlining operations, reducing staff requirements, and improving resource allocation. Institutions that adopt AI early can gain a competitive advantage in attracting students and talent. There are several challenges of AI in higher education such as AI relies on high-quality data to function effectively ensuring data security and integrity is crucial. AI algorithms can perpetuate biases if not designed with fairness and equity in mind. AI applications must be designed with ethical considerations in mind, such as privacy concerns and potential job displacement. Institutions may need to invest in training staff to develop the necessary technical expertise to integrate AI effectively. Students may need time to adjust to the use of AI in their educational experiences. AI has the potential to transform higher education by improving student outcomes, enhancing teaching practices, and increasing efficiency. However, it is essential to address the challenges associated with AI adoption, such as data quality and security, bias and fairness, ethical considerations, technical expertise, and student acceptance. As AI continues to evolve, institutions must prioritise the responsible integration of AI into their operations to ensure a positive impact on students, educators, and society as a whole.

## PROFESSIONAL DEVELOPMENT FOR THE AI ERA

As Artificial Intelligence (AI) continues to transform the higher education landscape, educators must adapt to new technologies and methodologies to remain effective and relevant. Professional development is essential for educators to stay up-to-date with AI trends, best practices, and pedagogical innovations. Educators should understand the basics of AI, including machine learning, deep learning, natural language processing, and computer vision. Educators should learn about AI applications in education, such as adaptive learning, personalised feedback, and intelligent tutoring systems. Educators should develop strategies for integrating AI into their teaching practices, such as designing AI-based learning activities, creating AI-powered assessments, and using AI to facilitate group work. Educators should develop digital literacy skills, including data analysis, data visualization, and programming languages like Python or R. Educators should learn how to effectively communicate with colleagues, students, and administrators about AI-related issues and opportunities. Educators should develop skills in data analysis and interpretation to inform instruction and decision-making. Educators should understand the ethical implications of AI in education, including bias in AI systems, data privacy, and intellectual property. Educators should learn about virtual learning environments, such as virtual reality (VR), augmented reality (AR), and online platforms like Canvas or Blackboard. Educators should learn about gamification and simulation techniques to engage students in active learning experiences. Educators should understand the concept of micro-credentials and competency-based education to provide students with flexible, stackable credentials. (Abulibdeh, et al. 2024; Cukurova, et al. 2024; Nyaaba & Zhai, 2024)

For professional development, online courses can provide educators with a flexible way to learn about AI-related topics. There is a need to attend conferences and workshops focused on AI in education to network with peers and stay up-to-date on best practices. Looking for a mentor who has experience with AI in education to provide guidance and support. Engage in peer coaching with colleagues to share knowledge and best practices. Request institutional support for professional development opportunities, such as funding for conferences or workshops. Encourage self-directed learning by providing resources, such as online tutorials or video lectures. Benefits of professional development include:

- Improved teaching practices: Educators can integrate AI into their teaching practices to enhance student engagement and outcomes.
- Increased student success: Educators can use AI-based tools to provide personalised feedback and support students' learning needs.
- Enhanced career opportunities: Educators who stay up-to-date with AI trends can enhance their career prospects and stay competitive in the job market.
- Better data analysis: Educators can use data analysis skills to inform instruction and improve student outcomes.
- Collaborative leadership: Educators who develop leadership skills can collaborate with colleagues to design innovative AI-based learning experiences. (Chen, 2024; Sharifuddin & Hashim, 2024; Wasito, 2024; Yusro et al. 2024)

By prioritizing professional development in the AI era, educators can stay current with the latest trends, technologies, and methodologies, ultimately enhancing their teaching practices and student outcomes.

## ADAPTIVE LEARNING: PERSONALISING THE HIGHER EDUCATION EXPERIENCE

Adaptive learning, a technology-enabled approach to education, offers numerous benefits that can revolutionize the way we learn. One of the most significant advantages is its ability to tailor instruction to each individual's unique learning style, pace, and abilities. By continuously assessing a student's progress and adapting the content and difficulty level accordingly, adaptive learning systems ensure that each learner stays engaged and motivated. This personalised approach also helps to address the needs of students who may be struggling or falling behind, allowing them to receive targeted support and catch up with their peers. Additionally, adaptive learning platforms can help reduce teacher workload by automating grading and assessment tasks, freeing up instructors to focus on more critical tasks (Slompy, et al. 2024). Furthermore, these systems provide real-time feedback and analytics, enabling educators to identify areas where students need extra support and make data-driven decisions to improve instruction. Overall, adaptive learning has been shown to improve student outcomes, increase academic achievement, and enhance the overall learning experience.

Implementing adaptive learning in educational settings can be a complex and challenging process. One of the primary challenges is ensuring that the technology is accurately assessing student knowledge and skills, and adapting to individual needs in a way that is fair and equitable. Additionally, implementing adaptive learning requires significant changes to teaching practices, which can be difficult for instructors who are accustomed to traditional methods. Moreover, ensuring that teachers have the necessary training and support to effectively integrate adaptive learning systems into their classrooms can be a barrier. Furthermore, the initial investment in adaptive learning technology and infrastructure can be substantial, which may be a challenge for schools or institutions with limited budgets. Moreover, ensuring the security and integrity of the adaptive learning platform is crucial, as it handles sensitive student data. Finally, scaling adaptive learning across large numbers of students and courses can be a logistical challenge, requiring significant resources and infrastructure. (Elimadi, et al. 2024; Gransden, et al. 2024; Jadan-Guerrero, et al. 2024)

To successfully implement adaptive learning, it is essential to follow best practices that ensure a smooth and effective transition. One of the most critical steps is to clearly define the learning objectives and outcomes, as well as identify the target audience and their needs. Additionally, it is crucial to choose an adaptive learning platform that is intuitive, user-friendly, and integrates with existing learning management systems. Teachers should receive thorough training on how to effectively use the adaptive learning platform, and ongoing support should be provided to address any technical issues or questions. Moreover, it is essential to monitor student progress and adjust the adaptive learning pathways regularly to ensure that they remain relevant and effective. Finally, regular evaluations and assessments should be conducted to measure the impact of adaptive learning on student outcomes and inform future improvements. By following these best practices, educators can harness the potential of adaptive learning to improve student engagement, achievement, and overall academic success.

As adaptive learning continues to evolve, future directions include the integration of emerging technologies such as artificial intelligence, machine learning, and data analytics to further personalise learning experiences. One promising trend is the development of more sophisticated assessment tools that can accurately measure complex skills and competencies, allowing for even more tailored instruction. Additionally, the increasing use of virtual and augmented reality technologies will enable immersive and interactive learning experiences that adapt to individual learners' needs. Another area of growth is the incorporation of social learning analytics, which will allow educators to track not only individual student progress but also group dynamics and collaboration patterns. Furthermore, the use of natural language processing and chatbots will enable more conversational and human-like interactions between students and adaptive learning systems. Finally, integrating data from multiple sources, such as learning management systems, educational games, and wearable devices, will provide a more comprehensive view of student learning and enable more precise adaptation. As these innovations emerge, adaptive learning is poised to play an increasingly important role in revolutionising education and enhancing student outcomes. In conclusion, adaptive learning has the potential to revolutionise the higher education experience by providing personalized learning experiences that cater to individual students' needs and interests. While implementing adaptive learning presents several challenges, improved student outcomes, increased engagement, and data-driven instruction make it a worthwhile investment for institutions seeking to improve student success.

## INTERACTIVE SIMULATIONS AND VIRTUAL ENVIRONMENTS IN HIGHER EDUCATION

Interactive simulations and virtual environments are increasingly used in higher education to enhance student learning and engagement (Familoni & Onyebuchi, 2024; Goi, 2024). These technologies allow students to experience complex, real-world scenarios in a safe and controlled environment, fostering a deeper understanding of abstract concepts and developing critical thinking and problem-solving skills. Interactive simulations and virtual environments offer numerous benefits for learners, including enhanced engagement, increased retention, and improved understanding of complex concepts. These immersive experiences allow students to interact with virtual objects, manipulate data, and make decisions in a safe and controlled environment, fostering a deeper sense of ownership and agency. Additionally, simulations can be tailored to individual learners' needs, providing personalised learning pathways and adapting to their pace and abilities. Virtual environments also enable learners to explore abstract concepts more concretely and tangibly, making complex ideas more accessible and memorable. Furthermore, simulations can be used to replicate real-world scenarios, allowing learners to develop critical thinking, problem-solving, and decision-making skills in a realistic and authentic context. Overall, interactive simulations and virtual environments have the potential to transform the learning experience, making it more engaging, effective, and enjoyable.

Interactive simulations and virtual environments come in various forms, each catering to different learning objectives and experiences. Examples include virtual labs, where students conduct experiments and investigations in a digital environment, such as chemistry simulations or physics labs; virtual reality (VR) experiences, which immerse learners in 3D environments, like virtual field trips or historical re-enactments; augmented reality (AR) overlays, which superimpose digital information onto real-world environments, such as museum exhibits or cityscapes; game-based simulations, which engage learners in interactive games and challenges to develop problem-solving skills; and virtual role-playing simulations, where students take on characters to practice communication, collaboration, and decision-making skills. Other examples include virtual whiteboards, where students collaborate on interactive diagrams and models; virtual breakout rooms, where learners work together to solve puzzles and challenges; and 360-degree videos, which provide panoramic views of real-world environments. These diverse types of interactive simulations and virtual environments offer educators a range of tools to create engaging and effective learning experiences.

To effectively implement interactive simulations and virtual environments, educators should follow best practices such as carefully aligning the simulation or environment with specific learning objectives and assessments, providing clear instructions and goals for learners, and incorporating opportunities for reflection and feedback. Additionally, educators should ensure that the simulation or environment is user-friendly and accessible on a variety of devices and that technical issues are addressed before implementation. It's also important to provide opportunities for learners to collaborate and communicate with each other, both within the simulation or environment and outside of it. Furthermore, educators should be prepared to facilitate discussions and debriefing sessions to help learners connect the simulation or environment to real-world applications and scenarios. Finally, it's crucial to continually evaluate and refine the simulation or environment based on learner feedback and assessment data to ensure its effectiveness in achieving the desired learning outcomes.

Future directions for interactive simulations and virtual environments include the integration of artificial intelligence and machine learning to create more realistic and responsive environments. Virtual and augmented reality is used to enhance immersive experiences and the development of personalized and adaptive simulations that adjust to individual learners' needs and abilities. Additionally, there is a growing emphasis on creating simulations and environments that focus on social-emotional learning, emotional intelligence, and soft skills development. Furthermore, the use of blockchain technology and other decentralised platforms is expected to increase, allowing for greater control over data ownership and security. Finally, the integration of virtual and augmented reality with other technologies, such as 5G networks and the Internet of Things (IoT), will enable the creation of even more sophisticated and interactive simulations and virtual environments that can be used in a variety of settings, from education to healthcare to corporate training. In conclusion, interactive simulations and virtual environments have the potential to revolutionise the way we learn in higher education. By providing a more immersive, interactive, and engaging learning experience, these technologies can improve student learning outcomes, increase student engagement, and reduce costs associated with traditional training methods.

## EDUCATION FOR SUSTAINABLE DEVELOPMENT AND THE ROLE OF AI

Education for Sustainable Development (ESD) refers to a type of education that aims to promote sustainable development by equipping individuals with the knowledge, skills, attitudes, and values necessary to contribute to a better future with greener environments that have a minimal carbon footprint by fully utilizing existing resources without depleting them so that future generations can also benefit from them. It encompasses various disciplines and addresses sustainability's social, economic, political, and environmental dimensions. Current studies have shown that Artificial Intelligence (AI) can be used to foster sustainability in higher education institutions (HEI) and act as an enabler in attaining the Sustainable Development Goals (SDGs). This can be achieved by improving the education delivery system and community engagements (Filho et al. 2024).

Artificial intelligence (AI) is an exceptionally powerful tool for analyzing vast amounts of data related to sustainability issues, including the environment, energy consumption, and socio-economic factors across various disciplines. The valuable insights gained from this analysis provide significant information on current trends and enable predictions of future scenarios with a high level of accuracy. This data can then be used to inform the development of effective educational programs and policies, giving educators and learners access to informed decisions and allowing them to take appropriate actions toward sustainable development with confidence. The widespread integration of AI in various fields like education, health care, finance, communication, and media has substantially increased society's productivity and economic outcomes and boosted international trade and competitiveness thus enhancing the development of nations with robust strategies for using AI. It is thus pivotal for the education sector to fully integrate AI and drive innovations in other sectors to achieve sustainable development (Chen & Zhu, 2024).

According to Huai (2024), the Minister of Education in China asserted that the modern world is characterized by rapidly changing technological and industrial revolutions (currently the Fourth Industrial Revolution (4IR) leveraging digital technologies like AI. This is soundly changing the education sector and the landscape of doing business in all other sectors of the economy by reshaping human society's thinking patterns, organizational structures, and operational modes on all fronts.

Education faces both new challenges and opportunities to drive further sustainable development and produce graduates who are fit for the 4IR in this 21st century and those to come. With its intelligent, automated, and high-precision data analysis and processing capabilities, educational AI can empower teaching and learning in many ways, such as simulating the roles of teachers, administrators, peers, partners, and competitors to promote communication and collaboration. All these are tenets for achieving the 17 SDGs and the global agenda 2030.

## Teaching Pedagogies

There is a big possibility of employing generative AI tools like Chat Generative Pre-trained Transformer (ChatGPT), Co-pilot, Poe, Bing, Grammarly, and others to enhance the development of teaching pedagogies to improve the quality of education from the elementary level up to higher education levels. This can help to mitigate the global shortage of teachers, particularly in STEM disciplines which directly affects SDG 4 on the provision of quality, accessible, and sustainable education. AI-powered adaptive learning platforms can tailor educational content and experiences to individual learners' needs and interests. This personalization can enhance engagement and motivation, making sustainability education more effective. AI algorithms can track learners' progress, identify knowledge gaps, and provide targeted resources and timely feedback, enabling learners to acquire relevant sustainability-related knowledge and skills. The use of AI may also result in the reduction of social inequalities, within and without the education sector. AI thrives in the virtual world which knows no geographical and socio-economic boundaries, thus yielding indirect positive impacts on other sustainable development goals across the globe (Arruda, Arruda, 2024).

## Virtual Lecturers

According to data from UNESCO, there is a global shortage of more than forty-four million lecturers, especially in economically challenged countries in much of Africa and parts of Asia. This poses a great challenge in attaining the global goal of providing quality basic education to all global citizens by 2030. Quality education is touted as the panacea for attaining all other SDGs and attaining sustainable development in all sectors of the economy because education is the bedrock for acquiring all skills, competencies, and attitudes required for development in any given sector. Lack of interest in the teaching profession due to unattractive incentives among other factors has been identified as a contributor to the shortage of teaching professionals. Since 2002, UNESCO has called for the need for long-term policies and sustainable strategies for mitigating this challenge. AI technologies seem to be able to fill this gap by suggesting solutions and generating tailor-made educational content for each class of student or teacher, leveraging the vast amount of data available and algorithms to process it (UNESCO, 2023).

AI algorithms have the potential to generate virtual simulations and modeling experiences that offer learners a safe and cost-effective way to engage in activities related to sustainable development. AI can also act as a virtual teacher, addressing the shortage of physical human teachers in certain countries. Virtual reality and simulations provide a collaborative and interactive learning platform that can be utilised in a global "classroom" setting. By sharing ideas and perspectives with peers from different parts of the world, learners can gain a deeper understanding of the subject matter. Such simulations can promote the development of critical thinking, and problem-solving skills. The AI-powered simulations can also facilitate personalised learning that adapts to the learner's pace and style of learning, ensuring that they have a more engaging and effective learning experience. AI presents opportunities for less privileged students to access quality education without requiring modern or expensive infrastructure (Gasevic et al., 2023).

## AI Tutoring Systems

AI-powered tutoring systems use machine learning algorithms to analyze the depth and breadth of learners' responses to given questions and provide personalized guidance and support to them, helping them navigate sustainability topics with ease and develop a deeper and more critical understanding of the issues being studied. AI systems can answer questions, offer explanations, and provide or suggest additional support resources required when necessary. Several AI assistants and chatbots like ChatGPT, Co-pilot, Poe, Bing, and Grammarly can assist learners and their teachers in finding relevant information and resources on various learning areas and also assist with correcting spelling and grammatical errors in written work, this fosters self-directed learning. In a nutshell, AI systems can adapt to particular students and adjust teaching pedagogies to reach each class of learner. Students enjoy personalized learning experiences that can be effectively designed by AI systems that can analyse vast amounts of available personal data like their learning styles, performance records, and personal progress, AI tools can come up with specific personalized learning methods that respond to their individual needs and preferences allowing students to progress at their own convenient pace, this has been seen to motivate and engage the learner (Adiguzel, Kaya, Cansu, 2023).

However, generative AI platforms like ChatGPT are not yet developed enough to provide very accurate information in scientific fields like Physics. This suggests that human teachers are still greatly needed to guide students. Emphasis is made that AI should be used as a tool or aide and not as a replacement for human teachers. This drives a point home that ChatGPT is not a very good problem-solving tutor. There is a real risk that the polished language and the capacity to exhibit logical reasoning chains may do significant damage by teaching unsuspecting students the wrong physics. This may be true for other learning disciplines (Gregorcic & Pendrill, 2023).

The Virtual Science Laboratory is a cutting-edge AI-powered tool created to transform secondary school students' science education. Students may explore the intriguing realm of scientific inquiry through its realistic simulations and interactive activities without being constrained by actual resources or equipment. The application provides a large variety of experiment simulations covering all STEM disciplines. Students can virtually adjust variables, take the results in real-time, and conduct data analysis to enhance their comprehension of fundamental scientific ideas which helps them develop critical thinking skills as they investigate, formulate hypotheses, and draw conclusions from their experiments. These skills and competencies are requisite for attaining sustainable development in education and the world at large (Liapakis et al., 2023).

## Generative AI Applications

Generative AI applications like ChatGPT can assist learners in many ways that human teachers cannot, for example in generating new content in text, images, or music form, from their trained parameters across Internet resources, published texts, and images to generate responses to user-provided prompts in a variety of conversational or academic styles, including journal papers, academic presentations. Hutson et al., (2024) posit that AI tools such as ChatGPT can support the writing process in the context of blended pedagogical practices. This suggests that AI is a vital tool in blended and flipped classroom scenarios where students learn from both the physical and virtual school environment as well as at home. It is worth noting that these AI technologies are not human-teacher replacers but are there to augment learning processes and supplement the much-needed human touch in education circles. Human teachers bring in the affection, analysis of real local problems, and personal understanding of students' circumstances and personalities, they assist students achieve social intelligence from the real world in a way machines cannot (Boscardin et al., 2024).

AI can contribute to sustainable resource management within educational institutions. For example, AI algorithms can analyze energy consumption patterns, water consumption, lighting, and heating/cooling systems, promoting efficient resource utilisation and optimizing energy usage in school buildings, leading to reduced environmental impact. Smart systems powered by AI can also monitor and control environmental monitoring and conservation issues.

## ETHICAL CONSIDERATIONS OF AI IN HIGHER EDUCATION

It is crucial to consider the ethical implications of integrating AI into education for sustainable development. Issues such as data privacy, algorithmic bias, basic human rights, social order and the digital divide need to be addressed to ensure equitable access and meaningful participation in AI-powered educational initiatives. Universities and their respective academics should focus on teaching students how to use ChatGPT and similar tools in ethical ways that foster critical thinking and problem-solving rather than merely downloading, coping and pasting information (García-Peñalvo, 2023; Feng & Zhang, 2024).

### Authenticity and Originality

The authenticity and quality of AI-generated assignments are of paramount academic importance concerning issues of plagiarism and integrity. It is crucial to ensure that AI generated content aligns with educational objectives, standards, and ethics. Cooper (2023) argued that other ethical concerns associated with AI include content moderation, environmental impact, and the risk of copyright infringement. Both students and educators must comprehend how AI-generated assignments are created, ensuring transparency in the process. Chatbots like Chat GPT can generate text that can pass as human-generated and thus impinge on authenticity. It is imperative for teachers and educational institutions to critically evaluate the place of AI in education and determine the circumstances and extent under which AI-generated assignments can be integrated to enrich the educational landscape without compromising academic ethics and standards. This chapter argues that stakeholders in education should embrace and use AI as a vital tool to assist in the generation of ideas, creative thinking and problem-solving and thus achieve sustainable development. AI should not be used as an alternative to critical thinking but as an aide. (Nitin Liladhar Rane, 2024).

Plagiarism arises when students present the work or ideas of others as their own, and AI tools have the unintended capacity to exacerbate this issue in multiple ways. In the first instance, ChatGPT produces text that can often pass as human-authored content. Consequently, when students employ this AI for their academic assignments or essays, they may inadvertently integrate entire or partial responses generated by ChatGPT without adhering to the necessary citations, thereby infringing upon established academic integrity norms. Some AI applications can be employed by educators to mitigate and detect acts of plagiarism and collusion by students. It should be noted that these programs are not 100% effective and accurate as asserted by Davis and Kumar (2023). Modern Educators have a mammoth task to protect the integrity of education to achieve sustainable development and discourage the collapse of educational outcomes by excessive reliance on AI by students at the expense of learning to produce original work. Teachers can employ programs like Open AI's Open Text Classifier, Turnitin, GPT Zero, Packback, and Hugging Face. Co, and AI Cheat Check (Shea, 2023).

## Human Rights and Educational Equity

Safeguard Human Rights and Educational Equity: stakeholders must ensure that the application of AI technology in education does not infringe on human rights to privacy, personal data security, and equitable access to quality education. All students, regardless of their backgrounds and social status should have equal access to the educational resources and opportunities brought about by AI technology. HEIs face the challenge of ensuring the fair and transparent use of GenAI applications while mitigating the risk of exacerbating existing socio-economic inequalities between low and high-income students and between native and non-native English speakers. Note that non-native English speakers may require more assistance from AI technologies to refine their English to meet global communication standards than native speakers (Xiao, 2023; Amano et al., 2023; Duah & McGivern, 2024).

## Data Privacy and Security

AI systems in higher education often rely on vast amounts of data, including personal information about students and educators. It is crucial to ensure robust data privacy and security measures are in place to protect sensitive and private information about students and teachers. Institutions should establish clear policies and procedures for data collection, storage, and usage, adhering to relevant data protection laws and regulations to ensure that information collected for educational purposes is strictly used for such purposes only. Individuals in the educational community should be able to access, manage, and control personal data processed by intelligent machines to prevent the unauthorized sharing of user information with other individuals or businesses. (Mhlanga, 2023; Chen, 2024).

## Human Autonomy

The concept of human autonomy pertains to an individual's capacity to make choices and pursue a path of action based on their convictions and values. This entails acting independently and making decisions that align with one's perspective. It is worth noting that the notion of human autonomy, along with other ethical principles, was established before the emergence of AI. Hence, it is plausible that certain concepts may require revision to address contemporary sociotechnical concerns.

Autonomy encompasses elements of self-rule, self-governance, and the ability to make decisions based on one's discernment.

AI technologies can analyze people and make decisions for them, including academic decisions. While this can be more efficient and sometimes more accurate than human-made decisions, it can also take away individual autonomy. AI developers should consider human autonomy and let people have the final say over AI suggestions. Humans are best suited to address modern socio-technical issues. Autonomy helps us understand problems from multiple perspectives including social, political, affective, and economic. In the context of technology, various advancements such as AI assistants and recommendation systems have the potential to promote individuals' autonomy by offering them alternatives tailored to their preferences. However, it is important to note that an excessive dependence on technology may impair students' independent and critical thinking abilities and render them passive receivers of information, not active creators. This is because intelligent recommendation systems may limit access to diverse and comprehensive information (Zhang, 2023). As such. Incorporating AI ethics education into digital literacy training is crucial to enable students to make informed decisions about integrating AI into their studies.

## Algorithmic Bias and Fairness

AI algorithms can inadvertently perpetuate bias if they are trained on biased or incomplete data. In the context of higher education, this bias can affect areas such as admissions, grading, and student support. Institutions should take measures to ensure algorithms are fair, transparent, and free from discriminatory biases. Regular audits and evaluations of AI systems should be conducted to identify and mitigate potential biases. In modern education, AI is used in various applications like intelligent tutoring systems, personalized learning platforms, and automated grading systems. It is thus essential to ensure that these systems are free from discriminatory bias. Incorporating ethical considerations and accountability in Human Resource Management decisions is essential if AI is responsible for selecting students for particular tasks or courses. In the case of a wrong decision, the question is- who is accountable? Is it the designer of the AI system, the operator, or the machine itself? AI should assist, not replace humans in decision-making. Oversight by humans is essential when using AI systems, and clear roles and responsibilities must be established for both humans and AI to ensure human agency and accountability are retained (Abatan et. al. 2024; Biu et. al. 2024).

## Equity and Inclusivity

AI should be designed and implemented in a way that promotes equity and inclusivity in higher education. Special attention should be given to addressing biases and ensuring that AI systems do not disadvantage certain student populations. Institutions should strive for equitable access to AI technologies and ensure that they do not exacerbate existing inequalities in education. AI-powered platforms and tools can facilitate collaboration and knowledge sharing among learners, educators, and other stakeholders from diverse backgrounds and geographic locations to promote sustainable development. These platforms can provide spaces for sharing best and novel practices, innovative ideas, and success stories. AI algorithms can also assist in identifying relevant networks and communities of practice, connecting individuals with shared sustainability interests and goals.

# EDUCATIONAL TECHNOLOGY POLICY AND AI INTEGRATION IN HIGHER EDUCATION

AI is an emerging and fast-developing technology in the 4IR and is taking all sectors by storm, the higher education sector, which directly feeds its graduates into the productive industrial and commercial sectors cannot afford to ignore AI otherwise it would be irrelevant to the community and fail to spearhead sustainable development. Against this backdrop, it is thus imperative to enact robust policy frameworks on generative AI integration and application in HEI. The AI Assessment Scale (AIAS) coherently seeks to address this phenomenon, albeit within sound ethical principles (Luo, 2024).

## Government Policies on AI

Looking at the wide applicability and impact of AI in modern education, several national governments have opted to promote and regulate AI adoption in various sectors of their economies including higher education to achieve sustainable development across the board. They do this by implementing a vast array of developmental policies. In the United Kingdom (UK) the National AI Strategy has been enacted, Japan has introduced the AI Strategy 2019 & Integrated Innovation Strategy 2020, China crafted the New Generation AI Development Plan for 2030, India put forward the National Strategy for Artificial Intelligence (NSAI), the United Arab Emirates (UAE) enacted the UAE Strategy for Artificial Intelligence (AI), South Korea introduced Toward AI World Leader beyond IT, and Canada has the Pan-Canadian AI Strategy. These policies spell out the role of AI, the ethical practices expected, and how AI should be used in various sectors. This shows that many countries in the globe are actively embracing AI and crafting measures to control and monitor its use. Many other countries particularly those in Africa should follow suit (Baum et al., 2023).

## Institutional Policies on AI

Institutions need to establish interdisciplinary committees or boards involving experts in AI, ethics, education, and relevant stakeholders to develop ethical guidelines and policies specific to AI implementation in higher education. Regular monitoring, evaluation, and open dialogue around the ethical implications of AI can help ensure that its integration aligns with educational values and promotes the well-being of all stakeholders involved. Across Asia, universities in Hong Kong (Cheung & Wong, 2023), Japan (Nagoya University, 2023), South Korea, Singapore, and India (Leung & Niazi, 2023) enacted a paradigm shift from banning GenAI and adapting their existing policies to accommodate it to enrich their curricula according to current trends and foster sustainable development. Prominent universities in the United States of America followed suit, for example (Harvard University, n.d.; Stanford University, 2023; Yale University, 2023). A call is made for the rest of the world including Africa to follow suit and enact robust policies governing the use of AI in higher education.

## Addressing Governance of AI: Data Privacy, Transparency, Accountability and Security

The Vice Minister of Education of China and Director of the National Committee of UNESCO emphasized at the 2024 WDEC that the expedited advancement of digital technology has brought forth unprecedented challenges and opportunities for global education, profoundly changing educational ideas, models, and paradigms. The Chinese government places great stress on the governance of digital education, adhering to the

Principle of maintaining balances between AI development and security and between AI innovation and moral considerations. The establishment of the digital education expert council committee and AI ethics committee and the formulation of regulation frameworks for educational AI are underway to meet the challenges of AI applications in education (China Youth Daily, 2024). It is also worth mentioning that previous AI policies in education did not anticipate the level of advancements that text-based GPT 3.5 and 4 can now achieve. Given the potential benefits and risks associated with the use of generative AI in education, it is important to develop a proper AI education policy that addresses these concerns and provides guidance on the responsible use of AI guidelines on the ethical use of AI technologies by emphasizing the key idea of human-centeredness and hence, human rights and values laid out in the Universal Declaration of Human Rights (UDHR) are advised to be adopted as the necessary foundation to further promote beneficial and appropriate use of AI technologies (UNESCO, 2023). Institutions should establish ethical guidelines for the use of student data in AI applications. Student data collected for AI purposes should be used solely for educational and support purposes and should not be exploited for commercial or non-educational purposes without explicit consent. Clear data governance policies need to be in place to regulate the collection, storage, and use of student data, ensuring compliance with relevant privacy regulations.

## Monitoring and Evaluating AI Implementation

To protect European Union (EU) citizens from the danger of abusive use of advanced technologies, the EU proposed its pillars (legal compliance, ethical alignment and sociotechnical robustness) to ensure the trustworthiness of AI and established a specific AI expert group to work on specific policy recommendations and guidelines. Moving forward, the ongoing efforts of national and international organizations to ensure the positive implementation of AI technologies will continue to prioritize discussions and the formulation of legal and ethical principles (AI regulation, 2023; UNESCO, 2023). However, until these principles are validated by real-time implementation of AI technologies, they will remain primarily predictive and prescriptive

## Ensuring Equity in Access to AI Technologies

AI integration policies should promote Inclusive and non-discriminatory learning environments to facilitate academic success among students with disabilities and other special educational needs (SEN). This will surely promote the attainment of SDG 4 and the global agenda 2030. Utmost care must be taken to adhere to ethical concerns and eliminate algorithmic biases that can exacerbate inequalities or bring about disadvantages to certain groups of students and teachers. Privacy and confidentiality of sensitive information should be kept and protected as such (Almufareh et al. 2024).

## Attributing AI Technologies

Attribution is an important aspect of AI policy in HEI. From previous discussions on the role of AI in education, policies should include clauses that require students to acknowledge the use of AI just like they do when citing academic sources. This will ensure the ethical credibility, integrity, and authenticity of the output product. Such policies should include clearly stated guidelines on how to attribute the contribution of generative AI to the student's work. There are several examples of ChatGPT being used to cheat on entrance exams in universities due to its ability to write college application essays, and it has also been tested in writing and passing an MBA exam and passed tests required for medical licenses and business degrees. These are examples where Generative AI applications can produce pieces of academic work that can pass as human-generated work. It is thus imperative to teach and encourage students to state the part of their work generated by AI or at least to acknowledge using AI technologies in their academic work so that assessments reflect what students have achieved. AI is part of our future, we need to embrace it, educators should make it very clear about expectations for students, and how they may or may not get help when they're preparing assignments (Erdem, 2023; Stannard, 2023).

## Providing Training and Support for Teachers, Technical Staff, and Students in AI Integration

To effectively implement AI tools into pedagogical practices in HEI, training and support are needed for teachers, technical staff and students. These people need both pedagogical and technical support. Recent studies stressed the necessity for students' understanding of generative AI as an essential component of digital literacy to enhance the quality of their work and not to be major contributors to it. Policies enacted must ensure that relevant 21st-century skills like critical thinking, communication, and problem-solving are upheld with the aid of AI. Proper training and support given to major stakeholders will empower them to overcome technological barriers, understand the functionalities of the tools, interpret the generated responses, and ensure ethical usage of AI with utmost confidence upholding data privacy and plagiarism issues. (Else, 2023; Bender, 2024).

## Rethinking Assessments and Examinations

Educators should make a paradigm shift and re-design assessments that require the application of knowledge and not test their ability to gather relevant information which could be easily done by AI applications. This is a call for problem-solving and project-based assessment strategies to be enacted. These will ultimately result in solving many societal problems and immensely contributing to sustainable development. Educators can also include assessments where students critically examine the loopholes of the current assessment methods and offer solutions. From these, it is envisaged that more insights that can drastically improve and update the current assessment methods will be discovered through engaging the students themselves, they can discuss the loopholes they are using to 'cheat'. As the use of AI in education and assessment becomes more prevalent, students and teachers must understand the principles behind the technology to maintain academic integrity and uphold ethical principles as discussed previously (Chan, 2023; Cotton et al., 2023). An AI education policy can teach students about the ethical considerations surrounding AI, such as bias and fairness, as well as the potential consequences of using AI in academic contexts. Universities can help ensure that graduates are equipped to contribute to the development of AI and to navigate the ethical, social, and economic issues that are likely to arise as AI becomes more widespread in the future.

Lecturers can apply AI-powered assessment tools to lessen their marking burdens and also improve efficiency. AI uses machine learning algorithms to analyze student responses and provide valuable insights into student learning outcomes in real time. These tools can assess a wide range of skills and competencies, including critical thinking, problem-solving, and creativity which are essential for sustainable development. AI can analyze essays and written responses to open-ended questions, providing educators with detailed feedback on student writing skills and content comprehension. Similarly, AI can assess student performance in interactive simulations and virtual laboratories, offering insights into their practical application of concepts and theories. This allows educators to identify patterns and trends in student performance, enabling them to intervene early if a student is struggling or provide additional challenges to students who are excelling (Ihemereze, et. al., 2023, Vashishth, et. al., 2024).

## Encouraging a Balanced Approach to AI Adoption

A balanced approach to AI adoption in HEI involves recognizing both the potential benefits and limitations of generative AI technologies. It is suggested that higher education institutions collaborate with AI designers to create systems that align with pedagogical principles and educational goals. Policy implications include flexible and adaptable curricula, professional development opportunities for educators, integration of AI ethics courses in the curriculum, continuous learning for students, and support of their self-directed learning (Abulibdeh et al., 2024). In the process of integrating AI into education, it is important to clarify the moral limitations of AI applications in regular instruction, scientific research, and social services, as well as formulate industry standards, governance regulations, and ethical norms for educational AI for AI to contribute to the safe, efficient, and sustainable development of education (People. cn, 2024b).

## Preparing Students for the AI-driven Workplace by Developing Student Holistic Competencies/Generic

An AI education policy can provide students with the prerequisite knowledge and skills to work with AI in a professional capacity in a real-world workplace. Secondly, AI has the potential to revolutionize many aspects of society, including education itself By educating students on AI, universities can help prepare them to be active participants in the development and implementation of AI technology, ensuring that it benefits society as a whole (Adiguzel et al., 2023).

# COMPETENCY-BASED LEARNING AND THE FUTURE OF HIGHER EDUCATION

Competency-based learning is a system of education that focuses on ensuring that all learners master academic knowledge and skills in particular fields and develop the expertise to apply it confidently. This approach shifts the primary focus of education to the desired outcomes for learners rather than the structure and process of the educational system. Competency-based learning refers to systems of instruction, assessment, grading, and academic reporting that are designed to allow students to advance at their own pace based on their ability to master a skill or competency, regardless of traditional measures such as grades and yearly curriculum bearing in mind that not all students learn at the same pace or in the same way. CBL provides a framework for teaching and assessment of learning that is personalized to each student's needs and abilities. Traditionally, to move forward with the curriculum, students are required to attain a minimum score or achievement to meet an educational standard within a given timeframe. This may be as simple as a list of successfully passed courses that reflect a variety of thoughts and opinions of educators, administrators, politicians, and professionals and/or may include workplace- or business-related skills and societal needs. CBL emphasizes what students can do rather than what they know. A three-domain competency model can be adopted structured around knowledge and information literacy, disciplinary and professional experience, and self-awareness and personal development as three interdependent aspects of competency (Hubbard, 2024).

For education to keep pace with the technologically advancing global marketplace, students need to learn “how to think” more than “what to think”. A student’s ability to quickly adapt to a changing marketplace and embrace new developments is anchored in their willingness to learn new things and on their critical thinking and problem-solving skills which are pivotal in this 4IR and 21$^{st}$ century. Adaptive learning experiences guide students to practice skills and build on their successes to demonstrate competency. In this context, competency can be defined as the attainment of excellence - not the meeting of a minimum standard (Rhoney et al., 2024).

Modern assignments need to build student competence and confidence in the appropriate use of digital tools and AI as these skills are required for success in multiple sectors of the 21st-century economy and in the future world and workplace (Ewen, 2023). A paradigm shift is thus required on how assessment of students is done, the proliferation of generative AI applications means that assessment design must be robust enough to ensure it is genuinely assessing student learning outcomes and competencies and not merely their ability to gather relevant information which AI can easily do. Assessments should shift towards the application of knowledge and demonstration of particular skills rather than simple recall of information. Teachers must teach students to think to be able to solve novel societal problems using modern technologies as tools to advance their competencies with a high degree of ethics and academic integrity (Francis & Smith, 2023).

Successful curriculum transformation requires a systemic and collaborative approach, involving the integration of technology-enhanced teaching and learning, project-based learning, and experiential learning opportunities. Faculty development, student-centered design, and continuous curriculum evaluation and improvement. The insights derived from this research contribute to the ongoing discourse on higher education reform and provide practical recommendations for educational leaders and policymakers seeking to align curriculum design with the demands of the technologically complex 21st-century knowledge economy with great emphasis on environmental issues and sustainable development. By embracing innovative and adaptive curriculum design strategies, higher education institutions can better prepare graduates to be productive global citizens in multicultural workplaces. While also enhancing institutional competitiveness and relevance in an increasingly digital and knowledge-driven world (Vela; Polo; Castillo, 2024; Love et al., 2023).

The education system should design focused training programs and professional development initiatives, ensuring that teaching and learning activities are aligned with both individual career goals and societal/global needs. This alignment is crucial for maintaining quality and efficiency in professional practices, and it also aids in the standardization of skills across a given organization or industry. This standardization is vital for consistent performance appraisal and quality assurance in professional outputs (Dai, 2023). Moreover, competence frameworks are dynamic and adaptable, capable of evolving with changing business environments, new technologies, and market trends. This adaptability ensures that the workforce remains agile and equipped with relevant skills. AI technologies can leverage machine deep learning to keep abreast with these changes and suggest strategies of relevant developments to stakeholders involved. It is worth noting that while CBL is being adopted by many countries as a global education policy, it is also largely affected by national history, politics, economy, and culture. Therefore, the points discussed in this chapter are not a one-size-fits-all, they are suggestions that may need modification to suit particular situations, nations, or cultures (Deng et al., 2023).

## CONCLUSION

In conclusion, the integration of AI with education for sustainable development (ESD) in higher education requires a comprehensive approach that addresses the professional development and assessment of educators, teaching and learning practices, and policies that promote the integration of AI with ESD. The integration of AI with ESD has the potential to revolutionize the way we learn, work, and interact, and it is essential to harness this potential to promote sustainable development and social justice. The integration of AI with ESD requires educators to develop new skills and knowledge in areas such as AI literacy, data analysis, and digital pedagogy. Professional development programs that focus on these areas can help educators better understand the potential and limitations of AI in education and develop effective teaching practices that incorporate AI. Assessment tools that evaluate the effectiveness of AI-based educational interventions can help identify improvement areas and provide feedback to educators. AI can enhance teaching and learning practices by delivering personalized learning experiences, automating routine tasks, and facilitating collaboration and communication among students and educators. However, it is essential to develop teaching practices that are designed to promote critical thinking, problem-solving, and collaboration among students. Educators should also be aware of the potential biases and limitations of AI-based educational tools and take steps to mitigate these issues. Policies that promote the integration of AI with ESD in higher education should prioritize equity, accessibility, and social justice. These policies should also provide support for educators as they develop new skills and knowledge in areas such as AI literacy, data analysis, and digital pedagogy. Additionally, policies should ensure that AI-based educational interventions are transparent, accountable, and inclusive.

## REFERENCES


Abatan, A., Jacks, B. S., Ugwuanyi, E. D., Nwokediegwu, Z. Q. S., Obaigbena, A., Daraojimba, A. I., & Lottu, O. A. (2024). The role of environmental health and safety practices in the automotive manufacturing industry. *Engineering Science & Technology Journal*, *5*(2), 531–542. DOI: 10.51594/estj.v5i2.830

Abatan, A., Obaigbena, A., Ugwuanyi, E. D., Jacks, B. S., Umoga, U. J., Daraojimba, O. H., & Lottu, O. A. (2024). Integrated simulation frameworks for assessing the environmental impact of chemical pollutants in aquatic systems. *Engineering Science & Technology Journal*, *5*(2), 543–554. DOI: 10.51594/estj.v5i2.831

Abulibdeh, A., Zaidan, E., & Abulibdeh, R. (2024). Navigating the confluence of artificial intelligence and education for sustainable development in the era of industry 4.0: Challenges and opportunities, and ethical dimensions. *Journal of Cleaner Production*, *437*, 140527. Advance online publication. DOI: 10.1016/j.jclepro.2023.140527

Adiguzel, T., Kaya, M. H., & Cansu, F. K. (2023). Revolutionizing education with AI: Exploring the transformative potential of ChatGPT. *Contemporary Educational Technology*, *15*(3), 429. DOI: 10.30935/cedtech/13152

Almufareh, M. F., Kausar, S., Humayun, M., & Tehsin, S. (2024). A conceptual model for inclusive technology: Advancing disability inclusion through artificial intelligence. *Journal of Disability Research*, *3*(1), 20230060. DOI: 10.57197/JDR-2023-0060

Arruda, E. P., & Arruda, D. P. (2024). Artificial intelligence for SDG4 of the 2030 agenda. Transforming education to achieve quality, equality, and inclusion. *Sustainable Economies*, *2*(2), 34. DOI: 10.62617/se.v2i2.34

Baum, K. B. (2024). From fear to action: AI governance and opportunities for all. *Frontiers of Computer Science*, *5*, 49.

Bender, S.M. (2024). Awareness of artificial intelligence as an essential digital literacy: ChatGPT and Gen-AI in the classroom. Retrieved from Changing English, 1-14: https://doi.org/DOI: 10.1080/1358684X.2024.2309995

Biu, P. W., Nwokediegwu, Z. Q. S., Daraojimba, O. H., Majemite, M. T., & Obaigben, A. (2024). Advancements in geo-data analytics: Implications for US energy policy and business investment. *World Journal of Advanced Research and Reviews*, *21*(1), 1422–1439. DOI: 10.30574/wjarr.2024.21.1.0172

Chan, C. (2023). A comprehensive AI policy education framework for university teaching and learning. *International Journal of Educational Technology in Higher Education, 20*(1), 38. DOI: 10.1186/s41239-023-00408-3

Chen, H. (2024). The ethical challenges of educational artificial intelligence and coping measures. A discussion in the context of the 2024 Science Insights Education Frontiers 2024; 20(2), 3263-3281. DOI: DOI: 10.15354/sief.24.re339

Cheung, W., & Wong, N. (2023, September 4). *Hong Kong universities relent to rise of ChatGPT, AI but keep eye out for cheats.* South China Morning Post. https://www.scmp.com/news/hong-kong/education/article/3233269/hong-kong-universities-relent-rise-chatgpt-ai-tools-teaching-and-assignments-keep-eye-out-plagiarism

China Youth Daily. (2024). A special report on the 2024 World Digital Education Conference.

Cooper, G. (2023). Examining science education in ChatGPT: An exploratory study of generative artificial intelligence. *Journal of Science Education and Technology, 32*(3), 444–452. DOI: 10.1007/s10956-023-10039-y

Cotton, D. R. E., Cotton, P. A., & Shipway, J. R. (2023). Chatting and Cheating: Ensuring academic integrity in the era of ChatGPT. *Innovations in Education and Teaching International.* Advance online publication. DOI: 10.1080/14703297.2023.2190148

Cukurova, M., Kralj, L., Hertz, B., & Saltidou, E. (2024). Professional Development for Teachers in the Age of AI.

Dai, D. (2023). Conceptual Frameworks Guiding Research on Talent Development. In Talent Development from the Qeios, CC-BY 4.0. Perspective of Developmental Science: A Guide to Use-Inspired Research on Human Excellence, 37-55. DOI: 10.1007/978-3-031-46205-4_3

Davis, M., & Kumar, A. (2023). 'Pay attention to it, ignore it or push on it': Brown professors discuss AI's impact on academic integrity. The Brown Daily Herald (February 8). https://www.proquest.com/wire-feeds/pay-attention-ignore-push-back-on-brown/docview/2774393345/se-2?accountid=10675

Deng, L. W., Wu, S., Chen, Y., Wang, Y., & Peng, Z. (2023). A comparative study of twenty-first-century competencies in high school mother tongue curriculum standards in China, the United States, and Finland. *Language, Culture and Curriculum, 36*(2), 142–160. DOI: 10.1080/07908318.2022.2072506

Deng, Y., Xu, H., & Wang, S. (2024). Governance of artificial intelligence risks: Models, tools, and strategies. *Reform, 2024*(1), 144–158.

Elimadi, I., Chafiq, N., & Ghazouani, M. (2024). Artificial Intelligence in the Context of Digital Learning Environments (DLEs): Towards Adaptive Learning. In *Engineering Applications of Artificial Intelligence* (pp. 95–111). Springer Nature Switzerland. DOI: 10.1007/978-3-031-50300-9_6

Erdem, E. (2023). ChatGPT: Exciting or terrifying? The Tufts Daily. https://www.proquest.com/wire-feeds/chatgpt-exciting-terrifying=tufts-daily/docview/2769546664/se-2?accontid=10675

Ewen, E. M. (2023). Mapping the potential of AI in the age of competence-based higher education. Retrieved from Wonkhe: https://wonkhe.com/blogs/mapping-the-potential-of-ai-in-the-age-of-competence-based-higher-education/

Familoni, B. T., & Onyebuchi, N. C. (2024). Augmented and virtual reality in our education: a review: analyzing the impact, effectiveness, and prospects of AR/VR tools in enhancing learning experiences. *International Journal of Applied Research in Social Sciences*, *6*(4), 642–663. DOI: 10.51594/ijarss.v6i4.1043

Feng, Y., & Zang, Y. (2024). *Moral myths in the era of artificial intelligence and counter-measures (J/OL)*. Jiangsu Social Sciences., DOI: 10.13858/j.cnki.cn32-1312/c.202240201.004

Filho, W. L., Ribeiro, P. C. C., Mazuti, J., Salvia, A. L., Marcolin, C. B., Borsatto, J. M. L. S., Sharifi, A., Sierra, J., Luetz, J., Pretorious, R., & Trevisan, L. V. (2024). Using artificial intelligence to implement the UN sustainable development goals at higher education institutions. *International Journal of Sustainable Development and World Ecology*, *31*(6), 726–745. Advance online publication. DOI: 10.1080/13504509.2024.2327584

Francis, N. (2023). Guidelines on Using AI in Academic Assessments. Retrieved from National Teaching: https://figshare.edgehill.ac.uk/articles/educational resources/Guidelines on Using_AI_in_Academic_Asseements_pdf/24259600

Garcia-Penalvo, F. J. (2023). The perception of Artificial Intelligence in educational contexts after the launch of ChatGPT: Disruption or panic? *Education in the Knowledge Society*, *24*, 1–9. DOI: 10.14201/eks.31279

Gasevic, D. S., Siemens, G., & Sadiq, S. (2023). (4)). Empowering learners for the age of artificial intelligence. *Computers and Education: Artificial Intelligence*, *100130*, 100130. Advance online publication. DOI: 10.1016/j.caeai.2023.100130

Goi, C. L. (2024). The Impact of VR-Based Learning on Student Engagement and Learning Outcomes in Higher Education. *Teaching and Learning for a Sustainable Future: Innovative Strategies and Best Practices*, 207-223.

Gransden, C., Hindmarsh, M., Le, N. C., & Nguyen, T. H. (2024). Adaptive learning through technology: A technical review and implementation. *Higher Education. Skills and Work-Based Learning*, *14*(2), 409–417. DOI: 10.1108/HESWBL-05-2023-0121

Gregoric, B. (2023). Research and Education on critical thinking in students plays a crucial role. *Physics Education*, *58*(3), 035021.

Huai, J. (2024). Promoting Jointly Application, Sharing and Innovation of Digital Education. Available at: http://en.moe.gov.cn/features/2024WorldDigitalEducationConference/KeynoteSpeech/202402/t20240201_111377.html

Hubbard, K. (2024). Plant biology education: A competency-based vision for the future. Plants, People, Planet. John Wiley & Sons Ltd, 1-11

Ihemereze, K. C., Eyo-Udo, N. L., Egbokhaebho, B. A., Daraojimba, C., Ikwue, U., & Nwankwo, E. E. (2023). Impact of monetary incentives on employee performance in the Nigerian automotive sector: A case study. *International Journal of Advanced Economics*, *5*(7), 162–186. DOI: 10.51594/ijae.v5i7.548

Jadan-Guerrero, J., Tamayo-Narvaez, K., Méndez, E., & Valenzuela, M. (2024, June). Adaptive Learning Environments: Integrating Artificial Intelligence for Special Education Advances. In *International Conference on Human-Computer Interaction* (pp. 86-94). Cham: Springer Nature Switzerland. DOI: 10.1007/978-3-031-61953-3_10

Leung, M., & Niazi, S. (2023, February 24). *Universities are on alert over ChatGPT and other AI-assisted tools*. University World News. https://www.universityworldnews.com/post.php?story=20230222132357841

Liapakis, S. Z., & Bougia, A. (2023). Ethical Use of Artificial Intelligence and New Technologies in Education 5.0. *J Artificial Intelligence Machine Learning & Data Science*, *1*(4), 119–124. DOI: 10.51219/JAIMLD/Anastasios-Liapakis/15

Love, H. C., Cross, J. E., Fosdick, B. K., Tofany, E., & Dickmann, E. M. (2023). Teaching team science: The key to addressing 21st-century global challenges. *Small Group Research*, *54*(3), 396–427. DOI: 10.1177/10464964221121349

Luo, J. (2024). A critical review of Gen-AI policies in higher education assessment: A call to reconsider the "originality" of students' work. *Assessment & Evaluation in Higher Education*, •••, 1–14. DOI: 10.1080/02602938.2024.2309963

Mhlanga, D. (2023). Open AI in education, the responsible and ethical use of ChatGPT towards lifelong learning. Education, the Responsible and Ethical Use of ChatGPT towards Lifelong Learning (February 11, 2023).

Nyaaba, M., & Zhai, X. (2024). Generative AI professional development needs for teacher educators. *Journal of AI*, *8*(1), 1–13. DOI: 10.61969/jai.1385915

People. cn. (2024b). The initiative of "Empowering Education Development with Artificial Intelligence" was announced at the 2024 World Digital Education Conference. Available at: https://edu.yunnan.cn/system/2024/01/31/032930479.shtm

Rhoney, D. C., Chen, A. M. H., Churchwell, M. D., Daugherty, K. K., Jarrett, J. B., Kleppinger, E. L., Nawarskas, J. J., Sibicky, S. L., Stowe, C. D., & Meyer, S. M. (2024). The Need for Competency-Based Education. *American Journal of Pharmaceutical Education*, *88*(6), 100706. DOI: 10.1016/j.ajpe.2024.100706 PMID: 38705241

Sharifuddin, N. S., & Hashim, H. (2024). Benefits and Challenges in Implementing Artificial Intelligence in Education (AIED) in ESL Classroom: A Systematic Review (2019-2022). *International Journal of Academic Research in Business & Social Sciences*, *14*(1), 146–164. DOI: 10.6007/IJARBSS/v14-i1/20422

Shea, J. (2023, February 4). VCU: Faculty and staff discuss the 'perplexing, exciting and scary' implications of AI, such as ChatGPT, on campus. VCU News. https://www.proquest.com/wire-feeds/vcu-faculty-staff-discuss-perplexing-exciting/docview/2772266645/se-2?accountid=10675

Slomp, E. M., Ropelato, D., Bonatti, C., & da Silva, M. D. (2024, March). Adaptive Learning in Engineering Courses: How Artificial Intelligence (AI) Can Improve Academic Outcomes. In *2024 IEEE World Engineering Education Conference (EDUNINE)* (pp. 1-6). IEEE. DOI: 10.1109/EDUNINE60625.2024.10500580

Stannard, E. (2023, January 30). ChatGPT will write you an essay in seconds using AI. So why aren't CT professors more concerned about it? Hartford Courant (Online). https://www.proquest.com/blogs-podcasts-websites/chatgpt-will-write-you-essay-seconds-using-ai-so/docview/2770810966/se-2?accountid=10675

UNESCO. (2023). *Global Education Monitoring Report 2023: Technology in Education- A Tool on Whose Terms?* UNESCO.

UNESCO. (2023). Ethics of Artificial Intelligence. Retrieved from: https://www.unesco.org/en/artificial-Intelligence/recommendation-ethics

Vashishth, T. K., Sharma, V., Sharma, K. K., Kumar, B., Panwar, R., & Chaudhary, S. (2024). AI-driven learning analytics for personalized feedback and assessment in higher education. In *Using Traditional Design Methods to Enhance AI-Driven Decision Making* (pp. 206–230). IGI Global. DOI: 10.4018/979-8-3693-0639-0.ch009

Vela, D. P. (2024). Transforming Higher Education: Effective Strategies for Contemporary Curriculum Design. *Educational Administration: Theory and Practice*, *30*(3), 1985–1993.

Wasito, B. (2024, February). Exploring Artificial Intelligence (AI) to anticipate changes in Professional Skills in the next ERA of Industrial Revolution 4.0. In *The Third International Conference on Government Education Management and Tourism* (Vol. 3, pp. 013-013).

Xiao, C. (2023). Digital Human Rights Research (master's thesis). Retrieved from Central South University of Forestry and Technology: https://doi.org/DOI: 10.27662/d.cnki.gznlc.2023.000313

Yusro, M., Misin, R., & Mauludin, M. A. (2024, February). Vocational Education Development Strategy in the Use of Artificial Intelligence in the Digital Era. In *5th Vocational Education International Conference (VEIC-5 2023)* (pp. 734-741). Atlantis Press. DOI: 10.2991/978-2-38476-198-2_100

Zhang, C., Gao, Y., & Janssen, M. (2023). Understanding the evolution of open government data research: Towards open data sustainability and smartness. *International Review of Administrative Sciences*, *89*(1), 59–75. DOI: 10.1177/00208523211009955

## KEY TERMS AND DEFINITIONS

**Artificial Intelligence (AI):** refers to the development of computer systems that can perform tasks that typically require human intelligence, such as learning, problem-solving, and decision-making. AI systems can be trained to perform specific tasks, such as language translation, image recognition, and data analysis.

**Education for Sustainable Development (ESD):** This is an approach to education that focuses on developing the knowledge, skills, and values necessary to address the complex social, economic, and environmental challenges facing our world. ESD aims to promote sustainable development by fostering a culture of critical thinking, problem-solving, and collaboration.

**Professional Development:** Professional development refers to the ongoing learning and growth of educators to improve their teaching practices, skills, and knowledge. Professional development can include workshops, training sessions, coaching, and mentoring.

**Assessment and Feedback:** Assessment and feedback refer to the processes used to evaluate student learning and provide feedback to students. Assessment can include quizzes, tests, projects, and performances, while feedback can include written comments, grades, and ratings.

**Adaptive Learning:** Adaptive learning refers to the use of technology to adapt the difficulty level of educational content to individual students' needs and abilities. Adaptive learning systems can adjust their content in real-time based on student performance.

**Personalized Learning:** Personalized learning refers to the use of technology to tailor educational content to individual students' needs and interests. Personalized learning systems can provide customized learning paths, adaptive assessments, and tailored feedback.

**Interactive Simulations:** Interactive simulations refer to virtual or digital environments that mimic real-world scenarios or situations. Interactive simulations can be used for training, education, or research purposes.

**Digital Literacy:** Digital literacy refers to the ability to effectively use digital technologies to access information, communicate with others, and solve problems. Digital literacy includes skills such as online searching, email communication, and software use.

**Digital Pedagogy:** Digital pedagogy refers to the use of digital technologies to support teaching and learning practices. Digital pedagogy can include the use of online platforms, social media, games, simulations, and multimedia resources.

**Educational Technology Policy:** Educational technology policy refers to the guidelines and regulations that govern the use of technology in education. Educational technology policy can include issues such as data privacy, online safety, and digital citizenship.

**Ethics of AI:** The ethics of AI refer to the moral principles and values that guide the development and use of artificial intelligence systems. The ethics of AI can include issues such as transparency, accountability, fairness, and safety.

**Competency-Based Learning:** Competency-based learning refers to an educational approach that focuses on student mastery of specific skills or competencies rather than seat time or credit hours. Competency-based learning systems can provide personalized learning pathways and assessments based on student performance.

# Compilation of References


"CC BY-SA 3.0 IGO Deed I Attribution-ShareAlike 3.0 Intergovernmental Organization I Creative Commons." https://creativecommons.org/licenses/by-sa/3.0/igo/

Abatan, A., Jacks, B. S., Ugwuanyi, E. D., Nwokediegwu, Z. Q. S., Obaigbena, A., Daraojimba, A. I., & Lottu, O. A. (2024). The role of environmental health and safety practices in the automotive manufacturing industry. *Engineering Science & Technology Journal*, *5*(2), 531–542. DOI: 10.51594/estj.v5i2.830

Abatan, A., Obaigbena, A., Ugwuanyi, E. D., Jacks, B. S., Umoga, U. J., Daraojimba, O. H., & Lottu, O. A. (2024). Integrated simulation frameworks for assessing the environmental impact of chemical pollutants in aquatic systems. *Engineering Science & Technology Journal*, *5*(2), 543–554. DOI: 10.51594/estj.v5i2.831

Abulibdeh, A., Zaidan, E., & Abulibdeh, R. (2024). Navigating the confluence of artificial intelligence and education for sustainable development in the era of industry 4.0: Challenges, opportunities, and ethical dimensions. *Journal of Cleaner Production*, *437*, 140527. DOI: 10.1016/j.jclepro.2023.140527

Abunaseer, H. (2023). The use of generative AI in education: Applications, and impact. Technology and the Curriculum: Summer 2023.

Adams, M., Bell, L. A., & Griffin, P. (Eds.). (2007). *Teaching for Diversity and Social Justice*. Routledge. DOI: 10.4324/9780203940822

Adiguzel, T., Kaya, M. H., & Cansu, F. K. (2023). Revolutionizing education with AI: Exploring the transformative potential of ChatGPT. *Contemporary Educational Technology*, *15*(3), 429. DOI: 10.30935/cedtech/13152

Aithal, P. S., & Aithal, S. (2023). Optimizing the use of artificial intelligence-powered GPTs as teaching and research assistants by professors in higher education institutions: A study on smart utilization. *International Journal of Management, Technology, and Social Sciences*, *8*(4), 368–401. DOI: 10.47992/IJMTS.2581.6012.0326

Akgun, S. and Greenhow, C. (2023). Artificial Intelligence in Education; addressing ethics Challenges in K-12 setting. AI ethic, 2(3): 431-440.

Akgün, S., & Greenhow, C. (2021, September). Artificial intelligence in education: Addressing ethical challenges in K-12 settings. *AI and Ethics*, *2*(3), 431–440. DOI: 10.1007/s43681-021-00096-7 PMID: 34790956

Akpan, V. I., Igwe, U. A., Mpamah, I. B. I., & Okoro, C. O. (2020). Social constructivism: Implications on teaching and learning. *British Journal of Educational Technology*, *8*(8), 49–56.

Akram, H., Abdelrady, A. H., Al-Adwan, A. S., & Ramzan, M. (2022). Teachers' perceptions of technology integration in teaching-learning practices: A systematic review. *Frontiers in Psychology*, *13*, 920317. DOI: 10.3389/fpsyg.2022.920317 PMID: 35734463

Al Balushi, J. S. G., Al Jabri, M. I. A., Palarimath, S., Maran, P., Thenmozhi, K., & Balakumar, C. (2024). *Incorporating Artificial Intelligence Powered Immersive Realities to Improve Learning using Virtual Reality (VR) and Augmented Reality (AR) Technology.* Paper presented at the 2024 3rd International Conference on Applied Artificial Intelligence and Computing (ICAAIC).

Al Braiki, B., Harous, S., Zaki, N., & Alnajjar, F. (2020). Artificial intelligence in education and assessment methods. *Bulletin of Electrical Engineering and Informatics*, *9*(5), 1998–2007. DOI: 10.11591/eei.v9i5.1984

Al Masry, N. O. (2022). The role of Artificial Intelligence technologies in improving the Jordan Students: A student Perspective. *Journal of the College of Education (Assiut)*, *30*(9), 265–290.

Al Samman, A. M. (2024, January). Harnessing Potential: Meta-Analysis of AI Integration in Higher Education. In *2024 ASU International Conference in Emerging Technologies for Sustainability and Intelligent Systems (ICETSIS)* (pp. 1-7). IEEE. DOI: 10.1109/ICETSIS61505.2024.10459420

Alam, A. (2021). *Cloud-based e-learning: development of conceptual model for adaptive e-learning ecosystem based on cloud computing infrastructure.* Paper presented at the International Conference on Artificial Intelligence and Data Science.

Alam, A. (2023). Developing a Curriculum for Ethical and Responsible AI: A University Course on Safety, Fairness, Privacy, and Ethics to Prepare Next Generation of AI Professionals. In *Intelligent Communication Technologies and Virtual Mobile Networks* (pp. 879–894). Springer Nature Singapore. DOI: 10.1007/978-981-99-1767-9_64

Al-Ansi, A. M., Jaboob, M., Garad, A., & Al-Ansi, A. (2023). Analyzing augmented reality (AR) and virtual reality (VR) recent development in education. *Social Sciences & Humanities Open*, *8*(1), 100532. DOI: 10.1016/j.ssaho.2023.100532

Alenezi, H. S., & Faisal, M. H. (2020). Utilizing crowdsourcing and machine learning in education: Literature review. *Education and Information Technologies*, *25*(4), 2971–2986. DOI: 10.1007/s10639-020-10102-w

Alfredo, R., Echeverria, V., Jin, Y., Yan, L., Swiecki, Z., Gasevic, D., & Martinez-Maldonado, R. (2024). Human-centered learning analytics and AI in education: A systematic literature review. *Computers and Education: Artificial Intelligence*, 100215.

Al-Husseiy, F. (2023). Artificial Intelligence in Higher Education: A New Horizon. In Kaddaoura, S. (Ed.), *Handbook of Research of Artificial Intelligence Methods and Applications in Computer Engineering*. I.G.I. global.

Allen, D., & Weyl, E. G. (2024). The real dangers of generative ai. *Journal of Democracy*, *35*(1), 147–162. DOI: 10.1353/jod.2024.a915355

Almufareh, M. F., Kausar, S., Humayun, M., & Tehsin, S. (2024). A conceptual model for inclusive technology: Advancing disability inclusion through artificial intelligence. *Journal of Disability Research*, *3*(1), 20230060. DOI: 10.57197/JDR-2023-0060

Al-Mugheed, K., Bayraktar, N., Al-Bsheish, M., AlSyouf, A., Aldhmadi, B. K., Jarrar, M., & Alkhazali, M. (2022). Effectiveness of game-based virtual reality phone application and online education on knowledge, attitude and compliance of standard precautions among nursing students. *PLoS One*, *17*(11), e0275130. DOI: 10.1371/journal.pone.0275130 PMID: 36327261

Al-Saidh, H. M. S., Al Balushi, F. A. M., & Al-Kaadbi, M. S. M. (2023). The availability of AI applications in Social Studies Curriculum in Basic Education Schools in the Sultanate of Oman. *Journal of Curriculum and Teaching Methods*, *2*(3), 1–14.

Altbach, P. G., Reisberg, L., & Rumbley, L. E. (2019). *Trends in Global Higher Education: Tracking an Academic Revolution.*

Amado-Salvatierra, H. R., Morales-Chan, M., Hernandez-Rizzardini, R., & Rosales, M. (2024, March). Exploring Educators' Perceptions: Artificial Intelligence Integration in Higher Education. In *2024 IEEE World Engineering Education Conference (EDUNINE)* (pp. 1-5). IEEE. DOI: 10.1109/EDUNINE60625.2024.10500578

Amara, K., Altinay, F., Altinay, Z., & Dagli, G. (2024). Artificial intelligence and sustainable educational systems. In *Computational Intelligence and Blockchain in Complex Systems* (pp. 199–204). Morgan Kaufmann. DOI: 10.1016/B978-0-443-13268-1.00011-X

Amaral, A., Tavares, O., Sá, C., & Sin, C. (2021). Equity in Higher Education: Evidence, Policies and Practices. Setting the Scene. In *Equity Policies in Global Higher Education: Reducing Inequality and Increasing Participation and Attainment*. Palgrave Macmillan.

Amoozadeh, M., Daniels, D., Nam, D., Kumar, A., Chen, S., Hilton, M., & Alipour, M. A. (2024, March). Trust in Generative AI among students: An exploratory study. In *Proceedings of the 55th ACM Technical Symposium on Computer Science Education* V. 1 (pp. 67-73). DOI: 10.1145/3626252.3630842

Anis, M. (2023). Leveraging artificial intelligence for inclusive English language teaching: Strategies and implications for learner diversity. *Journal of Multidisciplinary Educational Research, 12*(6), 54–70.

Arnold, P., Davids, J., & Reiser, M. (2024, June). Building Future Skills in Higher Education: An International Blended Project Seminar on Sustainable Development. In *Conference Proceedings. The Future of Education 2024.*

Arruda, E. P., & Arruda, D. P. (2024). Artificial intelligence for SDG4 of the 2030 agenda. Transforming education to achieve quality, equality, and inclusion. *Sustainable Economies*, *2*(2), 34. DOI: 10.62617/se.v2i2.34

Asad, M. M., Naz, A., Churi, P., & Tahanzadeh, M. M. (2021). Virtual reality as pedagogical tool to enhance experiential learning: A systematic literature review. *Education Research International*, *2021*(1), 7061623. DOI: 10.1155/2021/7061623

Asriadi, M. A., Hadi, S., Istiyono, E., & Retnawati, H. (2023). Does Differentiated Instruction Affect Learning Outcome? Systematic Review and Meta-Analysis. *Journal of Pedagogical Research*, *7*(5), 18–33.

Atlas, S. (2023). ChatGPT for higher education and professional development: A guide to conversational AI.

August, S. E., & Tsaima, A. (2021). Artificial intelligence and machine learning: an instructor's exoskeleton in the future of education. *Innovative Learning Environments in STEM Higher Education: Opportunities, Challenges, and Looking Forward*, 79-105.

Bahrami, M. R., Bahrami, B., Behboodi, F., & Pourrafie, S. (2023). *Teaching the future: the vision of AI/ChatGPT in education.* Paper presented at the KES International Symposium on Agent and Multi-Agent Systems: Technologies and Applications. DOI: 10.1007/978-981-99-3068-5_37

Bahroun, Z., Anane, C., Ahmed, V., & Zacca, A. (2023, August). Transforming Education: A Comprehensive Review of Generative Artificial Intelligence in Educational Settings through Bibliometric and Content Analysis. *Sustainability (Basel)*, *15*(17), 12983. DOI: 10.3390/su151712983

Baidoo-Anu, D., & Ansah, L. O. (2023). Education in the era of generative artificial intelligence (AI): Understanding the potential benefits of ChatGPT in promoting teaching and learning. *Journal of AI*, *7*(1), 52–62. DOI: 10.61969/jai.1337500

Baidoo-Anu, D., & Owusu Ansah, L. (2023). Education in the era of generative artificial intelligence (AI): Understanding the potential benefits of ChatGPT in promoting teaching and learning. DOI: 10.2139/ssrn.4337484

Baker, R. S. (2021). Artificial intelligence in education: Bringing it all together. *Digital education outlook: Pushing the frontiers with AI, blockchain, and robots*, 43-54.

Baker, R. S., & Inventado, P. S. (2014). Educational data mining and learning analytics. In Larusson, J. A., & White, B. (Eds.), *Learning Analytics: From Research to Practice* (pp. 61–75). Springer. DOI: 10.1007/978-1-4614-3305-7_4

Balliu, T. H., Sinanaj, X. A., Tapija, N. K., Durmishi, A., & Madhi, D. (2024). Analyzing the impact of entrepreneurial traits on business growth: A study of start-ups in Elbasan, Albania. *Multidisciplinary Reviews*, *7*(7), 2024152. DOI: 10.31893/multirev.2024152

Barlow, M., Heaton, L., Ryan, C., Downer, T., Reid-Searl, K., Guinea, S., & Lamb, A. (2024). The Application and Integration of Evidence-Based Best Practice Standards to Healthcare Simulation Design: A Scoping Review. *Clinical Simulation in Nursing*, *87*, 101495. DOI: 10.1016/j.ecns.2023.101495

Barua, P. D., Vicnesh, J., Gururajan, R., Oh, S. L., Palmer, E., Azizan, M. M., Kadri, N. A., & Acharya, U. R. (2022). Artificial intelligence enabled personalised assistive tools to enhance education of children with neurodevelopmental disorders—A review. *International Journal of Environmental Research and Public Health*, *19*(3), 1192. DOI: 10.3390/ijerph19031192 PMID: 35162220

Bashir, A. K., Victor, N., Bhattacharya, S., Huynh-The, T., Chengoden, R., Yenduri, G., Maddikunta, P. K. R., Pham, Q.-V., Gadekallu, T. R., & Liyanage, M. (2023). Federated learning for the healthcare metaverse: Concepts, applications, challenges, and future directions. *IEEE Internet of Things Journal, 10*(24), 21873–21891. DOI: 10.1109/JIOT.2023.3304790

Baum, K. B. (2024). From fear to action: AI governance and opportunities for all. *Frontiers of Computer Science, 5*, 49.

Beckingham, S., Lawrence, J., Powell, S., & Hartley, P. (Eds.). (2024). *Using generative AI effectively in higher education: Sustainable and ethical practices for learning, teaching and assessment*. Routledge. DOI: 10.4324/9781003482918

Bell, L. A. (1997). Theoretical foundations for social justice education. In Adams, M., Bell, L., & Griffin, P. (Eds.), *Teaching for diversity and social justice: A sourcebook* (pp. 3–15). Routledge.

Bender, S. M. (2024). Awareness of artificial intelligence as an essential digital literacy: ChatGPT and Gen-AI in the classroom. *Changing English, 31*(2), 161–174. DOI: 10.1080/1358684X.2024.2309995

Bengio, Y., LeCun, Y., & Hinton, G. (2015). Deep learning. *Nature, 521*(7553), 436–444. DOI: 10.1038/nature14539 PMID: 26017442

Bennani, S., Maalel, A., & Ben Ghezala, H. (2022). Adaptive gamification in E-learning: A literature review and future challenges. *Computer Applications in Engineering Education, 30*(2), 628–642. DOI: 10.1002/cae.22477

Bennett, M. J. (2013). *Basic Concepts of Intercultural Communication: Paradigms, Principles, & Practices*. Intercultural Press.

Berg, C. (2023). The case for generative AI in scholarly practice.

Bergan, S., Gallagher, T., & Harkavy, I. (2018). *Higher Education for Diversity, Social Inclusion and Community*. Council of Europe.

Beynaghi, A., Trencher, G., Moztarzadeh, F., Mozafari, M., Maknoon, R., & Leal Filho, W. (2016). Future sustainability scenarios for universities: Moving beyond the United Nations decade of education for sustainable development. *Journal of Cleaner Production, 112*, 3464–3478. DOI: 10.1016/j.jclepro.2015.10.117

Bhalla, R., Vidyasree, A., Chotai, N. A., Mahendher, S., & Agrawal, A. (2024). The gig economy and sustainable work practices in startups. *European Economic Letters, 14*(2), 1914–1915. DOI: 10.52783/eel.v14i2.1520

Bhandari, A. (2023). Bias in AI: A comprehensive examination of factors and improvement strategies. *International Journal on Computer Science and Engineering*, *10*(6), 9–14. DOI: 10.14445/23488387/IJCSE-V10I6P102

Bhullar, P. S., Joshi, M., & Chugh, R. (2024). ChatGPT in higher education - a synthesis of the literature and a future research agenda. *Education and Information Technologies*, *29*(16), 21501–21522. Advance online publication. DOI: 10.1007/s10639-024-12723-x

Bibri, S. E., & Allam, Z. (2022). The Metaverse as a virtual form of data-driven smart cities: The ethics of the hyper-connectivity, datafication, algorithmization, and platformization of urban society. *Computational Urban Science*, *2*(1), 22. DOI: 10.1007/s43762-022-00050-1 PMID: 35915731

Bibri, S. E., & Jagatheesaperumal, S. K. (2023). Harnessing the potential of the metaverse and artificial intelligence for the internet of city things: Cost-effective XReality and synergistic AIoT technologies. *Smart Cities*, *6*(5), 2397–2429. DOI: 10.3390/smartcities6050109

Biu, P. W., Nwokediegwu, Z. Q. S., Daraojimba, O. H., Majemite, M. T., & Obaigben, A. (2024). Advancements in geo-data analytics: Implications for US energy policy and business investment. *World Journal of Advanced Research and Reviews*, *21*(1), 1422–1439. DOI: 10.30574/wjarr.2024.21.1.0172

Black, P., & Wiliam, D. (2009, January). Developing the theory of formative assessment. *Educational Assessment, Evaluation and Accountability*, *21*(1), 5–31. DOI: 10.1007/s11092-008-9068-5

Blyth, R., Chia, A., & Warner, J. (2022). Self-branding strategies of online freelancers on Upwork. *Journal of Management Inquiry*, *31*(4), 410–424. DOI: 10.1177/10564926211035699

Bolton, E., & Emery, R. (2021). Using educational technology to support students' real world learning. *Applied Pedagogies for Higher Education: Real World Learning and Innovation across the Curriculum*, 343-369.

Booth, A., Martyn-St James, M., Clowes, M., & Sutton, A. (2021). *Systematic approaches to a successful literature review* (3rd ed.). SAGE Publications.

Bouteraa, M., Bin-Nashwan, S. A., Al-Daihani, M., Dirie, K. A., Benlahcene, A., Sadallah, M., Zaki, H. O., Lada, S., Ansar, R., Fook, L. M., & Chekima, B. (2024). Understanding the diffusion of AI-generative (ChatGPT) in higher education: Does students' integrity matter? *Computers in Human Behavior Reports*, *14*, 100402. DOI: 10.1016/j.chbr.2024.100402

Bozkurt, A., Junhong, X., Lambert, S., Pazurek, A., Crompton, H., Koseoglu, S., & Romero-Hall, E. (2023). Speculative futures on ChatGPT and generative artificial intelligence (AI): A collective reflection from the educational landscape. *Asian Journal of Distance Education*, *18*(1), 53–130.

Brahma, M., Tripathi, S. S., & Sahay, A. (2021). Developing curriculum for industry 4.0: Digital workplaces. *Higher Education, Skills and Work-based Learning*, *11*(1), 144–163. DOI: 10.1108/HESWBL-08-2019-0103

Brewer, J., Patel, D., Kim, D., & Murray, A. (2024). Navigating the challenges of generative technologies: Proposing the integration of artificial intelligence and blockchain. *Business Horizons*, *67*(5), 525–535. DOI: 10.1016/j.bushor.2024.04.011

Brighouse, H., & Swift, A. (2008). Putting educational equality in its place. *Education Finance and Policy*, *3*(4), 444–466. DOI: 10.1162/edfp.2008.3.4.444

Brock, J. K., & Von Wangenheim, F. (2019). Demystifying AI: What digital transformation leaders can teach you about realistic artificial intelligence. *California Management Review*, *61*(4), 110–134. DOI: 10.1177/1536504219865226

Brooks, A. L. (2021). Gaming, VR, and Immersive Technologies for Education/Training. *Recent Advances in Technologies for Inclusive Well-Being: Virtual Patients, Gamification and Simulation*, 17-29.

Brown, T. B., Mann, B., Ryder, N., Subbiah, M., Kaplan, J., Dhariwal, P., . . . Amodei, D. (2020). Language Models are Few-Shot Learners. *arXiv preprint arXiv:2005.14165.*

Brown, S., & Glasner, A. (Eds.). (1999). *Assessment Matters in Higher Education: Choosing and Using Diverse Approaches.* Open University Press.

Brown, T., & Katz, B. (2011). Change by Design. *Journal of Product Innovation Management*, *28*(3), 381–384. DOI: 10.1111/j.1540-5885.2011.00806.x

Bryant, J., Heitz, C., Sanghvi, S., & Wagle, D. (2020). *How artificial intelligence will impact K-12 teachers.* McKinsey & Company.

Bucea-Manea- oniş, R., Kuleto, V., Gudei, S. C. D., Lianu, C., Lianu, C., Ilić, M. P., & Păun, D. (2022). Artificial intelligence potential in higher education institutions enhanced learning environment in Romania and Serbia. *Sustainability (Basel)*, *14*(10), 5842. DOI: 10.3390/su14105842

Buchanan, B. (2020). Artificial Intelligence and Ethics: A Systematic Review of Bias and Fairness. *AI & Society*, *35*(4), 837–856.

Bucher, E., & Fieseler, C. (2016). The flow of digital labor: Microworkers' strategies for skill development. *Media and Communication*, *4*(3), 12–24. DOI: 10.17645/mac.v4i3.547

Bulathwela, S., Pérez-Ortiz, M., Holloway, C., Cukurova, M., & Shawe-Taylor, J. (2024). Artificial intelligence alone will not democratise education: On educational inequality, techno-solutionism and inclusive tools. *Sustainability (Basel)*, *16*(2), 781. DOI: 10.3390/su16020781

Burns, M. (2021). Technology in education. Background paper prepared for the 2023 Global Education Monitoring Report on Technology in Education. https://www.researchgate.net/publication/358358065_Technology_in_Education_Background_Paper_for_2023_Global_Education_Monitoring_Report

Cantarella, M., & Strozzi, C. (2021). Workers in the crowd: The labour market impact of the online platform economy. *Industrial and Corporate Change*, *30*(6), 1429–1458. DOI: 10.1093/icc/dtab022

Cant, R., Ryan, C., & Kardong-Edgren, S. (2022). Virtual simulation studies in nursing education: A bibliometric analysis of the top 100 cited studies, 2021. *Nurse Education Today*, *114*, 105385. DOI: 10.1016/j.nedt.2022.105385 PMID: 35569265

Cao, Y., Li, S., Liu, Y., Yan, Z., Dai, Y., Yu, P. S., & Sun, L. (2023). A comprehensive survey of AI-generated content (AIGC): A history of generative AI from GAN to ChatGPT. *arXiv preprint*, arXiv:2303.04226.

Casal, J. E., & Kessler, M. (2023). Can linguists distinguish between ChatGPT/AI and human writing?: A study of research ethics and academic publishing. *Research Methods in Applied Linguistics*, *2*(3), 100068. DOI: 10.1016/j.rmal.2023.100068

Çelik, İ., Dindar, M., Muukkonen, H., & Järvelä, S. (2022, March). The Promises and Challenges of Artificial Intelligence for Teachers: A Systematic Review of Research. *TechTrends*, *66*(4), 616–630. DOI: 10.1007/s11528-022-00715-y

Chaika, O. (2023). The role of artificial intelligence in higher education. *Молодь і ринок*, (6/214), 69-74.

Chan, C. K. Y. (2023). A comprehensive AI policy education framework for university teaching and learning. *International Journal of Educational Technology in Higher Education*, *20*(38), 1–25. DOI: 10.1186/s41239-023-00408-3

Chan, C. K. Y. (2024). Students' perceptions of 'AI-giarism': Investigating changes in understandings of academic misconduct. *Education and Information Technologies*, 1–22. DOI: 10.1007/s10639-024-13151-7

Chan, C. K. Y., & Colloton, T. (2024). *Generative AI in Higher Education: The ChatGPT Effect*. Taylor & Francis. DOI: 10.4324/9781003459026

Chan, C. K. Y., & Hu, W. (2023). Students' voices on generative AI: Perceptions, benefits, and challenges in higher education. *International Journal of Educational Technology in Higher Education*, *20*(1), 43. DOI: 10.1186/s41239-023-00411-8

Chemlal, Y., & Azzouazi, M. (2024). A Methodology for Evaluating and Reporting the Integration of Artificial Intelligence for Sustainability in Higher Education: New Insights and Opportunities. In *Engineering Applications of Artificial Intelligence* (pp. 113–130). Springer Nature Switzerland. DOI: 10.1007/978-3-031-50300-9_7

Chen, H. (2024). The ethical challenges of educational artificial intelligence and coping measures. A discussion in the context of the 2024 Science Insights Education Frontiers 2024; 20(2), 3263-3281. DOI: DOI: 10.15354/sief.24.re339

Chen, K., Chen, J., & Wang, C. (2023). The roles of empathy and motivation in creativity in design thinking. *Knowledge Management & E-Learning*, *15*(3), 468–486.

Chen, L., Chen, P., & Lin, Z. (2020). Artificial intelligence in education: A review. *IEEE Access : Practical Innovations, Open Solutions*, *8*, 75264–75278. DOI: 10.1109/ACCESS.2020.2988510

Chen, X., Xie, H., & Li, Q. (2022). *Vision, status, and topics of X Reality in Education* (Vol. 1). Elsevier.

Chen, X., Zou, D., & Cheng, G. (2021). Exploring the Integration of Artificial Intelligence into Education: A Review and Outlook. *Journal of Educational Technology & Society*, *24*(4), 83–97.

Cheong, L. Y. (2017). Evidence Based Education and the UN Sustainable Development Goals (SDGs) 2016–2030. *Children and Sustainable Development: Ecological Education in a Globalized World*, 85-92.

Cheung, W., & Wong, N. (2023, September 4). *Hong Kong universities relent to rise of ChatGPT, AI but keep eye out for cheats*. South China Morning Post. https://www.scmp.com/news/hong-kong/education/article/3233269/hong-kong-universities-relent-rise-chatgpt-ai-tools-teaching-and-assignments-keep-eye-out-plagiarism

China Youth Daily. (2024). A special report on the 2024 World Digital Education Conference.

Chiu, T. K. (2024). Future research recommendations for transforming higher education with generative AI. Computers and Education: Artificial Intelligence, 6, Article 100197.

Chiu, S. K., & Lee, J. (2019). Innovative experiential learning experience: Pedagogical adopting Kolb's learning cycle at higher education in Hong Kong. *Cogent Education, 6*(1), 1644720. DOI: 10.1080/2331186X.2019.1644720

Choi, O. K., & Cho, E. (2018). The mechanism of trust affecting collaboration in virtual teams and the moderating roles of the culture of autonomy and task complexity. *Computers in Human Behavior, 91*, 305–316. DOI: 10.1016/j.chb.2018.09.032

Chounta, I. A., Bardone, E., Raudsep, A., & Pedaste, M. (2022). Exploring teachers' perceptions of artificial intelligence as a tool to support their practice in Estonian K-12 education. *International Journal of Artificial Intelligence in Education, 32*(3), 725–755. DOI: 10.1007/s40593-021-00243-5

Christodorescu, M., Craven, R., Feizi, S., Gong, N., Hoffmann, M., Jha, S., & Turek, M. (2024). Securing the future of GenAI: Policy and technology. *Cryptology ePrint Archive*.

Chui, M., Hazan, E., Roberts, R., Singla, A., & Smaje, K. (2023). The economic potential of generative AI.

Cioca, L.-I., Ivascu, L., Filip, F. G., & Doina, B. (2024). *Digital Transformation: Technology, Tools, and Studies* (Vol. 253). Springer Nature. DOI: 10.1007/978-3-031-55952-5

Clarke, K. M. (2022). *Exploring the utility of crowdsourcing frameworks to inform the construction of a web-based 3D printing application (3DCrowdGo).* com, m. G. c. m. (2021). maxSIMhealth: An Interconnected Collective of Manufacturing, Design, and Simulation Labs to Advance Medical Simulation Training *Recent Advances in Technologies for Inclusive Well-Being: Virtual Patients, Gamification and Simulation* (pp. 141-176): Springer.

Cohen, L., Manion, L., & Morrison, K. (2011). *Research Methods in Education*. Routledge.

Colley, H., Hodkinson, P., & Malcolm, J. (2019). *Non-formal Learning: Mapping the Conceptual Terrain*. Springer.

Collis, B., & van der Wende, M. (2023). Designing the Future of Learning with AI: From Personalization to Global Inclusion. *Journal of Educational Technology & Society, 45*(2), 112–126.

Colucci, E., Davies, H., Korhonen, J., & Gaebel, M. (2022). Recognising and valuing non-formal and informal learning outcomes in higher education. *European Journal of Education, 57*(3), 387–405.

Connelly, C. E., Fieseler, C., Černe, M., Giessner, S. R., & Wong, S. I. (2021). Working in the digitized economy: HRM theory & practice. *Human Resource Management Review*, *31*(1), 100762. Advance online publication. DOI: 10.1016/j.hrmr.2020.100762

Conner, J. O. (2022). Applying experiential learning theory to student activism. *Journal of Further and Higher Education*, *46*(9), 1229–1242. DOI: 10.1080/0309877X.2022.2061843

Contreras, J. R. I., Castillo, E. F. R., Verdezoto, M. K. S., & Liliana, C. L. (2024). Exploring the Implementation of Artificial Intelligence in Higher Education: Advantages and Hurdles. *Migration Letters : An International Journal of Migration Studies*, *21*(S2), 233–243. DOI: 10.59670/ml.v20i8.6496

Contrino, M. F., Reyes-Millán, M., Vázquez-Villegas, P., & Membrillo-Hernández, J. (2024). Using an adaptive learning tool to improve student performance and satisfaction in online and face-to-face education for a more personalized approach. *Smart Learning Environments*, *11*(1), 6. DOI: 10.1186/s40561-024-00292-y

Cooper, G. (2023). Examining Science Education in ChatGPT An Exploratory Study of Generative Artificial Intelligence. *Journal of Science Education and Technology*, *32*(3), 444–452. Advance online publication. DOI: 10.1007/s10956-023-10039-y

Cotton, D. R. E., Cotton, P. A., & Shipway, J. R. (2023). Chatting and Cheating: Ensuring academic integrity in the era of ChatGPT. *Innovations in Education and Teaching International*. Advance online publication. DOI: 10.1080/14703297.2023.2190148

Crawford, J., Cowling, M., & Allen, K. (2023). Leadership is needed for ethical ChatGPT: Character, assessment, and learning using artificial intelligence (AI). *Journal of University Teaching & Learning Practice*, *20*(3), 02. DOI: 10.53761/1.20.3.02

Creswell, J. W., & Creswell, J. D. (2017). *Research design: Qualitative, quantitative, and mixed methods approaches* (5th ed.). SAGE.

Cukurova, M., Kralj, L., Hertz, B., & Saltidou, E. (2024). Professional Development for Teachers in the Age of AI.

Dai, D. (2023). Conceptual Frameworks Guiding Research on Talent Development. In Talent Development from the Qeios, CC-BY 4.0. Perspective of Developmental Science: A Guide to Use-Inspired Research on Human Excellence, 37-55. DOI: 10.1007/978-3-031-46205-4_3

Dai, C.-P., & Ke, F. (2022). Educational applications of artificial intelligence in simulation-based learning: A systematic mapping review. *Computers and Education: Artificial Intelligence*, *3*, 100087. DOI: 10.1016/j.caeai.2022.100087

Damaševičius, R., & Sidekerskienė, T. (2024). Virtual Worlds for Learning in Metaverse: A Narrative Review. *Sustainability (Basel)*, *16*(5), 2032. DOI: 10.3390/su16052032

Davis, M., & Kumar, A. (2023). 'Pay attention to it, ignore it or push on it': Brown professors discuss AI's impact on academic integrity. The Brown Daily Herald (February 8). https://www.proquest.com/wire-feeds/pay-attention-ignore-push-back-on-brown/docview/2774393345/se-2?accountid=10675

De la Torre, R., Onggo, B. S., Corlu, C. G., Nogal, M., & Juan, A. A. (2021). The role of simulation and serious games in teaching concepts on circular economy and sustainable energy. *Energies*, *14*(4), 1138. DOI: 10.3390/en14041138

Demaidi, M. N. (2023). Artificial intelligence national strategy in a developing country. *AI & Society*, 1–13. DOI: 10.1007/s00146-023-01779-x

Deng, L. W., Wu, S., Chen, Y., Wang, Y., & Peng, Z. (2023). A comparative study of twenty-first-century competencies in high school mother tongue curriculum standards in China, the United States, and Finland. *Language, Culture and Curriculum*, *36*(2), 142–160. DOI: 10.1080/07908318.2022.2072506

Deng, L., & Xie, J. (2019). The Digital Divide in Education: Issues and Solutions in the Context of AI. *International Journal of Information Management*, *50*, 47–56.

Deng, Y., Xu, H., & Wang, S. (2024). Governance of artificial intelligence risks: Models, tools, and strategies. *Reform*, *2024*(1), 144–158.

Diao, M., Kong, H., & Zhao, J. (2021). Impacts of ride-hailing on vehicle miles traveled and greenhouse gas emissions: The case of San Francisco. *Journal of Transpersonal Research*, *153*, 56–67. DOI: 10.1088/1748-9326/ad3285

Diaz, J., Gusto, C., Narine, L. K., Jayaratne, K. S. U., & Silvert, C. (2023). Toward Diversity, Equity, and Inclusion Outreach and Engagement in Extension Education: Expert Consensus on Barriers and Strategies. *Journal of Extension*, *6*(1), 21. DOI: 10.34068/joe.61.01.21

Dinca, C., Rousseaux, P., & Badea, A. (2007). A life cycle impact of the natural gas used in the energy sector in Romania. *Journal of Cleaner Production*, *15*(15), 1451–1462. DOI: 10.1016/j.jclepro.2006.03.011

Dörnyei, Z., & Al-Hoorie, A. H. (2017). The motivational foundation of learning languages other than global English: Theoretical issues and research directions. *Modern Language Journal*, *101*(3), 455–468. DOI: 10.1111/modl.12408

Drugova, E., Zhuravleva, I., Aiusheeva, M., & Grits, D. (2021). Toward a model of learning innovation integration: TPACK-SAMR based analysis of the introduction of a digital learning environment in three Russian universities. *Education and Information Technologies*, *26*(4), 4925–4942. DOI: 10.1007/s10639-021-10514-2 PMID: 33814955

Duarte, J., Morais, M., & Pereira, R. (2023). Hybrid Learning Environments: A Pathway to Inclusive Higher Education. *Journal of Educational Technology & Society*, *26*(2), 75–88.

Duong, M. T., Rauschecker, A. M., Rudie, J. D., Chen, P.-H., Cook, T. S., Bryan, R. N., & Mohan, S. (2019, November). "Artificial intelligence for precision education in radiology," *the British Journal of Radiology. The British Journal of Radiology*, *92*(1103), 20190389. DOI: 10.1259/bjr.20190389 PMID: 31322909

Dwivedi, Y. K., Kshetri, N., Hughes, L., Slade, E. L., Jeyaraj, A., Kar, A. K., Baabdullah, A. M., Koohang, A., Raghavan, V., Ahuja, M., Albanna, H., Albashrawi, M. A., Al-Busaidi, A. S., Balakrishnan, J., Barlette, Y., Basu, S., Bose, I., Brooks, L., Buhalis, D., & Wright, R. (2023). "So what if ChatGPT wrote it?" Multidisciplinary perspectives on opportunities, challenges and implications of generative conversational AI for research, practice and policy. *International Journal of Information Management*, *71*, 102642. Advance online publication. DOI: 10.1016/j.ijinfomgt.2023.102642

Eapen, T., Finkenstadt, D. J., Folk, J., & Venkataswamy, L. (2023). How generative AI can augment human creativity. *Harvard Business Review*, *101*(4).

Ebong, G. N., Matthew, U. O., Olofin, B., Andrew-Vitalis, N., Fatai, L. O., Waliu, A. O., & Oladipupo, M. A. (2024). *Multimedia Cloud Data Warehouse Design for Knowledge Sharing in the University Environment: A Proposed Digital Solution Implementing Interactive Learning Strategies in Higher Education*. IGI Global. DOI: 10.4018/979-8-3693-3559-8.ch010

Eden, C. A., Chisom, O. N., & Adeniyi, I. S. (2024). Integrating AI in education: Opportunities, challenges, and ethical considerations. *Magna Scientia Advanced Research and Reviews*, *10*(2), 6-13.

Efilti, P., & Gelmez, K. (2024). A deep dive into the impacts of empathy on design learning and teaching. *International Journal of Technology and Design Education*, *34*(2), 809–852. DOI: 10.1007/s10798-023-09835-9

EHEA. (2015). *The Bologna Process Revisited: The Future of the European Higher Education Area*.

Elbanna, A., & Idowu, A. (2021). Crowdwork as an elevator of human capital: A sustainable human development perspective. *Scandinavian Journal of Information Systems*, *33*(2), 4. https://aisel.aisnet.org/sjis/vol33/iss2/4

Elbanna, A., & Idowu, A. (2022). Crowd work, digital liminality, and the enactment of culturally recognised alternatives to Western precarity: Beyond epistemological terra nullius. *European Journal of Information Systems*, *31*(1), 128–144. DOI: 10.1080/0960085X.2021.1981779

Elo, S., Kääriäinen, M., Kanste, O., Pölkki, T., Utriainen, K., & Kyngäs, H. (2014). Qualitative content analysis: A focus on trustworthiness. *SAGE Open*, *4*(1). DOI: 10.1177/2158244014522633

Emma, S., Daniela, D., Glansa, Y., Elglis, C., Mutize, T., Morales, D., & Jose, A. C. (2022). The right to Higher Education: A Social Justice Perspective. UNESCO, 7.

Erdem, E. (2023). ChatGPT: Exciting or terrifying? The Tufts Daily. https://www.proquest.com/wire-feeds/chatgpt-exciting-terrifying=tufts-daily/docview/2769546664/se-2?accontid=10675

Erskine, M. (2019). Artificial intelligence, the emerging needs for human factors engineering, risk management and stakeholder engagement. *InProceedings of the World Engineers Convention, Engineers Australia*, Melbourne, Australia.

European Commission. (2018). Artificial Intelligence for Europe. *European Union.*

European Commission. (2020). White Paper on Artificial Intelligence: A European Approach to Excellence and Trust. European Union.

European-Commission. (2020). *European Education Area.*

Ewen, E. M. (2023). Mapping the potential of AI in the age of competence-based higher education. Retrieved from Wonkhe: https://wonkhe.com/blogs/mapping-the-potential-of-ai-in-the-age-of-competence-based-higher-education/

Fakhar, H., Lamrabet, M., Echantoufi, N., & Ajana, L. (2024). Towards a New Artificial Intelligence-based Framework for Teachers' Online Continuous Professional Development Programs: Systematic Review. *International Journal of Advanced Computer Science and Applications*, *15*(4). Advance online publication. DOI: 10.14569/IJACSA.2024.0150450

Familoni, B. T., & Onyebuchi, N. C. (2024). Augmented and virtual reality in us education: a review: analyzing the impact, effectiveness, and future prospects of ar/vr tools in enhancing learning experiences. *International Journal of Applied Research in Social Sciences*, *6*(4), 642–663. DOI: 10.51594/ijarss.v6i4.1043

Fealy, S., Irwin, P., Tacgin, Z., See, Z. S., & Jones, D. (2023). *Enhancing nursing simulation education: a case for extended reality innovation.* Paper presented at the Virtual Worlds. DOI: 10.3390/virtualworlds2030013

Fekih Zguir, M., Dubis, S., & Koç, M. (2021). Embedding education for sustainable development (ESD) and SDGs values in curriculum: A comparative review on Qatar, Singapore and New Zealand. *Journal of Cleaner Production, 319*, 128534. DOI: 10.1016/j.jclepro.2021.128534

Feng, Y., & Zang, Y. (2024). *Moral myths in the era of artificial intelligence and counter-measures (J/OL).* Jiangsu Social Sciences., DOI: 10.13858/j.cnki.cn32-1312/c.202240201.004

Ferrara, E. (2024). GenAI against humanity: Nefarious applications of generative artificial intelligence and large language models. *Journal of Computational Social Science, 7*(1), 1–21. DOI: 10.1007/s42001-024-00250-1

Fien, J. (2002). Advancing sustainability in higher education: Issues and opportunities for research. *Higher Education Policy, 15*(2), 143–152. DOI: 10.1016/S0952-8733(02)00005-3

Fieseler, C., Bucher, E., & Hoffmann, C. P. (2019). Unfairness by design? The perceived fairness of digital labor on crowd working platforms. *Journal of Business Ethics, 156*(4), 987–1005. DOI: 10.1007/s10551-017-3607-2

Filho, W. L., Ribeiro, P. C. C., Mazuti, J., Salvia, A. L., Marcolin, C. B., Borsatto, J. M. L. S., Sharifi, A., Sierra, J., Luetz, J., Pretorious, R., & Trevisan, L. V. (2024). Using artificial intelligence to implement the UN sustainable development goals at higher education institutions. *International Journal of Sustainable Development and World Ecology, 31*(6), 726–745. Advance online publication. DOI: 10.1080/13504509.2024.2327584

Finkelstein, S., Sharma, U., & Furlonger, B. (2019). The inclusive practices of classroom teachers: A scoping review and thematic analysis. *International Journal of Inclusive Education, 25*, 1–28.

Floridi, L. (2019). Establishing the rules for building trustworthy AI. *Nature Machine Intelligence, 1*(6), 261–262. DOI: 10.1038/s42256-019-0055-y

Floridi, L., Cowls, J., Beltrametti, M., Chatila, R., Chazerand, P., Dignum, V., Luetge, C., Madelin, R., Pagallo, U., Rossi, F., Schafer, B., Valcke, P., & Vayena, E. (2018). AI4People—an ethical framework for a good AI society: Opportunities, risks, principles, and recommendations. *Minds and Machines, 28*(4), 689–707. DOI: 10.1007/s11023-018-9482-5 PMID: 30930541

Floridi, L., Cowls, J., King, T. C., & Taddeo, M. (2020). How to design AI for social good: Seven Essential factors. *Science and Engineering Ethics*, *26*(3), 1771–1796. DOI: 10.1007/s11948-020-00213-5 PMID: 32246245

Floros, C. (2024). Rethinking algorithmic management in minor key: The case of housecleaning platform labour in Denmark. *Work, Employment and Society*, *38*(1), 67–84. DOI: 10.1177/09500170231112893

Fragoso, A., Javrh, P., Kelava, P., Kramberger, T., Ličen, N., Radovan, M., Rotar, D. B., Ermenc, K. S., Vidmar, T., Žagar, I. Ž., Žiljak, T., & Žnidaršič Žagar, S. (2024). *From Formal to Non-Formal: Education, Learning and Knowledge*. Cambridge Scholars Publishing.

Francis, N. (2023). Guidelines on Using AI in Academic Assessments. Retrieved from National Teaching: https://figshare.edgehill.ac.uk/articles/educational resources/Guidelines on Using_AI_in_Academic_Asseements_pdf/24259600

Freire, P. (1970). Pedagogy of the Oppressed. *Continuum : an Interdisciplinary Journal on Continuity of Care*.

Friend, M., Cook, L., Hurley-Chamberlain, D., & Shamberger, C. (2022). Co-Teaching: Principles, Practices, and Pragmatics in Inclusive Classrooms. *The Journal of Special Education*, *55*(2), 90–103.

Garcia, P., Smith, A., & Li, Y. (2022). The Democratization of Education: Online Learning Resources and Equity in Higher Education. *Journal of Higher Education Policy and Management*, *44*(3), 239–255.

Garcia-Penalvo, F. J. (2023). The perception of Artificial Intelligence in educational contexts after the launch of ChatGPT: Disruption or panic? *Education in the Knowledge Society*, *24*, 1–9. DOI: 10.14201/eks.31279

Gardner, J., O'Leary, M., & Li, Y. (2021, July). Artificial intelligence in educational assessment: 'Breakthrough? Or buncombe and ballyhoo?'. *Journal of Computer Assisted Learning*, *37*(5), 1207–1216. DOI: 10.1111/jcal.12577

Gasevic, D. S., Siemens, G., & Sadiq, S. (2023). (4)). Empowering learners for the age of artificial intelligence. *Computers and Education: Artificial Intelligence*, *100130*, 100130. Advance online publication. DOI: 10.1016/j.caeai.2023.100130

Gheyssens, E., Coubergs, C., & DeMaeyer, S. (2024). Differentiated Instruction as an Approach to Establish Effective Teaching in Inclusive Classrooms. *The Journal of Educational Research*, *62*, 23–45.

GHK. (2008). Inventory of innovative practices in education for sustainable development [Brussels: GHK Consulting.]. *Order*, •••, 31.

Ghotbi, N., Ho, M. T., & Mantello, P. (2022). Attitude of college students towards ethical issues of artificial intelligence in an international university in Japan. *AI & Society*, *37*(1), 283–290. DOI: 10.1007/s00146-021-01168-2

Gill, S. S., Xu, M., Patros, P., Wu, H., Kaur, R., Kaur, K., Fuller, S., Singh, M., Arora, P., Parlikad, A. K., Stankovski, V., Abraham, A., Ghosh, S. K., Lutfiyya, H., Kanhere, S. S., Bahsoon, R., Rana, O., Dustdar, S., Sakellariou, R., . . . Buyya, R. Transformative effects of ChatGPT on modern education: Emerging Era of AI Chatbots, Internet of Things and Cyber-Physical Systems, Volume 4, 2024, Pages 19-23, ISSN 2667-3452, https://doi.org/DOI: 10.1016/j.iotcps.2023.06.002

Gillissen, A., Kochanek, T., Zupanic, M., & Ehlers, J. (2022). Medical students' perceptions towards digitalization and artificial intelligence: A mixed-methods study. *Health Care*, *10*(4), 723. PMID: 35455898

Goh, C., Ma, Y., & Rizzo, A. (2024). Normative performance data on visual attention in neurotypical children: Virtual reality assessment of cognitive and psychomotor development. *Frontiers in Virtual Reality*, *5*, 1309176. DOI: 10.3389/frvir.2024.1309176

Goi, C. L. (2024). The Impact of VR-Based Learning on Student Engagement and Learning Outcomes in Higher Education. *Teaching and Learning for a Sustainable Future: Innovative Strategies and Best Practices*, 207-223.

Gong, B., Nugent, J. P., Guest, W., Parker, W., Chang, P. J., Khosa, F., & Nicolaou, S. (2019). Influence of artificial intelligence on Canadian medical students' preference for radiology specialty: A national survey study. *Academic Radiology*, *26*(4), 566–577. DOI: 10.1016/j.acra.2018.10.007 PMID: 30424998

Goralski, M. A., & Tan, T. K. (2020). Artificial intelligence and sustainable development. *International Journal of Management Education*, *18*(1), 100330. DOI: 10.1016/j.ijme.2019.100330

Gransden, C., Hindmarsh, M., Le, N. C., & Nguyen, T. H. (2024). Adaptive learning through technology: A technical review and implementation. *Higher Education. Skills and Work-Based Learning*, *14*(2), 409–417. DOI: 10.1108/HESWBL-05-2023-0121

Gregoric, B. (2023). Research and Education on critical thinking in students plays a crucial role. *Physics Education*, *58*(3), 035021.

Grimus, M. (2020). Emerging technologies: Impacting learning, pedagogy and curriculum Development. In Yu, S., Ally, M., & Tsinakos, A. (Eds.), *Emerging Technologies and Pedagogies in the Curriculum (pp* (pp. 127–151). Springer., DOI: 10.1007/978-981-15-0618-5_8

Gumel, A. A., & Abdullahi, A. B., & O, U. M. (2019). *The Need for a Multimodal Means of Effective Digital Learning through Data Mining and Institutional Knowledge Repository: A Proposed System for Polytechnics in Northern Nigeria.* Paper presented at the Proceedings of the 2019 5th International Conference on Computer and Technology Applications. DOI: 10.1145/3323933.3324068

Haefner, N., Parida, V., Gassmann, O., & Wincent, J. (2023). Implementing and scaling artificial intelligence: A review, framework, and research agenda. *Technological Forecasting and Social Change*, *197*, 1–11. DOI: 10.1016/j.techfore.2023.122878

Hagendorff, T. (2020). The ethics of AI ethics: An evaluation of guidelines. *Minds and Machines*, *30*(1), 1–22. DOI: 10.1007/s11023-020-09517-8

Hamilton, M. L., Smith, L., & Worthington, K. (2009). Fitting the methodology with the research: An exploration of narrative, self-study and auto-ethnography. *Studying Teacher Education*, *4*(1), 17–28. DOI: 10.1080/17425960801976321

Hamraz, A. R., & Hamidi, A. (2024). Digitalizing Administration Systems in an Under-Resourced Context: Ministry of Higher Education's E-Readiness. *Science and Education*, *5*(6), 37–50.

Hanushek, E. A. (2005). The economic value of improving local schools. Proceedings, Federal Reserve Bank of Cleveland, 59-72.

Hara, M. (2024). Roles of Artificial Intelligence in Education for Sustainable Development in Asia-Pacific Contexts. *Global Journal of Business and Integral Security*, *1*(2).

Hargreaves, A. (2007). Sustainable leadership and development in education: Creating the future, conserving the past. *European Journal of Education*, *42*(2), 223–233. DOI: 10.1111/j.1465-3435.2007.00294.x

Hashmi, N., & Bal, A. S. (2024). Generative AI in higher education and beyond. *Business Horizons*, *67*(5), 607–614. DOI: 10.1016/j.bushor.2024.05.005

Hatt, L., Davidson, J., & Carrion-Weiss, J. (2023). Design Thinking as Pedagogy in Practice. *International Journal of Management and Applied Research*, *10*(2), 95–105.

He, A. J., Zhang, Z., Anand, P., & McMinn, S. (2025). Embracing generative artificial intelligence tools in higher education: A survey study at the hong kong university of science and technology. *Journal of Asian Public Policy, 18*(1).

Heinz, P. (2021). Ethical and Legal Responsibility for AI. *Discover AI., 1*, 2. DOI: 10. 1007/ 544163-021-00002-4

Hernon, O., McSharry, E., MacLaren, I., & Carr, P. J. (2023). The use of educational technology in teaching and assessing clinical psychomotor skills in nursing and midwifery education: A state-of-the-art literature review. *Journal of Professional Nursing, 45*, 35–50. DOI: 10.1016/j.profnurs.2023.01.005 PMID: 36889892

Heyn, L. G., Brembo, E. A., Byermoen, K. R., Cruaud, C., Eide, H., Flo, J., Nordsteien, A., Overgaard, G., & Egilsdottir, H. Ö. (2023). Exploring facilitation in virtual simulation in nursing education: A scoping review. *PEC Innovation, 3*, 100233. DOI: 10.1016/j.pecinn.2023.100233 PMID: 38033419

Hiran, K. K., Doshi, R., & Patel, M. (2024). Modern Technology in Healthcare and Medical Education: Blockchain, IoT, AR, and VR: Blockchain, IoT, AR, and VR: IGI Global.

Holmes, W., Bialik, M., & Fadel, C. (2019). *Artificial Intelligence in Education: Promises and Implications for Teaching and Learning*. Center for Curriculum Redesign.

Holmes, W., Bialik, M., & Fadel, C. (2019). *Artificial intelligence in education: Promises and implications for teaching and learning*. Centre for Curriculum Redesign.

Holmes, W., Blalik, M., & Fadel, C. (2019). *Artificial Intelligence in Education: Promise and Implications for Teaching and Learning*. Center for Curriculum Redesign.

Holmes, W., & Porayska-Pomsta, K. (2022). *The Ethical of Artificial Intelligence in Education: Practice, Challenges and Debates*. Routledge.

Holstein, K., McLaren, B. M., & Aleven, V. (2019). Designing for complementarity: Teacher and student needs for orchestration support in AI-enhanced classrooms. *Artificial Intelligence in Education: 20th International Conference, AIED 2019, Chicago, IL, USA, June 25-29, 2019Proceedings, 20*(Part I), 157–171.

Hopcan, S., Polat, E., Ozturk, M. E., & Ozturk, L. (2023). Artificial intelligence in special education: A systematic review. *Interactive Learning Environments, 31*(10), 7335–7353. DOI: 10.1080/10494820.2022.2067186

Hou, H., Lai, J. H., & Wu, H. (2023). Project-based learning and pedagogies for virtual reality-aided green building education: Case study on a university course. *International Journal of Sustainability in Higher Education*, *24*(6), 1308–1327. DOI: 10.1108/IJSHE-06-2022-0197

Howard, J. L., Gagné, M., & Morin, A. J. S. (2020). Putting the pieces together: Reviewing the structural conceptualization of motivation within SDT. *Motivation and Emotion*, *44*(6), 846–861. https://www.oii.ox.ac.uk/research/projects/crowdlearn/?publications. DOI: 10.1007/s11031-020-09838-2

How, M. L., Cheah, S. M., Chan, Y. J., Khor, A. C., & Say, E. M. P. (2023). Artificial Intelligence for Advancing Sustainable Development Goals (SDGs): An Inclusive Democratized Low-Code Approach. In *The Ethics of Artificial Intelligence for the Sustainable Development Goals* (pp. 145–165). Springer International Publishing. DOI: 10.1007/978-3-031-21147-8_9

Huai, J. (2024). Promoting Jointly Application, Sharing and Innovation of Digital Education. Available at: http://en.moe.gov.cn/features/2024WorldDigitalEducationConference/KeynoteSpeech/202402/t20240201_111377.html

Huang, A. Y., Lu, O. H., & Yang, S. J. (2023). Effects of artificial Intelligence–Enabled personalized recommendations on learners' learning engagement, motivation, and outcomes in a flipped classroom. *Computers & Education*, *194*, 104684. DOI: 10.1016/j.compedu.2022.104684

Hubbard, K. (2024). Plant biology education: A competency-based vision for the future. Plants, People, Planet. John Wiley & Sons Ltd, 1-11

Huđek, I., & Širec, K. (2023). Unveiling the impact of the gig economy on sustainable development. In V. Bevanda (Ed.), *ERAZ Conference – Knowledge Based Sustainable Development: Vol. 9. Selected papers* (pp. 125–133). Association of Economists and Managers of the Balkans. DOI: 10.31410/ERAZ.S.P.2023.125

Hung, C.-C., Kao, H.-F. S., Liu, H.-C., Liang, H.-F., Chu, T.-P., & Lee, B.-O. (2021). Effects of simulation-based learning on nursing students' perceived competence, self-efficacy, and learning satisfaction: A repeat measurement method. *Nurse Education Today*, *97*, 104725. DOI: 10.1016/j.nedt.2020.104725 PMID: 33373813

Ihemereze, K. C., Eyo-Udo, N. L., Egbokhaebho, B. A., Daraojimba, C., Ikwue, U., & Nwankwo, E. E. (2023). Impact of monetary incentives on employee performance in the Nigerian automotive sector: A case study. *International Journal of Advanced Economics*, *5*(7), 162–186. DOI: 10.51594/ijae.v5i7.548

ITU. (2024). AI4Good global summit. Available online: https://aiforgood.itu.int (accessed on 27 May 2024).

Ivanov, S., Soliman, M., Tuomi, A., Alkathiri, N. A., & Al-Alawi, A. N. (2024). Drivers of generative AI adoption in higher education through the lens of the Theory of Planned Behaviour. *Technology in Society*, *77*, 102521. DOI: 10.1016/j.techsoc.2024.102521

Jacques, J. T., & Kristensson, P. O. (2019). Crowdworker economics in the gig economy. *CHI Conference on Human Factors in Computing Systems Proceedings (CHI 2019),* May 4–9, 2019, Glasgow, Scotland, UK. DOI: 10.1145/3290605.3300621

Jadan-Guerrero, J., Tamayo-Narvaez, K., Méndez, E., & Valenzuela, M. (2024, June). Adaptive Learning Environments: Integrating Artificial Intelligence for Special Education Advances. In *International Conference on Human-Computer Interaction* (pp. 86-94). Cham: Springer Nature Switzerland. DOI: 10.1007/978-3-031-61953-3_10

Jafari, F., & Keykha, A. (2024). Identifying the opportunities and challenges of artificial intelligence in higher education: A qualitative study. *Journal of Applied Research in Higher Education*, *16*(4), 1228–1245. DOI: 10.1108/JARHE-09-2023-0426

Jagatheesaperumal, S. K., Ahmad, K., Al-Fuqaha, A., & Qadir, J. (2024). Advancing education through extended reality and internet of everything enabled metaverses: Applications, challenges, and open issues. *IEEE Transactions on Learning Technologies*, *17*, 1120–1139. DOI: 10.1109/TLT.2024.3358859

Jain, D., Herrera, A., & Bernal, S. (2023). Decolonizing Higher Education: Addressing Equity, Diversity, and Inclusion in Academia, Innovate. *Journal of Education, Ageing, and Digital Technologies*, *7*, 985–1001.

Jain, K. K., & Raghuram, J. N. V. (2024). Gen-AI integration in higher education: Predicting intentions using SEM-ANN approach. *Education and Information Technologies*, *29*(13), 1–41. DOI: 10.1007/s10639-024-12506-4

Järvelä, S. (2006). *Personalised Learning? New Insights into Fostering Learning Capacity*. OECD Publishing.

Javaid, M., Haleem, A., & Singh, R. P.. (2023). An era of ChatGPT as a significant futuristic support tool: A study on features, abilities, and challenges. *Benchcouncil Transactions on Benchmarks. Standards and Evaluations*, *100089*. Advance online publication. DOI: 10.1016/j.tbench

Javaid, M., Haleem, A., & Singh, R. P.. (2023). Unlocking the opportunities through ChatGPT Tool towards ameliorating the education system. *Benchcouncil Transactions on Benchmarks. Standards and Evaluations, 100115*. Advance online publication. DOI: 10.1016/j.tbench.2023

Jha, N., Shankar, P. R., Al-Betar, M. A., Mukhia, R., Hada, K., & Palaian, S. (2022). Undergraduate medical students' and interns' knowledge and perception of artificial intelligence in medicine. *Advances in Medical Education and Practice*, *13*, 927–937. DOI: 10.2147/AMEP.S368519 PMID: 36039185

Jibril, A. U., Abdullahi, N. M., Ali, A. S., Abdulkadir, H., Matthew, U. O., & Haruna, K. (2022). Motivational aspects of digital games in learning process. *Science in Information Technology Letters*, *3*(1), 1–9. DOI: 10.31763/sitech.v3i1.885

Jobin, A., Ienca, M., & Vayena, E. (2019). The global landscape of AI ethics guidelines. *Nature Machine Intelligence*, *1*(9), 389–399. DOI: 10.1038/s42256-019-0088-2

Jones, R., & Williams, K. (2024). Diversity and Inclusion in Higher Education: A Comparative Analysis of Policy Implementation. *Higher Education Quarterly*, *34*(1), 77–84.

Kabudi, T., Pappas, I., & Olsen, D. H. (2021). AI-enabled adaptive learning systems: A systematic mapping of the literature. *Computers and Education: Artificial Intelligence*, *2*, 100017. DOI: 10.1016/j.caeai.2021.100017

Kalateh, F., & Kheiry, M. (2024). A Review of Stochastic Analysis of the Seepage Through Earth Dams with a Focus on the Application of Monte Carlo Simulation. *Archives of Computational Methods in Engineering*, *31*(1), 47–72. DOI: 10.1007/s11831-023-09972-3

Kang, J., Lim, S., & Park, H. (2023). Inclusive Teacher Professionalism: New Approaches in Teacher Education. *International Journal of Educational Research*, *101*, 112–125.

Kang, M., Yoo, Y., & Park, Y. (2012). Analyzing online mentoring process and facilitation strategies. *Procedia: Social and Behavioral Sciences*, *46*, 5158–5162. DOI: 10.1016/j.sbspro.2012.06.400

Kar, A. K., Choudhary, S. K., & Singh, V. K. (2022). How can artificial intelligence impact sustainability: A systematic literature review. *Journal of Cleaner Production*, *376*, 134120. DOI: 10.1016/j.jclepro.2022.134120

Karen, D. Wang, Eric Burkholder, Carl Wieman, Shima Salehi, & Nick Haber. (2023). *Examining the Potential and Pitfalls of ChatGPT in Science and Engineering Problem Solving*. https://arxiv.org/abs/2310.08773

Karpouzis, K., Pantazatos, D., Taouki, J., & Meli, K. (2024). Tailoring education with GenAI: A new horizon in lesson planning. *arXiv preprint*, arXiv:2403.12071. DOI: 10.1109/EDUCON60312.2024.10578690

Kaswan, K. S., Dhatterwal, J. S., & Ojha, R. P. (2024). AI in personalized learning. In *Advances in Technological Innovations in Higher Education* (pp. 103–117). CRC Press. DOI: 10.1201/9781003376699-9

Kayyali, M. (2024). *Immersive Technologies: Virtual and Augmented Reality in Higher Education Reshaping Learning with Next Generation Educational Technologies*. IGI Global.

Kazanidis, I., & Pellas, N. (2024). Harnessing generative artificial intelligence for digital literacy innovation: A comparative study between early childhood education and computer science undergraduates. *AI*, *5*(3), 1427–1445. DOI: 10.3390/ai5030068

Khlaif, Z. N., Ayyoub, A., Hamamra, B., Bensalem, E., Mitwally, M. A., Ayyoub, A., Hattab, M. K., & Shadid, F. (2024). University teachers' views on the adoption and integration of generative AI tools for student assessment in higher education. *Education Sciences*, *14*(10), 1090. DOI: 10.3390/educsci14101090

Kim, J., Lee, H., & Cho, Y. H. (2022). Learning design to support student-AI collaboration: Perspectives of leading teachers for AI in education. *Education and Information Technologies*, *27*(5), 6069–6104. DOI: 10.1007/s10639-021-10831-6

Kim, N. J., & Kim, M. K. (2022, March). Teacher's perceptions of using an artificial intelligence-based educational tool for scientific writing. *Frontiers in Education*, *7*, 755914. DOI: 10.3389/feduc.2022.755914

Kiong, L. V. (2024). *Metaverse Made Easy: A Beginner's Guide to the Metaverse: Everything you need to know about Metaverse, NFT and GameFi*. Liew Voon Kiong.

Kizilcec, R. F., Huber, E., Papanastasiou, E. C., Cram, A., Makridis, C. A., Smolansky, A., Zeivots, S., & Raduescu, C. (2024). Perceived impact of generative AI on assessments: Comparing educator and student perspectives in Australia, Cyprus, and the United States. *Computers and Education: Artificial Intelligence*, *7*, 100269. DOI: 10.1016/j.caeai.2024.100269

Klimova, A., Rondeau, E., Andersson, K., Porras, J., Rybin, A., & Zaslavsky, A. (2016). An international Master's program in green ICT as a contribution to sustainable development. *Journal of Cleaner Production*, *135*, 223-239. https://doi.org/ . JCLEPRO.2016.06.032DOI: 10.1016/J

Kolb, D. A. (1984). *Experiential learning: experience as the source of learning and develop- ment*. Prentice Hall.

Kopnina, H. (2020). Education for the future? Critical evaluation of education for sustainable development goals. *The Journal of Environmental Education, 51*(4), 280–291. DOI: 10.1080/00958964.2019.1710444

Kottmann, A., Vossensteyn, J. J., Kolster, R., Veidemane, A., Blasko, Z., Biagi, F., & Sánchez-Barrioluengo, M. (2019). *Social Inclusion Policies in Higher Education: Evidence from the EU. Overview of major widening participation policies applied in the EU 28.*

Kouijzer, M., Kip, H., Kelders, S. M., & Bouman, Y. (2024). The introduction of virtual reality in forensic mental healthcare–an interview study on the first impressions of patients and healthcare providers regarding VR in treatment. *Frontiers in Psychology, 15*, 1284983. DOI: 10.3389/fpsyg.2024.1284983 PMID: 38746916

Kozar, L. J., & Bolimowski, S. (2024). Gig economy and sustainable development: Bibliometric analyses and identification of future research directions. *Scientific Papers of Silesian University of Technology. Organization & Management/Zeszyty Naukowe Politechniki Slaskiej.Seria Organizacji i Zarzadzanie*, (194). Advance online publication. DOI: 10.29119/1641-3466.2024.194.11

Lake, D., Guo, W., Chen, E., & McLaughlin, J. (2024). Design Thinking in Higher Education: Opportunities and Challenges for Decolonized Learning. *Teaching & Learning Inquiry, 12*(1), 40–50. DOI: 10.20343/teachlearninqu.12.4

Lambrechts, W., Mulà, I., Ceulemans, K., Molderez, I., & Gaeremynck, V. (2013). The integration of competences for sustainable development in higher education: An analysis of bachelor programs in management. *Journal of Cleaner Production, 48*, 65–73. DOI: 10.1016/j.jclepro.2011.12.034

Langa, P. V., & David, M. E. (2021). *Crossing Boundaries in Higher Education: Rethinking Inclusion and Social Justice*. Routledge.

Langley, P., & Leyshon, A. (2017). Platform capitalism: The intermediation and capitalisation of digital economic circulation. *Finance and Stochastics, 3*(1), 11–31. DOI: 10.2218/finsoc.v3i1.1936

Laurillard, D., Rowe, F. A., & Rafferty, J. A. (2023). Enhancing Inclusive Learning through Digital Innovation: A Case Study in Optometry Education. *Journal of Inclusive Practice in Further and Higher Education, 15*(3), 245–250.

Lau, S., & Guo, P. (2023, August). From" Ban it till we understand it" to" Resistance is futile": How university programming instructors plan to adapt as more students use AI code generation and explanation tools such as ChatGPT and GitHub Copilot. In *Proceedings of the 2023 ACM Conference on International Computing Education Research-Volume 1* (pp. 106-121). DOI: 10.1145/3568813.3600138

Lee, A. V. Y., Tan, S. C., & Teo, C. L. (2023, November). Designs and practices using generative AI for sustainable student discourse and knowledge creation. *Smart Learning Environments, 10*(1), 59. Advance online publication. DOI: 10.1186/s40561-023-00279-1

Lee, J., Solat, F., Kim, T. Y., & Poor, H. V. (2024). Federated learning-empowered mobile network management for 5G and beyond networks: From access to core. *IEEE Communications Surveys and Tutorials, 26*(3), 2176–2212. DOI: 10.1109/COMST.2024.3352910

Lehdonvirta, V., Margaryan, A., & Davies, H. (2019). *Skills formation and skills matching in online platform work: Policies and practices for promoting crowdworkers' continuous learning (CrowdLearn).* Moray House School of Education and Sport, Centre for Research in Digital Education. Commissioned report.

Leicht, A., Heiss, J., & Byun, W. J. (Eds.). (2018). *Issues and Trends in Education for Sustainable Development.* UNESCO Publishing.

Leoste, J., Jõgi, L., Õun, T., Pastor, L., San Martín López, J., & Grauberg, I. (2021). Perceptions about the future of integrating emerging technologies into higher education—The case of robotics with artificial intelligence. *Computers, 10*(9), 110. DOI: 10.3390/computers10090110

Leung, M., & Niazi, S. (2023, February 24). *Universities are on alert over ChatGPT and other AI-assisted tools.* University World News. https://www.universityworldnews.com/post.php?story=20230222132357841

Liapakis, S. Z., & Bougia, A. (2023). Ethical Use of Artificial Intelligence and New Technologies in Education 5.0. *J Artificial Intelligence Machine Learning & Data Science, 1*(4), 119–124. DOI: 10.51219/JAIMLD/Anastasios-Liapakis/15

Li, H., Whalley, J., & Xing, C. (2021). Urban-rural inequality and higher education access in China. *China Economic Review, 67*, 101–115.

Li, J., Cao, H., Lin, L., Hou, Y., Zhu, R., & El Ali, A. (2024, May). User experience design professionals' perceptions of generative artificial intelligence. In *Proceedings of the CHI Conference on Human Factors in Computing Systems* (pp. 1-18). DOI: 10.1145/3613904.3642114

Lim, W. M., Gunasekara, A., Pallant, J. L., Pallant, J., & Pechenkina, E. (2023, July). Generative AI and the future of education: Ragnarök or reformation? A paradoxical perspective from management educators. *International Journal of Management Education*, *21*(2), 100790. DOI: 10.1016/j.ijme.2023.100790

Lin, H., & Chen, Q. (2024). Artificial intelligence (AI)-integrated educational applications and college students' creativity and academic emotions: Students and teachers' perceptions and attitudes. *BMC Psychology*, *12*(1), 487. DOI: 10.1186/s40359-024-01979-0 PMID: 39285268

Liu, J. Y. W., Yin, Y.-H., Kor, P. P. K., Cheung, D. S. K., Zhao, I. Y., Wang, S., Su, J. J., Christensen, M., Tyrovolas, S., & Leung, A. Y. (2023). The effects of immersive virtual reality applications on enhancing the learning outcomes of undergraduate health care students: Systematic review with meta-synthesis. *Journal of Medical Internet Research*, *25*, e39989. DOI: 10.2196/39989 PMID: 36877550

Liu, M., Ren, Y., Nyagoga, L. M., Stonier, F., Wu, Z., & Yu, L. (2023). Future of education in the era of generative artificial intelligence: Consensus among Chinese scholars on applications of ChatGPT in schools. *Future in Educational Research*, *1*(1), 72–101. DOI: 10.1002/fer3.10

Liu, Y. (2020). Challenges and Opportunities in Rural Education: The Case of China. *Journal of Rural Studies*, *78*, 150–158.

Liu, Y., Li, Y., Yang, S., Ren, T., Li, H., Hogg, A., Shah, P., Li, J., Zhang, Y., & Chhetri, A. (2022). A hybrid and non-formal music education connecting China's local family communities and cultures with Nepal. [IJI]. *International Journal for Infonomics*, *15*(1), 6. DOI: 10.20533/iji.1742.4712.2022.0218

Li, X., & Johnson, D. (2024). The Impact of Institutional Policies on Student Diversity and Inclusion Outcomes. *Studies in Higher Education*, *49*(2), 50–68.

Loi, D., Wolf, C. T., Blomberg, J. L., Arar, R., & Brereton, M. (2019). Co-designing AI futures: Integrating AI ethics, social computing, and design. *InProceedings of the 2019 on Designing Interactive Systems Conference*, San Diego, CA, USA. DOI: 10.1145/3301019.3320000

Lorente-Echeverria, S., Murillo-Pardo, B., & Canales-Lacruz, I. (2022). A systematic review of curriculum sustainability at university: A Key challenge for improving the professional development of teachers of the future. *Education Sciences*, *12*(11), 753. DOI: 10.3390/educsci12110753

Lougiakis, C., González, J. J., Ganias, G., Katifori, A., & Roussou, M. (2024). *Comparing Physics-based Hand Interaction in Virtual Reality: Custom Soft Body Simulation vs. Off-the-Shelf Integrated Solution.* Paper presented at the 2024 IEEE Conference Virtual Reality and 3D User Interfaces (VR). DOI: 10.1109/VR58804.2024.00094

Love, H. C., Cross, J. E., Fosdick, B. K., Tofany, E., & Dickmann, E. M. (2023). Teaching team science: The key to addressing 21st-century global challenges. *Small Group Research*, *54*(3), 396–427. DOI: 10.1177/10464964221121349

Lowell, V. L., & Ilobinso, A. C. (2023). Virtual reality in online higher education for learner engagement, interaction, and experiential learning. *The SAGE handbook of online higher education*, 458.

Lubowitz, J. H. (2023). ChatGPT, an artificial intelligence chatbot, is impacting medical literature. *Arthroscopy*, *39*(5), 1121–1122. DOI: 10.1016/j.arthro.2023.01.015 PMID: 36797148

Luckin, R. W., Holmes, M., & Griffiths, L. B. (2016). *Forcier Intelligence Unleashed: An Argument for AI in Education*. Pearson London.

Luckin, R., Holmes, W., Griffiths, M., & Forcier, L. B. (2016). *Intelligence Unleashed: An Argument for AI in Education*. Pearson.

Lumby, J., & Foskett, N. (2016). *International Perspectives on Leading and Managing Educational Institutions*. Bloomsbury Academic.

Luo, J. (2024). A critical review of Gen-AI policies in higher education assessment: A call to reconsider the "originality" of students' work. *Assessment & Evaluation in Higher Education*, •••, 1–14. DOI: 10.1080/02602938.2024.2309963

M. Cardona, R. J. Rodríguez, K. Ishmael, and U.S. Department of Education, "Artificial intelligence and the future of teaching and learning," 2023. [Online]. Available: https://tech.ed.gov/files/2023/05/ai-future-of-teaching-and-learning-report.pdf

Mafojane, M. A. J. (2021). *Changing perceptions regarding the use of information and communication technologies through subject-specific professional development: insights from a South African case study*. University of the Free State.

Mallam, S. C., Nazir, S., & Renganayagalu, S. K. (2019). Rethinking maritime education, training, and operations in the digital era: Applications for emerging immersive technologies. *Journal of Marine Science and Engineering*, *7*(12), 428. DOI: 10.3390/jmse7120428

Margaryan, A., Albert, J., & Charlton-Czaplicki, T. (2022). Workplace learning in Crowdwork Questionnaire (WLCQ): Measuring self-regulated learning and skill development in online platform work. *International Journal of Training and Development, 26*(3), 495–515. DOI: 10.1111/ijtd.12268

Marginson, S. (2016). *Higher Education and the Common Good.* Melbourne University Publishing.

Marougkas, A., Troussas, C., Krouska, A., & Sgouropoulou, C. (2024). How personalized and effective is immersive virtual reality in education? A systematic literature review for the last decade. *Multimedia Tools and Applications, 83*(6), 18185–18233. DOI: 10.1007/s11042-023-15986-7

Martin, R. (2014). *The Design of Business: Why Design Thinking is the Next Competitive Advantage.* Harvard Business Review Press.

Marvin, G., Hellen, N., Jjingo, D., & Nakatumba-Nabende, J. (2023, June). Prompt engineering in large language models. In *International Conference on Data Intelligence and Cognitive Informatics* (pp. 387-402). Singapore: Springer Nature Singapore.

Marzuki, W., Widiati, U., Rusdin, D., Darwin, , & Indrawati, I. (2023). The impact of AI writing tools on the content and organization of students' writing: EFL teachers' perspective. *Cogent Education, 10*(2), 2236469. DOI: 10.1080/2331186X.2023.2236469

Masanja, N., & Mkumbo, H. (2020). The application of open source artificial intelligence as an approach to frugal innovation in Tanzania. *International Journal of Research and Innovation in Applied Science, 5*, 36–46.

Matthew, U. O., Kazaure, J. S., Kazaure, A. S., Onyedibe, O. N., & Okafor, A. N. (2022). The Twenty First Century E-Learning Education Management & Implication for Media Technology Adoption in the Period of Pandemic. *EAI Endorsed Transactions on e-Learning, 8*(1).

Matthew, U. O. (2019). Information System Management & Multimedia Applications in an E-Learning Environment. [IJICTHD]. *International Journal of Information Communication Technologies and Human Development, 11*(3), 21–41. DOI: 10.4018/IJICTHD.2019070102

Matthew, U. O., Bakare, K. M., Ebong, G. N., Ndukwu, C. C., & Nwanakwaugwu, A. C. (2023). Generative Artificial Intelligence (AI) Educational Pedagogy Development: Conversational AI with User-Centric ChatGPT4. *Journal of Trends in Computer Science and Smart Technology, 5*(4), 401–418. DOI: 10.36548/jtcsst.2023.4.003

Matthew, U. O., Kazaure, A. S., Kazaure, J. S., Hassan, I. M., Nwanakwaugwu, A. C., & Okafor, N. U. (2022). Educational Technology Adaptation & Implication for Media Technology Adoption in the Period of COVID-19. *Journal of Trends in Computer Science and Smart Technology*, *4*(4), 226–245. DOI: 10.36548/jtcsst.2022.4.002

Matthew, U. O., & Kazaure, J. S. (2020). Multimedia e-learning education in nigeria and developing countries of Africa for achieving SDG4. [IJICTHD]. *International Journal of Information Communication Technologies and Human Development*, *12*(1), 40–62. DOI: 10.4018/IJICTHD.2020010103

Matthew, U. O., Kazaure, J. S., & Haruna, K. (2020). Multimedia information system (MIS) for knowledge generation and ICT policy framework in education: Innovative sustainable educational investment. [IJICTHD]. *International Journal of Information Communication Technologies and Human Development*, *12*(3), 28–58. DOI: 10.4018/IJICTHD.2020070102

Matthew, U. O., Kazaure, J. S., Ndukwu, C. C., Ebong, G. N., Nwanakwaugwu, A. C., & Nwamouh, U. C. (2024). *Artificial Intelligence Educational Pedagogy Development: ICT Pedagogy Development for Education 5.0 Educational Perspectives on Digital Technologies in Modeling and Management*. IGI Global. DOI: 10.4018/979-8-3693-2314-4.ch003

Matthew, U. O., Kazaure, J. S., & Okafor, N. U. (2021). Contemporary development in E-Learning education, cloud computing technology & internet of things. *EAI Endorsed Transactions on Cloud Systems*, *7*(20), e3–e3.

Mavroudi, E., Holmes, W., & Ibáñez, M. (2024). *Exploring the Impact of Artificial Intelligence in Teaching and Learning of Science: A Systematic Review of Empirical Research*. Springer.

McCowan, T. (2019). *Higher Education for and Beyond the Sustainable Development Goals*. Palgrave Macmillan. DOI: 10.1007/978-3-030-19597-7

McDonald, N., Johri, A., Ali, A., & Hingle, A. (2024). Generative Artificial Intelligence in Higher Education: Evidence from an Analysis of Institutional Policies and Guidelines. arXiv. McKinsey&Company. (2024). What is ChatGPT, DALL-E, and generative AI?

McDonald, P. (2023). Income generation on care work digital labour platforms. *British Journal of Industrial Relations*, *61*(1), 142–162. DOI: 10.1111/bjir.12625

McLaughlin, J. E., Chen, E., Lake, D., Guo, W., Skywark, E. R., & Liu, T. (2022). Design thinking teaching and learning in higher education: Experiences across four universities. *PLoS One*, *17*(3).

McPhail, C. J. (2021). Fostering Social Justice in Higher Education. Diverse: Issues in Higher Education. https://www.Diverseeducation.com./institutions-colleges/article/ 15108962/fostering-social-justice-in-higher-education

Menekaya, C. (2024). Gendered Innovations, and Skills for Societal Sustainability: Reflections on Today's Women and Women in the Bible. *International Journal of Gender Equity and Social Justice*, *1*(1), 1–15.

Mhlanga, D. (2023). Open AI in education, the responsible and ethical use of ChatGPT towards lifelong learning. Education, the Responsible and Ethical Use of ChatGPT towards Lifelong Learning (February 11, 2023).

Mhlanga, D. (2021). Artificial intelligence in the industry 4.0, and its impact on Poverty, innovation, infrastructure development, and the sustainable development goals: Lessons from Emerging Economies? *Sustainability (Basel)*, *13*(11), 5788. DOI: 10.3390/su13115788

Miao, F., Holmes, W., Huang, R., & Zhang, H. (2021). *AI and education–Guidance for policy-makers*. United Nations Educational, Scientific and Cultural Organization.

Miao, M., Rietdijk, R., Brunner, M., Debono, D., Togher, L., & Power, E. (2022). Implementation of web-based psychosocial interventions for adults with acquired brain injury and their caregivers: Systematic review. *Journal of Medical Internet Research*, *24*(7), e38100. DOI: 10.2196/38100 PMID: 35881432

Michel-Villarreal, R., Vilalta-Perdomo, E., Salinas-Navarro, D. E., Thierry-Aguilera, R., & Gerardou, F. S. (2023). Challenges and opportunities of generative AI for higher education as explained by ChatGPT. *Education Sciences*, *13*(9), 856. DOI: 10.3390/educsci13090856

Miller, D. (2003). *Principles of social justice*. Harvard University Press.

Mittelstadt, B. (2019). Principles alone cannot guarantee ethical AI. *Nature Machine Intelligence*, *1*(11), 501–507. DOI: 10.1038/s42256-019-0114-4

Mohamed Hashim, M., Tlemsani, I., & Duncan Matthews, R. (2022). A sustainable university: Digital transformation and beyond. *Education and Information Technologies*, *27*(7), 8961–8996. DOI: 10.1007/s10639-022-10968-y PMID: 35340534

Mohebi, L. (2021). Theoretical models of integration of interactive learning technologies into teaching: A systematic literature review. *International Journal of Learning. Teaching and Educational Research*, *20*(12), 232–254.

Mok, K. H., & Neubauer, D. (2020). *Higher Education in Asia: Equity, Access and the Social Dimension*. Springer.

Mollura, D. J., Culp, M. P., Pollack, E., Battino, G., Scheel, J. R., Mango, V. L., Elahi, A., Schweitzer, A., & Dako, F. (2020). Artificial intelligence in low-and middle-income countries: Innovating global health radiology. *Radiology*, *297*(3), 513–520. DOI: 10.1148/radiol.2020201434 PMID: 33021895

Montenegro-Rueda, M., Fernández-Cerero, J., Fernández-Batanero, J. M., & López-Meneses, E. (2023). Impact of the Implementation of ChatGPT in Education A Systematic Review. *Computers*, *12*(8), 153. Advance online publication. DOI: 10.3390/computers12080153

Moorhouse, B. L., Yeo, M. A., & Wan, Y. (2023). Generative AI tools and assessment: Guidelines of the world's top-ranking universities. *Computers and Education Open*, *5*, 100151. DOI: 10.1016/j.caeo.2023.100151

Morgan, D. L. (2023). Exploring the use of artificial intelligence for qualitative data analysis: The case of ChatGPT. *International Journal of Qualitative Methods*, *22*, 1–10. DOI: 10.1177/16094069231211248

Moturu, V. R., & Nethi, S. D. (2022). Artificial intelligence in education. In *Emerging IT/ICT and AI Technologies Affecting Society* (pp. 233–244). Springer Nature Singapore.

Mrass, V., Peters, C., & Leimeister, J. M. (2020). Crowdworking platforms in Germany: Business insights from a study & implications for society. In *82. Jahrestagung des Verbands der Hochschullehrer für Betriebswirtschaft (VHB)*, Frankfurt am Main, Germany. https://ssrn.com/abstract=3926265

Muhabbat, H., Mukhiddin, K., Jalil, H., Dustnazar, K., Farxod, T., Shavkat, M., Khulkar, K., & Jakhongir, S. (2024). The digital frontier: AI-enabled transformations in higher education management. *Indonesian Journal of Educational Research and Technology*, *4*(1), 71–88.

Naseer, F., Khalid, M. U., Ayub, N., Rasool, A., Abbas, T., & Afzal, M. W. (2024). Automated Assessment and Feedback in Higher Education Using Generative AI. In *Transforming Education with Generative AI: Prompt Engineering and Synthetic Content Creation* (pp. 433-461). IGI Global. DOI: 10.4018/979-8-3693-1351-0.ch021

Nazari, M., & Saadi, G. (2024). Developing effective prompts to improve communication with ChatGPT: A formula for higher education stakeholders. *Discover Education*, *3*(1), 45. DOI: 10.1007/s44217-024-00122-w

Ndunagu, J. N., Ukhurebor, K. E., & Adesina, A. (2023). *Virtual Laboratories for STEM in Nigerian Higher Education: The National Open University of Nigeria Learners' Perspective.* Paper presented at the Proceedings of the Technology-Enhanced Learning in Laboratories workshop (TELL 2023), CEUR Workshop Proceedings.

Neha, K., Kumar, R., & Sankat, M. (2024). AI Wizards: Pioneering Assistive Technologies for Higher Education Inclusion of Students with Learning Disabilities. In *Applied Assistive Technologies and Informatics for Students with Disabilities* (pp. 59–70). Springer Nature Singapore. DOI: 10.1007/978-981-97-0914-4_4

Neimann, T., Felix, J. J., Shliakhovchuk, E., & Hindman, L. L. (2022). *Policy and Practice Challenges for Equality in Education.* IGI Global.

Newton, M. H., Annetta, L. A., & Bressler, D. M. (2024). Using Extended Reality Technology in Traditional and Place-Based Environments to Study Climate Change. *Journal of Science Education and Technology, 33*(2), 208–227. DOI: 10.1007/s10956-023-10057-w

Nguyen, A., Ngo, H. N., Hong, Y., Dang, B. and Nguyen, B. P. T. (2023). Ethical Principles for Artificial Intelligence in Education. Education, and Information Technologies, 28, 4221-4241, 10639-022-11316-w.DOI: <ALIGNMENT.qj></ALIGNMENT>10.1007/s

Nguyen, T. H., Tran, D. N., Vo, D. L., Mai, V. H., & Dao, X. Q. (2022). AI-powered university: Design and deployment of robot assistant for smart universities. *Journal of Advances in Information Technology, 13*(1).

Nguyen, A., Kremantzis, M., Essien, A., Petrounias, I., & Hosseini, S. (2024). Enhancing student engagement through artificial intelligence (AI): Understanding the basics, opportunities, and challenges. *Journal of University Teaching & Learning Practice, 21*(06). Advance online publication. DOI: 10.53761/caraaq92

Nguyen, L. T., & Bui, T. D. (2023). Personalized Learning through Generative AI in Higher Education: Challenges and Opportunities. *Computers & Education*, •••, 182.

Nicol, D., & Macfarlane-Dick, D. (2006). Formative assessment and self-regulated learning: A model and seven principles of good feedback practice. *Studies in Higher Education, 31*(2), 199–218. DOI: 10.1080/03075070600572090

Nieto, S. (2010). *The Light in Their Eyes: Creating Multicultural Learning Communities.* Teachers College Press.

Nikolic, S., Wentworth, I., Sheridan, L., Moss, S., Duursma, E., Jones, R. A., Ros, M., & Middleton, R. (2024). A systematic literature review of attitudes, intentions and behaviours of teaching academics pertaining to AI and generative AI (GenAI) in higher education: An analysis of GenAI adoption using the UTAUT framework. *Australasian Journal of Educational Technology*. Advance online publication. DOI: 10.14742/ajet.9643

Nikolopoulou, K. (2025). Generative artificial intelligence and sustainable higher education: Mapping the potential. *Journal of Digital Educational Technology*, *5*(1), ep2506. DOI: 10.30935/jdet/15860

Nkambou, R., Panagiotopoulos, I., Kalou, A., Pierrakeas, C., & Kameas, A. (2023). *Adaptive Learning Spaces with Context-Awareness*. Lecture Notes in Computer Science. Springer.

Norman, D. A. (2013). *The Design of Everyday Things*. Basic Books.

Nyaaba, M., & Zhai, X. (2024). Generative AI professional development needs for teacher educators. *Journal of AI*, *8*(1), 1–13. DOI: 10.61969/jai.1385915

OECD. (2019). *AI in Education: Challenges and Opportunities for Sustainable Development*. OECD Publishing.

OECD. (2021). *Education for Sustainable Development: Learning for the Future*. OECD Publishing.

OECD-iLibrary. (2018). *PISA 2018 Results* (Vol. II). Where All Students Can Succeed.

Ofosu-Ampong, K. (2024). Beyond the hype: Exploring faculty perceptions and acceptability of AI in teaching practices. *Discover Education*, *3*(1), 38. DOI: 10.1007/s44217-024-00128-4

Onesi-Ozigagun, O., Ololade, Y. J., Eyo-Udo, N. L., & Ogundipe, D. O. (2024). Revolutionizing education through AI: A comprehensive review of enhancing learning experiences. *International Journal of Applied Research in Social Sciences*, *6*(4), 589–607. DOI: 10.51594/ijarss.v6i4.1011

Ong, Q. K. L., & Annamalai, N. (2024). Technological pedagogical content knowledge for twenty-first century learning skills: The game changer for teachers of industrial revolution 5.0. *Education and Information Technologies*, *29*(2), 1939–1980. DOI: 10.1007/s10639-023-11852-z

Onyebuchi, A., Matthew, U. O., Kazaure, J. S., Nwanagwaugwu, A. C., Nwamouh, U. C., & Adamu, U. A. (2022). Cloud based IoT Electronic Healthcare Data Warehouse Integration in emerging 5G Health Grid Ecosystem.

Onyebuchi, A., Matthew, U. O., Kazaure, J. S., Ebong, G. N., Ndukwu, C. C., Nwanakwaugwu, A. C., & Okey, O. D. (2024). *Cloud-Based IoT Data Warehousing Technology for E-Healthcare: A Comprehensive Guide to E-Health Grids Pioneering Smart Healthcare 5.0 with IoT, Federated Learning, and Cloud Security*. IGI Global.

Onyebuchi, A., Matthew, U. O., Kazaure, J. S., Okafor, N. U., Okey, O. D., Okochi, P. I., Taiwo, J. F., & Matthew, A. O. (2022). Business demand for a cloud enterprise data warehouse in electronic healthcare computing: Issues and developments in e-healthcare cloud computing. [IJCAC]. *International Journal of Cloud Applications and Computing*, *12*(1), 1–22. DOI: 10.4018/IJCAC.297098

Onyesolu, M. O., Nwasor, V. C., Ositanwosu, O. E., & Iwegbuna, O. N. (2013). Pedagogy: Instructivism to socio-constructivism through virtual reality. *International Journal of Advanced Computer Science and Applications*, *4*(9).

Open, A. I. (2022). *OpenAI Blog Introducing ChatGPT*. https://openai.com/blog/chatgpt

Open, A. I. (2024). ChatGPT: Optimizing language models for dialogue. https://openai.com/blog/chatgpt/

Ou, A. W., Stöhr, C., & Malmström, H. (2024). Academic communication with AI-powered language tools in higher education: From a post-humanist perspective. *System*, *121*, 103225. DOI: 10.1016/j.system.2024.103225

Oyekunle, D., Ugochukwu, O. M., Rosa, R. L., Rodriguez, D. Z., & Fatai, L. O. (2024). Novel Approaches in Clinical Simulation: Immersive Educational Technology to Enhance Nursing Education. *INFOCOMP Journal of Computer Science, 23*(1).

Oyekunle, D., Matthew, U., Waliu, A., & Fatai, L. (2024). Healthcare applications of Augmented Reality (AR) and Virtual Real-ity (VR) simulation in clinical ceducation. *Journal of Clinical Images and Medical Case Reports*, *5*(6), 3141.

Page, M. J., McKenzie, J. E., Bossuyt, P. M., Boutron, I., Hoffmann, T. C., Mulrow, C. D., ... & Moher, D. (2021). The PRISMA 2020 statement: an updated guideline for reporting systematic reviews. bmj, 372.

Panagopoulou, F., Parpoula, C., & Karpouzis, Kostas. (2023). Legal and ethical considerations regarding the use of ChatGPT in education. arXiv preprint arXiv:2306.10037. .DOI: 10.31235/osf.io/c5hf3

Park, C. J., Yi, P. H., & Siegel, E. L. (2020). Medical student perspectives on the impact of artificial intelligence on the practice of medicine. *Current Problems in Diagnostic Radiology*, *50*(5), 614–619. DOI: 10.1067/j.cpradiol.2020.06.011 PMID: 32680632

Parmar, S., & Patel, H. (n.d.). *Prompt engineering for large language model.*

Paszkiewicz, A., Salach, M., Dymora, P., Bolanowski, M., Budzik, G., & Kubiak, P. (2021). Methodology of implementing virtual reality in education for industry 4.0. *Sustainability (Basel), 13*(9), 5049. DOI: 10.3390/su13095049

Patel, A., & Martinez, L. (2024). Bridging Policy and Practice: Challenges in Implementing Equity in Higher Education. *Journal of Educational Policy and Administration, 29*(2), 89–105.

Patterson, C. A. (2020). Maintaining transmission: DIRECTV's work-at-home technical support, virtual surveillance, and the gendered division of labor. *Feminist Media Studies, 20*(4), 561–578. DOI: 10.1080/14680777.2020.1748947

Pavlik, J. V. (2023, January). Collaborating with ChatGPT: Considering the implications of Generative Artificial intelligence for journalism and media education. *Journalism & Mass Communication Educator, 78*(1), 84–93. DOI: 10.1177/10776958221149577

Pelletier, K., Brown, M., Brooks, D. C., McCormack, M., Reeves, J., Arbino, N., Bozkurt, A., Crawford, S., Czerniewicz, L., Gibson, R., Linder, K., Mason, J., & Mondelli, V. (2021). *2021 EDUCAUSE horizon report teaching and learning edition*. EDUCAUSE.

People. cn. (2024b). The initiative of "Empowering Education Development with Artificial Intelligence" was announced at the 2024 World Digital Education Conference. Available at: https://edu.yunnan.cn/system/2024/01/31/032930479.shtm

Peres, R., Shreier, M., Schweidel, D., & Sorescu, A. (2023). On ChatGPT and beyond: How generative artificial intelligence may affect research, teaching, and practice. *International Journal of Research in Marketing, 40*(2), 269–275. DOI: 10.1016/j.ijresmar.2023.03.001

Pesovski, I., Santos, R., Henriques, R., & Trajkovik, V. (2024). Generative AI for Customizable Learning Experiences. *Sustainability (Basel), 16*(7), 3034. DOI: 10.3390/su16073034

Pillai, R., Sivathanu, B., Metri, B., & Kaushik, N. (2024). Students' adoption of AI-based teacher-bots (T-bots) for learning in higher education. *Information Technology & People, 37*(1), 328–355. DOI: 10.1108/ITP-02-2021-0152

Porayska- Pomsta. K, Holmes, W. and Nemorin, S. (2023). The ethics of Artificial Intelligence in Education: In B. du Boulay, A. Mitrovic, and Yacet (Eds). The Handbook of AI in Education Edward Elgar Publishing Ltd.

Prather, J., Denny, P., Leinonen, J., Becker, B. A., Albluwi, I., Craig, M., & Keuning, H. (2023). The robots are here: Navigating the generative AI revolution in computing education. In *Proceedings of the 2023 Working Group Reports on Innovation and Technology in Computer Science Education* (pp. 108-159). DOI: 10.1145/3623762.3633499

Rahiman, H. U., & Kodikal, R. (2024). Revolutionizing education: Artificial intelligence empowered learning in higher education. *Cogent Education, 11*(1), 2293431. DOI: 10.1080/2331186X.2023.2293431

Ramalho, R., Adams, P., Huggard, P., & Hoare, K. (2015). Literature review and constructivist grounded theory methodology. In Ramalho, R., Adams, P., Huggard, P., & Hoare, K. (Eds.), *Forum Qualitative Sozialforschung/Forum: Qualitative Social Research, 16* (Vol. 3).

Rapanta, C., Botturi, L., Goodyear, P., Guàrdia, L., & Koole, M. (2020). Online university teaching during and after the Covid-19 crisis: Refocusing teacher presence and learning activity. *Postdigital science and education, 2*, 923-945.

Razzouk, R., & Shute, V. (2012). What is Design Thinking and Why is it Important? *Review of Educational Research, 82*(3), 330–348. DOI: 10.3102/0034654312457429

Rea, M., Lundmark, L., & Björk, M. (2021). Crowdsourcing as a tool for research: Methodological, fair, and political considerations. *Research Policy, 50*(4), 104155. Advance online publication. DOI: 10.1016/j.respol.2020.104155

Rekha, K., Gopal, K., Satheeskumar, D., Anand, U. A., Doss, D. S. S., & Elayaperumal, S. (2024, May). Ai-Powered Personalized Learning System Design: Student Engagement and Performance Tracking System. In *2024 4th International Conference on Advance Computing and Innovative Technologies in Engineering (ICACITE)* (pp. 1125-1130). IEEE.

Rhoney, D. C., Chen, A. M. H., Churchwell, M. D., Daugherty, K. K., Jarrett, J. B., Kleppinger, E. L., Nawarskas, J. J., Sibicky, S. L., Stowe, C. D., & Meyer, S. M. (2024). The Need for Competency-Based Education. *American Journal of Pharmaceutical Education, 88*(6), 100706. DOI: 10.1016/j.ajpe.2024.100706 PMID: 38705241

Rodríguez-Amigo, A., Fernández-Alvarado, J. F., & Fernández-Rodríguez, S. (2022). Case of study on a sustainability building: Environmental risk assessment related with allergenicity from air quality considering meteorological and urban green infrastructure data on BIM. *The Science of the Total Environment, 838*, 155910. DOI: 10.1016/j.scitotenv.2022.155910 PMID: 35577081

Roland, M. J. (2013). *Education reconfigured: Culture, encounter, and change.* Routledge.

Roscoe, R. D., Salehi, S., Nixon, N., Worsley, M., Piech, C., & Luckin, R. (2022). Inclusion and equity as a paradigm shift for artificial intelligence in education. In *Artificial Intelligence in STEM Education* (pp. 359–374). CRC Press. DOI: 10.1201/9781003181187-28

Roshanaei, M., Olivares, H., & Lopez, R. R. (2023). Harnessing AI to foster equity in education: Opportunities, challenges, and emerging strategies. *Journal of Intelligent Learning Systems and Applications, 15*(04), 123–143. DOI: 10.4236/jilsa.2023.154009

Rowe, P. G. (1987). *Design Thinking.* MIT Press.

Rudolph, J., Tan, S., & Tan, S. (2023). ChatGPT: Bullshit spewer or the end of traditional assessments in higher education? *Journal of Applied Learning and Teaching, 6*(1), 342-363.

Russell, S. J., & Norvig, P. (2016). *Artificial intelligence: a modern approach.* Pearson.

Ryan, G. V., Callaghan, S., Rafferty, A., Higgins, M. F., Mangina, E., & McAuliffe, F. (2022). Learning outcomes of immersive technologies in health care student education: Systematic review of the literature. *Journal of Medical Internet Research, 24*(2), e30082. DOI: 10.2196/30082 PMID: 35103607

Ryynänen, S., & Nivala, E. (2019). Inequality as a social pedagogical question. *International Journal of Social Pedagogy, 7*(1), 1–16. DOI: 10.14324/111.444.ijsp.2019.v7.1.008

Sætra, H. S. (2021). AI in Context and the Sustainable Development Goals: Factoring in the Unsustainability of the Sociotechnical System. *Sustainability (Basel), 13*(4), 1738. DOI: 10.3390/su13041738

Sahin, E., & Ozkan, M. (2024). The Role of AI in Supporting At-Risk Students: A Case Study of Generative AI in Higher Education. *Artificial Intelligence in Education, 30*(1), 105–120.

Sajja, R., Sermet, Y., Cikmaz, M., Cwiertny, D., & Demir, I. (2024). Artificial intelligence-enabled intelligent assistant for personalized and adaptive learning in higher education. *Information (Basel), 15*(10), 596. DOI: 10.3390/info15100596

Sakarneh, M. A., & Nair, N. S. A. (2014). Effective Teaching in Inclusive Classroom: Literature Review. *Journal of Education and Practice, 5*, 28–34.

Salas-Pilco, S. Z., Xiao, K., & Hu, X. (2022). Artificial Intelligence and Learning Analytics in Teacher Education: A Systematic Review. *Education Sciences, 12*(8), 12. DOI: 10.3390/educsci12080569

Salinas-Navarro, D. E., Vilalta-Perdomo, E., Michel-Villarreal, R., & Montesinos, L. (2024). Using generative artificial intelligence tools to explain and enhance experiential learning for authentic assessment. *Education Sciences, 14*(1), 83. DOI: 10.3390/educsci14010083

Sammalisto, K., Sundstrom, A., & Holm, T. (2015). Implementation of sustainability in universities as perceived by faculty and staff-a model from a Swedish university. *Journal of Cleaner Production, 106*, 45–54. DOI: 10.1016/j.jclepro.2014.10.015

Sampson, H., & Johannessen, I. A. (2020). Turning on the tap: The benefits of using 'real-life'vignettes in qualitative research interviews. *Qualitative Research, 20*(1), 56–72. DOI: 10.1177/1468794118816618

Samuel, Y., Brennan-Tonetta, M., Samuel, J., Kashyap, R., Kumar, V., Krishna-Kaashyap, S., Chidipothu, N., Anand, I., & Jain, P. (2023). Cultivation of human centered artificial intelligence: Culturally adaptive thinking in education (CATE) for AI. *Frontiers in Artificial Intelligence, 6*, 6. DOI: 10.3389/frai.2023.1198180 PMID: 38106981

Sanabria-Navarro, J. R., Silveira-Pérez, Y., Pérez-Bravo, D. D., & de-Jesús-Cortina-Núñez, M. (2023). Incidences of Artificial Intelligence in Contemporary Education. *Comunicar: Media Education Research Journal, 31*(77), 93–103. DOI: 10.3916/C77-2023-08

Sanchez-Carracedo, F., Sureda, B., Moreno-Pino, F. M., & Romero-Portillo, D. (2021). Education for Sustainable Development in Spanish engineering degrees. Case study. *Journal of Cleaner Production, 294*, 126322. DOI: 10.1016/j.jclepro.2021.126322

Sarai, L., Zockun, C. Z., & Cabral, F. G. (2023). Public administration and innovation: E-government in the international perspective. *Beijing Law Review, 14*(3), 1352–1371. DOI: 10.4236/blr.2023.143074

Sarshartehrani, F., Mohammadrezaei, E., Behravan, M., & Gracanin, D. (2024). *Enhancing E-Learning Experience Through Embodied AI Tutors in Immersive Virtual Environments: A Multifaceted Approach for Personalized Educational Adaptation.* Paper presented at the International Conference on Human-Computer Interaction. DOI: 10.1007/978-3-031-60609-0_20

Saunders, L. (2016). Teaching the reference interview through practice-based assignments. *RSR. Reference Services Review*, *44*(3), 390–410. DOI: 10.1108/RSR-04-2016-0025

Sauvé, L. (2005). Current in environmental education: Mapping a complex and evolving pedagogical field. *Canadian Journal of Environmental Education*, *10*, 12–37.

Schiff, D. (2022). Education for AI, not AI for education: The role of education and ethics in national AI policy strategies. *International Journal of Artificial Intelligence in Education*, *32*(3), 527–563. DOI: 10.1007/s40593-021-00270-2

Schriner, A., & Oerther, D. (2014). No really, (crowd) work is the silver bullet. *Procedia Engineering*, *78*, 224–228. DOI: 10.1016/j.proeng.2014.07.060

Scott, W., & Gough, S. (2003). *Sustainable development and learning: Framing the issues*. Routledge Falmer. DOI: 10.4324/9780203464625_chapter_4

Shaheen, H. A. M. (2023) Artificial Intelligence and the shift from Indoctrination to utilizing tools for sustainable education. Arab Journal for specific education. No26, 139-169. https:// search. Mandumad10.com/ Recrd/1355921

Sharifuddin, N. S., & Hashim, H. (2024). Benefits and Challenges in Implementing Artificial Intelligence in Education (AIED) in ESL Classroom: A Systematic Review (2019-2022). *International Journal of Academic Research in Business & Social Sciences*, *14*(1), 146–164. DOI: 10.6007/IJARBSS/v14-i1/20422

Shea, J. (2023, February 4). VCU: Faculty and staff discuss the ‘perplexing, exciting and scary’ implications of AI, such as ChatGPT, on campus. VCU News. https://www.proquest.com/wire-feeds/vcu-faculty-staff-discuss-perplexing-exciting/docview/2772266645/se-2?accountid=10675

Shen, Y., Heacock, L., Elias, J., Hentel, K. D., Reig, B., Shih, G., & Moy, L. (2023). ChatGPT and other large language models are double-edged swords. *Radiology*, *307*(2)230163. https://doi.org/. 230163DOI: 10.1148/radiol

Shorey, S., & Ng, E. D. (2021). The use of virtual reality simulation among nursing students and registered nurses: A systematic review. *Nurse Education Today*, *98*, 104662. DOI: 10.1016/j.nedt.2020.104662 PMID: 33203545

Shute, V. J., Ventura, M., & Kim, Y. J. (2013, November). “Assessment and learning of qualitative physics in Newton’s playground,” *the Journal of Educational Research. The Journal of Educational Research*, *106*(6), 423–430. DOI: 10.1080/00220671.2013.832970

Shwedeh, F., Salloum, S. A., Aburayya, A., Fatin, B., Elbadawi, M. A., Al Ghurabli, Z., & Al Dabbagh, T. (2024). AI adoption and educational sustainability in higher education in the UAE. In A. Al-Marzouqi, S. A. Salloum, M. Al-Saidat, A. Aburayya, & B. Gupta, B. (Eds.), Artificial intelligence in education: The power and dangers of ChatGPT in the classroom (pp. 201–229). Springer. DOI: 10.1007/978-3-031-52280-2_14

Silva, L., Mendes, A. J., & Gomes, A. (2020). *Computer-supported collaborative learning in programming education: A systematic literature review.* Paper presented at the 2020 IEEE Global Engineering Education Conference (EDUCON). DOI: 10.1109/EDUCON45650.2020.9125237

Sinanaj, X. A., Hazizi, T. B., Durmishi, L., Tapija, N. K., & Durmishi, A. (2024). Albanian challenges for sustainable development: Nature-based tourism sector evidence from entrepreneurs' point of view. *Multidisciplinary Reviews*, *7*(7), 2024153. Advance online publication. DOI: 10.31893/multirev.2024153

Singh, P., Pahuja, N., Kansal, M., Gurung, S., Shukla, U., & Gupta, S. (2024). *Enhancing Tourism Experiences and Preserving Cultural Heritage with AR and VR.* Paper presented at the 2024 2nd International Conference on Disruptive Technologies (ICDT). DOI: 10.1109/ICDT61202.2024.10489490

Slomp, E. M., Ropelato, D., Bonatti, C., & da Silva, M. D. (2024, March). Adaptive Learning in Engineering Courses: How Artificial Intelligence (AI) Can Improve Academic Outcomes. In *2024 IEEE World Engineering Education Conference (EDUNINE)* (pp. 1-6). IEEE. DOI: 10.1109/EDUNINE60625.2024.10500580

Smith, J., & Chen, Y. (2024). The Evolving Role of Higher Education in Promoting Social Justice. *International Journal of Higher Education and Policy*, *22*(3), 45–62.

Sorensen, E. K., & Andersen, L. K. (2022). Collaborative Learning and Social Mobility: The Role of Digital Platforms in Higher Education. *International Journal of Educational Technology*, *39*(4), 200–215.

Souza, A. M. C., Manzolli, J., Campos, C. D. S., & Rennó-Costa, C. (2022). *Playing the Hypercube–Using Augmented Reality to Enhance a Multimodal Musical Performance.* Paper presented at the Proceedings of the 24th Symposium on Virtual and Augmented Reality. DOI: 10.1145/3604479.3604530

Spitzberg, B. H., & Changnon, G. (2009). Conceptualizing intercultural competence. In Deardorff, D. K. (Ed.), *The SAGE Handbook of Intercultural Competence* (pp. 2–52). SAGE Publications. DOI: 10.4135/9781071872987.n1

Spricigo, C. B., Camilotti, B. M., Graham, C. R., & Baptista, R. (2023). An exploration of institutional and personal barriers to online academic engagement at a Brazilian university. *Educación XX1, 26*(2), 17-50.

SpringerOpen. (2024). Unveiling the evolution of generative AI (GAI): A comprehensive and investigative analysis toward LLM models (2021–2024) and beyond. *Journal of Electrical Systems and Information Technology, 11*(2), 101–125.

Squire, D., Gonzalez, L., & Shayan, C. (2024). Enhancing sense of belonging in nursing student clinical placements to advance learning and identity development. *Journal of Professional Nursing, 51*, 109–114. DOI: 10.1016/j.profnurs.2024.01.007 PMID: 38614668

Srnicek, N. (2017). The challenges of platform capitalism: Understanding the logic of a new business model. *Juncture, 23*(4), 254–257. DOI: 10.1111/newe.12023

Stables, A., & Scott, W. (2002). The quest of holism in education for sustainable development. *Environmental Education Research, 8*(1), 53–60. DOI: 10.1080/13504620120109655

Stannard, E. (2023, January 30). ChatGPT will write you an essay in seconds using AI. So why aren't CT professors more concerned about it? Hartford Courant (Online). https://www.proquest.com/blogs-podcasts-websites/chatgpt-will-write-you-essay-seconds-using-ai-so/docview/2770810966/se-2?accountid=10675

Stapleford, K., & Lee, K. (2024). *Online postgraduate education: Re-imagining openness, distance and interaction*. Taylor & Francis. DOI: 10.4324/9781003044048

Stenseth, H. V., Steindal, S. A., Solberg, M. T., Ølnes, M. A., Mohallem, A., Sørensen, A. L., & Riegel, F. (2022). Simulation-based learning supported by technology to enhance critical thinking in nursing students: Protocol for a scoping review. *JMIR Research Protocols, 11*(4), e36725. DOI: 10.2196/36725 PMID: 35373777

Stephens, J. C., Hernandez, M. E., Román, M., Graham, A. C., & Scholz, R. W. (2008). Higher education as a change agent for sustainability in different cultures and contexts. Higher education as a change agent for sustainability in different cultures and contexts. *International Journal of Sustainability in Higher Education, 9*(3), 317–338. DOI: 10.1108/14676370810885916

Sterev, N., Kostadinov, K., Yordanov, D., & Yorgova, T. (2023). Open entrepreneurial academic centres. [Ikonomicheski Izsledvania]. *Economic Studies Journal, 32*(4), 116–134.

Sterling, S. (2001). *Sustainable Education: Re-visioning Learning and Change*. Green Books.

Sterling, S. (2010). Transformative learning and sustainability: Sketching the conceptual ground. *Learning and Teaching in Higher Education*, *5*, 17–33.

Stern, C., Lizarondo, L., Carrier, J., Godfrey, C., Rieger, K., Salmond, S., Apóstolo, J., Kirkpatrick, P., & Loveday, H. (2020). Methodological guidance for the conduct of mixed methods systematic reviews. *JBI Evidence Synthesis*, *18*(10), 2108–2118. DOI: 10.11124/JBISRIR-D-19-00169 PMID: 32813460

Strzelecki, A. (2024). Students' Acceptance of ChatGPT in Higher Education: An Extended Unified Theory of Acceptance and Use of Technology. *Innovative Higher Education*, *49*(2), 223–245. DOI: 10.1007/s10755-023-09686-1

Su, J., & Yang, W. (2023). Unlocking the power of ChatGPT: A framework for applying generative AI in education. *ECNU Review of Education*, *6*(3), 355–366. DOI: 10.1177/20965311231168423

Sumak, B., Lopez-de-Ipria, D., Dziabenko, O., Correia, S. D., de Carvalho, L. M. S., Lopes, S., . . . Pusnik, M. (2024, May). AI-Based Education Tools for Enabling Inclusive Education: Challenges and Benefits. In *2024 47th MIPRO ICT and Electronics Convention (MIPRO)* (pp. 472-477). Institute of Electrical and Electronics Engineers.

Supriya, Y., Bhulakshmi, D., Bhattacharya, S., Gadckallu, T. R., Vyas, P., Kaluri, R., Sumathy, S., Koppu, S., Brown, D. J., & Mahmud, M. (2024). Industry 5.0 in Smart Education: Concepts, Applications, Challenges, Opportunities, and Future Directions. *IEEE Access : Practical Innovations, Open Solutions*, *12*, 81938–81967. DOI: 10.1109/ACCESS.2024.3401473

Sweller, J. (1988). Cognitive Load During Problem Solving: Effects on Learning. *Cognitive Science*, *12*(2), 257–285. Advance online publication. DOI: 10.1207/s15516709cog1202_4

Sywelem, M. M. G. (2024). Artificial intelligence and the sustainability of educational services: An overview. *World Journal of Social Sciences and Humanities*, *10*(1), 8–17. DOI: 10.12691/wjssh-10-1-2

Tabbakhian Khaziran, M. (2021). *The impact of the COVID-19 pandemic on nursing simulation use and the influence of simulation use on future admissions*. UCLA.

Tadeja, S. K., Bohné, T., Godula, K., Cybulski, A., & Woźniak, M. M. (2024). Immersive presentations of real-world medical equipment through interactive VR environment populated with the high-fidelity 3D model of mobile MRI unit. *Computers & Graphics*, *120*, 103919. DOI: 10.1016/j.cag.2024.103919

Taecharungroj, V. (2023). What Can ChatGPT Do?" Analyzing early reactions to the innovative AI chatbot on Twitter. *Big Data and Cognitive Computing*, *7*(1), 35. DOI: 10.3390/bdcc7010035

Tala, M. L., Müller, C. N., Nastase, I. A., State, O., & Georghe, G. (2024). Exploring university students' perceptions of generative artificial intelligence in education. Amfiteatru Economic Journal, 26(65), 71–88.

Tandon, A., & Rathi, S. (2022). Sustaining urban labour markets: Situating migration and domestic work in India's gig economy. *Journal of South Asian Development*, *17*(2), 135–157. DOI: 10.1177/09731741221118787

Tan, S. (2013). Harnessing Artificial Intelligence for Innovation in Education. In *Learning Intelligence: Innovative and Digital Transformative Learning Strategies* (pp. 335–363). Springer.

Tegtmeier, P., Weber, C., Sommer, S., & Tisch, A. (2022). Criteria and guidelines for human-centred work design in a digitally transformed world of work. *International Journal of Environmental Research and Public Health*, *19*(23), 15506. DOI: 10.3390/ijerph192315506 PMID: 36497580

Tejedor, G., Sanchez-Carracedo, F., & Segalas, J. (2022). Education for sustainable development in higher education: Introduction to a special issue. *Sustainability (Basel)*, *14*(17), 10530. DOI: 10.3390/su141710530

Thornhill, E., Sanderson, C., & Gupta, A. (2022). A grounded theory analysis of care-coordinators' perceptions of family growth associated with an experience of first episode psychosis. *Psychosis*, *14*(4), 355–367. DOI: 10.1080/17522439.2021.1971743

Thorp, H. H. (2023). ChatGPT is fun, but not an author. *Science*, *379*(6630), 313–313. DOI: 10.1126/science.adg7879 PMID: 36701446

Tight, M. (2020). *Education for All? The Legacy of International Commitment.* Routledge.

Ting-Toomey, S., & Chung, L. C. (2012). *Understanding Intercultural Communication.* Oxford University Press.

Tiwari, R. G., Agarwal, A. K., & Husain, M. (2023). 13 Integration of virtual reality in the e-learning environment. *Augmented and Virtual Reality in Industry 5.0, 2*, 253.

Tlili, A., Shehata, B., Adarkwah, M. A., Bozkurt, A., Hickey, D. T., Huang, R., & Agyemang, B. (2023). *What if the devil is my guardian angel ChatGPT as a case study of using chatbots in education.* Smart Learning Environments., DOI: 10.1186/s40561-023-00237-x

Tomusk, V. (2021). *The Bologna Process: A Critical Sociology of Higher Education in Europe*. Routledge.

Torrey, T., Woodruff, N., Matthew, C., & Jeromie, W. (2021). Educators' Interests, Prior Knowledge and Questions Regarding Augmented Reality, Virtual Reality and 3D Printing and Modeling. *TechTrends, 65*(4), 548–561. DOI: 10.1007/s11528-021-00594-9

Trevisan, L. V., Eustachio, J. H. P. P., Dias, B. G., Filho, W. L., & Pedrozo, E. A. (2024). Digital transformation towards sustainability in higher education: State-of-the-art and future research insights. *Environment, Development and Sustainability, 26*(2), 2789–2810. DOI: 10.1007/s10668-022-02874-7 PMID: 36624732

Tripathi, A., & Thakar, S. V. (2024). Ethical Use of AI for Academic Integrity: Preventing Plagiarism and Cheating. *Ethical Frameworks in Special Education: A Guide for Researchers, 91.*

Tugtekin, U., & Odabasi, H. F. (2022). Do interactive learning environments have an effect on learning outcomes, cognitive load and metacognitive judgments? *Education and Information Technologies, 27*(5), 7019–7058. DOI: 10.1007/s10639-022-10912-0

Tzotzou, M., Poulou, M., Karalis, T., & Ifanti, A. (2021). *Reflecting upon the Greek state-school teacher's changing role in the 21st century: an 'ecosystemic' approach.* Preschool and Primary Education.

Ullrich, S., Rausch, D., & Kuhlen, T. W. (2011). *Bimanual Haptic Simulator for Medical Training: System Architecture and Performance Measurements.* Paper presented at the EGVE/EuroVR.

UNESCO (Ed.). (2019). Artificial Intelligence in education: Challenges and opportunities for sustainable development. UNESCO Working Papers on Education Policy. https://bit.ly/3z6BQvN

UNESCO. (2014). Shaping the Future We Want: UN Decade of Education for Sustainable Development (2005-2014) Final Report. UNESCO Publishing.

UNESCO. (2015). *Education 2030: Incheon Declaration and Framework for Action*. UNESCO.

UNESCO. (2016). *Education for People and Planet: Creating Sustainable Futures for All.*

UNESCO. (2017). *Education for Sustainable Development Goals: Learning Objectives*. UNESCO Publishing.

UNESCO. (2019). Artificial Intelligence in Education: Challenges and Opportunities for Sustainable Development. 0https:///unescdoc. Unesco.org/ark

UNESCO. (2020). *AI in Education: Change at the Speed of Learning*. UNESCO IITE Policy Brief.

UNESCO. (2021). International Forum on AI and the futures of education developing competencies for the AI era.

UNESCO. (2023). Ethics of Artificial Intelligence. Retrieved from: https://www.unesco.org/en/artificial-Intelligence/recommendation-ethics

UNESCO. (2023). *Global Education Monitoring Report 2023: Technology in Education- A Tool on Whose Terms?* UNESCO.

UNESCO. (2023). *Global Education Monitoring Report. Technology in Education. A Tool on Whose Terms?* UNESCO.

UNESCO. (2023). Guidance for generative Artificial Intelligence in Education and Research, UNESCO Digital Literacy. https:///unescdoc. Unesco.org/ark

United Nations Educational, Scientific and Cultural Organization. (2012). *Education for sustainable development: source book*. Pars: UNESCO.

United Nations Educational, Scientific and Cultural Organization. (2017). *Education for sustainable development goals-learning objectives*. UNESCO.

United Nations Educational, Scientific and Cultural Organization. (2019). *Artificial Intelligence in education: challenges and opportunities for sustainable development*. UNESCO.

United Nations Educational, Scientific and Cultural Organization. (2020). *Education for sustainable development-roadmap: ESD for 2030*. UNESCO.

United Nations. (2015). Transforming our world: The 2030 Agenda for sustainable development; division for sustainable sevelopment goals. New York, NY, USA.

Upwork Community. (2024). From decades of traditional work to freelancing: Share your experience. *Upwork*. https://community.upwork.com/t5/Freelancers/From-decades-of-traditional-work-to-freelancing-Share-your/m-p/1115097

Vashishth, T. K., Sharma, V., Sharma, K. K., Kumar, B., Panwar, R., & Chaudhary, S. (2024). AI-driven learning analytics for personalized feedback and assessment in higher education. In *Using Traditional Design Methods to Enhance AI-Driven Decision Making* (pp. 206–230). IGI Global. DOI: 10.4018/979-8-3693-0639-0.ch009

Vela, D. P. (2024). Transforming Higher Education: Effective Strategies for Contemporary Curriculum Design. *Educational Administration: Theory and Practice, 30*(3), 1985–1993.

Venkatesh, V., Morris, M. G., Davis, G. B., & Davis, F. D. (2003). User acceptance of information technology: Toward a unifed view. *Management Information Systems Quarterly, 27*(3), 425–478. DOI: 10.2307/30036540

Verganti, R. (2009). *Design-Driven Innovation: Changing the Rules of Competition by Radically Innovating What Things Mean*. Harvard Business Press.

Verma, R. K., Gupta, S., & Illinich, S. (2024). *Technology-enhanced personalized learning in higher education Advances in Technological Innovations in Higher Education*. CRC Press.

Vinuesa, R., Azizpour, H., Leite, I., Balaam, M., Dignum, V., Domisch, S., Felländer, A., Langhans, S. D., Tegmark, M., & Nerini, F. F. (2020). The role of artificial intelligence in achieving the sustainable development goals. *Nature Communications, 11*(1), 1–10. DOI: 10.1038/s41467-019-14108-y PMID: 31932590

Vistorte, A. O. R., Deroncele-Acosta, A., Ayala, J. L. M., Barrasa, A., López-Granero, C., & Martí-González, M. (2024). Integrating artificial intelligence to assess emotions in learning environments: A systematic literature review. *Frontiers in Psychology, 15*, 1387089. DOI: 10.3389/fpsyg.2024.1387089 PMID: 38966729

Voss, E., Cushing, S. T., Ockey, G. J., & Yan, X. (2023). The use of assistive technologies including generative AI by test takers in language assessment: A debate of theory and practice. *Language Assessment Quarterly, 20*(4-5), 520–532. DOI: 10.1080/15434303.2023.2288256

Vygotsky, L. (1962). *Thought and language*. MIT Press. DOI: 10.1037/11193-000

Vygotsky, L. (1978). *Mind in Society: The Development of Higher Psychological Processes*. Harvard University Press.

Waeyaert, W., Lenaerts, K., & Gillis, D. (2022). Spain's 'Riders Law': New regulation on digital platform work. *European Agency for Safety and Health at Work (EU-OSHA)*. https://osha.europa.eu/en/publications/spain-riders-law-new-regulation-digital-platorm-work

Waghid, Z. (2014). (Higher) Education for social justice through sustainable development, economic development and equity. *South African Journal of Higher Education, 28*(4), 1448–1463.

Wang, L. (2023). *Equity, inclusion and the transformation of higher education.* UNESCO.

Wang, Y., Liu, C., & Tu, Y. F. (2021). Factors affecting the adoption of AI-based applications in higher education. *Journal of Educational Technology & Society, 24*(3), 116–129.

Wang, Y., Liu, X., Zhang, Y., Sang, X., & Wang, M. (2020). The first model of family education on the delivery of bilingual British NCC digital literacy qualifications in Dalian, China — Engaging and motivating children'. *Proceedings of the International Conference on Education in Mathematics, Science and Technology (ICEMST)*, Istanbul, Turkey, 21-24 March.

Ward, J. K., Comer, U., & Stone, S. (2018). On qualifying qualitative research: Emerging perspectives and the "Deer"(descriptive, exploratory, evolutionary, repeat) paradigm. *Interchange, 49*(1), 133–146. DOI: 10.1007/s10780-018-9313-x

Waseem, M., Das, T., Ahmad, A., Fehmideh, M., Liang, P., & Mikkonen, T. (2023). ChatGPT as a Software Development Bot: A Project-based Study. https://arxiv.org/abs/2310.13648

Wasito, B. (2024, February). Exploring Artificial Intelligence (AI) to anticipate changes in Professional Skills in the next ERA of Industrial Revolution 4.0. In *The Third International Conference on Government Education Management and Tourism* (Vol. 3, pp. 013-013).

Weerasinghe, S., & Perera, I. (2024). Optimized Strategy in Cloud-Native Environment for Inter-Service Communication in Microservices. *International Journal of Online & Biomedical Engineering, 20*(1), 40–57. DOI: 10.3991/ijoe.v20i01.44021

Wei, X., Kumar, N., & Zhang, H. (2025). Addressing bias in generative AI: Challenges and research opportunities in information management. *Information & Management, 62*(2), 104103. DOI: 10.1016/j.im.2025.104103

Wei, Z., & Yuan, M. (2023). Research on the current situation and future development trend of immersive virtual reality in the field of education. *Sustainability (Basel), 15*(9), 7531. DOI: 10.3390/su15097531

Wheelahan, L., & Moodie, G. (2022). Gig qualifications for the gig economy: Micro-credentials and the 'hungry mile'. *Higher Education, 83*(6), 1279–1295. DOI: 10.1007/s10734-021-00742-3 PMID: 34366441

Wilcox, K. C., & Lawson, H. A. (2022). Advancing Educational Equity Research, Policy, and Practice. *Education Sciences, 12*(12), 894. DOI: 10.3390/educsci12120894

Wilcox, R. L., Adem, P. V., Afshinnekoo, E., Atkinson, J. B., Burke, L. W., Cheung, H., & LeGallo, R. (2018). The Undergraduate Training in Genomics (UTRIG) Initiative: Early & active training for physicians in the genomic medicine era. *Personalized Medicine*, *15*(03), 199–208. DOI: 10.2217/pme-2017-0077 PMID: 29843583

Williamson, B., Eynon, R., Knox, J., & Davies, H. (2023). Critical Perspectives on Artificial Intelligence in Education: Political Economy, Discrimination, Commercialisation, Governance and Ethics. In B, Du. Boulay. A Mitrovic and K. Yacet (Eds). The Handbook of AI in Education Edward Elgar Publishing Ltd.

Williamson, B. (2017). Big data in Education. *Sage (Atlanta, Ga.).*

Winne, P. H., & Baker, R. S. (2018). The Potentials of Learning Analytics and AI to Improve Educational Practice. *British Journal of Educational Technology*, *49*(4), 610–626.

Wu, J. (2024). Enhancing Policies on Promoting Gender-inclusive and Equitable Quality STEM in Higher Education. Directions and challenges from a comparative analysis between Italy and China.

Xiao, C. (2023). Digital Human Rights Research (master's thesis). Retrieved from Central South University of Forestry and Technology: https://doi.org/DOI: 10.27662/d.cnki.gznlc.2023.000313

Yan, L., Martinez-Maldonado, R., & Gasevic, D. (2024, March). Generative artificial intelligence in learning analytics: Contextualizing opportunities and challenges through the learning analytics cycle. In *Proceedings of the 14th Learning Analytics and Knowledge Conference* (pp. 101-111). DOI: 10.1145/3636555.3636856

Yanow, D. (2000). *Conducting Interpretive Policy Analysis*. Sage Publications. DOI: 10.4135/9781412983747

Yeralan, S., & Lee, L. A. (2023). Generative AI: Challenges to higher education. *Sustainable Engineering and Innovation*, *5*(2), 107–116. DOI: 10.37868/sei.v5i2.id196

Yigitcanlar, T., & Cugurullo, F. (2020). The sustainability of artificial intelligence: An urbanistic viewpoint from the lens of smart and sustainable cities. *Sustainability (Basel)*, *12*(20), 8548. DOI: 10.3390/su12208548

Yin, L. W. (2013). *Inclusive leadership and employee voice: Mediating roles of psychological safety and leader-member exchange*. PhD Thesis. Hong Kong Baptist University.

Yusro, M., Misin, R., & Mauludin, M. A. (2024, February). Vocational Education Development Strategy in the Use of Artificial Intelligence in the Digital Era. In *5th Vocational Education International Conference (VEIC-5 2023)* (pp. 734-741). Atlantis Press. DOI: 10.2991/978-2-38476-198-2_100

Yusuf, A., Pervin, N., & Román-González, M. (2024). Generative AI and the future of higher education: A threat to academic integrity or reformation? Evidence from multicultural perspectives. *International Journal of Educational Technology in Higher Education*, *21*(1), 21. DOI: 10.1186/s41239-024-00453-6

Zaggl, M. A., Malhotra, A., Alexy, O., & Majchrzak, A. (2023). Governing crowdsourcing for unconstrained innovation problems. *Strategic Management Journal*, *44*(11), 2783–2817. DOI: 10.1002/smj.3505

Zailer, G., & Barak-Medina, E. (2024). Strategies for integrating generative AI into higher education: Navigating challenges and leveraging opportunities. *Education Sciences*, *14*(5), 503–509. DOI: 10.3390/educsci14050503

Zajda, J., Majhanovich, S., & Rust, V. (2006). Introduction: Education and Social Justice. *International Review of Education*, *52*(1/2), 9–22. DOI: 10.1007/s11159-005-5614-2

Zhang, C., Gao, Y., & Janssen, M. (2023). Understanding the evolution of open government data research: Towards open data sustainability and smartness. *International Review of Administrative Sciences*, *89*(1), 59–75. DOI: 10.1177/00208523211009955

Zhang, L., Ren, T., Xie, Y., Tian, Z., Tang, T., & Li, Y. (2022). Student Choirs and Virtual Social Practices by LivePBL: Linking Vocal Education with Project Based Learning. *Literacy Information and Computer Education Journal*, *13*(1), 7. DOI: 10.20533/licej.2040.2589.2022.0482

Zhang, Z., Dong, Z., Shi, Y., Price, T., Matsuda, N., & Xu, D. (2024, March). Students' perceptions and preferences of generative artificial intelligence feedback for programming. *Proceedings of the AAAI Conference on Artificial Intelligence*, *38*(21), 23250–23258. DOI: 10.1609/aaai.v38i21.30372

Zhen, H., & Yahaya, W. A. J. W. (2024). Use of Generative AI Tools to Facilitate Personalized Learning in the Flipped Classroom. In Transforming Education With Generative AI: Prompt Engineering and Synthetic Content Creation (pp. 327-349). IGI Global Scientific Publishing.

Zhong, R. (2020). Digital Divide in Education: Challenges and Solutions during the COVID-19 Pandemic. *Journal of Educational Technology & Society*, *60*(6), 18–24.

Zhou, M. (2011). The ethnic minority-majority gap in China's higher education. *Asian Ethnicity*, *12*(2), 145–156.

Zhou, Y., Ren, T., Chen, N., Li, J., Lu, K., Li, Y., Acharya, A., Shah, P., Hogg, A., & Liu, Y. (2023). Student virtual social practices between China and Nepal. *International Journal of Technology and Inclusive Education*, *12*(1), 6.

# About the Contributors

**Eleni Meletiadou** is an Associate Professor in Equity, Diversity and Inclusion (Management Learning and Education Specialist) and RILEAS and GEDI Research Group Director Director at London Metropolitan University Guildhall School of Business and Law, in London, UK. Her research interests include Education for Social Justice, Education for Sustainable Development, digital learning, gender diversity, inclusion and multilingualism.

***

**Temitope Samson Adekunle** received the B. Tech. (Hon's) degree in Pure Mathematics from the Federal University of Technology, Minna, Nigeria, the M.Tech. degree in Mathematics (Fluid Dynamics) from the Federal University of Technology, Minna, Nigeria and also MSc degree in Data Science from the University of Salford, Manchester, United Kingdom. He is a PhD student at the Department of Computer Science, Colorado State University, Fort Collins, United State. His major research focus is in the aspect of Artificial Intelligent and Machine Learning, Fluid Dynamics, Mathematics Modelling, Data Engineering, Simulation and Modeling, Big Data Mining.

**Sowmiya Baskar** is designated Assistant Professor in the Department of Computer Science, S.I.V.E.T College, Chennai. She completed her M.Sc Computer Science as a University topper at Bharathidasan University and an M.Phil at Periyar University. She qualified for both SET and UGC NET in Computer Science . She has completed a Ph.D. in Computer Science specializing in Digital Image Processing, machine learning, and deep learning at Bharathidasan University, Trichy. She has published research papers in Scopus, UGC care, and international conferences. She has also written a few books and book chapters. She served as a reviewer in reputed journals and a speaker at international conferences.

**Doris Chasokela** is a senior lecturer at the National University of Science and Technology. She holds a Doctor of Education; a Master of Engineering in Electrical Systems Control and Information Technology; a Bachelor of Technical in Electrical and Electronic Engineering; and a Diploma in Technical Vocational Education. She has 11 years of experience in Higher Education teaching and has supervised 15 postgraduate and over 40 undergraduate projects. She has published 16 articles and 3 textbooks. Her research interests are Engineering education, higher education, artificial intelligence, e-learning, and control.

**Stanley Ejiofor Chukwuebuka** is an accomplished academic and emerging researcher with a robust foundation in insurance and actuarial science. He earned his Bachelor of Science degree in Insurance and Actuarial Science from Imo State University, Owerri, Nigeria, where he gained comprehensive knowledge in risk management, financial analysis, and actuarial principles. Currently, Stanley is advancing his expertise by pursuing a Master's degree in Information Technology at Arkansas Tech University in Russellville, Arkansas, USA. His decision to specialize in IT underscores his forward-thinking approach and his recognition of the pivotal role technology plays in the modern financial and insurance sectors. Stanley is actively engaged in cutting-edge research, with a recent focus on "Generative Artificial Intelligence (AI) and Sustainable Development Goal 4 on Tertiary Education: Conversational AI with User-Centric ChatGPT-4." This research explores the transformative potential of AI in enhancing educational outcomes, particularly in higher education, and demonstrates his commitment to leveraging technological advancements for social good. Stanley's interdisciplinary academic journey equips him with a unique blend of skills, combining analytical acumen from his actuarial science background with advanced technological knowledge. This combination positions him to effectively address contemporary challenges in the insurance and education sectors, leveraging AI and IT to innovate and improve industry practices. Beyond his academic pursuits, Stanley is passionate about continuous learning and professional development. His commitment to integrating IT with insurance and actuarial science, coupled with his research on AI and education, highlights his drive to stay at the forefront of industry advancements and contribute meaningfully to the field. Stanley Ejiofor's dedication to excellence, his international educational experiences, and his innovative research make him a promising figure in the evolving landscapes of insurance, information technology, and education. His goal is to harness his diverse skill set to impact these industries positively, fostering innovation, efficiency, and sustainable development.

**Teuta Hazizi** is a Lecturer in the Business Administration Department at the Faculty of Business and Law, University of Elbasan "Aleksandër Xhuvani,"

Elbasan, Albania. She holds a degree in Business Administration and a Master's in Marketing from the University of Tirana, as well as a Master's in Risk and Financial Management, a joint program between the University of Bologna, Italy and the Catholic University Our Lady of Good Counsel in Tirana, Albania. In 2016, Dr. Hazizi earned her doctorate in Economic Sciences from the European University of Tirana. With approximately 23 years of experience in academia and industry, Dr. Hazizi has taught management, business communication, negotiation, and leadership since 2006. She began her academic career as a guest lecturer while managing roles at Customs House Elbasan and ProCredit Bank. In 2015, she transitioned to full-time lecturing. Dr. Hazizi has contributed to various national and international research projects, with publications in scientific journals and presentations at global conferences. She has also collaborated on research projects with London Metropolitan University, including studies on inclusive formative assessment, women in finance, and neurodiversity in higher education, led a UNIEL-funded project on leadership among new entrepreneurs in the natural tourism sector, and actually she is coordinating the Jean Monnet Project "European Entrepreneurship Ecosystem for the European Integration of Albania".

**JosephHlongwane** is an accomplished Physics educator and examiner with over 15 years of experience including curriculum designing and reviewing. He holds a Master degree in Physics Education with a distinction in Dissertation and a University Book Prize and is currently a lecturer at the National University of Science and Technology in Zimbabwe where he has spearheaded Physics Laboratory practical work and has successfully supervised Undergraduate and Masters Students, achieving above 80% annual pass rates. Joseph is passionate about Physics, Physics Education, Sustainable Development, and Artificial Intelligence in Education. He is an active researcher with several publications to his name and has made outstanding presentations at International Conferences. Joseph places utmost importance on his students; success and goes above and beyond to ensure that they achieve their full potential, becoming viable 21st-century global citizens with critical thinking and problem-solving skills to achieve the global agenda of 2030.

**Özgül Keleş** obtained his Bachelor's degree from Gazi University, Department of Science Education in 2001. She completed his Master's degree in 2003 and her Doctorate in Science Education at Gazi University in 2007. Between 2002 and 2008, she worked as a science teacher and also contributed to the writing of science and technology textbooks. She held the position of doctoral faculty member at Aksaray University Faculty of Education between 2008 and 2012, attaining the rank of associate professor doctor between 2012 and 2018. She has been a professor doctor since 2018. Furthermore, in 2014, she was a visiting researcher at the "Centre for

Sustainable Futures" at Plymouth University, with the support of the Council of Higher Education. She served as the Dean of the Aksaray University Faculty of Education between 2018 and 2021. Professor Dr. KELEŞ has been involved in numerous national and international projects, books, seminars and publications on education for sustainable development, ecological footprint, environmental education, science education and teacher education.

**Subhadip Kowar** is pursuing a PhD from UEM in Kolkata. He earned his MCA from Brainware University West Bengal, India, in 2023 and his BCA from Burdwan University, India, in 2021. He currently works as a Technical Assistant in the Department of Computer Science and Engineering (CSE CS & DS) at Brainware University in India. He has around 1.5 years of teaching experience. His research interests include Generative AI, machine learning for recommendation systems.

**Yuanyuan Li** is a distinguished Professor at the Music College of Capital Normal University in Beijing, China, specializing in vocal education and advancing music pedagogy for global citizenship education. During the COVID-19 pandemic, she co-founded the hybrid LivePBL (Linking Vocal Education through Project-Based Learning) project, collaborating with international teams to promote cultural and sustainable social development through music. LivePBL has been featured at major conferences, including the London International Conference on Education and QS Reimaging Education. Professor Li is a member of prestigious music associations and a judge for vocal competitions. Her students have won numerous awards, showcasing her effective teaching. She has led significant educational projects recognized by the Ministry of Education, including student-centred vocal teaching and nationwide cross-school online open courses on classical Chinese music.

**Ying Liu** is a lecturer at the London School of Science and Technology, UK, supporting HE for disadvantaged communities. He holds a PhD from TU Delft, an MEd from Cambridge, and an MBA from Durham. A former advisor to China's Ministry of Education, Dr. Liu has held research fellowships at Cambridge, Edinburgh, and Aberdeen. He leads international education projects and founded LivePBL, a hybrid learning program shortlisted by European eLearning and QS Reimagine Education 2023.

**Unmesh Mandal** serves as an Assistant Professor at the Department of Computer Science, Bidhan Chandra College, Rishra, Hooghly, West Bengal, India. He obtained his M.Sc. degree in Computer and Information Science from the University of Calcutta in 2014, followed by an M.Tech. degree in Computer Science and Engineering from the same university in 2016. He has teaching experience of more than 7 years. His research pursuits encompass a broad spectrum, focusing on areas such as Artificial Intelligence, Machine Learning, Deep Learning, as well as specialized domains like Time Series Analysis and Forecasting.

**Ugochukwu O. Matthew** presently is an Academic scholar with Hussaini Adamu Federal Polytechnic, Nigeria, in the Department of Computer Science with specialty in AI, Big Data Science, Cloud Computing, Internet of Things, Data Mining, Multimedia and E-Learning Education. A Member of Nigeria Computer Society (NCS), Nigeria Institute of Management (NIM), International Association of Computer Science & Information Technology (IACSIT), European Alliance for Innovation(EAI) and also a member of Teaching & Education Research Association (TERA). Ugochukwu O. Matthew hold Masters in Computer Applications from Bayero University Kano, Nigeria. Ugochukwu O. Matthew had reviewed several Journals and a member of Review Board Committee of Journals Indexed by Scopus and Web of Science including IEEE Access, SN Computer Science (Springer), International Journal of Information Communication Technologies & Human Development(IJICTHD), International Journal of Business Data Communications and Networking (IJBDCN), International Journal of Cloud Applications and Computing (IJCAC). Ugochukwu O. Matthew is a cofounder of U&J Digital Consult Limited, an IT and Educational Consulting Firm in Nigeria.

**Matthew Abiola Oladipupo** is the Lead Data Analyst at Perch Group Ltd in Manchester, United Kingdom. He earned his Master of Science in Data Science from The University of Salford and holds a Bachelor of Technology in Electronics and Electrical Engineering, as well as a Postgraduate Diploma, from Ladoke Akintola University of Technology. As a passionate scholar in Artificial Intelligence, he brings years of experience in researching machine learning and boasts a distinguished academic profile. His expertise spans across applied statistics and data mining techniques, enabling him to develop decision-making systems for business organizations. This involves collecting extensive datasets and transforming them into actionable insights and reports, aiding organizations in strategic decision-making, business improvement, and future trend prediction.

**Ajibola Olaosebikan** has a background in Industrial Engineering— where he honed his business, engineering and management skills. Understanding that challenges are local, and that solving them requires sustainable tailored solutions, Ajibola has three goals: to research local problems, develop globally acknowledged solution and make societal impactful by mainstreaming technical skills through teaching. Through his job exposure at Nestle and his master's degree in Applied AI and Data Science at Southampton Solent University—where he was also a Junior Data Scientist and worked collaboratively to deliver an AI-powered decision support system, he has developed capabilities in data analytics and engineering, applied artificial intelligence in business, software engineering and research in other to actualize these goals. Currently, he is pursuing the Food Market Vision (FMV) project. This project, that span areas such as route optimization, data acquisition and storage, process automation, cloud computing etc. is aimed at enhancing the core retailing processes in the Sub-Saharan Africa (Nigeria) informal food markets. Among others, this project's major objective is to ensure verified and real-time primary data and information needed to shape food policies are obtainable the source—the informal food markets. Ajibola's research interests spans across application of AI in Business, big data, data strategy, cloud computing. Ajibola's hobby is teaching and to further showcase this, he is building LearniT—a Learning Management System to educate interested users on developing end-to-end data and software projects.

**Victoria Enemona Oseni** is a passionate data scientist who just completed an MSc in Data Science from the university of Salford, Manchester United Kingdom. I have extensive experience in researching data analytics, Statistics and possess excellent communication skills in English. Having expertise in data collection, data analysis, and interpretation, I specialize in programming, data science, and Statistics. My aim is to develop detection and decision-making software for organizations that enables them to make informed business decisions, predict market trends, and improve their operations. My expertise includes analytical software, and proficiency in utilizing tools such as Python, SQL, R programming, Databricks and PySpark to deploy machine learning algorithms, data visualization, and business analytics to deliver value and solve business problems.

**David Oyekunle** is a highly esteemed expert with extensive education and experience in the fields of information technology research, project management, business analysis and artificial intelligence. He earned his Bachelor of Science degree in Statistics from the University of Ilorin in Nigeria. Furthering his education, he obtained a Postgraduate Diploma in International Business Administration and Management from the National Open University in Nigeria, and a (Summer online) Master of Business Administration in Leadership and Team Building from the University of New Haven in the United States of America. He excelled as a postgraduate research scholar at the University of Salford, graduating with a Master of Science degree in project management with distinctions. David significant organizational experience includes leading cross-functional teams, crafting strategic project policies, implementing logistics, ensuring adherence to risk standards and compliance, and analyzing vast datasets to uncover trends and patterns. Among his accomplishments are the successful implementation of intelligent lean management and Six Sigma with data analysis, the delivery of comprehensive business reports, and the utilization of technological innovation for more effective customer service improvements. Currently serving as an educational consultant at U& J Digital Consult Limited in Nigeria, David continues to contribute significantly to the fields of information technology and educational consulting. His research, published in global journals, spans various subjects, including strategic management, project management, international business, business informatics, and ethics in project management. Demonstrating his commitment to academic collaboration and human capital development, David actively participates in volunteer positions and committee memberships at conferences both locally and internationally. David aims to continue leveraging his expertise to drive innovation and excellence in the field of research, education, project management and information technology.

**Imelda Sejdini** is Associated Professor in the Department of Business Administration at the Faculty of Business and Law, University of Elbasan "Aleksandër Xhuvani." With a solid background in Business Administration and a specialization in Management, Prof. Sejdini has dedicated over 20 years to teaching and research in the fields of management and business ethics. Her academic journey includes a Ph.D. in Management from the University of Tirana. Prof. Sejdini has actively contributed to the academic community through publications in national and international journals, as well as presentations at conferences on topics related to her fields of study. In addition to her academic roles, Prof. Sejdini has collaborated on various projects funded by international organizations, focusing on topics like entrepreneurship, professional skills development, and enhancing the employability of graduates. She also serves as a consultant for both public and private sector entities, providing expertise on organizational development and human capital strategies. Prof. Sejdini's contributions to academia and industry make her a key figure in advancing the understanding and application of management principles in Albania.

**Aleck Sithole** is a lecturer at the National University of Science and Technology, Faculty of Science and Technology, Department of Technical and Engineering Education and Training. He holds a masters of Technology Education in Civil and Construction Engineering, Bachelor of Technical Education in Civil and Construction Engineering.

**Ting Zhao** is a Principal Lecturer and Scholar in Early Years Music Education at Beijing Youth and Politics Vocational College, China, with over a decade of experience. She has significantly impacted music education by integrating traditional and contemporary pedagogy. As a respected member of various music committees, she also served as an Associate of the Overseas Chinese Bureau, promoting global cultural exchanges. Ms. Zhao's research interest is in innovative teaching methods, child development, and technology in music education. She co-founded LivePBL, a hybrid teaching platform praised for enhancing teacher education through real-world scenarios.

# Index

## A



## C



## D



## E

## G



## H



## I



## L



## P

## R



## S



## T



## W



## Z

www.ingramcontent.com/pod-product-compliance
Lightning Source LLC
LaVergne TN
LVHW080607300926
849162LV00005B/1066
* 9 7 9 8 3 6 9 3 5 6 2 3 4 *